ECO-LABELLING AND INTERNATIONAL TRADE

Eco-Labelling and International Trade

Edited by

Simonetta Zarrilli, Veena Jha and René Vossenaar

Foreword by

Rubens Ricupero

Secretary General of UNCTAD

This book is published for and on behalf of
the United Nations

in association with
UNITED NATIONS CONFERENCE ON
TRADE AND DEVELOPMENT

First published in Great Britain 1997 by
MACMILLAN PRESS LTD
Houndmills, Basingstoke, Hampshire RG21 6XS and London
Companies and representatives throughout the world

A catalogue record for this book is available from the British Library.

ISBN 0–333–66547–3

First published in the United States of America 1997 by
ST. MARTIN'S PRESS, INC.,
Scholarly and Reference Division,
175 Fifth Avenue, New York, N.Y. 10010

ISBN 0–312–16579–X

Library of Congress Cataloging-in-Publication Data
Eco-labelling and international trade / edited by Simonetta Zarrilli, Veena Jha and René Vossenaar.
p. cm.
Papers from the United Nations Conference on Trade and Development.
"Published for and on behalf of the United Nations."
Includes bibliographical references and index.
ISBN 0–312–16579–X (cloth)
1. Eco-labelling—Congresses. 2. International trade—Congresses. I. Zarrilli, Simonetta, 1959– . II. Jha, Veena, 1959– . III. Vossenaar, René. IV. United Nations Conference on Trade and Development.
HF5413.E27 1997
382—dc20 96–41008
CIP

This book is printed on paper suitable for recycling and made from fully managed and sustained forest sources.

10 9 8 7 6 5 4 3 2 1
06 05 04 03 02 01 00 99 98 97

Printed in Great Britain by
The Ipswich Book Company Ltd
Ipswich, Suffolk

Contents

List of Tables

List of Boxes

List of Figures

Foreword

In June 1994 the UNCTAD Secretariat organised a workshop on "Eco-Labelling and International Trade". The workshop was chaired by H. E. Antti Hynninen and H. E. Aaron Siraj, Ambassadors to the United Nations Office at Geneva of Finland and Malaysia respectively and was attended by approximately 100 people, including eco-labelling practitioners, researchers from developing and developed countries, representatives from the business community, NGOs, international organisations and Geneva-based delegates.

The purpose of the workshop was to examine the possible effects of eco-labelling on export competitiveness and market access of firms in developing countries and countries in transition, to consider possibilities for strengthening international cooperation, and to discuss ways of moving towards greater compatibility between the environmental objectives of eco-labelling and the trade and sustainable development interests of developing countries.

This book brings together the papers presented at the workshop, which contain the results of conceptual and analytical work, as well as a great amount of practical information on existing or planned eco-labelling programmes. The added value of this book arises from the wealth of empirical details and viewpoints which are presented, from the expertise of the authors, most of whom are leading experts on this issue, and last but not the least, from the fact that it offers a development perspective. The workshop was organised under the aegis of a project funded by the International Development Research Center (IDRC) in Canada. Funds made available under the same project made it possible for several research teams in developing countries to carry out their studies and present them at the workshop. The IDRC's contribution is gratefully acknowledged.

Thanks are also due to the people whose work was vital to the publication of this book. These include the authors of the papers, the editor – Mr Udaya Kumar – and all the members of the Trade and Environment Section of the International Trade Division.

RUBENS RICUPERO
Secretary-General
United Nations Conference on Trade and Development (UNCTAD)

Notes on the Contributors

ABECEL is an association of Brazilian pulp exporters.

Mehmet Arda is the Chief of the Environmental Issues Section of the UNCTAD Secretariat. He is a commodities specialist.

Celik Aruoba is Professor of Economics at Ankara University. Some of his past posts in Turkey include Consultant to the Undersecretary of State for the State Planning Organisation, Prime Minister's Office, on Regional Planning and Agricultural Policy, 1978–79; Director of the Centre for Development Studies and Social Research (GETA) at Ankara University, 1979–82; Secretary-General, Turkish Economic Association, 1980–2.

Ximena Barrera works for the Environmental Economics Division at the Colombian National Planning Department.

Carlos A. Primo Braga joined the World Bank in 1991 and is currently a Senior Economist with the Telecommunications and Information Division, Industry and Energy Department. He received a degree in mechanical engineering from the Instituto Tecnologico de Aeronautica in 1976, his MA in economics from the University of Saõ Paulo in 1980, and his MSc (1982), and PhD (1984) in economics from the University of Illinois at Urban Champaign. Before joining the World Bank, he served as an economic consultant to many private companies, multilateral agencies, and governmental institutions in Brazil and abroad.

Laura B. Campbell has been with the United Nations Environment Programme since 1992. From 1992 to 1994 she served as the Deputy Co-ordinator of the Ozone Secretariat, and since 1994 she has worked on trade and environmental issues, particularly with respect to international Environmental Law at the National Law Center at George Washington University since 1987. From 1983 to 1985 she was a Fulbright Foreign Research Fellow at Tokyo University in Japan.

Mário C. de Carvalho Jr. currently is an associate researcher at Fundaçao Centro de Estudos do Comércio Exterior (FUNCEX) and associate professor at Universidade Estadual do Rio de Janeiro (UERJ).

Ramesh Chaitoo is a Research Associate at the Centre for Trade Policy and Law in Canada. He joined the Centre in 1993 after completing his MA in international affairs at the Norman Paterson School of International Affairs, Carleton University. Prior to his graduate studies, he was a Research Officer for the Caribbean Community Secretariat.

Janet Chakarian is currently at the Harvard Institute for International Development in Cambridge, Massachusetts, during a two-year leave from the World Trade Organization. At HIID, she is co-managing the Central and Eastern Europe Environmental Economics and Policy Project which is working to incorporate market-oriented environmental policies into the economic restructuring in these countries. At the WTO, she was in charge of the Committee on Trade and Environment and was the GATT representative to the UN Conference on Environment and Development. Prior to that she worked as a consultant to the World Bank on trade issues.

Rachel Crossley is an economist with the World Bank, International Trade Division, International Economics Department.

Pedro da Motta Veiga is currently Chief of Staff of the President of Brazil's National Development Bank. He was formerly General Director of the Foreign Trade Studies Foundation and Consultant for OECD, UNCTAD, IDB, LAIA and various private corporation.

Kilian Delbrück works for the Federal Ministry for the Environment in Germany as Deputy Head of Section.

David P. Elliot is a commodities specialist for tropical timber and agricultural raw materials in UNCTAD's Commodities Division. Since his appointment in 1974, he has held positions in the United Nations secretariat in Bangkok and Geneva.

Environmental Choice Program: understanding that Canadians had a high set of environmental values, Environment Canada decided to direct this market force toward environmental improvement. Accordingly, the Environmental Choice Programme was created in 1988 by Environment Canada to help Canadians make more environmentally informed decisions in their day-to-day purchasing. The Program invites companies which manufacture or provide products and services that are less stressful on the environment to apply for certification. After testing and verification that various environmental leadership criteria are met, companies are invited to contract with the program which allows them to use the Program's official mark, the EcoLogo (three doves intertwined to form a maple leaf) on their products or with their services.

Heraldiva Façanha is currently the General-Director of FUNCEX (Fundaçao Centro de Estudos do Comercio Exterior). She has been working at this institution for 19 years, in the positions of Researcher, Coordinator of Conjuncture and Assessor for the Directory.

Diana Gaviria is the Chief of the Environmental Economics Division at the Colombian National Planning Department. She was awarded her MA in international affairs (with a specialisation in economic and political development) from Columbia University in New York (1992) and a BSC in foreign service from Georgetown University in Washington, DC (1989). Her previous posts include Coordinator for Health Programs at the Presidency's Social Solidarity Network and Coordinator of the Columbian International Cooperation Strategy for the Environment at the National Planning Department.

Ineke Giezeman studied law at the University of Leiden, the Netherlands. During that period she subsequently worked as a manager of a laundry, in a travel agency and as an assistant to a member of the Dutch Parliament. From 1980 she worked for a regional employers' association and in 1989 she started her work for the board of Directors of a major flower-trading company. Since 1992 she has been director of Stichting Milieukeur International Organization for Standardization (ISO).

Maria Isolda P. Guevara is a Research Associate at the Centre for Trade Policy and Law in Canada. She joined the Centre after completing her MA in international affairs at the Norman Paterson School of International Affairs, Carleton University in 1991. She has collaborated on a number of the Centre's research reports commissioned by different organisations. Prior to pursuing graduate studies in Canada, she was a Project Officer at the Project Monitoring Group of the Private Development Corporation of the Philippines, a private development finance institution.

John Henry is Group Manager of Environment and Safety at Standards Australia, as well as being Secretary to ISO/TC 207/SC 3 Environmental

Labelling. A mechanical engineering by profession, he has been involved with consumer products for most of his working life, initially in manufacturing industry and for the past 14 years with Standards Australia, the Australian member body of (the Dutch eco-labelling organization). He has a strong involvement with product safety, including being a member of the New South Wales Product Safety Committee and the Commonwealth/State Consumer Product Advisory Committee (CPAC). His principal focus is now the environmental effects associated with the manufacture, marketing and supply of consumer products. He was a member of the ISO/IEC Strategic Advisory Group on the Environmental (SAGE), the forerunner to ISO/TC 107, and the SAGE sub-group on Environmental Labelling. He is also a member of the Chairman's Advisory Group (CAG) of TC 207.

Lily Ho was awarded her MA in international affairs (with a specialisation in economic and political development) from Columbia University in New York. She did a year's internship at the National Planning Department of Colombia.

ITC (International Trade Center) is the focal point in the United Nations system for providing technical cooperation to support governments and the business sectors in developing countries and economies in transition in their trade development efforts. It covers both export development and import management for commodities, manufactures and services. ITC's specific role is to deal with the operational aspects of trade promotion and development.

Zbigniew Jakubczyk graduated in 1983 from Engineering and Industrial Economics Department of the Academy of Economics in Wrocław. In the same year he began to work in the Economics Department at Wrocław, and he currently teaches courses in environmental economics, macroeconomics, microeconomics and the history of economic thought. Since 1989 he has worked with the Polish Parliamentary Commission of Environmental Protection and the Polish Ministry of Environmental Protection, Natural Resources and Forestry department.

Veena Jha is an Economic Affairs Officer in the Trade and Environment Section of the International Trade Division of UNCTAD. She has served as a consultant for the United Nations Conference for Environment and Development (UNCED), for the International Labour Office (ILO) and the United Nations Institute for Social Development.

She has been Professor and researcher at Queen's College at Oxford, the University of London where she completed her PhD in economics, Lady Spencer Churchill School of Management at Wheatley, and the School of Economics at the University of Delhi. She has published several articles on trade and environment issues in journals and other publications.

Saskia Jongma graduated in environmental economics at the Vrije Universiteit in Amsterdam and from 1993 environmental economics has taught there. She also became a part-time contract researcher at the Institute for Environmental Studies in Amsterdam. Since 1994, she has been involved in environmental research projects at the Economics Department of the Vrije Universiteit.

Vivien Liu graduated in economics and geography from the Chinese University of Hong Kong. She worked in the civil service of the Hong Kong Government for ten years, before joining the GATT Trade and Environment Division in 1992. She has acted as the Secretary for the Committee on Technical Barriers to Trade since then.

Anil Markandya is an environmental economist who was educated at York University and at the London School of Economics, where he obtained his PhD in 1974. He has held teaching positions at University College, London, and at the Universities of Princeton and Berkeley, California. Over the last 25 years, he has advised most of international organisations concerned with economic development, as well as a number of bilateral agencies. Among his numerous publications are the widely acclaimed *Blueprint for a Green Economy* and the *Earthscan Reader in Environmental Economics*. Currently he is Professor of Economics at Bath University. Previously, he worked as research associate with the Harvard Institute for International Development (HIID) and through HIID, he worked as a senior environmental policy adviser to the Russian Government.

Aaditya Mattoo is a member of the WTO Secretariat and works in the Trade in Services Division. He has a PhD in economics from the University of Cambridge.

Ricardo Sánchez is an economist from Colombia. At present he works as an adviser to the Environmental Policy Unit in the National Planning Department (DNP) in Bogota. Before joining DNP, he worked as a researcher for the journal *Estrategia Economica y Financiera* in the Macroeconomic Section.

Markku Simula is Adjunct Professor in the Department of Forest Economics at the University of Helsinki, and President of Indufor Oy, a consulting company specialising in forestry, forest industries and environmental management of natural resources. Dr Simula has been employed by the Food and Agriculture Organization and has worked as a consultant for development banks and international organizations. He has also served in the International Tropical Timber Organization. He has contributed to several books on forestry development in the developing world, trade and environment, and certification of forest management and timber products.

Harsha V. Singh is a member of the WTO Secretariat. He has a PhD in economics from the University of Oxford, and has worked in the GATT/WTO Secretariat since June 1995 in areas dealing with economic research, trade policy review, anti-dumping, subsidies/countervailing, safeguards, and trade environment. Earlier, he was a consultant to the ILO, UNCTAD, and the government of India (Bureau of Industrial Costs and Prices, Ministry of Industry).

Murray G. Smith is the Director of the Centre for Trade Policy and Law which was co-founded by the Norman Paterson School of International Affairs at Carleton University and the Faculty of Law of the University of Ottawa. He has held this position since 1990. Previously, he was Director of the International Economics Program of the Institute for Research on Public Policy from June 1987. Before that, he was with the C.D. Howe Institute, where he served as a Senior Policy Analyst and Canadian Research Director for the Canadian–American Committee. During the Tokyo Round of multilateral negotiations, he was Director of International Economic Relations in the British Columbia government.

Panayotis N. Varangis is an economist in the Commodity Policy and Analysis Unit of the World Bank dealing primarily with issues of agricultural markets, agricultural policies, commodity risk management and research in the area of commodity price behaviour. He has worked extensively on projects in several developing countries of Latin America and Africa. Prior to the World Bank, he worked as an instructor of economics at Columbia University and as a researcher at Hudson Institute.

He holds an MA in economics from Georgetown University, and a PhD in economics from Columbia University.

Harmen Verbruggen is Deputy Director of the Institute for Environmental Studies of the Vrije Universiteit, Amsterdam, the Netherlands. He has recently been appointed Professor of International Environmental Economics at the same university. He has served as an independent member of a number of Government Advisory Councils on environmental policy, and is the author of a great number of articles and studies on the interface of trade, environment and development.

Frits Verhees studied planning at the University of Nijmegen, the Netherlands. He worked with the Dutch Ministry of Environment, municipality of Hengelo, on environmental policy and the relation between environment and other governmental policies. Since 1992 he has worked as project manager for Stichting Milieukeur (the Dutch eco-labelling organization).

Maria Lúcia Vilmar holds an MSc in production engineering from the Universidade Federal do Rio de Janeiro, and is a researcher at same university.

René Vossenaar is Chief of the Trade and Environment Section of the International Trade Division of UNCTAD. Previously he was a researcher at the University of Tilburg in the Netherlands and worked for several years with the Economic Commission for Latin America and the Caribbean (ECLAC) in Santiago, Buenos Aires and Brasilia. He has been with UNCTAD since 198?. He has published several articles on trade and environment in the OECD and other publications.

Frans van der Woerd is a Senior Researcher at the Institute for Environmental Studies of the Vrije Universiteit, Amsterdam, the Netherlands. He has published various publications (in Dutch) about environmental cost–impact on business, and developments in business environmental management systems.

Poul Wendel Jessen works for the Danish Ministry of Environment and Energy.

Sophia Wigzell holds an MSc in environent and development from the University of Cambridge. She has been working on environmental issues in Thailand for four years, and is currently the Environment Coordinator at the Bangkok office of international law firm Baker & McKenzie.

Simonetta Zarrilli is an Economic Affairs Officer for the United Nations Conference on Trade and Development (UNCTAD) in Geneva, Switzerland. She joined UNCTAD in 1988 and spent her first three years doing work on international trade law. Prior to UNCTAD, she worked as Legal Officer with commodities trading companies in Italy. She was awarded an MA in European law from the College of Europe in Bruges, Belgium, and is a member of the Italian Bar Association. She has published a number of articles on trade and development-related issues.

1 Eco-Labelling: An Introduction and Review

Anil Markandya[1]

INTRODUCTION

As concern with the environment grows among the public, both in developed and developing countries, environmental issues are beginning to take more of a centre stage in economic and trade policies. One manifestation of this is the desire to inform consumers more fully about the products they purchase, not only with regard to those characteristics of commodities that affect their well-being directly (e.g. additives to food products), but also with regard to the impact of production processes on the environment in general. The practice of supplying information on the environmental characteristics of a commodity to the general public may be called eco-labelling. It is an expanding activity and one that generates many questions, as is clear from the articles in this volume.

From the papers presented here, there are eco-labelling schemes in operation in (or about to come into operation in) 17 countries.[2] In addition, the European Union (EU) is developing its own community-wide eco-labelling scheme. In fact it is very likely that several other countries are contemplating some form of eco-labelling scheme, and the level of interest in this issue across both developed and developing countries is very high.

It is evident from this volume that questions regarding the likely impacts of eco-labelling schemes are complex, with differences in concerns arising in "single issue schemes" and in broad multidimensional schemes; in perspectives taken by developed countries and those taken by developing countries; and problems arising in voluntary schemes as opposed to mandatory schemes. At the same time, it is becoming increasingly clear that some of the basic questions regarding the goals of eco-labelling and the design of effective schemes remain unanswered.

This introductory paper attempts to put the issues surrounding eco-labelling in perspective. Section I briefly describes the different schemes and classifies them according to coverage, legal status, source of certification etc. Section II goes on to examine the goals of different schemes. In so far as they are consumer-related, how can we assess their effectiveness? Similarly, if the goals are more related to encouraging industrial pollution control, how can we assess the effectiveness of the schemes with respect to those goals? Section III looks at the schemes from the perspective of developing countries and transition economies, while Section IV examines them from the developed-country, mainly EU, perspective. Section V considers the role of international institutions in ensuring an effective and equitable framework for eco-labelling.

I ECO-LABELLING SYSTEMS

Several systems of eco-labelling have been developed in recent years. As the paper by Environment Canada points out, there are three types of eco-labels. The first (type I labels) are labels established by third parties, which may be governmental organizations or private non-commercial entities, and which award labels to products and manufacturing processes. Such labels are distinct from single-issue labels (e.g. based on energy-efficiency criteria) by virtue of the fact that they are based on multiple criteria and the awarding authority has considered several environmental aspects of the commodity or the process, including the impacts that occur in the manufacturing, transportation and disposal of the product. The latter is referred to in the literature on eco-labelling as "life-cycle analysis (LCA)".[3] Type I labels are awarded on the basis of "scientific criteria", generally judged by an independent panel of experts along with industry representatives, and are awarded to approximately 15–20 per cent of the products in any one sector. In general, such schemes are voluntary, although some of the papers suggest compulsory eco-labelling schemes. Examples of type I labels are the Blue Angel scheme in Germany, the White Swan scheme in the Nordic countries, and most of the other national eco-labelling schemes.

The second type of eco-label is a single-attribute programme, often run by the company or the industry association, and deals with a specific attribute of the product. These may announce that the product is "energy efficient" in some specified sense, that the product does not use ozone-depleting substances, or that it is made from materials that are harvested in a sustainable way. In each case an independent body may make a verification of the claims. This may take many forms, e.g. of an industry overseeing body, a non-governmental organization (NGO), or an advertising standards agency. Claims are rarely based on a life-cycle analysis although that is not precluded. Examples include information on products that do not contain chloroflurocarbons (CFCs) and other ozone-depleting substances,[4] claims that pest management has not used insecticides (e.g. the Butterfly scheme in the Netherlands) and claims of good forestry practices (e.g. the Project Troppenwald in Germany).[5]

The third kind of eco-label provides quantified information, using an agreed set of indices. It is like a nutritional label, giving selected data about environmental impacts of the product, and making no judgment about the desirability of one impact relative to another. Such labels are rare in the environmental field – there is only one example of such a label, and little experience with it so far. Nevertheless, it is an important method of labelling, and should be included in any discussion of the subject.

As pointed out above, the literature is not altogether clear on whether eco-labels are voluntary or compulsory. Type I labels are essentially "voluntary" in the sense that not all producers are required to apply for them. On the other hand, some type II labels may be required for the sale of the products in certain markets (e.g. tropical timber), and these can then be considered mandatory. The same can apply, in a limited way, when government procurement policies require the product to have a type I label of a certain kind. The question of voluntary or mandatory therefore has to be judged relative to the market in which the product is sold.

The literature is also not clear, perhaps because the situation itself is confused, as to whether the label is awarded by an independent body or by the industry itself. In the case of type I labels, some independent assessment is considered essential, but the industry is also represented on the awarding body. In the case of type II labels, they can be firm-specific or industry-wide, or labels awarded by an independent body representing one or more interest groups such as those of consumers and environmentalists.

II WHAT ARE THE GOALS OF AN ECO-LABEL?

Before judging an eco-labelling system, it is important to consider the question, what are the goals of the scheme? The papers presented here point to three distinct objectives:

- First, there is the desire to give more information to the consumer about the environmental effects of what s/he is consuming.
- Second, there is a desire to raise environmental standards in the production of the commodity.
- Third, and this is not always admitted, there may be a desire to give producers in the country where the label is issued a competitive advantage over other producers.

In this section, all three objectives are considered. In each case, we shall inquire how the goals influence the nature of the eco-label.

A Consumer Information

The provision of fuller information to consumers is a desirable objective, as long as such information is accurate and not misleading. It can be misleading, however, in a variety of ways. The most obvious instance is when the information is factually incorrect. But the consumer can be misled also in cases where the data are incomplete, with information on more important impacts withheld and relatively unimportant issues given prominence. The width of coverage is therefore important, as are the relative weights given to different impacts.[6]

A more basic question that needs to be posed here is: what kind of information does the consumer want? This depends on the way in which the environment affects his/her well being. If the consumer cares about environmental impacts and damage to the environment, the label has to convey information that assists the consumer in making an evaluation of that damage. The label most suited for this purpose would be the type III label, which gives information on the magnitudes of different environmental impacts without giving relative weights to them. The consumer would then estimate the damage associated with the product and make a decision on whether to buy this product rather than another one with lower environmental impacts.[7] In actual practice, the information provided is much more limited. Often, consumers receive information in the form of a label that is awarded to all products that meet certain criteria specified for a product category. Some of criteria are of the "all-or-nothing" variety. For example, the criterion that the PCP content in the production of pairs of shoes should be less than 100 parts per million would mean that the producers qualify for the eco-label only if they meet the specified requirement. Other criteria are more flexible. For example, if the producer uses virgin pulp in the production of paper, a certain loading of points is given. The same load points system applies to other criteria too, and a label is awarded only if the number of load points is less than a specified number. From the point of view of information, such a system imputes certain weights to the different impacts, and these may not necessarily be the same as those of the consumer. Furthermore, there is an implicit threshold in the weighting system. If SO_2 emissions in excess of 0.3 kg/tonne from the production of wood pulp are given a loading of one point, and if the use of virgin pulp is given a loading of one point, it is implicitly assumed that: (a) both these impacts have equal value to the consumer, and (b) there is a threshold value at 0.3 kg/tonne in terms of SO_2 damages. The scientific evidence for the latter is weak and that for the former is non-existent. Hence, if the objective of the eco-label is to inform a consumer whose welfare is influenced by the level of damages, the present system of type I labels is arguably not the best method. Another important point to note about a system that seeks to inform consumers is that it would not treat damage caused in production in the country where the consumer is resident in the same way as damage caused in other countries. There is evidence to suggest that consumers in developed countries care about the environment in other parts of the world but their valuation of such damage is not the same as that for damage in their own "back yard".[8] Hence it would be inappropriate to require the same emissions standards or the same weights for foreign producers as for domestic producers if the objective is to inform domestic consumers about the environmental impact of a product.

Consumers may seek information about the environmental characteristics of a product not only for the damage caused, but because of the relative impacts of their consumption compared with that of their neighbours. There is a well-respected branch of economics that explains consumption behaviour in terms of relative effects and this may be appropriate to deal with the case of the environment. What matters is to be consuming a "cleaner" product compared to what most other people consume. In that case, the kind of information the eco-label should provide is on the characteristics of the product relative to average use – e.g. that it uses 50 per cent less energy, or emits 30 per cent less greenhouse gases than the average.

Although there is a major component of relative valuation in most eco-labelling schemes, few – if any – of them are purely relative, i.e. based on performance relative to an average for the industry. The present system of eco-label design is therefore an amalgam of relative and absolute criteria. It is often stated that the basis of the criteria is "scientific" but, given that the objectives are partly economic and social, it is impossible to have an eco-label that is fully objective and dependent only on scientific criteria. The sooner this is recognized, the better. The research effort needed then is to understand better what kind of information consumers want, what the benefits and costs of providing summary indicators as opposed to more detailed information are, and what relative weights should be used, if summary indicators are employed.

B Producer Information

Eco-labelling schemes are also aimed at encouraging producers to adopt better environmental practices. Thus, the label is only awarded to the "best" 10 or 20 per cent of products in the market, irrespective of absolute standards. Standards are set in such a way that cleaner technologies qualify for the award.

From the manufacturer's perspective, the incentive to apply for the label will be a function of the following:

- *The market premium that the eco-labelled good fetches over the non-labelled good*: the greater this premium the more attractive the label will be.
- *The costs of meeting the production requirements for the label over and above what it costs to produce the non-labelled good*: the greater this additional cost the less attractive it will be to try and obtain the label.
- *The prospects for falling producer costs as the level of output of the labelled good expands*: if there are "economies of scale" in the production of labelled goods, forward-looking companies may be willing to undertake production in the knowledge that costs will fall once a strong market position will have been established.[9]

There is little evidence regarding the size of the market premium. Some economists even deny that consumers are willing to pay any additional amount for a product that has general environmental benefits compared to its competitors.[10] The few pieces of empirical evidence presented in this volume point to a small premium for an eco-labelled product. Jha *et al.* quote the Singapore Green Label scheme as estimating a premium of about 5 per cent.[11] The paper by Crossley *et al.* quotes a study in the United States by van Ravensway and Hoehn that, for organic food, consumers are willing to pay as much as 5–7 per cent more on average.[12] Finally, the paper by Verbruggen *et al.* reports on the market for organically grown flowers in the Netherlands.[13] Such products have a "GEA" label and a price premium of 30 per cent over non-labelled products, but only a 1 per cent share of the market. This is one of the few guides to the elasticity of demand for the green market.

This kind of information is critical both for producers to evaluate potential benefits from seeking a label, as well as for authorities that are designing labels. Yet it seems to have been rarely systematically collected and seldom used.

Even within the countries in which they are awarded, the labels have not always had an identifiable impact in terms of sales of products under the relevant categories. In the Blue Angel scheme in Germany, for some commodities such as low pollutant coatings, the share of labelled products in the market is significant. However, that may have been the case even without the label.

More information is available on eco-labelling premia for timber products.[14] The surveys for tropical timber forests are not clear, however, on whether there will be any demand impact from a rise in price for timber from "sustainably managed forests". If the rise in price is less than the premium a section of the public is willing to pay, and if the supply that comes from the eco-labelled source is no more than the demand of that section of the public, there should be no impact on total demand. If the increase in supply of eco-labelled timber is greater than the demand of the environmentally conscious public there could be a demand impact, which will depend partly on the price elasticity of demand of the "environmentally indifferent" consumers. Estimates of this impact are partially available for tropical timber, but not for other products.

On other aspects of the economics of eco-labelling too, there is precious little evidence, again with the exception of forestry. For forestry products, it is estimated that the additional cost of harvesting from a well-managed forest could range from 10 to 20 per cent of the current price of $350 per cubic metre.[15] To that, we have to add certification costs. If the average premium that consumers are willing to pay (including those who are willing to pay nothing) is, say, 10 per cent, one would need detailed information on how the costs are distributed among the different suppliers before estimating what the supply for the labelled product would be. This supply information would then have to be combined with the demand estimates to arrive at an overall evaluation of the impacts of the labelling scheme. Crossley *et al.* start such an analysis and find that the revenues from certification are limited due to the size of the ecosensitive market and the size of the premium. The next step is to bring in the cost side and that has yet to be done.

Another issue of potential importance is the impact of eco-labelling on the industrial structure of the sector in which it is introduced. If labels are awarded to larger producers who already have access to the technology for cleaner production, and if there is a strong demand for such products from the public, one many see a big shift in demand to such firms, at the expense of smaller enterprises that cannot afford to obtain the label. This will have implications for competition policy, as well as for the dynamics of enterprise development and growth. This question comes up in the context of the impact of the label on developing-country producers, but is relevant for other countries as well. Reviews of existing schemes in the papers in this volume do not say much about such impacts. Perhaps they are not important. However, a systematic analysis of the effects on industrial structure would be desirable.

To conclude, much needs to be known about the incentive structure of eco-labels for producers, if a scheme is to be designed to be as effective as possible. The present schemes have too much of an *ad hoc* structure, as far as their industrial impacts are concerned.

C Protection of Domestic Markets

A number of the papers in this volume note that the introduction of an eco-label in one country may have impacts on the imports of competing products from other countries that cannot easily acquire the label (or cannot acquire it on the same terms as home-country manufacturers). This issue is dealt with in more detail in Section III. At this point it is useful to ask what kind of scheme a country would design and what other measures it would take, if it wanted to restrict foreign competition?

A scheme will have a trade bias if:

- it is specified in terms of technology that domestic producers have special access to;
- it gives special attention to local manufacturers when setting the criteria by which the label is awarded and not consulting with foreign suppliers; or
- it requires foreign producers to meet the same criteria, including those that are not important in the country of the manufacturer.[16]

These factors can be exacerbated when the labelling scheme is supported by procurement policies that favour the labelled product. For example, government purchasing rules may say that only products that carry the label may be eligible for tender.

There is no doubt that trade issues of eco-labelling are of great concern to actual and potential exporters. The discussion in Section III shows that some developing-country producers are concerned about the possible impact of proposed schemes. In Section IV papers reviewing some of the schemes from the developed-country perspective show that, implicitly, restricting competition from abroad was at least part of the motive. In Section V, some possible solutions for dealing with this question are examined, particularly the role of international agencies in ensuring a "level playing field" in the context of eco-labelling schemes.

III ECO-LABELLING: DEVELOPING COUNTRIES AND TRANSITION ECONOMIES

The papers in this volume provide the views of teams from Brazil, Colombia, Poland and Thailand. Primarily these papers deal with proposed schemes, principally those being considered by the EU. However, it is important to note that most existing schemes in industrialized countries have not much impact on the trade of these non-OECD countries.[17] This is primarily because the products covered in the existing labelling schemes are mainly ones that are traded between OECD countries.

The concern expressed in the papers in this volume, especially those from Brazil and Colombia, has to do with forthcoming labelling programmes. The Brazilian survey[18] is very clear that the proposed EU and other European labels in the areas of textiles, pulp and paper, and footwear will be difficult for some Brazilian firms to acquire. The principal difficulties identified are:

- Small companies will find it difficult to make the necessary investments to acquire the labels whereas the larger companies have already started making necessary modifications to their production processes. Suppliers of chemicals do not easily provide smaller firms with the products that meet labelling requirements, while bigger manufacturers are in a position to negotiate the supplies of such chemicals. These larger companies are facing additional costs but, so far, have not lost market sales.

- It is difficult to meet eco-labelling criteria when the inputs used were themselves imported. This is the case with raw cotton and leather that is imported into Brazil. The costs of obtaining supplies and verifying that they met the conditions were judged to be high.
- Some of the requirements of the eco-labels put countries such as Brazil at a disadvantage *vis-à-vis* the countries of the EU and are of little relevance in environmental terms. For example, consider the requirements for sulphur dioxide and nitrogen oxides emissions. Technologies meeting these requirements have been developed in the EU because such pollutants are important there. In developing countries where they are less important, they have not been developed, and the label would make it necessary to import them. Adapting existing production systems to meet these conditions will be costly and may reduce the competitive advantage that Brazil has in these areas.
- Some of the conditions for the eco-label unfairly penalize countries such as Brazil because they place a penalty on materials that Brazil uses, or give preference to materials that are not readily available in the country. An example is the use of virgin pulp in the paper industry. Such pulp receives 0.9–1.2 penalty points (to get an eco-label a producer must have less than a certain number of penalty points) even though the pulp comes from sustainable forests. Conversely, favouring recycled paper by giving credit for waste reduction benefits developed countries where more recycled material is available, and where collection and recycling are subsidized.
- The setting up of the labelling guidelines was done without sufficient consultation with producing countries such as Brazil. "No attention was paid [in establishing the criteria for the eco-labels] to the fact that in non-EU countries positive environmental results might be achieved in ways different from those tagged as top priority in Europe, and that solutions appropriate to Europe may not be valid for other regions."[19]

Similar comments emerge from the paper by Ho *et al.*[20] for Colombia. The paper stresses the costs of complying with the EU standards, which it estimates to be very high. These costs are believed to be much higher for Colombian producers than for EU producers because of the way the criteria are framed. The authors also argue that some of the standards are not set on criteria that are transparent. For example, the justification for the requirement that the maximum amount of lead permissible in water in textile production is only 0.004 mg/l is not clear, except perhaps that EU production technology meets that criterion.

The paper on Poland[21] notes that eco-label standards for wood products for the German market are being met by 80 per cent of those applying for certification (it does not say what proportion of producers applied for certification). On textiles it notes that the present ECO-TEX requirements of the German market are being fulfilled by Polish producers, but that the stricter EU proposals being formulated under the leadership of Denmark are unlikely to be met "without pressure of EU importers and EU institutions promoting these proposals".[22] It is also pointed out that meeting these stricter standards will be very expensive and beyond the reach of many Polish producers.

In a related survey of the issues, some Polish authorities warn against too much optimism over taking advantage of "green consumerism" in the West but at the same time acknowledge that Poland will have to respond to such changes. They state: "The market for ecological products and so called 'health foods' in EFTA [European Free Trade Association] and EU countries expands quickly but . . . it is subject to a very strong competition and exceptionally strict and fully observed regulations. We emphasize this fact because all the programs of ecological agriculture development in Poland are to a significant extent linked to the expansion of 'green product' exports".[23] At the same time, it notes that Poland does have favourable conditions for eco-agriculture because of its large rural population, low labour costs and low pesticide use. With regard to the last point, however, it notes that the current trend of manufacturers of some pesticides that are banned in developed countries to aggressively market their products in Poland is proving an obstacle to the development of eco-agriculture.

None of the above studies comment on the possibility of selling in the EU market without the label after it has been introduced. All the papers note that these markets are very price-sensitive. If, therefore, a developing-country producer can sell at a small price discount over the EU producer who has to bear some extra cost, s/he may be able to keep market share. The limited evidence available suggests that customers are willing to pay about a 5 per cent premium for the eco-label. If so, the price discount may not have to be large. In addition, developing countries could promote their products positively. One way is through their own eco-labels. Another is to make the point that although they do not carry the EU label, it is for reasons that are not environmentally damaging. Such "negative" advertising could be effective, and the case for it is strong. These are areas where further research would be useful.

All the countries from which papers have been included in this volume have their own eco-labelling schemes. All of them are new: either just introduced or about to be introduced. In the case of Brazil, the main reason for setting up the scheme was to counter the impacts of the schemes in developed countries, which were affecting the exports of Brazilian firms. The "Green Seal" scheme is based on work under way at the International Organization for Standardization (ISO) which should give the scheme international credibility. Another Brazilian scheme for forest product certification, CERFLOR, also aims to offer a credible alternative to the EU proposals. In terms of the domestic market, the labels are seen as relatively unimportant.

The proposed Colombian scheme is based on the German system of eco-labelling, its goals being both export promotion and the enhancement of domestic environmental consciousness. It is too early to comment on the impacts of the scheme, but the level of interest among domestic producers appears to be high.

In Poland, the process of eco-labelling is getting under way, with the ultimate aim of harmonizing with the EU standards. The aim here is clearly to integrate within the European market. At the same time, there appears to be a range of eco-labels in place for plastics, dyestuffs and lamps. As far as one can tell, these labels are offered to influence both domestic and foreign markets.

Unfortunately, these papers generally look at eco-labelling in their countries as a defensive measure. Although that is important, there is also a proactive dimension to eco-labelling for developing countries. There are other studies that suggest that developing countries may actually turn the eco-labelling system to their advantage by marketing their own "eco-friendly" products more aggressively.[24] The development of "green food" labels in China and "green cotton" in India and the possible use of natural fibres such as jute in packaging are cases in point.

The possibilities can be seen by looking at the case of India, which has recognized the profitability of some environmentally friendly products and is promoting them in a number of ways. One of the most important is organically grown cotton (or "green cotton"). The federal government has identified 1000 ha of land in two states for producing organic cotton on a pilot scale. Of course, this is only a start (India has 8 million ha under cotton) but a promising one. The benefits are not only to the producers, who can receive a 20 per cent price premium over cotton grown using chemicals, but also to the country where more than half the pesticide consumption is accounted for by cotton production. India is also beginning to grow some naturally coloured cotton, thus avoiding the use of dyes. This fetches a very high premium in foreign markets. Hybrid seeds for this, however, are still being locally developed, as India was unsuccessful in obtaining them from the United States where such cotton is grown.[25] A similar promotion is taking place for jute and its products, which lost much of their market due to competition from synthetic products, but are now seen as eco-friendly. If terms can be agreed for their use in packaging to the European markets, they may have a big increase in demand. Other products where exporters recognize the benefits of environmentally friendly production are food products and leather.

The paper by Arda[26] stresses the potential for developing countries to promote the environmental friendliness of some of their products. He notes, however, that there are some problems that have to be addressed if such ventures are to be successful. Prime among them is information: about the quality of the product and about its environmental friendliness. Related to that is the need for proactive marketing and promotion of products.

In conclusion, a number of developing countries view the proposed eco-labelling for products such as textiles, wood, pulp and paper, and leather as attempts to give a competitive advantage to countries where the criteria for labels have been defined. They offer some credible evidence to support their case. However, they do not comment on the extent of the impact (it is still premature), nor do they comment on the possibility of countering such eco-labelling through price competition or alternative eco-labelling proposals.

With respect to the role of developing-country eco-labelling schemes, the papers in this volume mostly see them as a defensive measure, although the paper by Arda offers some suggestions on how the schemes can be more proactive, as does the paper by Jha and Zarilli.[27] Indeed, there is considerable potential for this, as the examples quoted above demonstrate. Whatever the purpose of introducing a scheme in these countries, they will be successful only if there is credibility in the labels awarded. This may require some international certification. Furthermore, the schemes will need cooperation with the importing countries, to define the appropriate labels and even to modify the importers' own labelling schemes. Finally they will require active promotion about their qualities.

IV ECO-LABELLING: THE PERSPECTIVE FROM THE EU

There are three papers in this volume that look at the issue from the perspective of EU: Delbrück (who examines the German "Blue Angel" Scheme); Jessen (who comments on the EU current eco-labelling proposals); and Verbruggen *et al.* (who review the eco-labels in the Dutch horticultural sector).

The paper by Delbrück is a review of the Blue Angel scheme which was introduced in Germany in 1977. The scheme appears to be popular and successful with over 1200 firms having sought the label, 10 per cent of which were non-German. None of these was from a developing country, and the only non-EU/EFTA country was Yugoslavia. This is attributed to the fact that the products covered are not normally imported from developing countries. Further, it is noted that there has not been any complaint about the scheme being a trade barrier. The paper goes on to suggest that a multilateral approach to eco-labelling would be desirable, to ensure harmonization and mutual recognition. Although both these aspects of an eco-labelling scheme are desirable, there is a negative side to unifying the eco-labelling process that needs to be addressed.

The paper by Jessen comments on the process by which the EU is developing its eco-labelling scheme. This was started in March 1992. The paper recognizes the problem of harmonization of standards when the environmental problems of countries differ. For example, in countries where sewage treatment plants have phosphate precipitation equipment, the inclusion of phosphates in detergents is not such a serious matter as in countries where they do not. To have a single system for both countries would mean finding a compromise on phosphate levels in detergents which may not serve the interests of either party.

The EU labelling process has to avoid setting EU standards for the rest of the world. Taking the labelling of paper products as an example, Jessen's article points out that the process has been transparent and wide consultation has been sought. This is contrary to the perception, for example, in the Brazilian paper.[28] The paper does not answer many of the criticisms of the EU schemes in the developing-country papers. It does note, however, that the introduction of political and ethical criteria in trade preferences will increase within the EU. Complementary to the eco-labelling schemes there are proposals for reductions in tariffs below the most-favoured nation (MFN) levels for products that meet criteria with respect to child labour, animal testing, etc. The possibility that such measures will complement the eco-label is something that developing countries will certainly need to respond to. The paper by Verbruggen *et al.* is most supportive of the developing-country view, that, in large measure, the eco-labelling schemes have a protectionist intent. Looking at four Dutch horticultural schemes they find:

- The schemes do not treat domestic and foreign products equally. Foreign producers are not represented on the panels that set criteria.
- No account is taken of the specific environmental conditions in the country where the flowers are grown. For example, Dutch growers use large amounts of energy to cultivate their products. Developing countries where sunlight is used would have an advantage but are penalized by including the costs of international shipping of the flowers. On the other hand, Dutch shipping costs to international markets are not included.
- The environmental accounting systems and monitoring procedures needed for some of the schemes are costly and difficult to meet.
- Two schemes (the "Butterfly" for fruits and vegetables, and the GEA label for organically grown flowers) are only open to Dutch growers, and foreign suppliers are therefore excluded. Extending the schemes to them is constrained by the complex verification procedures and product-range requirements.

The paper concludes by recognizing that, although each country has the right to establish eco-labelling criteria that reflect its environmental concerns, it should not impose those on other countries. Only those aspects of the criteria that are relevant to the importing country's environment or to the global environment should be applied to the imported product. Although this may seem to be a reasonable approach it has not met with much approval in the developed countries. As Jha *et al.* note, in the Canadian eco-label case (EcoLogo), it was suggested that the evaluation of final products entirely produced off-shore be based on only that part of the product life cycle which occurs in Canada, i.e. use and disposal. However, this proposal was discarded because it raises a number of concerns notably that (a) it will not be beneficial to global environments, and (b) that it will create double standards and discriminate against domestic producers.[29]

In spite of these comments, the issue may be worth reconsidering. The global aspect could be handled by including such criteria for the award of all eco-labels. The argument about discrimination is no more relevant than that about reverse discrimination when importing-country standards are imposed on the exporter. Perhaps the most equitable way to deal with strictly local environmental impacts at the production stage is for each country to recognize the labelling system of the other.

To conclude, the EU has not convincingly demonstrated that its proposed eco-labelling measures will not be trade-discriminatory. Indeed some of the existing schemes, such as those in the Netherlands, appear to be discriminatory, although their impact is probably small. The best way to tackle some of the issues is through mutual recognition of those aspects of each country's scheme that only impinge on the environment in the country where production has taken place. A number of papers in this volume make this point. How such mutual recognition would operate, and what role international institutions should play in the eco-labelling debate is the subject of the next section.

V THE ROLE OF INTERNATIONAL INSTITUTIONS

There are three important roles that international institutions such as the World Trade Organization (WTO), ISO and others can play with regard to eco-labelling. First, the question of what constitutes technical barriers to trade has to be resolved by the WTO. Second, bodies such the ISO can play a part in developing acceptable criteria for eco-labels. Third, they can assist in establishing rules for the mutual recognition of labels. On the issue of eco-labelling and barriers to trade, the position is fairly clear in principle. In the context of the General Agreement on Tariffs and Trade (GATT), it was recognized that it was crucially important to provide access for foreign suppliers to participate and raise their trade concerns in the process through which product criteria and threshold levels for awarding eco-labels were decided. Their having access to certification systems and the awarding of labels on the same terms as domestically produced goods was critical. The selection of product categories as well as the setting of criteria tend to reflect local environmental conditions, and this may result in difficulties for foreign producers. The GATT working group on Environmental Measures and International Trade recognized that the influence of local industry in the choice of products or criteria should not result in inadvertent protective consequences. The criteria should be based on sound scientific evidence and foreign suppliers should have access to the design stage of the scheme. With respect to eco-labelling criteria based on processes and production methods (PPMs), foreign suppliers' access to an eco-label may be restricted if their own preferred PPMs are not the same as those required in the overseas market, or if establishing that they meet the process standards involves substantial additional cost.[30] As there may be legitimate reasons for diversity in environmental regulations across countries, these can result in different production methods, and an eco-label may be restrictive if it effectively imposes the production methods of the country of origin on other countries. Given these rules and the evidence presented in this volume, it is doubtful whether the some of the EU schemes would satisfy the condition that they not be technical barriers to trade.

There has long been a practice in the trade arena of harmonizing standards for traded commodities, to facilitate commerce and to have agreed definitions of what is being bought and sold. This has largely been done through the ISO. In the area of eco-labelling this organization attempts to "establish agreed procedures and principles to underpin all current and future eco-labelling schemes and . . . providing some of the infrastructure necessary for the schemes to move closer together".[31] The ISO is concerned with the whole range of issues on how criteria are developed and how the differences between the criteria adopted in different countries can be reconciled. As has been noted, this requires consultation between those setting the criteria and the producers engaged in international trade. The ISO provides a forum for such multilateral consultations. It is also working on defining principles for the establishment of criteria that could be the basis of any future system of mutual recognition.

Another group that has been seeking agreement on procedures and criteria in this field is the Global Eco-labelling Network (GEN).[32] This is a body of approximately twelve countries concerned with setting rules on the kinds of organizations that may award eco-labels and the procedures they must follow. It is just starting its activities. These activities are all desirable and can be seen, in part, as an attempt to resolve the trade issues that arise in relation to eco-labelling. Clearly the key issues will be (a) agreement on criteria to be adopted and (b) mutual recognition of some criteria across schemes for the same product in different countries. Although it is commendable that criteria should be agreed upon, this should not be seen as implying that every country must have the same environmental preferences or weights for different factors. None of the papers explicitly suggests that this is desirable but it is nevertheless something to warn against. One paper suggests that harmonization should be based on agreed WHO standards, codes of ethic on international trade in chemicals, etc.[33] Although this is attractive in some respects, the difficulty is that ambient conditions in different countries will not be equally affected by the activities of the manufacturers. In one country releases of chemicals might seriously affect water quality while in another the same releases could easily be assimilated. Hence international agreement on ambient standards (which is not universally observed anyway) cannot form the basis of how the labels are awarded.

Notes

1. This introductory review draws, in addition to the various contributions in this volume, on the ongoing work at under the joint UNCTAD/UNDP project on "Reconciliation of Environmental and Trade Policies". The author wishes to thank R. Vossenaar, V. Jha, S. Zarrilli and many others who have contributed to the several workshops organized on trade and the environment for many of the ideas expressed in this review.
2. They are Brazil (Green Seal and CERFLOR schemes), Canada (Environmental Choice Program), Colombia (no name given as yet), France (NF Environnement scheme), Germany (Blue Angel scheme), India (Eco-mark scheme), Japan (Eco-mark scheme), Korea (Eco-mark scheme), New Zealand (Environmental Choice), Poland (no name as yet), The Netherlands (Milieukeur, FAH, Butterfly and GEA), The Nordic countries (White Swan scheme in Iceland, Finland, Norway and Sweden, and the Good Environment Choice programme in Sweden); Singapore (Green Label scheme), and the United States (Green Seal).
3. Life-cycle analysis does not generally extend to the environmental impacts of those commodities that are used in the production of commodities that go into the manufacturing process. Thus, indirect effects are not addressed, and the analysis is sometimes referred to as limited life-cycle analysis.
4. This generally does not mean that the product has not used CFCs in the production processes involved. Hence it is an example of a claim that is not based on a life-cycle analysis.
5. The distinction between the different types of eco-labels is not always clear. For example, some products may have only one environmental impact, in which case their label will amount to a single-issue label.
6. An example given by Jha and Zarrilli is that of labelling schemes where roll-on deodorants are excluded from the scheme which deals only with aerosols. Though roll-ons are even more environmentally friendly, the consumer may be misled into believing that aerosols are to be preferred to roll-ons because the latter do not have a label. See Veena Jha and Simonetta Zarrilli, "Eco-labelling Initiatives as Potential Barriers to Trade: A Viewpoint from Developing Countries", in this volume.
7. Traditional economic theory takes the view that consumers would not pay anything extra for a good that had a general improving effect on the environment, if it did not affect them directly. It is argued that they would

choose to "free ride". However, much of the evidence on eco-labelling shows that this is not the case, and that there is a willingness to pay for general environmental improvements that have no direct benefits.

8. See, for example, T. Tietenberg, *Environmental and Resource Economics* (Chicago: Scott Foresman, 1992), and A. Markandya and J. Richardson, *The Earthscan Reader in Environmental Economics* (London: Earthscan, 1992).
9. The French scheme appears to place some importance on this aspect, so it is anticipated that, as the eco-labelled good is established, its costs of production will be no more than those of non-labelled goods. However, there is no empirical evidence to support this
10. See A. Jaffe, S. Peterson, P. Portney and R. Stavins, "Environmental Regulations and the Competitiveness of US Industry", Report prepared for the United States Department of Commerce, The Economic Resources Group, Cambridge, Mass., 1993.
11. V. Jha, R. Vossenaar, and S. Zarrilli, "Ecolabelling and International Trade", UNCTAD Discussion Paper, no. 70, October 1993.
12. See Rachel Crossley, Carlos A. Primo Braga and Panayotis N. Varangis, "Is There a Commercial Case for Tropical Timber Certification?", in this volume. See also E. van Ravensway and J. Hoehn, "Consumer Willingness to Pay for Reducing Pesticides in Food: Results of a Nation-wide Survey", Discussion Paper, Department of Agricultural Economics, Michigan State University, 1991.
13. Harmen Verbruggen, Saskia Jongma and Frans van der Woerd, "Eco-labelling and the Developing Countries: The Dutch Horticultural Sector", in this volume.
14. The paper by Crossley *et al.* in this volume cites the following studies: (a) D. Winterhalter and D. L. Cassens, "United States Hardwood Forests: Consumer Perception and Willingness to Pay", Discussion Paper, Purdue University, Department of Foresty, August 1993, who state that 34 per cent of United States consumers were willing to pay 6–10 per cent more for "sustainable wood"; (b) Gerstman and Meyer (1991) who find a 1–5 per cent premium from 75 per cent of consumers; (c) a Purdue University survey (D. Winterhalter, "Consumer Perception and Willingness to Pay: Results of two National Surveys", Purdue University, May 1994) also estimating a 1–5 per cent premium but among 57 per cent of the population and a 6–10 per cent premium among the top 36 per cent; and (d) a study in the United Kingdom by Gazali and Simula (paper presented at the ITTO Conference, Colombia, May 1994) that found a 13 per cent premium for tropical timber products from sustainably managed forests.
15. Crossley *et al.*, this volume. The cost analysis is only partial and does not include, for example, all the benefits of sustainable management. Moreover the cost is expected to fall as common principles and criteria are applied.
16. An example would be to place a requirement on SO_2 emissions in the production process. In a country where such emissions are not a matter of concern (the levels may be very low relative to the assimilative capacity) the emissions requirements would impose extra costs.

17. See also A. Markandya, "Reconciliation of Environment and Trade Policies: Synthesis of Country Case Studies", MIMEO, 1994.
18. Pedro da Motta Veiga, Mário C. de Carvalho Jr, Maria Lúcia Vilmar and Heraldiva Façanha, "Eco-labelling Schemes in the European Union and their Impact on Brazilian Exports", in this volume.
19. Veiga *et al.*, in this volume.
20. Lily Ho, Diana Gaviria, Ximena Berrera and Ricardo Sánchez, "The Potential Impact of EU Eco-labelling Programme on Colombian Textile Exports", in this volume.
21. Zbigniew Jakubczyk, "Eco-labelling Schemes in Poland", in this volume.
22. Ibid.
23. B. Fiedor, S. Czaja, A. Graczyk and J. Rymarczyk, "Linkages between Environment and Trade: A Case Study of Poland", UNCTAD, Geneva, 1994. A summary of this repor has been published as "Trade, Environment and Development: Lessons from the Empirical Studied: The case of Poland", UNCTAD, TD/B/WG.6/Misc. 10, November 1995.
24. See Markandya, op. cit.
25. Financial Times, 16 June 1994.
26. Mehmet Arda, "Environmentally Preferable Commodities", in this volume.
27. Jha and Zarrilli, in this volume.
28. Veiga *et al.*, in this volume.
29. Jha *et al.*, op. cit.
30. J. Chakarian, "Eco-labelling and GATT", in this volume.
31. J. Henry, "ISO and Eco-labelling", in this volume.
32. Environmental Choice Programme, Environment Canada, "Dealing with the Trade Barrier Issue", in this volume.
33. L. B. Campbell, "International Environmental Standards: Their Role in the Mutual Recognition of Eco-labelling Schemes", in this volume.

2 Eco-Labelling and International Trade: The Main Issues

René Vossenaar[1]

INTRODUCTION

A Background

Eco-labelling aims to promote the consumption and production of environmentally more "friendly" products by providing information to consumers on their environmental effects, in principle based on a life-cycle approach. This paper points out that while eco-labelling is essentially aimed at environmental purposes, it may at times result in discrimination against foreign producers and act as a non-tariff barrier to trade. Developing countries are becoming more exposed to the effects of eco-labelling as some of the new product categories which are being selected for eco-labelling are of export interest to them. In addition, in the case of these product categories, upstream environmental effects may be seen as more important than those related with consumption and disposal. Thus, criteria tend to be developed regarding raw materials and production processes, which may be difficult to comply with for foreign producers. This paper examines the possible environmental and, in particular, trade effects of eco-labelling on developing countries. It reviews the main issues which are currently being deliberated in a number of forums, including the United Nations Conference on Trade and Development (UNCTAD). It draws considerably from reports prepared by the UNCTAD secretariat to aid deliberations on eco-labelling in the Ad Hoc Working Group on Trade, Environment and Development.[2]

B Eco-Labelling Principles

This paper focuses on eco-labels awarded by a third party for products which meet preset environmental criteria, or "type I" eco-labels in the

Table 2.1 Overview of eco-labelling programmes

Country/group	*Name of the programme*	*Date of creation*
Germany	Blue Angel	1977
Canada	Environmental Choice Program	1988
Japan	EcoMark	1989
Nordic countries	White Swan	1989
United States	Green Seal	1989
Sweden	Good Environmental Choice	1990
New Zealand	Environmental Choice	1990
India	Ecomark	1991
Austria	Austrian Eco-label	1991
Australia	Environmental Choice	1991
Republic of Korea	Ecomark	1992
Singapore	Green Label Singapore	1992
France	NF-Environnement	1992
Netherlands	Stichting Milieukeur	1992
European Union	European Flower	1992
Croatia	Environmentally Friendly	1993

Source: UNCTAD, TD/B/WG.6/2, Box 2.

terminology used by the International Organization for Standardization (ISO). Currently there are more than 20 type I eco-labelling programmes (see Table 2.1).

In principle, eco-labelling follows a comprehensive, multi-criteria and life-cycle approach with a view to informing the consumer about a real reduction of environmental stress, and not merely a transfer of impacts across environmental media or stages of the product's life cycle. In practice, however, the use of life-cycle analysis (LCA) varies widely across eco-labelling programmes. For example, in the programmes of the European Union (EU) and the Netherlands the most relevant environmental aspects are first identified on the basis of a matrix which considers a list of environmental aspects at different stages of the product's life cycle. Specific criteria are then developed addressing these aspects. The French programme is probably the most rigorous with regard to LCA. In other programmes, however, the criteria refer to only one or some environmental aspects and only part of the product's life cycle. For example, the German and Japanese eco-labelling programmes usually focus on one environmental aspect, normally related to the use and disposal stages of a product's life cycle.

While LCA is considered a useful approach from an environmental point of view, its use may create practical and conceptual problems, in particular when international trade is involved. The simple fact that LCA requires a large amount of information may cause practical problems when products or materials are imported. In addition, specific process and production method (PPM)-related criteria which are based on the domestic conditions and priorities in the importing country may be less appropriate in other countries, in particular developing countries, where environmental conditions and priorities tend to be different.

C Possible Discriminatory Effects on Foreign Producers

To some extent, difficulties that may be encountered by foreign suppliers in obtaining an eco-label represent the normal disadvantages of the exporter versus the domestic producer. However, certain aspects of eco-labelling, such as the cradle-to-grave approach, may add a specific dimension to such difficulties. There is concern that, although the criteria for granting labels are the same for domestic and foreign suppliers, eco-labelling may *de facto* discriminate against foreign producers, in particular from developing countries. Possible discriminatory effects can be attributed to a number of factors:

- Eco-labelling tends to be based on domestic environmental priorities and technologies in the importing country and may overlook acceptable products and manufacturing processes in the country of production. Eco-labelling criteria often lack flexibility to reflect relevant local environmental conditions and priorities in the country of production.
- The definition of product categories, and the determination of criteria and limit values may favour domestic over foreign producers. Eco-labelling criteria may be specified in terms of technology to which domestic firms have easier access.
- Eco-labelling may require foreign producers to meet criteria which are not relevant in the country of production.[3] Thus, technologies which have been developed to deal with pollutants which are important in the importing country, but less important in the country of production, would need to be imported if a firm wishes to qualify for a label.[4]
- Environmental infrastructures may differ widely across countries (e.g. municipal waste water treatment plants; solid waste treatment plants; recycling stations).[5]
- Ensuring supplies of chemicals and other materials which are

acceptable for use in eco-labelled products may be difficult for foreign producers, in particular in developing countries. Foreign suppliers of inputs to eco-labelled products may also be discriminated against.

- Certain parameters used for calculating the environmental effects of products throughout their life-cycle may be based on information collected in the importing country or countries with comparable environmental conditions, and may overestimate environmental impacts in the country of production. For example, parameters used to estimate the energy used in the manufacturing of products may not reflect the conditions in the country of production.

I TRADE AND COMPETITIVENESS EFFECTS OF ECO-LABELLING

Since the use of an eco-label is voluntary, exporting firms have the option of either applying for the label (focusing competitiveness on non-price factors) or selling unlabelled products (focusing competitiveness on price factors). Eco-labelling promotes product differentiation on the basis of environmental quality and may have effects on competitiveness.

At the time of drafting, no developing-country producer was using a "type I" eco-label to market products in any OECD country. Although data on refused applications are not available, it is likely that developing-country producers have not yet applied for such labels. Producers in developing countries may nevertheless have been affected in two ways. First, eco-labelling may have reduced the competitiveness of unlabelled products in a particular market. It has been reported, for example, that Norway's imports of fine paper originating in Brazil declined significantly after the introduction of an eco-label.[6] Second, eco-labelling may have had effects on suppliers of materials used for manufacturing eco-labelled products. It is difficult to know whether such effects have already arisen. However, the major concern of Brazilian exporters of pulp with a recently introduced EU eco-label on tissue paper referred precisely to such indirect effects. And eco-labelling in footwear could have effects on leather tanneries in developing countries.

The effects of eco-labelling on developing countries depend basically on the choice of product categories selected for eco-labelling, the relative size of the market for eco-labelled products,[7] compliance costs (including the costs of testing and verification) in combination with possible price premiums for eco-labelled products, and the administrative costs of using the labels (such as fees). In some cases, eco-labelling may affect suppliers of materials rather than the manufacturers of products included in eco-labelling programmes.

So far, developing countries may not as yet have been significantly affected by eco-labelling because products that have been included in eco-labelling programmes in general are not very significant in terms of developing countries' trade (with the possible exception of paper and paper products). However, proposals for eco-labels for timber and timber products are of key concern and interest to a number of developing countries. With regard to other export products, developing countries are also becoming more exposed to the effects of eco-labelling. For example, the EU is in the process of establishing eco-labels for footwear and certain textiles (T-shirts and bed linen). In the Netherlands, the "Stichting Milieukeur" has already established criteria for shoes within the national eco-labelling programme. In 1991, as much as 91 per cent of all shoes sold in the Netherlands were imported (at least 84 per cent in the case of leather shoes and 97 per cent in the case of footwear made from other materials). Developing countries accounted for 35 per cent of all imports and 82 per cent of extra-EU imports in 1993. At a recent meeting of UNCTAD's Ad Hoc Working Group on Trade, Environment and Development, developing-country participants expressed concern about this trend and questioned the rationale for establishing eco-labelling criteria for products which are principally imported, in particular when such criteria related to the use of specific materials or PPMs.

The case studies presented in this volume provide some indication of key factors determining compliance costs in product categories which are of export interest to these countries. It is to be noted, however, that since producers in developing countries have not yet applied for eco-labels, these studies are not based on detailed analyses of the costs of adjustments needed to qualify for an eco-label, but rather on preliminary consideration of the perceived degree of difficulties that firms may encounter in complying with different criteria (in case they would apply for a label), based on interviews with manufacturers, exporters, and industry associations.[8]

These case studies indicate that the possible impacts of eco-labelling programmes on the competitiveness of firms in developing countries could, for analytical purposes, be classified in three broad categories: (i) costs of materials; (ii) capital costs; and (iii) costs of testing and verification. In addition, it was found that in each of these cases possible effects were substantially different for small and medium-sized firms as compared to large firms.

A key question is whether targeting a potential market niche for eco-labelled products could allow firms to recover – through price premiums and/or increased market shares – the costs involved in adjusting their production processes and in securing materials that comply with the eco-labelling criteria. However, at times price premiums may be difficult to obtain. It follows that incurring additional costs with a view to obtaining eco-labels may involve a certain economic risk.

II ENVIRONMENTAL EFFECTS OF ECO-LABELLING

Measures which inform and educate the consumer on a product's environmental advantage, such as eco-labels, can create demand pressure and encourage innovation leading to reduced environmental impacts of production and consumption. Whether and how much eco-labelling has already contributed to reducing environmental stress is difficult to assess. Existing evidence of positive environmental effects which could be attributed to eco-labels is limited to specific cases. For example, it has been reported that a few years after the introduction of eco-labels for oil and gas heating appliances under the German Blue Angel programme, emissions of sulphur dioxide, carbon monoxide, and nitrogen oxides were reduced by more than 30 per cent and that the energy efficiency of these appliances had improved significantly. Also, after the introduction of an eco-label, the market share of low-solvent paints and varnishes went up from 1 per cent to 50 per cent while the amount of solvents released into the environment were estimated to have been reduced by some 40 000 tons.[9] Unfortunately, however, there are no studies which have tried to make a systematic assessment of the effects of existing eco-labelling programmes on the environment. What can be said is that the environmental effects of eco-labelling depend largely on the relevance and significance of eco-labelling criteria as well as the market share of eco-labelled products, which in turn depends on consumer preferences for eco-labelled products and the responsiveness of producers and suppliers. Thus in order for eco-labelling to be an effective marketing instrument, there must be public awareness of eco-labelling programmes and eco-labelled products, and producers must be interested in making a significant volume of eco-labelled products available in the marketplace.

Table 2.2 Number of product categories and of products under different eco-labelling programmes (February/March 1995)

	Product categories for which criteria have been established	*Eco-labels granted*			
		Product categories	*Manufacturers*	*Of which foreign*	*Products*
Canada	31	15	116	17	1500
EU	5	1	1	–	8
Germany	81	61	1058	175	4353
Japan	65	63	1039	22	2322
Netherlands	20	4	10	3	40
Nordic countries	31	15	182	19	–

Source: UNCTAD, TD/B/WG.6/5, Box 1.

A useful way of analysing the possible environmental effects of eco-labelling is to examine consumer awareness and the response of producers. Eco-labelling programmes are becoming increasingly known among consumers, and polls indicate that many consumers declare that they are willing to pay a premium for environment-friendly products. Consumer concerns may focus on particular environmental issues, such as recycling and deforestation. Thus, eco-labels may play a relatively significant role in sectors such as paper and timber products. In some other sectors, however, consumer concerns may be less significant. Institutional buyers may also provide a market for eco-labelled products. In this context, public procurement guidelines in OECD countries increasingly pay attention to environmental factors, although in general eco-labelled products are not favoured explicitly.

Experience shows that it may be difficult to implement eco-labels which are successful in terms of producers' response. For example, Canada's Environmental Choice Programme (ECP) has developed criteria for 31 product categories, but eco-labels are being used in only 15 of these categories (see Table 2.2). And a large part of ECP's licensing revenues are derived from only two product categories: paint and fine paper. ECP has now established an action plan aimed at increasing the presence of eco-labelled products in the marketplace.[10]

The more successful programmes in terms of number of products using eco-labels are the German "Blue Angel" and the Japanese EcoMark.[11] However, approximately half of the eco-labelled products in Germany belong to only a few categories, especially low-pollutant coatings, recycled paper products and recycled cardboard products.

A Effects on Developing Countries

In theory, eco-labelling in OECD countries may have positive environmental and trade effects in developing countries, but such effects will likely be modest. Large firms in developing countries who possess the financial and technological means to invest in environmental improvements may be able to qualify for an eco-label and sell in premium markets. However, as mentioned above, incurring additional costs with a view to obtaining eco-labels may involve a certain economic risk. A key question from an environmental point of view is whether the required adjustments to qualify for an eco-label in export markets are also appropriate in the context of the economic, technological and environmental conditions in the producing country. Eco-labelling criteria which are objective, understandable and realistic are more likely to provide incentives to developing-country producers to design and manufacture products which comply with these criteria.

A number of developing countries and countries in transition have established their own eco-labelling programmes (e.g. India, Republic of Korea and Singapore) or are in the process of doing so. As in the case of developed countries, the purpose of such programmes is to contribute to environmental improvements by providing information to consumers and to encourage producers to shift to more environment-friendly production processes. Eco-labelling and the associated education process may contribute to heightened consumer awareness of environmental issues. However, since the domestic market for eco-labelled products tends to be small, the conservation of export markets and the improvement of export competitiveness are often among the key objectives. In order to be successful, eco-labelling programmes aim at some form of mutual recognition with similar programmes in OECD countries.

III TAKING DEVELOPING-COUNTRY INTERESTS INTO ACCOUNT

The preceding sections have indicated why eco-labelling programmes have raised concerns among developing-country producers. From a trade point of view, there is concern that eco-labelling may adversely affect export competitiveness and act as a non-tariff barrier to trade. From an environmental point of view, there is concern that eco-labelling criteria which address local environmental problems and priorities of the industrialized countries may be irrelevant or inappropriate for other countries, but especially so for developing countries.

Taking account of the interests of developing countries in the development of eco-labelling programmes will in the first place require improved transparency as well as the association of developing countries with the process of determining criteria for products of export interest to them. Technical assistance also has an important role to play. The implementation of guiding principles, currently being developed by ISO, as well as an examination of the relationship between eco-labelling and the rules and principles of the WTO are also useful. In the long run, the acceptance by eco-labelling agencies in industrialized countries of different but "equivalent" environmental criteria which take account of the environmental conditions in developing countries, as well as mutual recognition, could also serve developing countries' interests.

A Transparency

Eco-labelling is a fairly transparent process at the domestic level, but foreign producers may find it difficult to express their views and concerns. To some extent this can be explained by the fact that eco-labelling has been considered primarily as an instrument of domestic environmental policy, which has not been perceived as having significant trade effects.

In certain aspects, the possible trade effects of eco-labelling are similar to those of technical standards and regulations. In this context, the experience acquired through the WTO Agreement on Technical Barriers to Trade could be used as a basis for mitigating adverse trade effects of eco-labelling. WTO rules, however, may be less well adapted for other aspects of eco-labelling, such as the life-cycle approach and the use of PPM-related criteria.

There is a need to analyse the requirements for improved transparency of eco-labelling programmes as well as ways and means to achieve such improvements. It may be useful to analyse such requirements at different stages of the eco-labelling process, in particular (i) in the selection of products and the formulation of criteria, and (ii) in the public-review process.

Eco-labelling processes are generally open to public participation.

Various interest groups participate in the relevant bodies but such participation is normally limited to domestic interest groups. At present, foreign producers are not able to participate directly in the stages of product selection and formulation of criteria: they have to rely on public-review processes.[12]

B Technical Assistance

Technical assistance and capacity-building efforts in the area of eco-labelling and certification may help in reducing the potential negative effects of eco-labelling on developing countries and may assist producers in taking advantage of trading opportunities that may arise for environment-friendly products. Technical assistance in capacity-building could also be useful in supporting developing countries wishing to establish their own eco-labelling programmes and in promoting mutual recognition of eco-labelling programmes. Technical assistance is also needed to facilitate the effective participation of developing countries in future international deliberations on eco-labelling, in particular in ISO. Furthermore, the establishment in developing countries and countries in transition of standardization bodies – or training of existing bodies – to conduct testing and certification in the producing country could reduce associated costs.

C Dealing with the PPMs Issue

The application of specific PPM-related criteria to imported products may pose certain problems, in particular when such products originate in countries where environmental and developmental conditions are significantly different from those in the importing country. Not all eco-labelling programmes use PPM-related criteria. It is often argued that life-cycle analysis and the use of PPM-related criteria are necessary to provide information to the consumer. However, it could be asked to what extent eco-labels that do not take account of different environmental conditions in the country of production could provide relevant information to the consumer.[13] One option could be to avoid PPM-related criteria in the case of product categories that are largely produced by developing countries. If PPM-related criteria are used, a number of options could be considered, on a case-by-case basis, to avoid or mitigate adverse effects on trading partners. It may at times be desirable to exempt foreign producers from the requirement to comply with specific process-related criteria.[14]

It may also be possible to limit the requirements for products originating in developing countries to comply with existing regulations in the country of production. It is to be noted that environmental regulations in developing countries are often quite stringent, but enforcement may be more difficult. Eco-labelling could perform a useful function if it provides incentives to comply with existing environmental standards.

Another approach would be to exercise special caution when designing PPM-related requirements in areas where imports are predominant.[15] Thus, PPM-related requirements and limit values for product categories which include significant imports, in particular from developing countries, could be designed in such a way that adverse effects on producing countries are avoided. In other cases, concepts such as "equivalency" and mutual recognition, discussed in the next section, may be useful in dealing with the PPM issue.

D Equivalencies and Mutual Recognition

The concept of equivalencies in the context of eco-labelling implies that when comparable environmental objectives can be achieved in different ways, taking into account the specific environmental conditions of each country, different criteria can be accepted as a basis for awarding eco-labels. The concept could be applied in two different circumstances. Firstly, the eco-labelling programme of the importing country might accept compliance with certain environmental requirements or the achievement of certain environmental improvements in the exporting country as "equivalent" to compliance with specific criteria and thresholds established in its own programme, even when no eco-labelling programme exists in the exporting country. Secondly, the concept of "equivalent" standards is generally considered as a basic condition for mutual recognition of eco-labelling programmes.

When discussing equivalencies it may be useful to make a distinction between product-related and process-related criteria. Product-related criteria address environmental impacts of a product on the environment of the importing country, associated with its consumption and disposal phase. Possibilities for establishing "equivalent" product-related criteria may be relatively limited, compared to the case of PPM-related criteria. Since the domestic environment of the importing country would not be affected by PPMs addressing local environmental problems in the exporting country, there would be extra scope for accepting as equivalent environmental criteria which better reflect the environmental conditions and priorities in the exporting country.

Current experience with the concept of equivalencies is limited to the area of product measures. References to "equivalent" standards can be found in the Agreement on Technical Barriers to Trade (TBT Agreement)[16] and in the Agreement on Sanitary and Phytosanitary Measures (SPS Agreement),[17] negotiated in the Uruguay Round. These references seem to recognize that certain "objectives" or "appropriate levels of protection" may be achieved by different, but "equivalent" standards.

Mutual recognition of eco-labels may help to avoid or mitigate adverse effects on trade while contributing to environmental objectives in a way that takes account of differences in environmental conditions between countries.

The interest in mutual recognition of eco-labelling has been growing, partly as a result of concerns that the emergence of different eco-labelling programmes in an increasing number of countries might adversely affect trade as well as create confusion among consumers. Mutual recognition, however, is not yet widely accepted. Environmental groups may be concerned that mutual recognition could imply that products that do not meet the same stringent criteria of the domestic programme are nevertheless awarded the corresponding eco-label. Domestic producers may be concerned about possible effects on competitiveness. Mutual recognition requires a confidence-building process. Acceptance by consumers and environmental interest groups requires credibility of the exporting country's programme.

Mutual recognition is of key interest to developing countries and an important long-term objective in establishing eco-labelling programmes in some of these countries. Mutual recognition, however, does not serve only trade interests. Mutual recognition appears to be a basic condition for eco-labelling to have significant positive environmental effects in developing countries.

E Eco-Labelling and the WTO

Strengthened international cooperation and increased transparency are of key importance in avoiding or mitigating possible adverse trade effects of eco-labelling. An important question in this context is the relationship of eco-labelling with the WTO, in particular the TBT Agreement.

Contrary to what is often argued, the fact that eco-labelling is a voluntary instrument or is implemented by non-governmental bodies does not by itself mean that eco-labelling would not be covered by the TBT Agreement. Voluntary standards implemented either by central government, local government, non-governmental bodies or regional bodies are in fact covered by the Code of Good Practice for the Preparation, Adoption and Application of Standards (Annex 2 to the TBT Agreement). However, the use of criteria regarding PPMs which are not related to the (eco-labelled) product may be critical in the context of the relationship between eco-labelling and WTO rules. There may be some concern that a clear recognition that eco-labelling falls under the provision of the TBT Agreement may create a precedent for recognizing non-incorporated PPMs in the WTO. It may also be possible to negotiate a separate code on eco-labelling and other voluntary instruments in the WTO.

IV CONCLUSIONS

Eco-labelling can be an effective instrument of environmental policy-making, provided it is non-discriminatory, transparent and based on an open process, including, where relevant, the involvement of foreign producers. If these conditions are not met, eco-labelling can also act as a non-tariff obstacle to trade.

In certain aspects, the possible trade effects of eco-labelling are similar to those of technical standards and regulations. The experience acquired in dealing with the trade effects of technical standards and regulations, for example through the WTO Agreement on Technical Barriers to Trade, could be used as a basis for mitigating adverse trade effects of eco-labelling.

In addition, eco-labelling could have trade effects with which the international trade rules are less familiar. For example, the life-cycle approach and the use of PPM-related criteria involve complex issues, in particular when international trade is involved. These aspects of eco-labelling point to the need for a broad concept of transparency.

ISO's work on guiding principles for eco-labelling is expected to contribute significantly to the credibility of eco-labelling programmes and to avoid discrimination. However, it is likely that eco-labelling will continue to cause concern, in particular to developing countries. A number of issues still need to be resolved:

- the relationship between eco-labelling and the provisions of the multilateral trading system, in particular the Agreement on Technical Barriers to Trade (an issue included in the terms of reference of the WTO Committee on Trade and Environment);

- the transaction costs that may arise from the co-existence of different eco-labelling schemes; it is to be noted that current work in ISO is not aimed at establishing uniform eco-labelling criteria across programmes;
- the PPM-issue;
- mutual recognition and equivalencies.

This paper has examined several possibilities to take into account the interests of foreign producers, including those from developing countries, in the elaboration of eco-labelling criteria. In the short run, it seems useful to improve transparency and to be particularly cautious in the use of PPM-related criteria in product categories where imports, particularly from developing countries, are predominant. In the longer run, exploring the scope for "equivalencies" and mutual recognition between eco-labelling schemes seems a useful approach. UNEP and UNCTAD are cooperating on these issues.

Notes

1. The opinions expressed in this paper are those of the author and do not necessarily reflect the views of UNCTAD. The designations and terminology employed are those of the author.
2. See UNCTAD, TD/B/WG.6/2 of 6 October 1994 and TD/B/WG.6/5 of 28 March 1995.
3. An example would be to place a requirement on sulphur dioxide emissions in the production process. In a country where such emissions are not a matter of concern (the levels may be very low relative to assimilative capacity) the eco-labelling requirement would impose extra costs, without leading to any significant environmental improvements. See A. Markandya, "Eco-labelling: An Introduction and a Review", in this volume.
4. For example, requirements in the European Union may refer to sulphur dioxide and nitrogen oxides. Since such pollutants are important in the European Union, technologies have been developed. In developing countries, where these pollutants are less important, technologies have not been developed. An eco-label would thus make it necessary to import such technologies.
5. Differences in environmental infrastructures across countries have a large impact on valuations of what is a "cleaner product". For example, if municipal waste-water treatment plants already have phosphorus cleaning, as in Denmark, the use of phosphorus would be preferred to other calcium-binding substances. Another example refers to fly-ash. A number of countries have built up infrastructure to allow to use fly-ash as a raw

material in the cement industry (in Denmark, practically all fly-ash is used in cement production). Thus, certain activities that produce fly-ash, such as burning of coal, are valued differently as compared to other countries. See Helle Petersen, "A Possible (International) Implementation Strategy for Product Oriented Environmental Policy Measures", in *International Workshop on Product Oriented Environmental Policy*, Workshop Proceedings, The Hague, 30 September–1 October 1993.

6. UNCTAD, TD/B/40(1)/6 of 6 August 1993.
7. It is often mentioned that eco-labelling will in any case be applied to only a small portion of the market for a given category of products. Some programmes indeed set thresholds at a high level so that initially only a small part of the products in a certain category would be eligible for the eco-label. For example, Canada's ECP used to work with a target of around 20 per cent of the market. In other programmes, such as Japan's EcoMark, however, criteria are set independently of what proportion of firms are expected to be able to comply with the criteria, and a larger portion of firms may obtain the label. To the extent that eco-labelling programmes become more market-oriented, the argument that trade effects are insignificant as market shares for eco-labelled products are in any case small becomes more difficult to defend.
8. Developing-country producers tend to focus competitiveness on price factors and may therefore show little interest in eco-labels. Producers in more advanced developing countries may focus efforts on upgrading product quality with a view to selling in premium markets. Eco-labels may have a bearing on such efforts.
9. See R. V. Hartwell and L. Bergkamp, "Eco-labelling in Europe: New Market-related Environmental Risks?", *BNA International Environmental Daily*, 20 October 1992, and M. Porter and C. van der Linde, "Green and Competitive", *Harvard Business Review*, September–October 1995, pp. 120–34.
10. ECP hopes to expand the number of product categories for which eco-labels will be operative by 60 new categories. As part of its plan, ECP is putting more emphasis on market orientation, public-awareness building (e.g. through cooperation with licensees in the fields of advertising and marketing) and new approaches to eco-labelling criteria. For example, a study has been commissioned to identify and prioritize possible product and service categories, based on the estimated environmental benefits of their inclusion in the programme, their sales volumes (considering both household expenditure and government procurement) and possible industry response.
11. In both programmes product-specific award criteria tend to focus on the use and disposal stages of the product's life cycle (see UNCTAD, TD/B/WG.6/2, Box 4).
12. In most eco-labelling programmes, there is a public-review process of draft criteria before final product criteria are published. Any interested party, including foreign producers, can take advantage of this process. To some extent, transparency provisions in existing eco-labelling programmes may not differ substantially from those of the TBT Agreement. However, the ability of foreign producers to participate in the review process depends on many factors, such as the timely dissemination of information

on new product categories being selected for eco-labelling, the length of the review process and the ability to be physically present and to devote time to the process. It may thus be necessary to improve the review process when imports are significant, for example through improved notification procedures. See also Maria Isolda P. Guevara *et al.*, "Canada's Environmental Choice Programme and Its Impact on Developing-Country Trade", in this volume.

13. See also A. Markandya, op. cit.
14. For example, in the case of eco-labels for footwear in the Netherlands, foreign producers are exempted from the requirement to process solid waste containing chromium (through recycling, deposit in a secure dumping site, or incineration whereby chromium is reclaimed) if such waste is not considered as chemical waste in the country of production.
15. Environmental Choice Program, Environment Canada, "Eco-labelling and PPMs: The international Context", paper presented at the OECD Workshop on Eco-labelling and Trade, London, 6–7 October 1994.
16. The reference in the TBT Agreement is as follows: "Members shall give positive consideration to accepting as equivalent technical regulations of other members, even if these regulations differ from their own, provided they are satisfied that these regulations adequately fulfil the objectives of their own regulations" (Article 2.7).
17. The SPS Agreement includes the following reference: "Members shall accept the sanitary and phytosanitary measures of other Members as equivalent, even if these measures differ from their own or those used by other Members trading in the same product, if the exporting country objectively demonstrates to the importing Member that its measures achieve the importing Member's appropriate level of sanitary or phytosanitary protection" (Article 14).

3 Eco-Labelling, the Environment and International Trade

Aaditya Mattoo and Harsha V. Singh[1]

INTRODUCTION

Eco-labelling has been introduced in a number of countries[2] for a wide variety of products.[3] This chapter analyses the effects of eco-labelling both on the environment and on international trade. It first establishes the conditions under which the introduction of labelling would have a beneficial impact on the environment and suggests an appropriate empirical test. Then it assesses the consequences of labelling schemes for international trade. Four factors are identified as important: the distribution of environmental concern, the structure of the market, the nature of environment-friendly technology and the precise form of labelling policy.

A labelling scheme is often perceived as a voluntary tax borne by a section of consumers (those who are concerned about the environment) to finance a subsidy to a section of the producers (those who produce environmentally friendly goods). But such a scheme could also lead to a negative demand shock for another section of producers, i.e. those who do not or cannot produce goods deemed to be environment-friendly. Thus, the conditions of entry into the environment-friendly segment of the market, i.e. the conditions for acquiring the label, assume crucial significance.

In the context of international trade, the most obvious question is whether these conditions discriminate between domestic and foreign producers. Even if the same standard is set, there may be effective discrimination on account of unequal access to environment-friendly technology. Similarly, if foreign producers initially had lower costs, the effect may be a greater increase in foreign costs than in domestic costs. However, it is not only manifestly discriminatory measures which might be cause for concern. In markets characterized by strategic interaction between firms, the introduction of eco-labelling could lead to outcomes favouring the relatively high-cost producers even when the standards implicit in the labelling schemes are not discriminatory *per se*.

The various products covered by eco-labelling involve different types of market situations, ranging from competitive markets to oligopoly. This paper will begin with an analysis of eco-labelling in a competitive situation, and then consider some aspects of eco-labelling in an oligopolistic model.

In section I, a simple model is presented to show when eco-labelling (henceforth "labelling") would have desirable consequences for the environment. The empirical relevance of the result and the implications for policy are also examined. Section II provides a stylized example which shows that the introduction of labelling in one country could have adverse terms-of-trade and welfare consequences for its trading partners. Section III considers some trade and welfare consequences of labelling in more general situations, in each case drawing implications for policy. Section IV illustrates the implications of the market structure, the nature of the environmentally friendly technology and the precise form of labelling policy.

I ENVIRONMENTAL IMPACT OF ECO-LABELLING IN AN INTEGRATED MARKET

A Possible Adverse Effects

The labelling of products to indicate whether or not they have been produced by methods friendly to the environment is widely regarded as an appropriate, though partial, response to environmental problems. It is expected that labels will enable consumers to discriminate between products, leading to reduced demand and hence reduced output of products produced by methods detrimental to the environment. This section, based on a paper by Mattoo and Singh,[4] shows that in certain cases, eco-labelling could lead to an adverse effect on the environment.

In the market, there are some consumers who are concerned about environmental problems and others who are not.[5] Even though labelling does not remedy the negative externality imposed by unconcerned consumers on those who are concerned, it may stimulate concern for the environment and increase the demand for environment-friendly

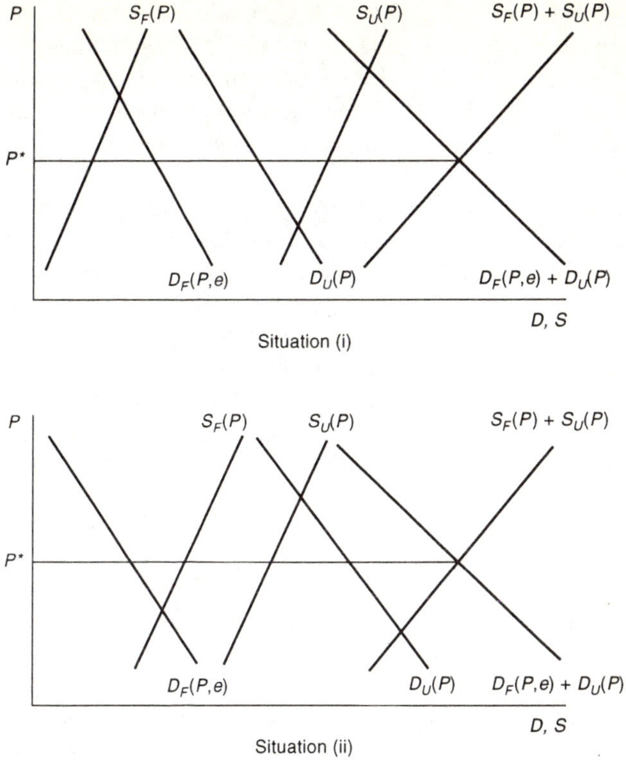

Figure 3.1 The effect of eco-labelling in alternative situations

products. However, it is precisely this consequence of labelling which can lead to perverse results. In certain plausible cases, the differentiation of products due to labelling may lead to increased sales of products made by both environment-friendly and environment-unfriendly methods.

A simple example will make clear the intuitive rationale for such a result. Say, the market for a particular undifferentiated good was in equilibrium at a certain price *P* with 100 units being supplied and demanded (see Figure 3.1). Let us assume that 50 units were being demanded by consumers who are potentially concerned about the environment, and 50 by those who are not. Now labelling is introduced and products are differentiated according to whether they are produced by environment-friendly methods (F) or environment-unfriendly methods (U). Let us further assume that concerned consumers buy only F products while the unconcerned buy either or both, depending on the price. If the quantity produced of F products at price *P* was less than 50 (Situation (i) in Figure 3.1), the price of such products would increase relative to *P* and the price of U products would fall. In this case, labelling would achieve its objective of discouraging production by environment-unfriendly methods.

However, consider the possibility that the quantity produced of F products at price *P* was greater than 50 (situation (ii) in Figure 3.1). Then, if only concerned consumers buy F products, there will be a tendency for the price of F products to fall relative to *P*. This will prompt unconcerned consumers also to buy F products, i.e. perform arbitrage until a uniform price is established for both F and U products. Now, if conditions of demand and supply are unchanged, then the post-labelling uniform price will be the same as *P*, and labelling will achieve little. However, the problem arises if concerned consumers are willing to pay even slightly more for the certainty of purchasing a product produced by an environment-friendly method than they were for the undifferentiated product. Then aggregate demand in the post-labelling situation will be greater than aggregate demand in the pre-labelling situation. The uniform price post-labelling will then be higher than *P*. This implies that the production of both F and U products is likely to increase.

It has been assumed that concerned consumers behave somewhat rigidly, in that they necessarily consume only environmentally friendly products. Concerned consumers are more likely to be willing to pay up to a maximum premium for the labelled product, and in equilibrium, the price difference between the labelled and the unlabelled product will be equal to the premium that the marginal concerned consumer in the labelled segment is willing to pay. However, allowing consumers to balance their environmental concerns against price differences would only widen the range of situations in which labelling leads to increased production by environment-unfriendly methods. Supplies of the two categories of the product have been treated as fixed. It may be argued that in the longer run there are possibilities of augmenting these supplies and for producers to switch methods of production. But whether the producers have an incentive to do so will depend, in the first instance, on the impact of consumer behaviour on market prices, which has been the subject of this section.

It should also be noted that even when labelling results in a decline in the output of the unlabelled product, it is not necessary that the absolute level of "pollution" will be reduced. While there will be a reduction in the level of "pollution" per unit output, the absolute level of "pollution" may increase because of the higher production of the labelled product. Thus, if the environmental concern is with the absolute level of "pollution", rather than the "pollution" per unit of output, then labelling may not be useful even when it results in lower production of the unlabelled product.

B Some Empirical Examples

The discussion above shows that labelling reduces the output of U products only if, at the pre-labelling undifferentiated equilibrium price, *P*, the quantity demanded by concerned consumers is greater than the quantity supplied by the environment-friendly method. Thus the comparison of these two magnitudes constitutes the appropriate empirical test of whether it is desirable to introduce labelling. If the stated inequality does not hold, labelling will at best be ineffectual and at worst lead to adverse consequences for the environment. Consider the following two examples.

Since 1991, tuna imported into the United States market can be labelled "dolphin-safe" only if it fulfils certain conditions.[6] Methods perceived to be dolphin-unfriendly could be used for harvesting tuna, either on the high seas by a vessel engaged in drift-net fishing, or in the eastern tropical Pacific Ocean by a vessel using purse seine nets. Crude estimates suggest that before the labelling requirement was introduced, tuna caught by methods which qualified as "dolphin-friendly" was over 80 per cent of the total tuna supplied to the United States market. On the other hand, market surveys suggest that the percentage of demand originating from environmentally concerned consumers was significantly smaller.[7] Thus, it would seem that the tuna market conformed to Situation (ii) in Figure 3.1, i.e. before labelling was introduced, demand originating from concerned consumers was smaller than the supply from dolphin-friendly methods. On that basis, we would have expected a uniform price to emerge post-labelling, which would be higher than the price in the pre-labelling equilibrium if concerned consumers were willing to pay more for tuna which was clearly dolphin-friendly than they had been willing to pay for undifferentiated tuna. Evidence for these predictions is hard to find because the United States imposed an embargo on dolphin-unfriendly tuna which virtually coincided with the coming into force of the labelling requirement.[8] But our reasoning would suggest that in the absence of the embargo, the quantity of tuna caught by both dolphin-unfriendly and dolphin-friendly methods would probably have increased.

Eco-labelling programmes have also been introduced to discourage the use of tropical timbers from forests which are not sustainably managed.[9] The European Community has been developing an eco-labelling programme and supporting legislation for several years, and similar programmes have been started in other parts of the world.[10] On the supply side, it has been estimated that production of tropical timber is only 14–15 per cent of the total production of timber (softwood and hardwood).[11] Moreover, not all tropical timber comes from unsustainable sources, so the proportion actually produced by environment-unfriendly methods is likely to be much smaller. On the consumption side, surveys reveal, as noted above, that not all European consumers are concerned. Furthermore, as Varangis *et al.* point out, China, Japan and the Republic of Korea account for almost half of the world's tropical timber imports, and "if consumers in major Asian importing countries do not show a preference for certified timber products, while consumers in Europe and North America do, large scale trade diversion in tropical timber trade is likely to take place".[12] This trade diversion is identical to the switch in consumption patterns of the environmentally concerned and unconcerned consumers (or countries, as the case may be) which is an aspect of our model.

However, the conclusion that "the rejection of tropical timber products due to eco-labelling in Europe and United States would reduce the value of these products and make them more attractive for Asian importers"[13] is a valid description of only the intermediate dynamics. The price of tropical timber may initially fall after the introduction of labelling, prompting unconcerned consumers to buy tropical timber until a uniform price for both kinds of timber is established, but our analysis suggests that the eventual equilibrium price might be higher.[14] This is because the production and consumption statistics suggest that we might again be in Situation (ii) of our model (see Figure 3.1). Furthermore, it has been estimated that consumers in Europe are willing to pay a "green premium" in the order of 5–15 per cent more for sustainably produced timber products.[15] Thus aggregate demand in the post-labelling situation is likely to be higher than in the pre-labelling situation. Hence, the final equilibrium price of all timber is likely to be higher than the price before labelling was introduced, but it is too early to establish whether this is actually happening.

C Certain Implications for Policy

In the two cases we used as examples, environment-friendliness of production methods was determined by exogenous criteria. The adverse effect on the environment arose because the proportion of total quantity supplied which qualified as environment-friendly was greater than the proportion of demand originating from potentially concerned consumers. A clear prescription for policy is that the criteria for determining environmental friendliness must be endogenous, i.e. dependent on the market share of different production methods. In effect, policy makers should ensure, in their choice of criteria, that the proportion of total supply which qualifies as environment-friendly before labelling is less than the proportion of demand from potentially concerned consumers. In several labelling programmes, such as the programme of the Swedish Society for the Conservation of Nature, the market share of product types is irrelevant in determining whether they qualify for labels.[16] However, in some cases, labelling policy has already reflected the concerns raised in this paper, though it is not necessarily for the reasons we have identified as crucial.[17] For instance, in the case of the German programme, the product market share is also examined and products already holding a dominant market share are not included in the programme.[18] In Canada, as well, the programme has ensured that only about 10–20 per cent of the eligible market would qualify for the label.[19] Over time these percentages, which seem to have been set more or less arbitrarily, would increase as the product category as a whole would improve its environmental norms. Standards could then be raised so that a small proportion of environmentally superior goods qualify for labelling. The discussion in this paper has provided not only a rationale for taking market shares into account, but also provided a precise ceiling on the proportion of total supply that could be allowed to qualify as being environment-friendly, i.e. it must be less than the proportion of environmentally concerned consumers.[20]

Certain dynamic effects of policy may now be examined. Consider first the effect of policies that are designed to enhance environmental consciousness among consumers.[21] If the result of these efforts were "widened" awareness, i.e. more consumers became concerned, then the likelihood of the adverse situation (ii) would diminish. However, if the result were only "deepened" awareness, i.e. the already concerned consumers were willing to pay even higher premiums, and we were in Situation (ii) to begin with, then the adverse consequences could be worsened.

Therefore, in general, unless policy makers are well-informed about the underlying conditions of demand and supply, the consequences of indirect measures like labelling are not always predictable. There may thus be a case for providing more direct incentives for the use of environment-friendly production methods. Encouraging the move of producers from the unlabelled to the labelled segment of the market would have a much more immediate effect on mitigating "environmental unfriendliness".[22]

II ADVERSE TERMS-OF-TRADE EFFECTS

In this section we illustrate the possible adverse impact on trading partners of the introduction of labelling in a particular country. Consider the following stylized example. There are two countries: N, in which all consumers are concerned about the environment, and S, in which nobody is. Country N introduces a labelling scheme such that all its production meets the labelling requirements while that of country S does not. In effect, the demand from environmentally concerned consumers and the supply of environment-friendly producers in Figure 3.1 can be seen as demand and supply in country N, while the demand from unconcerned consumers and the supply of unfriendly producers can be seen as country S magnitudes.

It is possible to show that, in certain situations, *the introduction of eco-labelling worsens the terms of trade for, and reduces the welfare of, country S.* If S were a net exporter of the product before labelling was introduced – corresponding to Situation (i) – then welfare is reduced as the introduction of labelling leads to reduced demand and a decline in the price of S exports. If S is a net importer of the product pre-labelling (corresponding to Situation (ii)), then welfare declines because the willingness of the N consumer to pay more for the labelled product leads to an increase in the price of S imports.

The example above is obviously highly stylized. In reality, not all N consumers are likely to be concerned and not all S consumers are likely to be unconcerned. Similarly, not all N production may qualify for the label and at least some S production may qualify. However, the basic result of adverse terms-of-trade consequences would survive a significant dilution of the assumptions. The crucial conditions are that there be significant asymmetries in environmental concern between countries, and that labelling schemes favour producers in the concerned country.

III EXTENSION OF THE MODEL TO MORE GENERAL SITUATIONS

A Labelling with International Trade

For a fuller analysis, consider a situation where two countries, country 1 and country 2, are trading with each other, and each could have both concerned and unconcerned consumers as well as friendly and unfriendly production. The pre-labelling equilibrium price is *P*, and at this price, country 1 could be either a net exporter or net importer of the product. The introduction of ecolabelling in country 1 (taken in isolation) could result in:

(a) excess demand in the labelled segment in country 1 at price *P*; or
(b) excess supply in the labelled segment in country 1 at price *P*.[23]

The implications of labelling by country 1 could be analysed for a number of situations, including those in which labelling is also introduced in country 2 and those in which there is mutual recognition of labels. This section provides the more interesting results of the analysis.

The introduction of labelling can lead to a change in the pattern as well as the volume of international trade. For instance, consider a highly environmentally conscious country which, prior to labelling, was a net importer of a good but also had significant domestic production by polluting methods. The introduction of labelling may then create an exportable surplus of the product if it is not economically feasible for domestic producers to opt for cleaner methods. It is also possible that the level of trade of the unlabelled product could increase even if the overall production of that product declines. Consider the situation when in country 1 there is greater domestic supply of the environment-friendly good than domestic demand for that product at the pre-labelling price. Section I showed that adverse environmental consequences are possible in this situation. The interaction with country 2 will result in an improvement in the environmental situation in country 1 only if there is offsetting demand for the environment-friendly good from that country. *If the trading partner is a country where consumers have low environmental concern, then international trade is unlikely to ameliorate the possible adverse environmental effects of labelling.* Moreover, if labelling involves not merely the selection of certain technologies currently in use as environmentally friendly, but the setting of standards which are higher, then the additional cost involved could worsen the adverse environmental impact of labelling. In such a situation, assistance in transfer of technology would improve the environmental effect of labelling.

Now consider the situation when in country 1 domestic demand is greater than domestic supply for the environment-firendly good at the pre-labelling price. *Then the environmental situation in country 1 would worsen under international trade only if there is offsetting excess supply of the environment-friendly good from abroad, i.e. the overall situaion would be similar to Situation (ii) in Figure 3.1.*

B Mutual Recognition

When considering the issue of mutual recognition, it is important to address the question of whether the labelling criteria in different countries are based solely on local or global environmental effects. If environmental problems are local, then, *ceteris paribus*, it is unlikely to be in a country's interest to recognize the environmental labels of a trading partner. Essentially, by denying mutual recognition, a country can create additional import competition for its own unfriendly production, and lead to reduced local production by such methods.[24] However, obtaining foreign recognition of domestic labels may be desirable in so far as it encourages local exporting firms to switch to more friendly technology. Thus, with local environmental problems, mutual recognition may be advantageous for a country if there is significant environmental concern amongst foreign consumers.

With global environmental problems, unilateral recognition of foreign labels may be desirable, particularly when there is little environmental concern among foreign consumers. This would be one way of allowing domestic concern to induce changes in foreign technologies so that more environmentally friendly technologies are promoted abroad. Conversely, if there is substantial environmental concern among consumers abroad, then mutual recognition would assist the process of promoting environmentally friendly technologies at home.

Lack of mutual recognition would generally result in different prices for the labelled product in the two countries. Mutual recognition would result in an integration of the labelled markets and the establishment of a uniform equilibrium price. Prior to mutual recognition, some concerned consumers may have chosen to consume the unlabelled good because the price of the labelled good was much higher than that of the unlabelled product. Mutual recognition, in so far as it leads to a decline in the prices of labelled goods in one country, would encourage some concerned consumers to switch from unlabelled to labelled goods. The converse would happen in the other country. The net impact on the environment would depend on the elasticities of demand and supply in the two countries.

Another aspect which emerges from the analysis is the likely conflict between fulfilling the objective of reducing production of environmentally unfriendly products and the objective of increasing income levels of some of the countries involved. Thus, even when labelling in country 1 results in an improvement in the environmental situation, it could also result in a lower income level of country 2 if the latter country is an exporter of the product for which labelling is established in country 1. The decline in income may, for a variety of reasons, impede the attainment of the environmental objective. This adverse effect on income could be mitigated by an introduction of a labelling scheme in country 2 which is recognized in country 1.

IV MARKET STRUCTURE, TECHNOLOGY AND THE NATURE OF LABELLING POLICY

In this section, we look at some of the implications of the prevailing market structure, the nature of the environmentally friendly technologies and the precise form of labelling policy. For the policy-maker the question is the following: given the current level of environmental concern, where should the standard be set? If it is set too high, the implicit costs will deter most firms from acquiring labels. If it is set too low, most firms may acquire the label but there may be little improvement in their production technology. The optimal standard, from the environmental point of view, may involve the switching of a fraction of the firms so that environmental damage is minimized. An interesting question relates to who these firms are likely to be: the initially high-cost firms or the initially low-cost firms?

As an illustration, consider an oligopolistic market which is supplied by both domestic and foreign firms. The firms are Cournot oligopolists, so that differences in marginal costs are reflected in differences in market shares. When labelling is introduced, each firm takes into account the benefits and costs of acquiring a label. The benefits depend on the width and depth of environmental concern, i.e. how large a segment of consumers is concerned and the premium they are willing to pay for environmentally friendly goods. The costs of meeting labelling conditions depend both on the standard set and on the nature of the environment-friendly technology.

Depending on the nature of the environment-friendly technology, there may be a change in the firms' marginal costs, fixed costs or both. For instance, the switch in methods could involve a change in the quality of variable inputs like fuel, in which case marginal costs are affected, or a change in the quality of fixed inputs like machinery, in which fixed costs are affected. In some cases, there may even be a choice between the two: a firm could use cleaner fuel or install a catalytic converter.

It is obvious that even identical labelling standards can be discriminatory if some producers have to incur greater costs to meet them than other producers. If the labelling standard is set at a level where all firms have an incentive to acquire labels, then *labelling could have the effect of raising foreign rivals' costs in a segment of the market*. Access to the labelled segment may involve increased costs for all firms, but, if domestic firms are initially closer to the standard, then there will be a greater increase in the costs of their foreign rivals. In oligopolistic competition, this could mean a decline in market share and profits of foreign firms.[25] This is necessarily true when the basis for the initial difference in costs between producers is differences in, say, the environmental standards of their products or production methods.

However, there are many situations in which differences in costs between producers arise not because of the environmental aspects of their products or production methods, but due to factors such as differences in efficiency or access to cheaper inputs. In such a situation, let us define a *non-discriminatory labelling standard* as one that entails an identical incremental cost to all producers. An example would be a situation in which all producers initially use diesel as a fuel and are required by the standard to change to petrol, but this does not affect the absolute difference in their costs due to differences in efficiency or access to cheaper complementary inputs. It can be shown that even when standards are subject to such strict requirements of non-discrimination, their imposition may sometimes alter the market outcome in favour of the relatively high-cost producers.[26]

Such discriminatory consequences arise when a firm choosing to meet a certain standard must do so for its entire output, rather than only for the portion sold in the labelled segment. Even though firms are known to sell products with different standards to different segments of the market, such separability is sometimes not feasible either for economic or legal reasons. When technology is subject to economies of scale, it may simply not be profitable for the firms to supply different segments of the market from different plants. Alternatively, the standard may have to be met by the firm rather than its product, on the basis of the conditions of production for its entire output, such as its aggregate emission of harmful gases or the manner in which it carries out product tests. In such "non-separable" situations, it is possible to show that: *relatively high-cost firms are likely to have the greatest incentive to acquire environmental labels when the standards imply an identical increase in marginal costs for all firms.* The criteria of environmental friendliness may then conflict with comparative advantage in the determination of trade.

However, when the standards require an increase in fixed costs, relatively low-cost firms are likely to have the greatest incentive to acquire environmental labels. The criteria of environmental friendliness then need not conflict with comparative advantage in the determination of trade.

Consider first the case where fulfilling the conditions implicit in a label implies an identical increase in marginal costs for all firms. The high-cost firm has a greater incentive to meet such standards. First, an increase in constant marginal costs leads to a larger decline in the profits of the low-cost firm than of the high-cost firm for the following reason. An increase in a firm's marginal costs has a direct effect on its profits, and an indirect effect through induced changes in the rivals' output and hence market price. Under reasonable assumptions, both effects have a negative sign, and their magnitude depends on the firm's initial output. Since the low-cost firm initially produces a larger output than the high-cost firm, any cost increase has a greater adverse impact on its profits.

Now it may seem that the low-cost firm also obtains greater benefits from meeting a standard because it makes larger profits from a monopoly position in the labelled segment of the market. However, it is *relatively* less attractive for the low-cost firm to gain exclusive access to a segment of the market. For the low-cost firm, the increase in profits from creating a monopoly position in the concerned segment derives from the exclusion of a relatively inefficient rival, while for a high-cost firm, the increase in profits arises from excluding a relatively efficient rival. In other words, entry by a high-cost firm hurts a low-cost firm less than entry by a low-cost firm hurts a high-cost firm. Thus, the low-cost firm incurs greater costs and obtains smaller benefits from meeting a standard than does a high-cost firm.

It is possible that the profits of both types of firms could increase, through a form of product differentiation in quality which reduces the intensity of competition in the industry. The profits of high-cost firms increase when a label is acquired, despite the implied increase in costs, because they obtain exclusive access to a segment of the market. The low-cost firms, which do not acquire the label, lose access to a segment of the market, but become relatively more competitive in the market for goods perceived to be environmentally unfriendly. Thus if foreign producers were relatively efficient prior to labelling, they would have an incentive to specialize in low-environment-quality products while high-cost domestic producers produce the "environment-friendly" labelled good.

However, if meeting the conditions for a label implied incurring a certain fixed expenditure in, for example, cleaning operations, the outcome is different. Relatively efficient producers make higher absolute profits in the labelled segment of the market and thus are more willing to incur the necessary expenditures. Suppose labels are given *ex post* to 10 or 20 per cent of the most environmentally friendly producers. In such a situation, it is the relatively efficient firms which have the greatest incentive to become environment-friendly. Environment-friendliness will not be in conflict with comparative advantage.

Finally, consider the case where there are economies of scale in production and where access to environment-friendly technology is restricted, for instance by patents. In this case, first of all, the market structure itself could be changed by the introduction of labelling: for instance, a competitive market may be transformed with a labelled monopolist operating along with an unlabelled competitive fringe. Moreover, if a domestic firm has privileged access to the labelled segment of the market, it obtains an advantage in scale over other rivals. The scale advantage translates into lower marginal costs and higher market shares even in unlabelled markets. *Hence, restricted access to the labelled segment can lead to loss of competitiveness even in the non-labelled segment.* The labelled segment, in this case, is analogous to a protected home market which confers a competitive edge abroad – so that import protection serves to promote exports.[27]

V CONCLUSIONS

This chapter first showed that eco-labelling could, in certain cases, lead to an adverse effect on the environment. A precise empirical test was suggested to establish when labelling could be usefully introduced. Then it was demonstrated how the introduction of labelling in one country could lead to adverse terms-of-trade effects for its trading partners. More generally, it emerged that labelling could lead to changes in the volume and pattern of international trade. As far as the domestic environmental effect was concerned, the existence of concerned consumers abroad was in certain situations conducive to desirable outcomes. Similarly, with local environmental problems, mutual recognition of environmental labels would be in a country's interest if there was significant environmental concern amongst foreign consumers. However, with global environmental problems, lack of concern among foreign consumers would be a strong reason for recognizing foreign labels, and thus transmitting abroad the concern of domestic consumers. Mutual recognition was also suggested as a means of dealing with the possible adverse income effects on trading partners of the introduction of labelling. The effects of labelling were shown to depend on the prevailing market structure, the nature of the environment-friendly technology and the precise form of environmental policy. In particular, in some cases, labelling policy could induce changes in the pattern of trade away from the dictates of comparative advantage.

Notes

1. The views expressed in this paper are strictly those of the authors, and should not be ascribed to any other person or to any organization.
2. Labelling programmes have become increasingly popular. See OECD, *Environmental Labelling in OECD Countries* (Paris: OECD, 1991). The Federal Republic of Germany issued its first environmental label in 1978. By 1991, the programme had 3,600 labelled products in 64 product categories. Programmes have been in operation in Canada and Japan since 1988, while other programmes have either already started or are under consideration in the European Union, Norway, Sweden, Finland, Austria, Australia and New Zealand. For a survey of the most important labelling programmes, see V. Jha, R. Vossenaar, and S. Zarrilli, "Eco-Labelling and International Trade", UNCTAD Discussion Paper, no. 70 (October 1993).
3. Examples of product categories subject to, or under consideration for, eco-labelling are batteries, certain types of paper, textile detergents, tone cartridges for copying machines and for laser printers, furnaces and oil burners, marine engines, cleaning agents for cars, fluorescent tubes and light bulbs, reused plastics, sprays with CFCs, reusable diapers, non-asbestos brake linings, aluminium cans with stoppers, filters for kitchen sinks, water

valves, paints and varnishes, textiles and insulation materials, shampoos, detergents, refrigerators, ceramic tiles, footwear, cat litter, bulbs, dishwashers, washing machines, and organic additives.

4. A. Mattoo and H. V. Singh, "Eco-Labelling: Policy Considerations", *Kyklos*, vol. 47 (1994), pp. 53–65.
5. A number of consumer surveys, though differing in their estimates, confirm that social attitudes to the environment range from complete lack of concern to a willingness to intervene directly. For instance, a study by the Roper Organization suggested that a quarter of the United States' adult population were environmentalists, slightly more than half were not, and the attitudes of the remaining quarter were not well defined. V. Jha quotes survey evidence which suggests that slightly over half of the consumers in North America purchased a product that they felt was better for the environment, boycotted a specific product which they felt was bad for the environment, or boycotted products made by a company which they felt was damaging the environment. See Roper Organization, Inc., "The Environment: Public Attitudes and Individual Behaviour", A study conducted for S.C. Johnson and Son, Inc., 1990; and V. Jha, "Green Consumerism, Eco-Labelling and Trade", mimeo, UNCTAD, Geneva, 1993. See also OECD, op. cit.
6. This was a requirement under the Dolphin Protection Consumer Information Act, 1990. See US Government Committee on Foreign Affairs and Committee on Foreign Relations, *Legislation on Foreign Relations Through 1991*, Washington, DC, 1992.
7. See, for example, the studies referred to in note 5. Of course, the relevant statistic is not the proportion of concerned consumers, but the share of such consumers in total demand.
8. The embargo was imposed under the Marine Mammal Protection Act of 1972, as subsequently amended. See US Government, op. cit.
9. At present there is significant debate on the appropriate definition of "sustainable" forest management.
10. R. Mori provides details of the Austrian tropical timber labelling scheme, which was introduced in 1992 but then withdrawn in 1993. See R. Mori, "Environmental Labelling and Trade", mimeo, Institut de Hautes Etudes Internationales, Geneva, 1993.
11. See P. N. Varangis, C. A. P. Braga and K. Takeuchi, "Tropical Timber Trade Policies: What Impact Will Eco-Labelling Have?", *Wirtschaftspolitische Blatter*, vol. 3/4 (1993) pp. 338–51.
12. Ibid.
13. Ibid.
14. When we say "uniform" price, we abstract from differences in prices which reflect variations in the non-environmental characteristics of different types of timber.
15. Varangis *et al.*, op. cit.
16. OECD, op. cit., pp. 62–3; and V. Jha, op. cit.
17. V. Jha *et al.* state that "in most systems, the threshold levels are deliberately kept at a high level, in order to stimulate competition among the manufacturers for the label and to stimulate public confidence in the label". See V. Jha *et al.*, op. cit., p. 6.
18. OECD, op. cit., p. 45.

19. Ibid., p. 50.
20. If the small share of the production of labelled product results in lack of information about them, this could be dealt with by increasing publicity about the label and the products that are labelled.
21. This could be either due to "unconcerned" consumers becoming environmentally conscious, i.e. they become willing to pay a premium for the labelled product, or due to the existing environmentally conscious consumers willing to pay a larger premium.
22. In a dynamic situation, where it is possible for producers to switch technology, the move of producers from the labelled to the unlabelled segment may lead to a narrowing of price differences. This may, in turn, induce a shift from the unlabelled to the labelled segment of certain consumers who are willing to pay the new, lower price premium.
23. There is, of course, also the special case of equality of demand and supply in the labelled (and unlabelled) segment in country.
24. It is open to question whether one country should impose on another its preferences on the policy choice for dealing with a local problem.
25. See T.G. Krattenmaker, and S.G. Salop, "Anticompetitive Exclusion: Raising Rivals Costs to Achieve Power over Price", *Yale Law Journal*, vol. 96 (1986), pp. 209–95.
26. See A. Mattoo, "Discriminatory Consequences of Discriminatory Standards", mimeo, 1995.
27. P. R. Krugman, "Import Protection as Export Promotion: International Competition in the Presence of Oligopoly and Economies of Scale", in H. Kierzkowski, ed., *Monopolistic Competition and International Trade* (Oxford: Oxford University Press, 1984).

4 Eco-Labelling Schemes in the European Union and their Impact on Brazilian Exports

Pedro da Motta Veiga, Mário C. de Carvalho Jr, Maria Lúcia Vilmar and Heraldiva Façanha*

INTRODUCTION

Although eco-labelling programmes are voluntary and accessible to both domestic and foreign producers, the industry of the importing country is often in a position to influence the conceptualization and implementation of these programmes, making it necessary for foreign suppliers – particularly from developing countries – to make additional efforts to maintain the competitive edge of their exports. In so far as the criteria and parameters of these eco-labelling schemes are related to the life cycle of the products and therefore include the production process, they point to the need to meet certain standards in the countries of origin of products. The broad scope of life-cycle analysis suggests that eco-labelling systems, although not mandatory, may affect the production of input materials and raw materials for the export industry, thus effectively acting as barriers to the entry of products exported from the developing countries – although the production of these goods may not have any environmentally hazardous transborder effect.

Although only a small number of export products of interest from the developing countries are covered by eco-labelling schemes in force today, there is a clear increase in these figures. In fact, of the 25 categories of products for which criteria are being set under the aegis of the European Union (EU), at least eight (various types of paper, packaging, textiles, ceramics, footwear and refrigerators) are on the list of Brazilian exports in varying quantities. On the other hand, in so far as the so-called "dirty" industries are perceived as constituting a large proportion of exports from developing countries, it may be assumed

Table 4.1 Brazilian exports: selected sectors (million of dollars)

Sector	*1980*	*1985*	*1990*	*1991*	*1992*	*1993*
Footwear	407.655	968.668	1183.589	1245.397	1473.529	1945.178
Textiles	915.666	1000.607	1248.069	1358.970	1463.256	1382.438
Natural threads & fabrics	614.701	598.864	594.656	603.235	541.143	404.475
Artificial threads & fabrics	90.170	125.849	226.817	268.725	351.113	308.391
Clothing	210.795	275.894	426.596	487.010	571.000	669.572
Overall Total	20 132.401	25 639.011	31 413.756	31 260.459	35 861.525	38 782.679

Source: DTIC/SECEX/MICT.

Table 4.2 Brazilian exports: selected sectors (percentage share in exports)

Sectors	*1980*	*1985*	*1990*	*1991*	*1992*	*1993*
Footwear	2.02	3.78	3.77	3.94	4.11	5.02
Textiles	4.55	3.90	3.97	4.30	4.08	5.02
Natural threads & fabrics	3.05	2.34	1.89	1.91	1.51	1.04
Artificial threads & fabrics	0.45	0.49	0.72	0.85	0.98	0.80
Clothing	1.05	1.08	1.36	1.54	1.59	1.73

Source: DTIC/SECEX/MICT.

that eco-labelling initiatives could result in a negative impact on natural resource-intensive industries and on heavy polluters, for whom the costs of compliance with environmental criteria in relation to total production and investment costs could be particularly high.

Although there has been a steady growth in Brazil's industrial exports (see Tables 4.1 and 4.2) over the past few decades, the export drive has not always taken environmental factors into account. At the same time, Brazilian industrial exports since mid-1980s suggests a reduction in competitiveness-gains indicators, due to the country's macroeconomic crisis and its implications on the dynamics of productive investments. This means that, in the international market, Brazilian export industry may be vulnerable to environmental regulations and non-mandatory initiatives that could increase production costs and investments for its export products or for input materials.

This chapter analyses the actual and potential impacts of eco-labelling systems in the EU for Brazil's textile and footwear sectors. Sections I and II provide analyses of the structural characteristics of the textile and footwear sectors in Brazil and a brief assessment of the competitive position of these sectors in the international market. An assessment of the sectorial impacts of EU eco-labelling systems on the Brazilian industry is also provided. Finally, Section III provides some conclusions concerning the impact of the eco-labelling schemes in the EU on Brazilian exports in the two sectors analysed, the establishment of systems of this type in Brazil, and the conditions necessary to endow them with credibility and ensure international acceptance.

I ECO-LABELLING SYSTEMS IN THE EU AND THE BRAZILIAN TEXTILE SECTOR

A Structural Characteristics and Competitive Position

Brazil's textile industry is characterized by technological and managerial heterogeneity. Within the same market segment one can observe the coexistence of:

- modern companies that operate with advanced technological standards and strategies;
- partially modernized companies with updated equipment at strategic stages or old machinery run under rigid quality controls with advanced design skills; and
- a large number of companies with outdated technological and managerial standards.

The textile industry underwent a concentration process during the second half of the 1980s: among the 6000 companies that operated in 1986 only 4300 survived by 1991. The cotton knits industry as well as the bed, table and bath linens industry registered higher degrees of concentration. These industries constitute a major portion of Brazil's textiles exports, accounting for 51 per cent in 1992.

Textile exports from Brazil are strongly concentrated in a relatively small number of companies.[1] Among the 456 companies that exported textile products from Brazil, the ten largest firms accounted for 46 per cent of the total exports, and the share of the twenty largest firms was as high as 60 per cent of the total. It should be noted that all are sizable companies with over 500 employees. This concentration of exports in a small number of major companies results from the technological and organizational heterogeneity of the textile industry. These companies adopted the international market as an important variable in the formulation of their growth strategy.

The large textile companies from Brazil face relatively fewer obstacles in domestic and foreign markets – they are more closely attuned to international trends, and have their own funding as well as access to sources of financing for modernization and expansion. However, most companies lack the level of technological updating crucial for ensuring competitive positions in markets. Furthermore, they are also threatened by imported synthetic fabrics, fibres and threads.

The major trends in exports in this sector over the past few years are summarized in Tables 4.3 and 4.4. Brazilian textile exports have registered moderate growth since 1980. Between 1985 and 1990, growth rates were higher than during the previous five years, but from 1990 through 1993, the pace of expansion became slower. Textile exports were distributed in different regional markets, with the North American and Western European markets and Japan accounting for 64 per cent of Brazilian exports in 1985 and 61 per cent in 1992. The principal factor responsible for this downturn is the appreciable growth in Brazilian textile exports (in the three segments listed in Tables 4.3 and 4.4) to the Latin American Integration Association (LAIA) countries.[2] Between 1985 and 1992, exports to the LAIA region rose by almost 300 per cent to represent 27.4 per cent of the total, and in contrast with a total sectorial export expansion of 46 per cent. Nevertheless, OECD countries remain the principal destination for Brazilian textile exports. According to data given in Tables 4.3 and 4.4, in 1992 textile exports played a particularly important role in the list of Brazilian foreign sales to the United States, Canada and the EFTA countries, in addition to LAIA. This factor is linked to the weight of clothing exports in the list of textiles channelled to these countries and regions.

In 1985, the threads and fabric segments represented 72.5 per cent

Table 4.3 Brazilian textile exports, 1985/92 (millions of dollars)

Sectors	*USA*	*Canada*	*EU*	*LAIA*	*Japan*	*EFTA*	*Others*	*Total*
1985								
Textiles	228.339	56.000	279.512	100.914	32.327	42.653	260.862	1 000.607
Natural threads & fabrics	89.293	18.236	202.180	34.026	32.290	28.620	194.219	598.864
Artificial threads & fabrics	18.061	18.837	22.409	20.604	0	2.886	43.052	125.849
Clothing	120.985	18.927	54.923	46.284	0.037	11.147	23.591	275.894
Overall total	6 955.930	427.510	6 227.434	2 230.670	1 397.792	797.002	7 602.673	25 639.001
1990								
Textiles	270.444	56.659	412.504	134.479	59.290	44.644	270.049	1 248.069
Natural threads & fabrics	37.872	11.605	235.103	38.976	57.073	12.328	201.699	594.656

Artificial threads & fabrics	67.080	11.983	53.306	41.767	0.894	6.188	45.599	226.817
Clothing	165.492	33.071	124.095	53.736	1.323	26.128	22.751	426.596
Overall total	7 718.426	521.574	9 870.062	3 193.685	2 348.517	621.825	7 139.667	31 413.756
1992								
Textiles	365.951	47.171	389.089	400.334	50.228	43.041	167.442	1 463.256
Natural threads & fabrics	123.805	14.315	133.538	115.664	48.745	9.667	95.409	541.143
Artificial threads & fabrics	67.663	9.854	69.552	138.364	0.130	2.701	62.849	351.113
Clothing	174.483	23.002	185.999	146.306	1.353	30.673	9.184	571.000
Overall total	6 933.230	401.475	10 627.516	7 591.924	2 306.067	436.661	7 564.632	35 861.525

Table 4.4 Brazilian textile exports, 1985/92 (percentage share in exports)

Sectors	*United States*	*Canada*	*EU*	*LAIA*	*Japan*	*EFTA*	*Others*	*Total*
1985								
Textiles	3.28	13.10	4.49	4.52	2.31	5.35	3.43	3.90
Natural threads & fabrics	0.26	4.27	3.25	1.53	2.31	3.59	2.55	2.34
Artificial threads & fabrics								
Clothing	0.26	4.41		0.92	0.00	0.36	0.57	0.49
1990								
Textiles	3.50	10.86	4.18	4.21	2.52	7.18	3.78	3.97
Natural threads & fabrics	0.49	2.22	2.38	1.22	2.43	1.98	2.83	1.89
Artificial threads & fabrics	0.87	2.30	0.54	1.31	0.04	1.00	0.64	0.72
Clothing	2.14	6.34	1.26	1.68	0.06	4.20	0.32	1.36
1992								
Textiles	5.28	11.75	3.66	5.27	2.18	9.86	2.21	4.08
Natural threads & fabrics	1.79	3.57	1.26	1.52	2.11	2.21	1.26	1.51
Artificial threads & fabrics	0.98	2.45	0.65	1.82	0.01	0.62	0.83	0.98
Clothing	2.52	5.73	1.75	1.93	0.06	7.02	0.12	1.59

Source: DTIC/SECEX/MICT.

of total textile exports, while in 1992 they accounted for only 52.5 per cent, reflecting the increasing importance of the clothing segment in Brazil's foreign sales. This development is in step with world textile trade trends, today concentrating increasingly in prepared fabrics, cotton knitwear and clothing. In the threads and fabrics segment, artificial (synthetic) products have become increasingly important in Brazil's exports, reducing the share of natural threads and fabrics – a trend also noted in world textile trade.

Exports for this sector remain strongly linked to intermediate or finished products using natural fibres, particularly cotton. Approximately 47 per cent of threads and 73 per cent of textiles exported in 1991 by Brazil used cotton. Among textile products that incorporate natural fibres (cotton, silk, jute) grown in Brazil, within the textile sector, the largest market shares on the international market were for certain types of cotton skeins, where Brazil's participation reached 6.5 per cent of the global market, with cotton bed sheets reaching 4.7 per cent.

The specialization and competitive edge of Brazil in cotton products is also clearly proven by the level of utilization of its export quotas under the Multifibre Agreement. In exports to the EU, the product that is effectively limited through regularly filling its quotas with a high percentage of use is cotton threads. Cotton-knit shirts and T-shirts, brushed or smooth, also feature an upward trend in filling their quotas. This characteristic makes the sector particularly sensitive to life-cycle analyses of products using environmental criteria related to the production and use of cotton fibres. Managers of large export companies seem well aware of this fact, and are attempting to incorporate this variable into their strategies. With regard to water pollution indicators, sectorial indices are well below the average for the industry (7.3 g/$, against 18.2 g/$, respectively for biochemical oxygen demand (BOD) and 0.1 per cent g/$ against 0.4 g/$, for heavy metals). For BOD, the pollution abatement rates are approximately 48 per cent.

The same trend has been observed with respect to air pollution indictors, as the emission of particulates (24.25 g/$) is appreciably lower than the industrial average of 41.34 g/$. The same occurs with emissions of SO_2 (13.44 g/$ and 31.95 g/$ respectively) and to a lesser extent of nitrogen oxide (11.21 g/$ and 13.88 g/$ respectively).

These figures for the textile sector in general should be treated only as a point of reference, while examining specific segments such as T-shirts and bed linens. These segments are far more concentrated than the sectorial average. The large- and medium-sized companies in these segments are located in Santa Catarina State in Southern Brazil, characterized by heavy immigration of European industrial workers, particularly from Germany. These companies export cotton bed clothes and T-shirts to the Western European countries as well as to other parts of the world. The two largest production groups in the cotton knitwear segment (both from Santa Catarina) are powerful exporters with approximately 50 per cent of the net operational revenues for this segment in Brazil. In the case of bed, table and bath linens, the three largest companies – all exporters to Europe located in Santa Catarina – held 75 per cent of the revenues for this segment in Brazil in 1992.

The São Paulo textile park exports cotton or synthetic products to the American continent and the Middle East, with sales to Europe being virtually negligible. The two largest T-shirt exporters in Santa Catarina earmark just over 50 per cent of their total exports for Western Europe, principally Germany; in 1993 this represented $56 million. Germany alone absorbed $16 million in T-shirts this same year from these two companies. These two major T-shirt exporters accounted for 80 per cent of foreign sales of this product in 1993.

In the cotton bedclothes segment, export supplies are concentrated. Here also the same export pattern as for T-shirts is seen: large companies in Santa Catarina exporting cotton products to the European market. Almost all the products in this segment exported to Europe come from large companies in Santa Catarina: three of them alone accounted for 65 per cent of total Brazilian exports world-wide in 1993. Major export companies are already adapting pollution abatement strategies, and one of them is even a member of the ECO-TEX consortium. These companies are also among the first to develop quality management systems in the textiles sector.

B Eco-Labelling Scheme in the EU and Brazilian Textile Exports

A variety of private eco-labelling schemes are currently being proposed by countries in the European Union and by Austria.[3] The German textile industry has proposed a product label – MST – and a process-related label – MUT. Under both schemes, criteria cover air, soil and water pollution during the production process. German industry has already introduced processes targeting compliance with criteria for use of power, chemical products and pollution emissions, which places it in a favourable position compared to imported products. Additionally, very strict criteria on the use of dyestuffs may also impose the need to import this type of material from Germany on export companies aiming at the German market,[4] in addition to discriminating against natural dyes produced by developing countries.

The ECO-TEX scheme, developed by an association of German and Austrian research institutes, defines criteria that basically focus on controlling the possible impacts of the use of textiles on human health. Production standards are similar to those of German labels, and the effects expected on competition in the domestic markets of countries that institute them will tend to be the same as these schemes.

Under the aegis of the eco-labelling schemes launched by the European Union in 1992, Denmark was appointed as the lead country to develop and propose eco-criteria for T-shirts and bed linen made of cotton or blends of cotton and polyester. The criteria developed refer to different stages in the life cycle of the products and in particular to the raw materials production process, the fabric manufacturing process, and finished products to a lesser extent. These may thus constitute a benchmark not only for the specific products which are today under analysis (T-shirts and bed linen) but also for textile products in general. In its current format, the proposal submitted by Denmark covers the criteria and parameters described in Box 4.1.

Box 4.1 Eco-criteria for textiles: T-shirts (100 per cent cotton or blends of cotton/polyester) and bed linen

1. **Mechanical and physical properties:**
   - ISO 5077 to 7768, wash and wear test

2. **Colour fastness of dyeings and prints:**
   - to water (din 54006), rubbing (54021), perspiration (54020), domestic and commercial laundering (54017)

3. **Materials:**
   - 100 per cent cotton or blend of cotton/polyester

4. **Energy consumption – production:**
   - polyester – fibre: 50 MJ PE/kg fibre, mechanical process: 150 MJ PE/kg textile, wet treatment: 165 MJ PE/kg textile (for bed linen), 50 MJ PE/kg textile

5. **Consumption of water during wet treatment:**
   - 245 l/kg (for 100 per cent cotton), 140 l/kg (for 100 per cent polyester), pro-rata (for blends)

6. **Waste water parameters (in manufacturing process):**
   - EC directive on urban waste water (91/271/EEC), COD 50 kg/

tonne of textile, AOX 0.025 kg/tonne of textile (DIN 38409), maximum accepted coloration (DIN 38494)

7. **Volatile organic compounds:**
   - production of polyester fibres – 10 g/kg of fibre, wet treatment – no chemical containing VOC, halogen containing organic solvents considered as a source of VOC

8. **Pesticides and chemicals during cotton growing:**
   - hazardous to environment – persistent and/or bioaccumulativity not to be used, hazardous to health – not to be used, no pesticides containing heavy metals

9. **Catalysts during polyester production:**
   - antimony catalyst – not to be used

10. **Lubricants:**
    - only mineral oils of pharmaceutical quality (in spinning, knitting and weaving)

11. **Detergents and compelling agents:**
    - no surface active agents where degradation results in formation of stable toxic metabolites, DTDMAC, DSDMAC, DHTDMAC, NTA, EDTA – not to be used

12. **Bleaching agents:**
    - not to be used: containing chlorine and chlorine compounds

13. **Dyes, pigments and carriers (in manufacturing process):**
    - benzidine-based dyes, azo-dyes based on other aromatic amines, dyes containing or consuming heavy metals – not to be used; carcinogenic (or suspected) and dyes with acute toxic effects (LD 50< 200 mg/kg bw) not to be used, carriers containing chlorine or other halogens – not to be used

14. **Flame retardants:**
    - based on heavy metals or halogenated – not to be used, FR systems releasing formaldehyde – not to be used

15. **Crease-resistant finishes:**
    - releasing formaldehyde – not to be used

16. **Occupational conditions:**
    - 89/391/EEC – Council Directive on the introduction of measures to encourage improvements in the safety and health of workers at work: written assessment of risks

17. **Cotton dust:**
    - 0.2 mg/m^3 (8 h – TWA) – at all life-cycle stages

18. Noise:
- 85 dB (at all life-cycle stages)

19. Final products:
- substances and parameters – limits for chemical residues in the final products

To assess the potential impact of the EU labelling scheme on Brazilian exporters, some major companies in the clothing sector in Santa Caterina who export product categories included in the scheme were interviewed. As these companies are better equipped to carry out the adaptations and make the investments required by the foreign market, the assessment based on the experience of these companies does not reflect the possible negative impact of the proposed scheme on companies with lower levels of qualification. Given the extreme heterogeneity of Brazil's textile and clothing industries, the implications of this scheme may vary substantially, depending on the export experience of the companies concerned, the age of their equipment, and their growth strategies. Large companies with limited exports to Europe showed little concern over this issue. With regard to the Santa Catarina clothing industry, the companies interviewed accounted for an appreciable proportion of Brazilian exports of T-shirts and bed linen to the EU. All were keenly aware of the environmental requirements of European consumers, the irreversible nature of the trend expressed by these requirements, and the implications thereof on exports and the production and marketing strategies of these companies. They constitute the core of the leading companies in the textile sector in the introduction of quality management systems (ISO-9000 and 9001) as well as the functioning of quality control circles (Circulos de Controle de Qualidade, CCQs) and other participative programmes.

All the five companies interviewed were coping with environmental demands made directly by their European importers, particularly the Germans. Although these requirements have not yet had much effect on their exports, they have generated additional costs on account of the tests carried out for certifying exported products. The requirements formulated by the importers covered various aspects of the production process, such as:

- use of production processes that give rise to pollutive discharges during local production by the company;
- use of raw materials considered as toxic; and

- use of production processes considered as virtually unacceptable in terms of the emission of noise or air pollution.

The principal source of information on eco-labelling schemes for the export companies was their European clients, with suppliers and technical literature playing a subsidiary role. The companies felt that they could comply with requirements stipulated by their clients with regard to the environmental impact of their production. Compliance would involve:

- alterations in the production process;
- increased demands for compliance with environmental standards in the procurement policy for input and raw materials by the companies;
- the installation of pollutant emission control equipment; and
- changes in the presentation and packaging of products.

The interviews suggested that the leading companies in the Brazilian clothing sector are already to a large extent adapting to requirements imposed by the criteria of the eco-labelling scheme proposed in the EU. There is a high capacity to comply with these criteria and a trend to channel investments towards resolving shortfalls under some criteria. With regard to compliance with these criteria, the severest difficulties are found with respect to the use of pesticides in cotton-growing, waste-water parameters during the manufacturing process, and noise. The principal difficulties encountered by the companies in complying with the criteria refer to relationships with the suppliers of input materials (e.g. cotton, pigments, etc.), outdated equipment, higher product prices in a market where competition is price-based, and a lack of market stimulation, linked to the fact that the demand is not very exigent in environmental terms.

With regard to cotton production, until recently cotton bought by the Brazilian clothing industry was produced almost completely in Brazil, with low pesticide use and harvested almost completely by hand. With large-scale cotton imports by Brazilian industry on the rise, the companies interviewed admit that they are not in a position to state that the cotton is pesticide-free.

Chemical input materials are supplied to the textile industry by a restricted group of multinational companies with production plants in Brazil. Their supply of products in Brazil depends on the characteristics of local demand, which is generally not very exigent with regard to quality and environmental criteria. This means that chemical companies continue to produce in Brazil input materials that are no longer used in Europe or the United States, or may even be banned in these countries. The demand in Brazil for products compatible with environmental regulations and European national legislation thus originates in major textile and clothing companies, with high export levels to EU member countries. Although they exert pressure on chemical industries to supply – either through local production or imports – the input materials required by legislation in the European countries, the major export companies were unwilling to pay higher prices for these input materials, as this would affect the competitiveness of their prices on foreign markets. As noted below, this fact reflects the specific market power of the major export companies, and this pattern of relationship with the chemical industry does not correspond to the small and medium-sized textile and clothing companies in the segment.

Compliance with criteria for water consumption and – to a lesser extent – energy, highlights the perception that compliance with these requirements may introduce sizeable economic and financial savings for the company, through reduced expenses on these input materials and through the rationalization of production processes. One leading cotton-knit clothing manufacturer and Brazil's largest exporter recycles 600 tons of cotton waste per month, which is sold to third parties for producing string, cotton batting, eiderdowns and towels. It is also implementing a conservation programme for energy resources, both renewable and non-renewable, which will allow it to save 300 tons of oil per month, reducing the emission of air pollutants and replacing oil by natural gas. It has cut the amount of water used for each kilogram of cotton knit produced by 30 per cent, down to 120 litres/ kg, targeting 100 litres/kg in the near future. The smaller companies, by contrast, consider that the investment to comply with EU eco-criteria will increase their production costs.

The economic and financial restrictions which characterize the vast majority of Brazil's textile and clothing companies at the moment, and the effects of these constraints on the investment capacity of firms constitute the benchmark for assessing the possibilities and difficulties of complying with the eco-criteria defined by Denmark for the EU eco-labelling scheme.[5] Compliance with most of the criteria presented essentially depends on renovation of machinery and equipment for most companies. The sharp drop in the domestic consumption of products manufactured by this sector, together with rising imports, challenges companies with the need to adapt in order to survive. However, the vast majority of small and medium-sized companies are not in a position to make investments in modernization. Reduction in consumption is accompanied by shrinking demands for quality on the domestic market, so that companies that are not orientated towards exports find investments in modernization of equipment and concern with environmental criteria somewhat remote from their priorities.

This suggests that the key variable for defining the capacity – and the motivation – of companies to invest in modernizing the production process, whether or not this is done specifically to comply with environmental criteria, is the importance of exports in corporate strategy, particularly in view of the increasing gap over the past few years between quality requirement levels in the domestic and foreign markets, especially the EU and the United States. Even among export companies, there are substantial differences among the production processes and products earmarked for the local and foreign markets. These differences involve the quality of threads used, use of chemical input materials, and the quality of the final product.

In non-exporter companies, the dominant trend on the domestic market prevails, where the demand for quality is concentrated to an increasing extent in upper income segments. Due to the limited investment capacity of the vast majority of companies, the conclusion is that the most difficult criteria to comply with are those involving the production of raw materials which lie beyond the control of companies. Other areas of difficulty also involve criteria and parameters where compliance depends on investments, renovation of machinery and equipment, particularly in the case of small and medium-sized companies. Restrictions in this case are not based on access to technology but rather on investment costs. Compliance with the criteria related to the use of chemical input materials essentially depends on the level of requirements of the demand, as well as the market power and negotiating capabilities possessed by textile companies in their relationships with suppliers in the chemical sector. On the one hand, the limited requirements of domestic demand do not force textile companies to replace the chemical input materials used. On the other hand, the sales policies of companies in the chemical sector raise an additional obstacle to this substitution, due to the impact on the costs of these materials. Only major companies will be in a position to negotiate reasonable price conditions with chemical firms for the acquisition of new materials. However, criteria where compliance demands investments in renovating machinery and changes in relationships with the suppliers of raw materials and input materials are those where non-exporter companies as well as small and medium-sized companies in Brazil may well find the greatest difficulties in adaptation.

Criteria on the emission of waste water are complied with by most of the leading export companies in this sector, and Brazilian legislation requires companies to build waste-water treatment systems. The criteria and parameters seem reasonable, provided that company treatment systems are properly designed and operated. In Brazil, this depends to a very large extent on the supervisory capacities of the environmental control agency at the state level, which means that legislation is only implemented and routinely enforced in Southern Brazil.

The use of bleaching agents containing chlorine and chlorine compounds has already been abandoned or is being phased out by the vast majority of Brazilian companies. This means that Criterion no. 12 may be considered as not posing a problem for these companies. With regard to the use of flame retardants and crease-resistant finishes releasing formaldehyde (nos 14 and 15), this depends on the destination of the product, whether the domestic or a foreign market. Many companies that produce for the domestic market use these input materials.

In sum, for small and medium-sized companies, no criterion is easy to comply with, on account of the shortage of funds for investment and the lack of adequate incentives to encourage them towards compliance. These difficulties increase in step with more stringent requirements (associated with the criteria) for new investments, and the capacity and power of negotiation with the suppliers of raw and input materials. For major export companies, on the other hand, none of the criteria present great difficulties, as investments in modernization of equipment are a prerequisite for the participation of these companies in the international market. As they export to markets that are more environmentally demanding, their growth strategies, together with incentives to make additional investments in modernization and environmental management, increase and may become economically profitable. Nevertheless, it should be noted that even for these companies, compliance with certain requirements, e.g. with respect to waste-water treatment and the use of pesticides and chemicals, may prove difficult.

II THE FOOTWEAR SECTOR

A Structural Characteristics and Competitive Position

Brazil ranks fourth in the world's footwear sector: its 1990 output consisted of 42 per cent plastic and rubber and 41 per cent leather footwear, with the remaining 17 per cent concentrated in sports shoes.

Approximately 28 per cent of Brazilian footwear production was exported that year, but the export profile differs substantially from the production profile. In fact, 92 per cent of exports consists of leather footwear, which makes this segment an essentially export activity: almost two-thirds of output is earmarked for foreign markets. This fact warrants particular attention as Brazil's leather sector has an extremely high rate of residual pollution, particularly heavy metals.

In addition to channelling most of its leather footwear to exports, these activities take place in a very specific pattern of industrial organization characterized by concentration in two regional centres in southern Brazil: Novo Hamburgo in Rio Grande do Sul state (women's footwear) and Franca in São Paulo (men's footwear). This regional polarization of production has attracted new producers, as well as manufacturers of input materials and equipment, while spurring the development of technological and information infrastructure in these production centres. In addition to underwriting the participation of small and medium-sized companies in the international market, this structuring endowed Brazil's export footwear sector with flexibility in adapting to constantly changing rules and conditions for competing in global markets. This explains the sector's remarkable growth in exports over the past few years, despite the entry of new competitors from South-East Asia in the international market.

Thus, while the total footwear production is relatively concentrated in a few major companies, in the leather footwear export segment, production is distributed among large, medium and small companies. The concentration of production in this segment shows 28 per cent of total revenues for the eight largest companies in 1992, while the number of export companies rose from 294 in 1975 to 487 in 1992.

Brazil's footwear production sector has gone through three distinct periods over the past 15 years (see Tables 4.5 and 4.6). The first phase, between 1980 and 1985, was characterized by marked growth in exports (up 138 per cent over the period), due principally to expansion fuelled by demand in the United States. During this phase, Brazil expanded its share in the international market, although this growth was concentrated in one single market, i.e. the United States. The second phase, between 1985 and 1990, is marked by relative stagnation of the total amount exported by this sector (up only 22 per cent over the period) and by a shrinking international market share, down from 2.1 per cent to 1.8 per cent in the world-wide market and from 5.0 per cent to 2.8 per cent in the North American market. The entry of competitors from South-East Asia in this market and transformations in

Table 4.5 Brazilian footwear exports, 1985/92 (millions of dollars)

Sectors	*USA*	*Canada*	*EU*	*LAIA*	*Japan*	*EFTA*	*Others*	*Total*
1985								
Footwear	820.172	25.237	64.366	5.452	0	2.258	51.183	968.668
Overall total	6 955.930	427.510	6 227.434	2 230.670	1 397.792	797.002	7 602.673	25 639.011
1990								
Footwear	853.192	43.460	198.579	24.150	6.653	27.125	30.430	1 183.589
Overall total	7 718.426	521.574	9 870.062	3 193.685	2 348.517	621.825	7 139.667	31 413.756
1992								
Footwear	1 017.824	47.444	283.107	51.961	8.291	18.935	45.967	1 473.529
Overall total	6 933.230	401.495	10 627.516	7 591.924	2 306.067	436.661	7 564.632	35 861.525

Table 4.6 Brazilian footwear exports, 1985/92 (percentage share in exports)

Year	*USA*	*Canada*	*EU*	*LAIA*	*Japan*	*EFTA*	*Others*	*Total*
1985	11.79	5.90	1.03	0.24	0.00	0.28	0.67	3.78
1990	11.05	8.33	2.01	0.76	0.28	4.36	0.43	3.77
1992	14.68	11.82	2.66	0.68	0.36	4.34	0.61	4.11

Source: DTIC/SECEX/MICT.

the North American retail market forced suppliers to adopt quick-response practices, explaining Brazil's loss of position in the United States and prompting Brazilian producers to adopt cost-cutting strategies while upgrading products. The third period, between 1990 and 1993, suggests that the adaptation to these new market conditions was highly successful: exports increased by 64 per cent in three years and maintained the trend towards market diversification within OECD countries. In 1992, exports to the United States represented 69 per cent of the total, against 72 per cent in 1990 and 85 per cent in 1985. The EU, which in 1985 absorbed 7 per cent of Brazil's footwear exports, in 1992 accounted for 19 per cent of this total. Consequently, the participation of footwear in Brazil's list of exports rose from 3.8 per cent in 1990 to 5 per cent in 1993. Technological updating and managerial modernization were implemented in the industry, primarily in response to competition from South-East Asian producers. A recent study of the competitive nature of Brazilian industry noted that in the footwear sector some areas show technological lags, with a probable blunting of competitive advantages in relation to competitors from South-East Asia.[6] Small companies, hampered by tight finances, face more difficulties in investing, which tends to accentuate the technological heterogeneity of this sector. The use of basic microelectronic equipment, although not unknown in these companies, is still not very wide-spread. The dissemination of computer-aided design (CAD) is limited to a few companies, and the same applies to stitching machines, die-cutters and equipment fitted with microprocessors.

These recent technological and organizational changes have not resulted in any significant change in the relationships of the footwear industry with the leather supply sector, which has been perceived as responsible for emissions of high volumes of pollution (BOD and heavy metals) as well as for the highest rates of residual water pollution in

Brazilian industry (878.9g /$ in BOD and 30.3 in heavy metals) in which the abatement rates reached 54 per cent for BOD and 62 per cent for heavy metals.[7] As a recent UNIDO study noted, "although tanneries have effluent wastes treatment installations, it is estimated that they are not used in an efficient manner".[8] Low-pollution processes are being adopted very slowly; treatment plants represent investments and heavy operational costs, particularly for small and medium-sized companies, and only in a few places is it possible to establish joint-use plants. The impossibility of arranging adequate disposal of liquid wastes and mud may force the shutdown of installations which are not in a position to make the necessary investments.

Two tendencies may reshape the quality of the relationships between the leather and footwear sectors over the next few years. On the one hand, Brazil's major footwear companies are becoming vertically integrated, acquiring tanneries and leather treatment plants in order to guarantee the quality of their products and delivery periods. On the other hand, the integration process of the MERCOSUR Southern Cone Common Market has streamlined the access of Brazilian footwear manufacturers to leather produced in the other countries of this subregion. The former development implies the internalization by major companies of pollutive stages in the production processes of footwear input materials. Environmental requirements and regulations targeting the production and preparation of leather will have a direct impact on these companies. In contrast, the latter development implies the import of input materials, thus transferring the issue of adapting productive processes to environmental regulations to the companies in various MERCOSUR countries.

B The EU Eco-Labelling Scheme and Brazilian Footwear Exports

The Netherlands were appointed by the EU as the lead country for the definition of product categories and for the development of criteria and parameters for granting the eco-label for footwear.[9] The preliminary proposal for the Netherlands eco-label mentions footwear made out of leather, rubber, EVA, nylon, polyester and cotton, provided their combined share in the total weight of the shoe is at least 90 per cent. These criteria and parameters cover the five phases of the life cycle of the product: acquisition of raw materials, production of materials, fabrication of the product, use of the product and waste-processing. The environmental aspects considered for each of the phases in the life

Box 4.2 Factors to be considered in an environmental assessment of footwear

Main aspects/ environment measures	*Partial aspects*	*Acquisition of raw material (1)*	*Production of materials (2)*	*Manufacture of product (3)*	*Use of product (4)*	*Waste processing (5)*
Raw materials	1. Depleting scarce renewable raw materials	(+)	–	–	–	–
	2. Depleting non-renewable raw materials	+	–	(–)	–	–
	3. Total quantity of raw materials use	–	+	+	–	–
Energy	4. Depleting non-renewable energy sources	+	+	+	–	–
	5. Total energy used	+	+	+	–	–
Emissions	6. Acid emissions	–	+	–	–	+
	7. Fertilizing emissions	–	–	(–)	–	–
	8. Greenhouse gas emissions	–	+	+	–	+
	9. Ozone-depleting emissions	–	(–)	+	–	+
	10. Emissions of substances toxic for flora and fauna	+	++	–	–	++
	11. Emissions of substances toxic for man (smog)	–	++	+	–	++
	12. Emissions of waste	–	–	–	–	–
	13. Radiation emissions	–	–	–	–	–

Nuisance	14. Release of substances causing odours					
	15. Noise nuisance for user/environment	?	++	+	–	–
	16. Risk of catastrophes	–	–	–	–	–
	17. Effects on nature/landscape/quality of life	–	–	–	–	+
Waste	18. Quantity of waste produced in processing	–	++	++	–	++
	19. Quantity of waste after processing (final waste)	–	++	++	–	++
	20. Quantity of chemical waste	–	++	++	–	++
Re-usable	21. Total product re-usable	–	–	–	–	(+)
	22. Parts of total product re-usable	–	(+)	(+)	–	(+)
	23. Materials can be recycled	–	–	–	–	+
Repairable	24. The product can be repaired	–	–	–	++	–
Lifespan	25. Technical lifespan of product	–	–	–	++	–

Notes:
++ substantial
\+ reasonable
– not substantial
? unknown
(–) still unsure

cycle of the product cover the use of raw materials (renewable and non-renewable), energy consumption (including non-renewable), discharges and emissions, various forms of nuisance (health and environmental hazards), wastes, reutilization of products and parts thereof (including through recycling) and the reparability and durability of the product.

Box 4.2 presents the principal environmental factors and aspects to be considered during the production phase of materials and raw materials (hides for tanning and chemical or plant-based tanning agents) for the production of leather footwear, relevant factors for the fabrication phase of footwear as well as those pertinent to the phases of product use and waste processing. The box also indicates in which aspects the environmental impact of the various phases of the life cycle of the product are considered substantial (++), reasonable (+), non-substantial – unknown (?) and uncertain (–).

A preliminary assessment based on the information provided in Box 4.2 suggests that major concerns are concentrated on energy consumption, the emission of toxic substances and the quantities of waste produced during the production phase of materials, energy consumption and waste production during footwear fabrication phase, and finally, emissions of toxic substances, wastes, reparability and durability during the use and waste-processing phases. The criteria and parameters defined on the basis of these concerns focus particularly on the production of leather footwear.

1 Raw Materials

(1) Energy content no greater than 95 MJ/pair (60 for children's footwear).
(2) Constraints on the use of chemicals and dyestuffs in processing raw materials.

2 Leather Production

(1) Emissions of chromium <120 mg/pair.
(2) Pentachlorophenol (PCP) content in the leather <100 p.p.m.
(3) Treatment of leather with water-based materials and not volatile organic substances (VOs). For VOs no greater than 150 mg/m^3.
(4) during the leather tanning process, waste water should be disposed of in a biological water purification installation
(5) contaminated chrome waste should be recycled unless the chrome waste is not discharged/recycled as chemical waste in the country where the waste originates

3 Footwear Production

(1) Criteria identical to item (3) above.

4 Quality and Performance Requirements

There is a lengthy list of requirements for the various components in footwear, all with defined parameters and testing methods, with specified checking procedures. These requirements cover, among other matters, resistance to splitting, sweat, rubbing and abrasion, water, repeated bending, dry and wet, and are specific for upper leather, inner leather, insole leather, non-leather, insole materials, rubber and synthetic sole materials etc.

5 Average Energy Content

For all materials that could be used in the production of footwear eligible for the eco-label, this establishes an energy content grid which includes the energy content of raw material and that of processing.

Brazil's major business associations representing the export sector are keenly aware of European eco-labelling initiatives. However, this issue is often accorded less priority than that of maintaining a competitive edge in export product prices within the context of competition with Asian manufacturers, especially China. The widespread feeling is that efforts to comply with eco-labelling criteria would increase production costs and product prices, making them still more vulnerable to competitive prices of Asian products.[10]

Large companies have begun being concerned about the difficulties in obtaining information, e.g. as on input materials, as their suppliers are not yet capable of providing this. With respect to the criteria covering chemicals and dyestuffs, Brazilian companies are already taking steps to ensure the safety of chemical products and dyestuffs used in production processes. Many of the products under restrictions mentioned in the EU document are no longer in use. The substitution of these products resulted in higher final costs for footwear, which are, however, difficult to measure without detailed study. As to chromium emissions, with the present effluent waste treatment systems, tanneries currently discharge double the required limit. New investments would be required in order to upgrade the efficiency of existing treatment stations. The use of PCP as a leather preservative is already banned in Brazil. Imported leathers should comply with the guarantee certificates ensuring that PCP is not used. With increasing leather imports from neighbouring countries, this requirement will tend to have an increasingly marked effect on the relationships between Brazilian footwear companies and Uruguayan or Argentine tanneries. The emission of volatile substances into the atmosphere is a major problem during the leather finishing stage. Water-based products for finishing leather are available, and the replacement of products based on organic solvents is already under way. At other production stages, the emission of volatile organic substances is virtually negligible.

In general, tanneries have biological water purification systems. Bleaching takes place with chlorine, while the footwear sector uses raw or unbleached cotton. Although the footwear industries use expanded plastic material, the expansion agents used are not chlorine-based. Brazilian companies already comply with requirements regarding the use of tolerence diisocyanate/methylene diphernyl isocyanate in polyurethane, and limits for sulphur and nitrous dichloromethome in relation to PUR. The use of nitrous dichloromethome is reportedly insignificant, and the figure of 2 per cent for sulphur concentrations is considered somewhat low, to the extent of undermining the quality of some products. It is suggested that the parameter should be raised to 3 per cent.

Brazilian footwear companies are in a position to comply with the quality and performance requirements, which involve using high-quality components, thus affecting costs. With respect to energy use, a superficial analysis noted no major problems. It should be noted that almost all power used in this sector is hydroelectric. There is concern about the constraints on the use of PVC linings, coatings and soles, considered a basic material in the production process. Companies are aware of products that can replace PVC, but these products boost the cost of materials by at least 20 per cent. In the specific case of coatings, this increase may as high as 100 per cent. Business associations feel that some companies in this sector are already finding difficulty in exporting to some countries in Europe, particularly Germany, due to rising restrictions on the use of PVC in footwear. Requirements covering the use of glue and adhesives would lead to increased costs and may lead to a reduction in the productivity of companies.

In general, Brazil's companies are perceived to be in a position to produce footwear that meets eco-labelling standards, but that costs would be appreciably higher than for conventional products, although no data are available to measure these cost increases. The adaptation of the production process and the use of materials complying with these requirements becomes viable only if plans are afoot to develop a line of products targeting a market niche that can pay for footwear with the characteristics required under this scheme. Even under this hypothesis, companies would need time to adapt to these criteria and parameters, especially as this adaptation involves relationships between the producers and the suppliers of their input materials (leather, plastics and chemicals). The Brazilian footwear sector feels that many of the difficulties in adapting to these criteria arise from the fact that this demands changes in the production process of leather – a core material for Brazilian exports.

Historically, the relationship between the leather and footwear sectors in Brazil has been characterized by a low level of cooperation. Companies in the footwear sector have responded to this situation through verticalization (purchase of tanneries) and increased imports from neighbouring countries (Argentina and Uruguay). In turn, this has prompted the leather sector to shift towards modernization which may over the medium term streamline compliance with eco-labelling requirements.

III CONCLUSIONS

The environmental regulations in OECD countries – particularly the EU – are generally perceived by Brazilian exporters as a threat to the maintenance of positions won by Brazilian products in the markets of these countries over the past two decades. Eco-labelling schemes were seen as featuring two characteristics that point in opposite directions. On the one hand, as they are not mandatory, the threat represented by these schemes is, at least in principle, lightened. On the other hand, as this involves an analysis of the entire life cycle of the product, they embody a massive potential for discrimination between imported and domestic products based on the assessment of the various uses of inputs, as well as processing and production methods. This assessment, due to the criteria and parameters that guide it, necessarily implies the upgrading of a specific standard that is not only environmental but also technological and economic, covering the production and interface among various stages of production chains. Criteria and parameters that take into account the various sustainable alternatives for the use of input materials and production methods may reduce the discriminatory impact.

In sum, the impact of eco-labelling schemes on Brazilian exports depends, among other factors, on the specific characteristics of the formulation and implementation of these schemes. The experience of the footwear sector and the T-shirts and bed linen segment, with strong traditions of exports in Brazil, indicate that aspects related to the consumer market, to the pattern of competition, and to the production structure also influence the capacity of eco-labelling schemes to act as barriers to trade:

- The pre-existence of a consumer preference for specific environmentally friendly products and production methods endows the eco-labelling system with a high capacity to guide consumer choices, creating a voluntary (rather than regulatory) discrimination that is still more relevant as it blocks products with a high level of substitutability.
- If the pattern of competition in market segments where companies operate is primarily price-based, compliance with criteria may undermine the market position of these companies. However, at the same time, concern over the discriminatory effects of the eco-labelling scheme decreases, as the market will not sanction such discrimination and will maintain its preference for low prices. Apparently, this is the case with the Brazilian footwear sector: the perception that the costs of adapting the production process to these criteria are high is accompanied by a relative lack of concern with regard to the effects of the introduction of this scheme on the market shares of the Brazilian footwear industry in the EU. On the other hand, if the demand for ecologically differentiated products should create segmentation in the consumer market, this would act as a significant incentive for upgrading the production process to comply with eco-labelling criteria, principally in the case of companies where exports to the EU have a high share in total foreign sales.
- The analysis of the life cycle of the product shows, in the case of the Brazilian footwear, textile and clothing sectors, the weight of the items related to the production of raw materials and input materials in eco-labelling schemes proposed by the EU. In both these sectors, Brazilian companies repeatedly mention difficulties in complying with criteria covering these items, which involve imports to an increasing extent. Additionally, these difficulties may also reflect the tradition of troubled relations between the input materials production sectors and the finished goods production sectors, in a closed economy where levels of protection were administered by the government, frequently in response to pressures from sectorial interests. This means that any effort to channel back

to earlier stages in the production chain the information and demands required by these eco-criteria – principally when compliance involves investments in equipment and machinery in the input materials production sector – seems a particularly difficult task for the finished goods production sector.

It should also be noted that the transformation of eco-labels into a trade barrier also depends on the economic and financial capacity of companies in the sector studied to implement the adaptations required in their production processes and products. In the case of Brazil it has been noted that this capacity varies from sector to sector, in function of the size of the company and the weight of its exports – as well as the EU export market in the company's growth strategy. This is even more so for the large majority of small and medium-sized companies in Brazil, where these requirements involving renovation of equipment and redefinition of the patterns for relationships with suppliers and customers seem totally unobtainable within the current economic and financial context of the country.

Even for major export companies, the costs of compliance have been considered high, principally when this involves new investments in fixed assets. In the case of the textile industry, it has also been indicated that testing and certification costs are far heavier than might been assumed *a priori.*

Reduction in the vulnerability of Brazilian exports to eco-labelling schemes would basically involve the following initiatives at the international level:

- the adoption of non-discriminatory criteria and parameters, especially by schemes being implemented in the EU, as well as a decision-making process compatible with the provisions of the General Agreement on Tariffs and Trade (GATT); and
- the development of multilateral initiatives leading to consensus on the preparation of guidelines for formulating and implementing national and supra-national eco-labelling schemes, which would serve as a basis for mutual recognition among different national schemes.

At the national level, the following elements are crucial:

- increased awareness within export sectors, with respect to the eco-labelling initiatives under way in other countries as well as to their own production processes, including through the systematic preparation and dissemination of technical data on the use of input and raw materials and the manufacturing processes of companies of these sectors;

- broader fora for discussion and negotiation among sectors producing input materials and exportable finished goods, seeking the establishment of mechanisms for cooperation that also lead to the modernization of these sectors with a consequent reduction in vulnerability attributable to specific characteristics of Brazil's production structure;
- development of a national eco-labelling scheme, technical cooperation with countries that have already implemented eco-labelling schemes, and the exploration of compatibility between Brazilian and other schemes leading to mutual recognition among schemes; and
- joint efforts by the Brazilian Government and the private sector to assess the initiatives under way in the EU, and seeking in multilateral fora the compliance of such schemes with the Agreement on Technical Barriers to Trade developed in the context of GATT.

Notes

* This chapter is an abridged version of the study presented at the UNCTAD workshop on "Eco-labelling and International Trade" held in Geneva, June 1994.

1. O. L. Garcia, "Competitivade da indústria têxtil", in *ECIB – Estudo da Competitivade da Indústria Brasileira* (UNICAMP/UFRJ/FDC/FUNCEX, 1993).
2. LAIA: member countries – Argentina, Boliva, Brazil, Chile, Colombia, Ecuador, Mexico, Paraguay, Peru, Uruguay, Venezuela.
3. See Veena Jha and Simonetta Zarrilli, "Eco-labelling Initiatives as Potential Barriers to Trade: A Viewpoint from Developing Countries", in this volume.
4. Ibid.
5. The EU scheme on textiles was discussed in detail with the technical staff of the Chemical and Textile Industry Technological Centre of the National Industrial Apprenticeship Service (CETIQT/SENAI) of the National Confederation of Industry in Rio de Janeiro. The following paragraphs are based on this discussion.
6. A. B. Costa, "Competitividade da indústria de calçados", in *ECIB – Estudo da Competitividade da Indústria Brasileira* (UNICAMP/UFRJ/FDC/FUNCEX, 1993).

7. R. Seroa da Motta, "Política de controle ambiental e competitividade", in *ECIB – Estudo da Competitividade da Indústria Brasileira* (UNICAMP/UFRJ/FDC/FUNCEX, 1993).
8. UNIDO, "La competitividad internacional de la industria de cueros y calzados en el Mercosur", mimeo, 1993.
9. The criteria on which this analysis is based are those developed by the Netherlands for its national eco-labelling programme.
10. Interviews were carried out with representatives of business associations, individual companies, and the Footwear, Leather and Similar Products Technological Centre (CTCAA) in the Vale dos Sinos Production and Export complex in Rio Grande do Sul State in Southern Brazil. The CTCCA replied in writing to the questionnaire forwarded by UNCTAD to FUNCEX. The following paragraphs rely on the information furnished by CTCAA and on the interviews.

5 Eco-Labelling of Tissue and Towel Paper Products in the EU: A Brazilian Perspective

ABECEL[1]

I THE BRAZILIAN PULP INDUSTRY AND THE ENVIRONMENT

The pulp industry in Brazil has been making a concerted effort to conform to principles of sustainable development. All the pulp produced comes from carefully managed tree plantations, and no wood from tropical rain forests is used. Furthermore, the industry makes extensive use of renewable resources since a major share of the energy used comes from biomass. Advanced pollution control technologies are also used by the industry, and these include secondary, and in one case tertiary, treatment of effluents.

II BRAZILIAN PULP EXPORTERS AND EU ECO-LABELS

Brazilian exporters actively support the use of eco-labels in the European Union (EU) because such labels may function as uniform indicators of environmental and consumer standards throughout the EU, and because they may provide the market with a new marketing mechanism that will enable a new ecological impetus to be given to consumers, manufacturers, and traders.

However, pulp exporters from Brazil feel that an eco-labelling scheme should be

- open, clear and transparent, and based on sound technical and scientific information;
- non-discriminatory towards products, producers, countries and regions;

- simple to apply and based on full life-cycle analysis; and
- based on internationally agreed standards.

III EU ECO-LABEL FOR TISSUE PRODUCTS: THE BRAZILIAN EXPERIENCE

Brazilian exporters of pulp and their association, ABECEL, have felt that the decision-making process for the EU label for tissue products has not been adequately transparent. There has been considerable difficulty in obtaining relevant information from the EU and from the Danish Lead Body. There has been no formal mechanism for third countries to submit their views and recommendations. It is understood that the EU is in the process of changing this procedure, and an improvement in this situation would indeed be very welcome.

Brazilian exporters have also been concerned about certain aspects of the criteria used for awarding labels, and they feel that it is unfair to penalize wood from sustainably managed plantation forests. In addition, the concept of "consumption of renewable resources" has been defined so as to exclude wood waste, sawdust, trimmings from saw mills, thinnings and thin wood, thus exempting these materials from load points. This is discriminatory against planted forests, and the Brazilian plantation forests have been particularly affected by this. Moreover, the criteria seem to display an unreasonable double bias towards recycling. If used as purchasing guidelines, these may result in adverse impact on developing-country suppliers.

ABECEL feels that the scheme fails to provide consumers with the information necessary for making informed environmental choices. The eco-label may, in effect, function as a serious non-tariff barrier, especially if governments use the criteria as purchasing conditions. Such a situation may mean extra-territorial application of EU laws and regulations on environment and health, and this is incompatible with the General Agreement on Tariffs and Trade.

However, Brazilian pulp exporters welcome the new guidelines of the Commission of the EU, which provide that, through the Consultative Forum, third-country producers will have access to the information available to EU producers and that they will be able to submit their views on the scheme before the final decision is made. If these guidelines are effectively implemented, third countries may be able to participate actively in the discussions from the outset.

IV QUESTIONS AND SUGGESTIONS

Brazilian pulp exporters are very eager to have confirmation that non-EU producers will have access to the same information available to EU producers, and that they will be able to participate at every stage of the decision-making process. One suggestion in this respect would be that major third-country producers such as ABECEL should be invited to submit data, observations and comments to the Consultative Forum, the Lead Competent Body, and the officials of the Commission. However, it remains unclear as to how the Consultative Forum will ensure that the points of view of non-EU producers are adequately represented. It also remains to be clarified whether the Consultative Forum will ensure that the views of non-EU producers with respect to criteria are brought to the attention of the officials of the Commission and the member states, even in instances where such views differ substantially from the views of European industries. Another issue that remains to be resolved concerns the determination of instances when criteria will be modified according to regional differences in environmental conditions. Furthermore, the market shares of labelled paper products need to be specified, and this should be compared with the situations in other product groups.

The new guidelines explicitly state that the Consultative Forum will be able to nominate its representatives to the *ad hoc* working group. Non-EU producers should be included in the working group. The role of the European Environmental Agency (EEA) in the new mechanism would need to be specified. Finally, the Commission should specify that the labelling criteria for tissue products do not create a precedent for the eco-labelling of other paper products, so that the discrimination discussed above does not continue.

Note

1. ABECEL is an association of Brazilian pulp exporters. The members of ABECEL are Brazilian market pulp producers such as Aracruz Cellulose, S. A., Bahia Sul Cellulose, S. A., Cenibra-Cellulose Nipo-Brasileira, S. A., Jari Cellulose, S. A., and Riocell. They produce 2.1 million tons of pulp every year and employ 23 000 persons. Of their total exports of pulp and paper, 38 per cent are directed to the EU.

6 The Potential Impact of the EU Eco-Labelling Programme on Colombian Textile Exports

Lily Ho, Diana Gaviria, Ximena Barrera and Ricardo Sánchez

The Colombian textile industry produces an average of 75 000 cubic metres of material per year. The textile industry represents 8.6 per cent of Colombia's total industry aggregate value, and generates approximately 50 000 jobs through direct employment (see Table 6.1). Production in this sector is semi-capital-intensive. The process of technological reconversion has implied a major shift from non-qualified to qualified labour. This change towards capital-intensive production has affected the cost structure in the industry. Table 6.2 summarizes the current situation of some sectors of the industry.

Colombia initiated a process of rapid economic liberalization at the beginning of the 1990s. Most of the Colombian industries, which had earlier been protected, were not prepared for the stiff competition they began facing from foreign firms. Average tariff rates for textiles dropped from 37.9 per cent to 18 per cent during this period.

The downward trend in the Colombian textile sector has been influenced during the past year by the revaluation of the peso against the dollar (mainly caused by a surplus of international reserves),[1] and the economic crisis in Venezuela, one of Colombia's main trading partners.

The situation in world textile markets also had an adverse impact on Colombia. While the sector grew at an annual rate of 6.5 per cent in the 1980s, the growth rate dropped to 2.3 per cent in the past two years (1994/95). This has resulted in a massive stock accumulation of textiles on account of the decrease in demand, and has led to unconventional trade policies and practices by some countries for the creation of new markets.

One of the main inputs used in the textile sector is cotton, representing

Table 6.1 Textile industry as a percentage of total industry

Variables	*1985*	*1989*	*1990*	*1991*
Number of establishments	6.7	6.6	6.6	6.6
Total personnel employed	10.8	10.8	10.8	10.9
Net production value	7.7	7.8	7.9	8.1
Aggregate value	10	10.2	10.3	8.6
Net investment	26.5	10.6	9.5	12
Energy consumption	10	9.9	9.5	9.5
Fixed assets value	15.2	14.6	13	13.6

Source: "El Sector Textil Colombiano", Notas Empresariales, National Planning Department, 1994.

Table 6.2 Growth of some Colombian industries (percentages)

Sector	*1990*	*1991*	*1992*	*1993*
Textiles	2.7	0	7.1	–7.1
Clothing	6.9	–2.8	4.2	–2.2
Leather	17.7	9.2	–3.6	–8.3
Shoes	–7.5	22.40	1.0	–3.5
Total industry	6.6	–1.8	5.7	3.9

Source: Fedesarrollo, *Coyuntura Económica Latinoamericana*, September 1994.

roughly 60 per cent of the total fibre consumption. Low international prices and increases in imports have also influenced local production trends. In 1993, cotton imports doubled, while production and harvested area decreased by 3.6 per cent and 38.4 per cent respectively, in 1994.[2]

Despite all the adverse effects mentioned above, the industry took advantage of the new commercial agreements with countries in the Latin American region and opened new markets. Figures 6.1 and 6.2 show this.

Although Colombia's main importers continue to be the United States, the European Union (EU) and Venezuela, Colombian textile exports have registered a decline in recent years. Table 6.3 summarizes the changes in Colombian textile exports to their major destinations in the year 1993–4.

The information used in this study was obtained through interviews

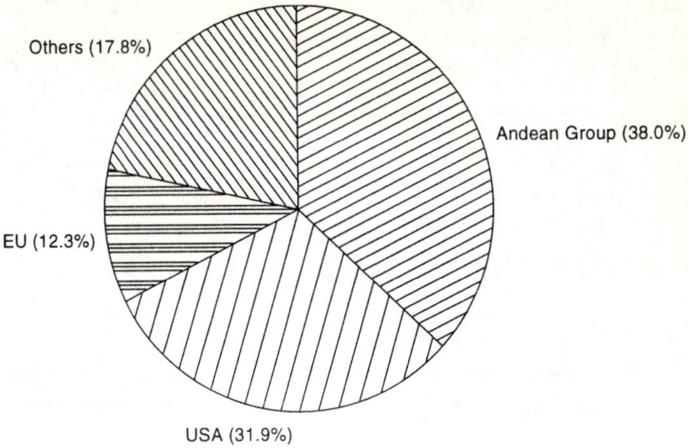

Figure 6.1 Direction of Colombian textile exports, 1993

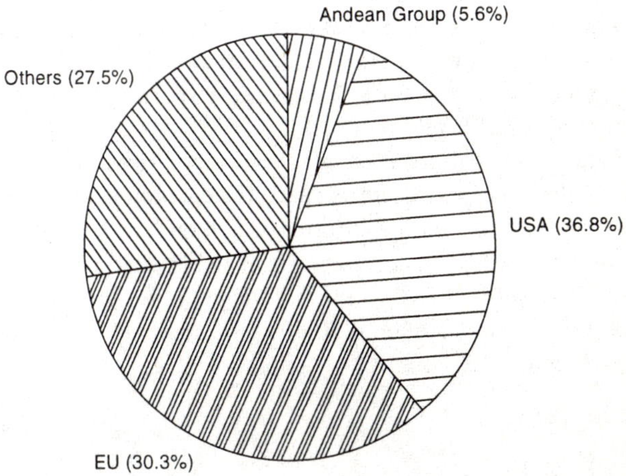

2

Figure 6.2 Direction of Colombian textile exports, 1990

conducted with several textile firms in Medellin and Bogotá. In addition, ASCOLTEX (the association of textile producers) held meetings with several large textile companies, both in Medellin and in Bogotá, to discuss the eco-labelling proposal. In Medellin, representatives from the following textile companies attended the meeting: Everfit, Tejicondor,

Table 6.3 Colombian textile export growth (January 1993–May 1994)

Country	*Growth rate (per cent)*
United States	3.8
Canada	–8.7
Mexico	131.8
Venezuela	–10.7
EU	2.8
Other European countries	–14.5
Japan	–75.5
Total	6.8

Source: Fedesarrollo, op. cit.

Fabricato, Coltejer, and Satexco. Ascoltex participated actively in the distribution and the analysis of eco-labelling schemes, and made comments on earlier versions of this paper.

These interviews were conducted as part of a larger survey for which 67 exporting firms were interviewed. Nine of these were textile exporting firms, with four of them located in Medellin industrial area, three in Bogotá and two in Cali. The average share of exports in their total production was 28 per cent.

Most of these firms did not report large environmental investment. Only four of the nine textile firms interviewed indicated having done any type of mitigation action (pollution treatment). It is estimated that their investments are less than 2 per cent of their total production costs. The case of Tejicondor is an exception, though. This company, as noted below, has invested more than $250 000 in treatment plants and other pollution mitigation activities.

I EU ECO-LABELLING PROGRAMME AND COLOMBIAN EXPORTERS

The initial reaction of Colombian firms to the EU eco-labelling programme was rather negative. However one year later, these same industries consider that the draft eco-criteria developed under the programme will be expensive to meet but they are aware that they will have to make environment-related investments in the future in order to compete in international markets. Colombian exporters are conscious that environmental standards are constantly becoming stricter, and have expressed fears that this may have an impact on their competitiveness.

The criteria established by the EU were discussed with each firm, and the following points emerged from the survey:

- Almost all Colombian firms surveyed consider they are close to compliance with the European eco-labelling scheme. Firm B, for example, studied the criteria for water consumption during wet treatment; for the production of flat cloth, they use 246 litres of water per kilogram in one of their plants, whereas the EU criteria is 245 l/kg for flat cloth and 260 l/kg for cotton; in another plant, they consume 268 l/kg both for cotton and flat cloth.
- Firm A considered that it could comply with all the standards, except noise levels, which have been set at 85 dB. It recently invested approximately US$ 10 million in state-of-the-art technologies, which have lesser noise levels than older equipment. However, even with this new technology, they would not be able to meet European noise standards, as the noise level in this plant fluctuates between 95 and 100 dB. They also find it difficult to calculate the quantity of water needed for the cotton process or the polyester process separately, as required by the EU standards, since there is a vertical production system. Firm C also stated that it would be difficult to comply with the water standards, because their technology is older than in other firms.
- Firm D, which exports 40 per cent of its products to Spain, considers that the quality of products improved after environment-related investments were made. However, they are willing to change their production processes and adopt the EU eco-label only if the benefits exceed the costs.
- All firms stated that they comply with occupational-safety conditions, and have made investments to ensure better safety and health conditions for their workers. This is largely a result of the stringent labour conditions imposed by the Ministries of Health and Labour. Colombian producers stated that one of the largest costs they would face if they applied for an eco-label is monitoring residue limits on final products. Here there is a pronounced need for transfer of equipment and know-how by developed countries. Currently, it is not clear who will carry the financial burden of the auditing.

Nevertheless, some Colombian firms such as Tejicondor reported that compliance with environmental requirements from German importers in recent years has led them to focus their exports on other markets, with more flexible regulations. They are conscious that the European market is very important to them, and are willing to adjust their production processes in the medium term to attain the required standards. Most firms stated, however, that since new investments are subjected to a strict cost–benefit analysis, the costs of an EU eco-label currently exceed the benefits by far. Nevertheless, all firms will adopt EU criteria once they have been harmonized on an international basis.

Small and medium-sized firms, on the other hand, are especially vulnerable, as their scarce resources prevent them meeting labelling requirements. As industries are forced to grapple with increasingly strict environmental measures and green consumerism, the small firms will suffer the most. The economic consequences could be serious in the near future, as small and medium-sized enterprises make up of 93 per cent of the number of companies found in Colombia, and contribute about 33 per cent of minor exports. Colombian textile firms are afraid that the eco-label could be used as a protectionist measure against non-European imports. They feel that this is especially the case in the private labelling schemes, such as MST (designed by the German textile industry) and Steilmann (developed by the largest German producers of garments), where German producers set standards which are relatively easy for themselves to meet. Even though these private schemes do not appear to be as strict as the EU eco-label (two firms, Tejicondor and Satexco, specifically stated that they do not use most of the restricted chemicals and compounds listed), it is none the less more costly and more inconvenient for foreign exporters to obtain the label, than for German producers.

Colombian producers also want more transparency in the process of setting standards. They do not understand why, for example, 0.004 mg/l was set as the maximum amount of lead permissible, or why minute amounts of formadelhyde cannot be allowed for the EU eco-label. They wonder to what degree (and at what costs) do these standards contribute to environmental conservation. Since fulfilling the criteria involves costly investments, the firms would like to see scientific justification for the determined levels. European eco-labels seem to have been designed with European technology and production processes in mind, and the situation in developing countries is seldom taken into account. Coltejer, which manages 220 products, explained that the structure of large textile firms in Colombia is different from those in Europe. In Colombia, large firms produce a whole gamut of products, involving most of the textile production processes. This constitutes a major difference with respect to European firms characterized by one-product processes, which find compliance with efficiency standards easier.

In addition, textile industries and the Government consider the proposed eco-labelling schemes protectionist since their requirements pertain not only to product standards but also to process standards. Both feel that there is no reason for the European governments or the private eco-labelling schemes to make requirements on local water and air pollution standards when these do not affect European consumers. They are also suspicious of the fact that these schemes are mainly directed towards products that are also produced in Europe, such as leather, textiles and flowers. Other products, potentially more harmful to the European consumer and to Colombia's environment, such as coffee and fruit, are not submitted to the same requirements.

Colombian producers also perceive verification procedures to be a major difficulty. Especially in the criteria related to cotton growing and other production processes, they do not see how compliance can be proven without costly visits on the part of European inspectors. The producers themselves would also have to spend time, effort and money verifying that the cotton they use complies with the standards, and in most cases they do not have the facilities or the resources to test the cotton or their own products. Therefore, they view the eco-label as a *de facto* non-tariff barrier.

Now that producers are focusing on product quality, some complaints have arisen to the effect that quality may be affected by stricter environmental standards. Satexco was required by the German importer Steilmann to avoid bleaching with chlorine. Satexco used this chemical for quality considerations. The closest substitute would be peroxide, which is somewhat less costly, but which does not whiten effectively and also affects the resistance of the thread. Another company, Enka, was forced by its headquarters to eliminate asbestos in production. The recommended substitutes were mineral fibers and magnesium silicate. Once again, the industry contends that quality is affected with more environmentally friendly substitutes. Enka claims that substitutes can only be used at temperatures below 3000° Celsius. Graphite is used at higher temperatures, and therefore substitution is not complete.

Investment in pollution control has been primarily a result of national environmental requirements. All Colombian firms have invested substantial resources in environmental protection in order to comply with national legislation.[3]

While these firms are investing in environmental requirements, Colombia's regulations differ somewhat from European norms, as they currently emphasize to a greater degree end-of-the-pipe air and water pollution control, as distinct from energy consumption and the use of chemical inputs used in the industrial process. With the creation of the Ministry of the Environment, all norms related to processes involving industrial pollution, application of non-approved chemicals and water pollution, amongst others, will be revised. These reforms may make Colombian standards less stringent than European standards, because there is a general consensus both at the private and public level that any viable legislation should take into account the social and economic realities of Colombia. Economic instruments will also be used to attain environmental standards.

Finally, companies view environmental conservation as a matter of priorities. In their opinion, textiles are not a high priority in comparison with other industries such as chemicals that are much more contaminating. Overall, they perceive cotton textiles as safe products, and suggest that the EU concentrate on other products where the benefits of the environmental measures will exceed the costs.

Suggestions made by Colombian firms include the following:

- information should be provided to developing countries on the most recent developments in environmental measures, including through translations into national languages, of important regulations;
- sources of easy long-term credit should be arranged for firms so that they can have access to the financial resources necessary for compliance with environmental criteria;
- consultations and assistance need to be provided, aimed at transfer of know-how and technology to mitigate environmental impacts;
- exporting companies, particularly from developing countries, should be given adequate time and advance warning to adjust to new environmental requirements;
- an alternative eco-labelling programme may be created, with eco-criteria more consistent with developing-country conditions and environmental priorities; this programme would be based on eco-criteria that are less strict than those proposed by the EU; however, it would provide a concrete incentive for firms to improve their environmental performance, as it would be more accessible; and
- standards should not be based on a complete life-cycle analysis, as this would pose difficulties, given the large number of firms involved in the production of the final good.

II PROPOSALS FOR A COLOMBIAN ECO-LABELLING PROGRAMME

At present, Colombia is developing its own eco-labelling programme, based on the systems already implemented in Germany and in other European countries. While modelled on some of these schemes, the eco-labelling programme will adapt to the specific domestic conditions in terms of requirements and products. The project is spearheaded by the Colombian Ministries of the Environment and Foreign Trade, and has the technical support of the National Planning Department.

The objectives of the Colombian eco-label are:

- to promote environmental conservation in several sectors, addressing a variety of aspects, including polluting emissions, energy use and natural resource exploitation;
- to provide the domestic industry with means and incentives to increase its competitiveness through the implementation of environmental strategies; and
- to assist Colombian export firms in penetrating foreign markets, especially those in which "green consumerism" and the implementation of environmental measures are evident.

The eco-label is being designed to address both domestic and export concerns. Colombian companies have clearly expressed their desire to have a Colombian label certifying Colombian products, and not directed solely towards export markets. Related to this is the need perceived by environmentalists to increase environmental consciousness among domestic consumers and producers. On the other hand, export sectors are increasingly confronting environmental demands in their markets, and are interested in the label as a means to promote a "green" image for their products. This eco-labelling programme will include a parallel process of developing environmental action plans with the related industries. As such, the focus will be on mitigating and preventing pollution, and the eco-label will just be the result of this process.

The considerations made by companies regarding the eco-labelling programme were mostly practical: is it environmentally feasible to apply an eco-label to a certain product? Does the eco-label provide a realistic incentive to the industry in mind? Have eco-labelling criteria already been developed abroad which may be adapted to Colombia, or will eco-criteria need to be developed from scratch?

The eco-labelling programme has not defined specific products, but will probably begin working with industries interested in promoting eco-labelling schemes, such as flowers and detergents.

The criteria will be drafted with the following in mind:

- use of life-cycle analysis as a tool to assess the main environmental impacts of the product;
- review of industrial literature and applied production processes to identify state-of-the-art technology and processes that are ecologically more sound;
- analysis of eco-criteria already developed by other eco-labelling schemes, and their adaptation to the Colombian context;
- issues of quality and security; and
- existence of Colombian environmental laws.

At present, the procedure for developing eco-labelling criteria is envisioned as a two-tiered process: elaboration at the expert level, followed by approval by the decision-making body. An independent body, with the assistance of specialized advisers, would design the criteria and the related verification requirements. The resulting draft would be presented to an expert committee which would include representatives from the Government, industry, consumers, environmental groups, and other interested parties. If the document were accepted by other experts, it would be forwarded to a Certification Committee which would act as the final decision-maker. The following institutions could be members of the Committee: the Ministry of Environment, which would chair the Committee, the Ministries of Foreign Trade and Development, consumer associations, industries associations, and the press.

The entire certification process should be designed to be as transparent and voluntary as possible. As a result, participation from all sectors of society will be actively encouraged. It is expected that the industry will play a significant role in the development of criteria, since much of the expertise lies with the companies. This participation should be somewhat balanced by the presence of neutral institutions such as universities or laboratories.

The level of interest among Colombian companies regarding the eco-label has been very high. A meeting in which a possible eco-label was introduced was attended by 130 firms. The national flower association (Asocolflores) is currently developing its own eco-labelling programme within a regional context.

The National Planning Department's trade-environment survey, conducted among export firms, indicated that three out of every four companies were willing to apply for a Colombian eco-label if it existed for their product. The main reasons cited were that the label was good for the environment, that it improved the company's image and that it was indispensable for the international market. Approximately one out of every eight firms stated that they would not apply for the label. Some of the firms indicated that they would apply for the label only if the market demanded it.

Other firms have urged an early establishment of the Colombian eco-label. Over half of those surveyed had a favourable opinion of this initiative, but a few commented that the Colombian eco-label would be of very little use in export markets if it were not recognized by foreign eco-labelling schemes. Two out of every three companies indicated that they would be willing to implement an education/publicity campaign regarding the eco-label, which is critical for raising environmental consciousness among consumers. Of the remainder, half did not respond and the other half declined to participate in such a campaign.

At present, there are several major issues concerning the establishment of the Colombian eco-label. There are discussions taking place on whether the label should focus primarily on the product or take its entire life cycle into account. In addition, the question of how the standards should be set is also being discussed. Colombian legislation is very stringent at present, but registers low levels of compliance and enforcement. There are also a number of environmental problems, such as ground water pollution, which are not covered by existing laws or standards.

It is expected that, with the creation of the Ministry of Environment, Colombian environmental legislation will be reformed. Industries and some members of the Government feel that setting eco-labels equivalent to Colombian legislation is self-defeating because this legislation does not reflect the reality of the country, and would therefore be difficult to comply with. As a result, some members feel that standards should be independent of the current legislation, that they should be gradual and increasingly demanding, and that there should be time targets to reach standard levels equivalent to domestic and foreign norms.

Colombian manufacturers expressed their preference for having requirements related to production processes among the eco-criteria. The call for more comprehensive criteria stemmed from competition-related considerations, as some firms were afraid that some competitors should get an "environmental approval" based on the product alone, despite the use of highly polluting processes. The argument was that if the objective of the eco-label is to improve the environmental performance of the Colombian industry, the production side cannot be ignored.

Verification was also considered an important issue. In situations where it may not be possible to take the firm's declaration at face value, audit and tests by an independent body may be required before the eco-label can gain credibility among the public. The difficulty lies in the scarcity of qualified laboratories and institutions which can independently assess compliance with the criteria.

Notes

1. Gradual devaluation had been used as the main mechanism for gaining competitiveness in international markets for more than 20 years.
2. Ministry of Agriculture, August 1994.
3. Tejicondor has initiated an environmental management plan which involves educational campaigns, a reduction of water consumption by 50 per cent, solid-waste disposal systems, and air pollution control. The cost of this programme is estimated at US$1 million.

7 Eco-Labelling in the EU and the Export of Turkish Textiles and Garments

Celik Aruoba

INTRODUCTION

This paper examines the probable impact of various European eco-labelling programmes, especially the eco-labelling scheme of the European Union (EU) on the export of textiles and garments from Turkey to European markets. The research for the paper was carried out in the form of interviews with representatives of various institutions and companies.[1] Section I summarizes the basic positions of the bodies interviewed, while section II provides a summary of the conjectures that emerged during an item-by-item analysis of the list of criteria used in the EU eco-labelling programme.

I RESPONSES TO ECO-LABELLING

In recent years, in response to increasing public interest in environmental matters in European countries, a new product has emerged in the European market. This new product is known under a variety of names such as "eco-garment", "eco-textile", "green wear" and "bio-garment". At present, two factors seem to restrict the wider use of eco-garments:

- specifications of existing production technologies and the limited supply of obligatory inputs (e.g. raw materials such as cotton, natural soap and environment-friendly dyes) make it technically difficult to produce eco-garments in large quantities; and
- the new investment needed and the prices and costs of obligatory production inputs make production of eco-garments more expensive.

At least for the time being, only a limited number of import companies, especially in Northern European countries such as Sweden, Denmark, and Germany where sufficient demand exists for this new product, demand and purchase eco-garments. It is interesting to note that these companies, which also purchase "regular" merchandise, assign two different sets of criteria for regular products and eco-products.

One segment of Turkish textiles and garments manufacturing industry believes that Turkey has a comparative advantage at profitably producing and supplying this new product, and various Turkish companies are in the process of (a) investing to encourage the production of organically grown and also naturally coloured cotton in various parts of the country; (b) importing organically grown and also naturally coloured cotton, as well as yarns and fabrics produced from these raw materials (e.g. from the United States and from India);[2] (c) investing in machinery and equipment in order to establish an approved ecofactory;[3] (d) actively using advertising and other promotional methods to market their eco-garment products in European countries; and (e) applying to obtain an eco-label (or more than one) from an assessment and labelling institution in Europe, particularly the "Öko-Tex 100 standard label" which is considered as the most important and influential eco-labelling programme among Turkish manufacturers and exporters. It can be maintained that these companies have been successful in their efforts, and that for the past three years they have been widening their reach and marketing high quality, high priced eco-garments and eco-collections in various European countries.

The textile and garments manufacturing and exporting sectors in Turkey argue that the interest in environmental matters and the approach of certain manufacturing and trading companies to profit from this interest have given rise to a new industry in Europe: that of assessment and labelling institutions and companies. According to the manufacturers interviewed, the number of these institutions is quite high and is on the increase. There are considerable differences among the norms and standards imposed by the different labelling institutions. Besides, the services offered by these institutions are very expensive. On the other hand, a number of Turkish companies are in the process of applying to various eco-labelling schemes to maintain their marketing strategies.[4] Some of the interviewees claimed that the situation was similar in the case of ISO 9000 series, when numerous Turkish companies paid – and are still paying – large fees to European assessment companies in order to obtain certificates. Most of the interviewees believe that due to the restrictive nature of their norms and standards, eco-labelling schemes in their present stature will only help to create a new product that cannot be produced in large quantities and that will fall far short of meeting world textile and garment demand. They feel that these schemes may not seriously contribute to the adoption of environmentally sounder practices such as the promotion of less hazardous pesticides, wider and more efficient application of waste-water treatment, and the development and production of environmental friendly and economically affordable dyes and chemicals.

Another generally agreed point among Turkish textile and garment manufacturers is that the environmental restrictions aiming trade in general, and eco-labelling programmes – specifically the rules and procedures for applying for and obtaining labels – in particular, are non-tariff barriers to trade and may easily emerge as sources of discrimination in European markets (a) between European companies and exporting-country companies, and more importantly (b) among exporting countries themselves. Turkish exporters are particularly worried about the rise of Chinese textiles exports to European countries.

As for fulfilling the norms set by various European eco-labelling schemes in general and the criteria suggested by the EU eco-labelling programme for T-shirts and bed linen in particular, the representatives of the Turkish textiles and garments sector claim that the exporting segment of the industry would not confront technical difficulties except, perhaps, in cases of (a) pesticides used in cotton growing, and (b) dyes and certain chemicals that are solely provided by the European chemical companies. Difficulties in these two areas are also faced by other suppliers, including European and North American manufacturers, who do not produce eco-garments but regular merchandise.

According to the manufacturers interviewed, the costs of complying with the criteria would be very high, and this is especially so in the case of textile manufacturing companies. Some of the immediately observable sources of additional costs in the EU criteria list, even for modern and relatively environment-friendly companies, can be listed as follows:

- use of approved dyes;
- prohibition of formaldehyde;
- use of approved chemicals;
- removal of colouration from waste water;
- cost of applying for the eco-label;
- cost of tests and other assessment procedures; and
- other additional costs.

The manufacturers also believe that those prerequisites will necessarily increase the import demand of the industry. This new demand necessarily will be directed towards European companies in order to facilitate approval by the assessing and labelling bodies. The increase in the costs of textile production would understandably be passed on to garment manufacturers. Garment manufacturing companies which produce eco-garments, on the other hand, face different and considerable costs. One T-shirt manufacturer who exports his eco-collections to northern European markets and imports "licensed fabrics manufactured with organic cotton", both from India and the United States, in order to make these collections, claimed that these imports cause a 60 per cent rise in his production costs.

II ANALYSIS OF CRITERIA FOR T-SHIRTS AND BED LINEN

A Definition

The number of items (T-shirts as defined and bed linen) included in the EU eco-labelling programme, at least for the time being, is very limited. These two items are only a small portion of the textiles and garments trade. Other eco-labelling programmes in Europe cover a wider range of products. Import companies, especially for the eco-garments and eco-collection, enforce norms on various accessories such as buttons, zippers, etc. Due to this limitation, the EU eco-labelling programme is not expected to act as a guideline for some kind of standardization among numerous European environmental-norm catalogues. Other eco-labelling programmes – international, national and private, such as the Öko-Tex – are expected to continue to strengthen their positions in the mean time. The lists of norms for T-shirts and for bed linens are almost identical.

B Fitness for Use

In general, the textile and garment manufacturers feel that national and international standards specified in this part of the criteria list have nothing to do with ecological concerns. They define in detail various test procedures within the scope of the so-called "quality standards" which are subjected to thorough and continuous tests and inspections,[5] not only for T-shirts and bed linen as defined in the document mentioned above, but for all kinds of products, by the importing companies,[6] and the costs of all these tests and inspections are usually borne by the manufacturers. In other words, for a company that applies to obtain the EU eco-label, these criteria may emerge as a source of overlapping, confusion and unnecessary additional costs, since in the short and medium term, it may not be possible to persuade individual import companies to agree on this label, due to differences in expected standards and assessment methods.

Several Turkish manufacturing and export companies argued that some of the tests and assessment methods were subjective, and that evaluation by a bureaucratic body could result in discrimination. The EU criteria for T-shirts and bed linen identify test and assessment methods, but do not specify expected "rating limits" for itemized fitness-for-use standards.

1 Mechanical and Physical Properties

Textiles: method for assessing the appearance of durable press fabrics after domestic washing and drying (ISO 7768, AATCC 135 and DIN 53 870) In general, European companies expect a minimum fabric rating of DP-3, especially for T-shirts. Turkish textiles constantly maintain a level of DP-3 or DP-4 ratings. Tests are performed by various national laboratories, including the Textile Laboratory at the Istanbul Technical University,[7] TSE laboratories and certain private sector laboratories operated by export and invoicing companies. Import companies sometimes demand that quality and fitness tests be conducted in certain European laboratories. A number of large-scale European and North-American import companies retain and operate their own laboratories.

Textiles: determination of dimensional change in washing and drying (ISO 5077) Dimensional stability is considered one of the most important quality attributes. The maximum limit of dimensional change approved by importers from the United States and from Europe is 5 per cent in length and width. Ensuring dimensional stability is often a matter of costs. For high-quality, expensive merchandise, and in cases where import companies insist, dimensional changes are reduced by extra washing. In certain cases, absolute dimensional stability is obtained by: (i) industrial type washing with an extra cost of $0.20–0.25/kg, or (ii) a 50 per cent sanforization process (Rutrix method without the use of chemicals) of the knitted material with an extra cost of $0.35–0.40/kg. Shrinking by chemical processes has generally been abandoned for textiles and garments, especially for export items. Manufacturers and exporters claim that importers increasingly demand that all fabric should be given a pre-shrinking mechanical finish with a compactor. The industry, accordingly, invests in such machinery.

2 Colour Fastness

Colour fastness of dyeings and prints to wear (DIN 54 000, ISO 105-E01); to rubbing (DIN 54 021, ISO 105-X12); to perspiration (DIN 54 020, ISO 105-E04); and to domestic and commercial laundering (DIN 54 017, ISO 105-C06) All colour fastness tests, especially those for washing as well as dry and wet rubbing, are conducted in various private and public laboratories in Turkey in accordance with the test norms and standards listed above. Some import firms, such as Hennes and Mauritz, AB in Sweden and Marks and Spencer in the United Kingdom, carry out their own colour fastness tests in their laboratories. Almost all European companies demand ratings of three or four for colour fastness to washing and dry rubbing, and a rating of three for wet rubbing.

C Materials for the Product

Turkey's principal exports are 100 per cent cotton T-shirts and bed-linen. Blending of cotton and polyester for export is not a common practice. Turkey exports polyester yarns.

D Energy Consumption

None of the firms interviewed calculate the consumption of energy during manufacturing in the manner described in European Union's list of criteria. Two firms, one from Istanbul and the other from Cukurova, agreed to make such calculations, but eventually did not provide any response.

E Water Consumption

The criteria set by the EU with respect to water consumption during wet treatment is 245 litres/kg of material. This is perceived as too high by the textile manufacturers interviewed from Istanbul, who claim that the common practice involves a water consumption of 60–90 litres/kg at the material manufacturing phase for T-shirts and bed-linen.[8]

Textile manufacturing plants in Cukurova (Adana and Tarsus) consume much more water. Administrators of these companies pointed out that the amount of water consumption depends on the technology used, and evaluate the limits set in the EU criteria as reasonable. Established early, these plants use older technologies.

Manufacturers from Istanbul stressed the need to establish an optimum level of consumption for water, as the price of water as well as that of waste-water discharge charged by the municipalities is very high. Furthermore, excess consumption of water also means higher energy consumption, and the price of energy is very high in Turkey. One manufacturer pointed out that at the dyeing stage, the proportion of energy cost to total cost in his firm is 18 per cent. Comparable figures for Germany and Italy are 16 per cent and 22 per cent respectively.

F Waste-Water Parameters

Environmental norms and standards in Turkey, specified in various legal documents including the *Regulation for Control of Water Pollution*, are in general consistent with the norms in the EU. Turkish waste-water regulation (*Regulation for Control of Water Pollution* of 4 September 1989) sets the maximum limits of allowance for chemical oxygen demand (COD) between 250 and 400 ppm, and the maximum limits of allowance of BOD between 80 and 90 ppm for different stages in the manufacturing process, for two-hour composed samples.

Textile manufacturers in Istanbul feel that the COD limit stipulated by the EU (50 kg/ton) is very high. One manufacturer claimed that the COD of his factory's waste water is approximately 12 kg/ton. According to him, the COD and BOD of waste water discharge of this factory are 210 ppm and 75 ppm respectively.

None of the textile factories in the Cukurova region have waste-water treatment plants. Administrators of these companies confessed that they have serious problems both with the Government and with various European import companies. They all claimed that despite severe technological and financial difficulties, they were in the process of establishing waste-water treatment plants.

Regarding the maximum accepted colouration of waste-water discharges (DIN 38 494), textile manufacturers from Istanbul insisted that the cost of removing colour from waste water was prohibitively high. One manufacturer, whose factory has biological and chemical waste water treatment plants, explained that he uses "environmentally-approved", European-made reactive dyes on cotton, and that about 60 per cent of the dyestuff reacts with natural fibre, while about 25 per cent of the dyestuff goes into waste water. Although the factory releases non-toxic and non-poisonous waste water into the sewage system after treatment in the biological unit, the colour reacts with the carbohydrates and dyes the waste water. In other words, the colour cannot be removed by biological treatment, and chemical treatment would be necessary for this. The manufacturer argued that in addition to being several times more expensive than biological treatment, chemical treatment also could harm the environment on account of the use of various chemicals during this process.

With respect to the amount of absorbable organo-halogens (AOX) in waste water discharges (DIN 38 409), the survey could not obtain analysable data.

The survey could not obtain data on emissions of volatile organic compounds by polyester manufacturing plants. Textile manufacturers claimed that halogen-containing organic solvents were not used in Turkey.

G Pesticides and Chemicals used in Cotton Cultivation

Cotton, one of the most important cash and export crops in Turkish agriculture, is erosive, exceedingly irrigated, consumes high levels of fertilizers, and is treated with a variety of chemicals to prevent insect infestations and plant diseases. It is grown intensively in the fertile and irrigated plains and valleys of western and southern Turkey – in Antalya, irrigated plains of the Aegean coast – and in the Cukurova plain on the north-eastern Mediterranean coast. Since the 1960s, farmers have become increasingly inclined to grow cotton without any rotation with other crops that are less prone to soil erosion and that might decrease the need for fertilizer nutrients and chemical inputs.

1 Use of Chemical Inputs in Cotton Cultivation

Use of insecticides and pesticides and herbicides in cotton cultivation administers a severe environmental impact. Irrigated agriculture provides an appropriate habitat for various damaging insect populations and wild weed growth, giving way to increasing levels of chemical use by the cotton grower.

(a) Use of insecticides More than 11 different kinds of insects are classified as active and harmful during cotton growing in Turkey. Especially, the "red spider" (*Tetranychus* spp.) and the "pink worm"

(*Pectinophora gossypii*) in western Anatolia and the "white fly" (*Bemesia tabaci*) in southern Anatolia, particularly in the Cukurova region, are considered to be the most dangerous species.

Although efforts have been made to develop and apply biological control measures, the main means of insect control remains the spraying of various pesticides and insecticides. In addition to hand-operated spray machinery, motorized and tractor-mounted spraying machines and spraying from aeroplanes are used in Turkey. It is estimated that approximately 60 per cent of the cotton growing area in Turkey is sprayed from aeroplanes. The number of sprayings in a session differs among regions: for more than 70 per cent of the cotton-growing area in Cukurova, there are more than six sprayings per session, while the figure is lower for the Aegean and Antalya regions.

There is a large variety of insecticides and pesticides in the Turkish market. Producing and importing companies aggressively promote their products, and it is generally felt that farmers are inclined to apply overdoses. Extensive use of aerial spraying also induces pesticide application beyond acceptable limits from an environmental point of view. Insecticides and pesticides, herbicides, and drugs and chemicals used against plant diseases are all supplied in the Turkish market mainly by a small number of large transnational companies of United States or European origin. They produce these chemicals in solely-owned or joint-venture production plants in Turkey, or import these products and distribute them. Research and product development are carried out by these firms, and production technologies and know-how are strictly protected.[9]

(b) Plant diseases and use of chemicals A variety of plant diseases affect cotton growing in Turkey. Diseases such as *Verticillium* wilt and *Rhizoctonia solani* are dominant in Cukurova (Adana) region, Antalya and the Aegean plains. Although efforts to control and combat plant diseases by biological means and to develop host plant resistance continue and increase, for the time being the major procedure remains the use of drugs and chemicals for seed treatment and soil preparation. Spraying is widely used in soil preparation in all cotton growing regions. PCNP, Busan 72 A and Rhizolex are among the major drugs used for seed treatment and chemical control.

(c) Weeds and the use of chemicals Harmful weeds are active in Turkey's cotton growing regions. Species such as *Sorghum halepenese* and *Cyperus rotundus* are active in many regions. Before and during

the growing season, in addition to biological control measures, mechanical destruction and hand hoeing are widely used in order to remove hazardous weeds. However, in all cotton growing regions, the most ubiquitous weed combating method is pre-germination and post-germination chemical application. Major herbicides used include Trifluralin, Alachlor, Fusilade Super and Gallant.

The prices of insecticides, pesticides and herbicides are not subsidized in Turkey. However, high levels of subsidy paid to the output as well as the availability of cheap credit from agricultural banks and credit cooperatives provide sufficient motivation for elevated use of chemicals.

Cotton cultivation in Turkey consumes large quantities of water, leading in turn to leaching of chemicals into the sea, surface water and ground water. Although precise figures are not available on toxic impact, concentration levels and other conditions of chemicals in the waters and soils of cotton growing regions, the potential environmental consequences of chemical contamination of waters and soils in Turkey appear alarming.

2 *Organic Cotton Cultivation and Use*

An interesting development in recent years in the textiles and garments export scene in Turkey is the increase in efforts to cultivate organic cotton. Certain textile producing and exporting companies in Istanbul, Izmir and Adana exporting to Northern European markets, especially to Sweden and Germany, have been investing in and financing the cultivation of organic cotton in the western and southern cotton growing regions in Turkey. A list of criteria for organic cotton has been prepared by some import companies and textiles producers in Turkey, and this has gained wide-spread recognition. The major criteria for organic cotton, according to this list, are:

- soil should be unplanted for at least six months before cultivation, in order for it to be cleansed of past residues;
- cotton should be hand-planted and hand-picked;
- chemical fertilizers should not be used (organic fertilizers are allowed);
- insecticides, pesticides and herbicides should not be used (biological control is allowed; harmful weeds should be combated only by hand hoeing);
- harvested cotton should be stored separately;
- organically grown cotton should be ginned separately;

- lint cotton should be packed in pressed bales and be clearly marked for easy identification;
- packed lint cotton should immediately be transported to special warehouses to wait for spinning; and
- organic cotton lint should be spun separately.

Some Turkish companies employ experts from Germany and Sweden acknowledged by European importing firms for controlling, labelling and verifying the organic cotton growing procedure.

However, some of the garment producing and exporting companies in Turkey import licensed 100 per cent cotton yarns of organically grown cotton from the United States and from India. In order to produce biological/ecological garments, organic cotton is not enough. Processes related to manufacturing and packaging would also need to fulfil biological/ecological requirements. These requirements include washing of fabric without bleach or chemicals, dyeing factories with acceptable waste-water management systems, and packaging in recycleable cartons or paper bags.

H Lubricants

Henkel, an ISO 9000 TQM awarded company, is considered to be the most important supplier of lubricants used in spinning, knitting and weaving processes in polyester production. Representatives of Henkel stated that the main ingredient of lubricant mineral oil used in polyester yarns and fabrics production is spindal oil B, and this oil is solely produced by the Aliaga refinery (Izmir) of the giant public company Petkim in Turkey. Henkel purchases this oil from Petkim and produces various lubricants for the textile industry in compliance with existing formulations and prescriptions. According to the representatives of Henkel, Petkim faces difficulties to maintain the same chemical structure on account of the differences in crude oil processed in Aliaga refinery, and spindal oil B produced by Petkim generally contains 8–10 per cent aromatic groups. The production of mineral oils in this manner is not consistent with United States Pharmacopoeia specifications for medicinal white oils.[10] Mineral oils specified in EU criteria list are not used for 100 per cent cotton products, and paraffin is used instead.

I Detergents and Complexing Agents

The textile manufacturers interviewed for the survey claimed that chemicals that cause the formation of stable toxic metaboilites, such as alkylophenolethoxylates, are not used in detergents and complexing agents. Similarly bis (hydrogenated tallow alkyl) dimethyl ammonium chloride (DTDMAC), distearyl dimethyl ammonium chloride (DSDMAC) and di (hardened tallow) dimethyl ammonium chloride (DHTDMAC) are not used either. Phosphanetes are used instead of these.

The manufacturers also stated that they did not use NTA. However, EDTA is used, including in household detergents. One Cukurova (Adana) textile manufacturer stated that EDTA was used specifically for blended fabrics.

In the case of eco-garments, importing companies generally demand, and manufacturing and exporting companies in Turkey guarantee, that fabrics and garments are washed only in pure water and with natural soap. Using natural soap instead of detergents also has an impact on costs.

J Bleaching Agents

Export-oriented textile manufacturers from Istanbul stated that they did not use bleaching agents containing chlorine or chlorine compounds. They use hydrogen peroxide for bleaching. On the other hand, administrators of large-scale textile manufacturing firms from Cukurova (Adana and Tarsus) maintained that they produced a wide range of fabrics for different kinds of markets and needs, and that they use almost all kinds of bleaching agents, including chlorine-containing compounds. One manufacturer from Istanbul pointed out that hypochloride is only half as expensive as sodium chloride and that it is seven times cheaper than hydrogen peroxide.

Importers of eco-garments often demand that the fabric or garment should be bleached before dyeing. Like the prohibition of softener use, this is one of the few cost-reducing requirements in "eco-textiles" production. However, it is difficult to produce good-looking fabrics or garments in this manner.

K Dyes, Pigments and Carriers

The Turkish textile industry principally uses dyes imported from various European and Asian countries, especially Taiwan and India.[11] European dyes in general are 40–45 per cent more expensive than Asian dyes. Some of the manufacturers claimed that the marketing efforts of European dye manufacturers such as ICI, Bayer, Cybe and Zeneca have increased with the rise of import restrictions in European and North American markets. These companies claim that their production processes comply with the environmental regulations in Western countries, and they offer to supply environment-friendly dyes to Turkish manufacturers. Some dye manufacturing companies from Europe such as Zeneca also offer information and education services to Turkish textile manufacturers on various environmental matters.

It is claimed that benzidine-based dyes and azodyes based on various aromatic amines are used in various segments of the Turkish textile industry. Dyes that contain heavy metals are also in use.[12] However, dyes that are carcinogenic or with an acute toxic effect were not used in Turkey due to the standards used by manufacturers, especially from Europe, and to the strict import licensing procedures and controls of the Government. Carriers containing chlorine or other halogens are also not used by textile manufacturers and dyeing factories in Turkey, mainly because of the prevalent technology in the industry.

European importers of eco-garments impose stricter norms for dyes and dyeing methods, including requirements such as "all dyestuff should be 100 per cent soluble in water and water-based; only reactive dyes should be used; when dyeing knitted fabrics low impact dyes – fully enclosed high pressure jet machines – with low water to fabric ratio should be used; when dyeing woven fabrics, Jugger or Foulard machines should be used".[13] These import companies do not insist on many of these norms in their regular imports.

L Flame Retardants

Manufacturers, especially of children's wear, who export to the United States market use flame retardants at the request of the importing companies. These are in accordance with international standards and those set by the importer.

M Crease-Resist-Finishes

Formaldehyde is an important input in textile production, and almost all manufacturing companies use it to various extents at different stages of production. European eco-labelling schemes for textiles allow limited use of formaldehyde – usually between 20 and 300 ppm for different kinds of garments. Although importers allow the use of formaldehyde in the production of their regular imports, it is prohibited in the production of eco-garments.[14]

N Occupational Conditions

None of the manufacturers interviewed hand out written assessments of the risks to safety and health at work as part of job applications. None of them carry out measurements of occupational exposure to cotton dust and therefore do not have any perception on compliance with the suggested EU standard of 0.2 mg/m^3 (8h-TWA). However, cotton dust seems to appear as an important problem at all stages of manufacturing, adversely affecting the health and efficiency of workers as well as product quality. In order to tackle this problem, firms try to establish various systems including vacuuming infrastructures. Manufacturers do not carry out measurements on occupational exposure to noise either. The suggested EU standard is 85 dB. Noise constitutes an important problem, particularly at the weaving stage, and weaving workers usually wear ear plugs while at work.

Notes

1. The bodies interviewed comprised: (a) four textile manufacturing companies from Istanbul; (b) three Cukurova (Adana and Tarsus) textile manufacturing companies; (c) three garment manufacturing firms from Istanbul; (d) the President of the Istanbul Garments Exporters Association; (e) one cotton cultivator from Cukurova; (f) one cotton exporter from Cukurova; (g) two chemical manufacturers from Istanbul; (h) Ministry of Agriculture; (i) General Directory of Foreign Trade; (j) Union of Istanbul Textiles and Garments Exporters; and (k) Istanbul Chamber of Industry.
2. One Cukurova textile company, interviewed during this study, imports naturally coloured (brown and cream) organic cotton from Ozbekhistan. The company, exhibiting the fabrics and garments produced with this imported cotton in various textiles and garments fairs in Europe, hopes to enter the European market like various other Turkish companies.
3. This term has also been used by the Swedish company Hennez and Mauritz, AB, in a leaflet prepared and distributed among Turkish exporters to specify the "ecocotton textile and garment standards".
4. In the course of the research conducted for this paper, the author located one company that had already obtained an Öko-Tex 100 Label. Due to its geographical location (Denizli), the representative of this firm could not

be interviewed. The price lists of Forschungsinstitut Hohenstein, the German institution that supplies Öko-Tex labels, however, have been widely distributed among textile and garment manufacturing and export firms in Turkey.

5. These tests are normally carried out with the guidelines instituted by ISO, DIN or other similar norms (e.g. AATCC), varying in accordance with the expectations and recommendations of the importing company.
6. In many instances, quality standards are also tested and inspected by the national standards labelling body, the Turkish Standards Institute (TSE) at the manufacturers' expense.
7. The Textile Laboratory at the Istanbul Technical Unversity is also supported by the Union of Textile Exporters. The laboratory is well-equipped, and the ITU Research Center is currently planning to apply for membership in the International Association for Research and Testing in the field of Textile Ecology founded by the Hohensteiner Institute in Germany.
8. A manufacturer from Istanbul, of high quality 100 per cent cotton material for export, provided the following figures for water consumed per kilogram of dry material at different stages of production: bleaching – 12 litres, dyeing – 8 litres, soaping – 16 litres, washing – 16 litres, and softening – 8 litres, accounting for a total of 60 litres/kg.
9. Major companies supplying insecticides, pesticides, herbicides and other agricultural chemicals for cotton cultivation in Turkey include Rhone-Phoulenc, Bayer, Hoechst, Sandoz, ICI, Ciba Geigy, Tarim Koruma-Henkel, Hektas and Fow Elanco.
10. Here it should be recalled that Turkey exports large amounts of polyester yarns to European textile manufacturing companies.
11. Some Turkish manufacturers are in the process of establishing joint venture manufacturing plants with Indian producers. Some of the interviewed sources argued that these efforts would prove futile due to the pressure exerted by European companies.
12. It is difficult to produce some colours, ironically including green, without the use of heavy metals.
13. See Hennez and Mauritz, AB, *H&M Product Sheet, Eco-Cotton: Turkey*.
14. For example, Hannez and Mauritz allow 10 ppm formaldehyde in their regular imports while banning its use at all stages in the production of ecogarments. See *H&M Product Sheet, Eco-Cotton: Turkey* and *H&M Textile Test Standard*.

8 Thailand and Eco-Labelling

Sophia Wigzell[1]

INTRODUCTION

Eco-labelling, as part of a general movement towards greener markets overseas, is seen in some government and business circles in Thailand as presenting more potential opportunities than barriers to Thai producers. Technical and financial barriers are not generally perceived to be insurmountable in the event that the market gains to be made through this approach are seen as adequate rewards for the capital investments made. Those sectors of the community who are concerned with environmental quality have an even more favourable attitude towards green markets overseas. International concerns for the environment and the emerging markets for cleaner technologies and "greener" products are seen as providing a part of the necessary economic incentive to encourage Thai producers to behave more responsibly with regard to the environmental effects of industrial production. To understand these perspectives, it is necessary to consider the position of the Thai economy and the Thai environment at present.

Thailand's economic growth over the last three decades has been rapid. Real gross domestic product (GDP) growth rate averaged 7 per cent in the 1970s. During the world-wide recession in the early 1980s, the Thai economy suffered a temporary set-back, with the GDP growth rate averaging around 5 per cent annually. However, in the latter half of the 1980s, Thailand emerged as one of the fastest growing economies in the world, with the annual GDP growth rate averaging 10 per cent. Despite a recent slow-down in economic growth, Thailand still maintains its economic growth rate at the level of an average 8 per cent per annum in the early 1990s.

The outstanding economic performance over the past three decades can be attributed, for the most part, to the sharp increases in export products. Trade-to-GDP ratios have risen, and the Thai economy has shown increasing interdependence with world markets. The contribution of exports to GDP has risen sharply. In the 1960s, export values of goods and services was 10.8 billion baht, accounting for 15.6 per cent of GDP. The proportion grew to 35.4 per cent or accounted for 886.6 billion baht in 1992.[2]

By 1985, the share of manufactured produce in total export had surpassed that of agricultural produce. Highly export-oriented industries include garments, textiles, electrical and non-electrical machinery, canned and frozen food, jewellery, electronic parts and components, leather products, footwear, toys, plastic products, ceramics and miscellaneous products.

Since 1989, textiles exports have become the leading Thai export product, the textiles industry alone accounting for 20 per cent of manufactured exports. More recently, the manufacture of electrical appliances has emerged as one of the fastest growing export sectors. In 1992, electrical appliances accounted for 9.5 per cent of all manufactured exports, compared with only 2.4 per cent in 1988.

It may become necessary for Thai manufacturers and exporters fully to understand and adjust to the new eco-labelling requirements in their markets in order to maintain such market share, especially since Thailand's competitive advantage in labour-intensive industries is likely to come increasingly under threat as China and Vietnam open up to trade, and from other South-East Asian countries such as Indonesia. Another concern is that rapid technological change in the form of computer-integrated manufacturing, for example, will reduce the demand for labour-intensive exports from countries such as Thailand. The most serious impediment to Thailand's ability to emulate the performance of the senior newly industrializing economies in repeatedly upgrading technological levels of production will be its acute shortage of technically skilled secondary-school graduates.

Possible options for Thai manufacturers could include investing in more capital-intensive technologies (a move being seriously considered by many textile producers), upgrading the quality of products being traded, and placing more emphasis on education at higher levels as well as on local research and development. Alternatively, Thai producers could invest in production facilities in countries where labour rates are lower. Anyhow, Thai manufacturers may need to be able to enter special segments of markets such as that for eco-labelled products.

It should be noted here that the growth of environmental concerns, both domestically and world-wide, is regarded to be of considerable potential importance for Thai growth.

> Domestic issues of erosion, deforestation, and the fouling of fishing grounds are serious. This sort of resource depletion, extending now

> even into neighbouring countries, is likely to slow Thai growth. Similarly, the increase in pollution and congestion in Bangkok is a major threat to both public health and economic growth. Attention to these issues must be an increasingly important priority for Thai economic development policies.[3]

The Government and some private sector firms are observing overseas "green" markets with interest, as they offer the potential for combining efforts at sustainable development with a search for new market niches for Thai exports. With more attention directed towards improving human resource development to support upgrading technology, and the appropriate capital investments, international "green" markets should not be inaccessible to Thai producers.

In general, the larger producers[4] could be expected to have sufficient capital to invest in cleaner technologies (and indeed, most large production plants are already required to have waste-water treatment facilities, and other pollution-control equipment). Middle-scale industries should still be able to invest in cleaner technologies, given the tariff reductions on imports of technologies for environmental protection, and the availability of soft loans for such equipment. The necessary infrastructure, in the form of central waste-water treatment plants and other facilities, could be provided for small-scale and household industries.[5] Given the impressive economic growth rates of the last two decades, and the concentration of wealth in the manufacturing sector, it is perhaps not unreasonable to expect such investments. None the less, without the necessary incentives, be they national policy changes,[6] increasing the effectiveness of enforcement, or growth in green markets at home and abroad, it is unlikely that many producers will consider environmental protection as a high priority for investment.

The rapid industrialization of the last thirty years has resulted in a number of serious environmental problems including urban congestion, air and water pollution, deforestation, salinization, and soil erosion. In particular, the rapid growth of the Thai economy during the late 1980s and early 1990s, which proceeded with little attention given to the infrastructural needs of growth, has exacerbated the environmental problems associated with production.[7] The centralized nature of production in the Kingdom has concentrated industry-related environmental problems in the following provinces: Bangkok, Samut Prakarn, Samut Sakhon, Nakorn Pathom, Nonthaburi, Pathum Thani, Rayong, Chonburi and Chachoengsao.[8]

Rapid, unplanned urbanization, and infrastructure bottle-necks in these provinces have also produced pollution problems from non-industrial sources. Seventy-five per cent of the biochemical oxygen demand (BOD) in Thailand's most polluted rivers comes from untreated sewage and other domestic wastes.[9] Vehicle emissions, as well as dust from construction and from roads are the largest contributors of suspended particulate matter (SPM), a serious health hazard in the capital.

I ENVIRONMENTAL LEGISLATION AND ITS IMPLEMENTATION

The key piece of environmental legislation in the Kingdom of Thailand is the *Enhancement and Conservation of National Environment Quality Act of 1992*[10] (hereafter referred to as *NEQA 1992*, or the Act). This comprehensive piece of legislation updates and strengthens existing laws within a policy framework outlined in the Seventh National Economic and Social Development Plan. Implicit in this plan as referred to in the Act is the polluter-pays principle. A number of fundamental changes have been made in environmental management under the new law in Thailand: the public sector is now eligible to apply user charges on central treatment plants and the polluters are responsible for damages resulting from their pollution discharges. The Royal Thai Government is looking for innovative and appropriate market instruments to provide economic incentives for industries to take responsibility for their waste. Different methods for implementing the polluter-pays principle are being considered at a number of levels.[11] It is likely, however, that market instruments will continue to be used in conjunction with command and control instruments for maximum effectiveness.

Apart from *NEQA 1992*, the most important legal instrument in Thailand for the control of pollution is the *Factories Act 1992*. Under the *Factories Act 1992*, a licensee to operate a factory is obliged not to release polluted water, toxic waste or other emissions resulting from the operation of his factory that may have adverse effects on the environment. The licensee also has an obligation not to cause any danger, damage or nuisance to persons or properties existing in or near the factory through the operation of the factory.

Emissions standards are set by the Ministry of Science, Technology and Environment (MOSTE) after recommendation by various expert bodies and with the approval of the National Environment Board (NEB).

These standards are published in the Government Gazette. In addition, in cases where the Governor of a Province sees fit, he has the power, by publishing in the Government Gazette, to set standards over and above the standards provided by MOSTE. In addition, areas where the intensity of production is the sole cause of pollution problems may be designated pollution-control zones and case-specific emissions standards and technical requirements may be imposed on the entire zone.

The Minister of Science, Technology and Environment can also, under advice from the Board of Toxic Waste Control, designate categories of industries whereby the licensee has the duty to build, attach or provide a system of waste treatment and pollution control in accordance with the provisions fixed by the official in charge of toxic control. Where a central waste treatment/disposal facility is available, the factory operator is responsible for the service costs at the rate provided for by the *NEQA 1992* and other related Acts. In such cases and unless the factory owner has his own treatment/disposal facilities already in compliance with the provisions fixed by the official in charge of toxic control, all wastes are required to be released to the Central Waste Treatment Plant for treatment and disposal.

Over and above the standards set either by the Minister of Science, Technology and Environment or the Governor of a Province, the *Factories Act 1992* also contains provisions to set standards on a case-by-case basis. Under the *Factories Act 1992*, the Department of Industrial Works (DIW) is responsible for the following: licensing systems before construction; licensing systems before operation; license renewals; factory expansion licenses; treatment design services; provision of central treatment facilities; and provision of training for treatment operations. Before approval of any licenses, license renewals or factory expansions, the DIW can set specific standards for the factory operator; for example, zero emissions to a public waterway.

By virtue of the *Factories Act 1992*, in cases where the official has found that a licensee to operate has violated or failed to perform in accordance with this Act, or the operation of the factory may cause danger, damage or nuisance to persons or properties existing in or near the factory, the official has the authority to order the licensee to cease the violation, or modify, or improve, or behave within the law within a designated period of time. If deemed appropriate, the official may, with the approval of the Permanent Secretary of State for Industry or person entrusted by him, seal or tie any machinery in order to prevent its continued use.

Further, where necessary, the Permanent Secretary of State for Industry or person entrusted by him has the power to order the licensee to stop totally or partially from operating the factory, and improve the factory's performance during a specified period of time. If after that time has elapsed no appropriate action has taken place, the factory may be closed down and the license to operate revoked. Factory licensees are entitled to appeal against the order of the official within 30 days of the date of the order to close being known. The decision of the Minister on the appeal is final.

Prior to the enactment of *NEQA 1992* and the *Factories Act 1992*, the effectiveness of existing legislation for environmental protection was restricted at least in part by the lightness of the penalties for non-compliance. To a large extent this has been addressed in the newer legislation.[12]

There are a number of practical problems with the design of environmental regulations in Thailand. Although the environmental regulations and standards are national in scope, the environmental conditions of the different regions in the Kingdom vary greatly. In particular, standards based on concentrations of effluent at the end of pipe are problematic. In some areas, the levels of freshwater in rivers and streams change with the seasons, and an acceptable concentration in the rainy season will be completely unacceptable in the dry season. In addition, no consideration is given to the concentration of industries in the locality. Each factory may therefore abide by the standards set, but the total load of biochemical oxygen demand, for example, may far exceed the carrying capacity of the river. As the environmental emissions standards are based on concentrations rather than on absolute volume, a typical response from the industry has been to add water to the effluent in order to reduce the concentration of outflows.[13] Unfortunately, water availability is a serious problem in Thailand. In addition, such standards do nothing to encourage reuse of water, water conservation and waste minimization approaches to environmental emission problems.[14]

Since the upgrading of Thailand's environmental legislation in 1992 through the enactment of the Enhancement and Conservation of *National Environmental Quality Act of 1992* as well as the *Factories Act 1992*, environmental legislation is perceived to be quite stringent. The establishment of offices of environmental protection at national level in the Ministry of Science, Technology and the Environment, and the National Environment Board, reflects the importance which the Government currently places on environmental issues in the Kingdom. However, there is a need for basic research and data collection on the environment in the Kingdom as a prerequisite for designing effective standards.[15]

In the last two years, there have been significant advances in upgrading the government departments responsible for enforcement of this legislation. A change in the emphasis of legislation towards market instruments and the development of innovative ways to implement the polluter-pays principle may well assist in providing part of the necessary pressure for industries to comply with current legislation. Operation of the Environment Fund and other forms of assistance to industry in implementing environmental protection are also significant steps forward in providing effective institutions for environmental protection. Likewise, an increase in severity of the penalties for non-compliance may also serve as incentives to comply.

A number of government officials, trade association leaders and business leaders have also been looking to external incentives to encourage a more responsible attitude towards environmental protection. Overseas demands for greener products, and drives for the introduction of environmental management systems are seen as offering the potential to provide the economic incentives to implement more environmentally sound business practices in the Kingdom. Other members of the business community are skeptical about the effectiveness of this, as compliance with the majority of such demands is still voluntary. However, purchasing requirements for eco-labelled products from importing countries are in the same line as the international quality standard, ISO 9000, and this may effect a change in the situation. Further, the release of the draft environmental management standard, ISO 14 000, has been met with considerable interest on the part of Thai manufacturers with some of the larger companies expressing their intentions to gain certification within the next two years.

In addition to the lack of effective enforcement as an incentive to implement environmentally sound technologies, prices for natural resources including energy and water in the Kingdom are low. Clean technologies based on pollution prevention and waste minimization have slow returns. Given the initial costs of such equipment[16] and the high maintenance costs, there are very few economic advantages to implementing more "eco-efficient" technologies. The only exceptions to this would tend to be in those industries where natural resource requirements and constraints on production provide the incentive for the introduction of cleaner production technologies, e.g. water conservation and recycling in the pulp and paper industry. For the majority of Thai producers, environmental protection inevitably does involve increased costs. This situation contrasts with that in many of the OECD countries. However, eco-labelling can provide an incentive for investing in cleaner technologies if labelled products are provided additional marketing advantages.

Some of the better-known domestic companies operating in the Kingdom do take care to maintain a "clean" image, as the environment becomes an issue of national importance. The petrochemical, chemical and cement industries, in particular, are seen to be better than average at operating at levels which go beyond mere compliance. The establishment of the Thai Green Label scheme may provide economic incentives to such activities, since it will enhance the green market segment in domestic markets.

Although some individual members of the Government have been trying to raise interest in the trade implications of overseas environmental concerns for several years, the Government as a whole has only recently begun to recognize the importance of these issues. A paper on the interlinkages between trade and the environment, produced by the Department of Export Promotion in 1995, states that it is essential that those departments of the Government with responsibilities concerning trade and industry begin planning information campaigns to emphasize the importance of producing "environmentally sound products" for export.

In general, the attitude of the government is to abide by the decisions of Thailand's key markets, and to encourage Thai producers to fulfil the needs of overseas buyers. Eco-labels are here seen as an opportunity to increase the market share of Thai products. Little consideration seems to have been given to the costs involved in changing production technologies, inputs, packaging techniques, etc. The attitude is rather that Thai producers must adapt to the needs of the key markets, and that export levels must be maintained. This view would also appear to reflect the view of many manufacturers in Thailand.[17]

II THE THAI GREEN LABELLING SCHEME

Currently, Thailand is developing a national eco-labelling scheme. The Working Group responsible for spearheading the "Thai Green Labelling Scheme" is the Thailand Business Council for Sustainable Development (TBCSD).[18] TBCSD was founded in October 1993, when it was first mooted that the Council should establish a national eco-labelling scheme as one of five Council projects. On approval by the Council members, plans for the national eco-labelling scheme were formulated and approved at subsequent meetings and interested members of the Council were asked to join a special Working Group. The Thai Green Labelling Scheme has been officially accepted as the national eco-labelling scheme of Thailand by the Ministry of Industry, and work is now commencing on product criteria (see Box 8.1).

The TBCSD Working Group is composed of associates from leading corporations who are members of TBCSD. It was initially stressed that the associates nominated to represent the "Thai Green Labelling scheme" should come from diverse professions such as the manufacturing sector, retailers and lawyers.

The development of the national scheme referred to the prior experience of three models: the German Blue Angel scheme, the Canadian Environmental Choice Program, and the Japanese Ecomark system. While the first two schemes formed the core consultation base of the Thai labelling programme, the exact scope and nature of the Thai scheme will respond to the specific domestic needs of Thailand.

The Green Labelling Board comprises 18 members from various sectors, five from the Government, seven from NGOs and concerned associations, and six from business sectors appointed by the Ministry of Industry.

III THE IMPACT OF CURRENT ECO-LABELLING SCHEMES ON THAI PRODUCTS

The impact on Thai products of the eco-labelling schemes in Thailand's key markets, i.e. North America, East Asia and Europe, has been negligible. None of the Thai Export Promotion Offices in those countries had heard of any product from Thailand which had either been granted or refused an eco-label. Nor did the majority of the products for which eco-labelling criteria have been drawn up apply to products which are key exports from Thailand.

Where life-cycle analysis has been used in drawing up product criteria for an eco-label, this has tended to be through a review approach highlighting the key stages of the life cycle. The majority of labels awarded thus far have concentrated on the environmental effects of consumption. Few Thai producers showed concern about the potential negative effects of eco-label, when they were informed about their

Box 8.1 Work plan for the Thai Green Labelling Scheme

Phase 1

Activity Establish a committee on green labelling consisting of representatives from several organizations such as the Federation of Thai Industry, the Board of Trade of Thailand, TISI, interested consumer groups and TBCSD members (TEI will serve as the Secretariat)
Time Frame One month
Expected outcome Report on the composition of the established committee, its role and responsibilities

Activity Review and evaluate the existing eco-labelling programs. Propose a practical "Thai Green Labelling scheme"
Time frame One month
Expected outcome Report on the evaluation of the existing ecolabelling schemes and the proposed Thai version

Activity Select the product categories; establish criteria for green labelling and threshold levels
Time frame Five months
Expected outcome Report on the selection of product categories, criteria and threshold levels

Activity Organize a seminar to introduce the "Thai Green Labelling scheme" to the general public. Publicize the scheme among industries
Time frame Two months
Expected outcome Report on the comments of the seminar

Phase II

Activity Encourage industries to apply for the label
Time frame Two months
Expected Outcome Report on the numbers of applied industries

Activity Review and evaluate the performance of the scheme after operation
Time frame Two months
Expected outcome Report on the results of the evaluation

existence and about the methodology used in establishing product specifications.[19] This may change as more rigorous approaches to life-cycle analysis are used. In addition, eco-labelling schemes in Canada, Japan, Scandinavian countries and the European Union are all planning to develop labels for textiles. These schemes will have an impact on this key export product from Thailand.

Notably, the cost of applying for labels under all these schemes may be prohibitive unless some of that cost is absorbed by the buyers or importers. Likewise, the costs of inspection would be prohibitive for some schemes under current practice. A system such as that used by the International Organization for Standardization (ISO), whereby local standards institutes would be responsible for verification and spot checks, would be less discriminatory.

One of the biggest problems facing Thai producers with regard to eco-labels based on a rigorous life-cycle analysis is the inadequate understanding of the environmental effects of production, and the tendency to concentrate on end-of-pipe solutions to environmental problems. The introduction of environmental management systems might well serve to support a given manufacturer in assessing the costs and benefits of applying for an eco-label.

In addition, if a given product were to be assigned a label designating that all component parts of the product had been produced by companies with an approved environmental management system in place, this might provide a means by which local differences in environmental effects and in environmental concerns could be reflected, while still ensuring that producers have an incentive to take the environmental impacts of their production processes into account.

Attitudes towards the Ecotextile label established by the German textile industry are exemplary of the attitude of textiles manufacturers in general. German buyers who have been trying to persuade their suppliers to produce garments eligible for the Ecotextile label complain of a general lack of interest. Textiles manufacturers are concerned that the market niche for such products is not sufficiently large to justify changes in product standards. (This may well be justified, in the light of the impact of the economic recession in Europe on the demand for eco-textile.) When pressed to provide eco-textile, some producers said that they would prefer to switch to alternative markets (for example, the Middle East) than to change production inputs. In response, some buyers are looking to other countries such as Malaysia, where producers are more responsive. However, as other labels for textiles are approved, they may provide incentives for textile producers to respond to demands for more environmentally friendly garments. Thai producers in general have a reputation for short-termism, and for adopting a wait-and-see attitude to new developments in markets. However, once convinced of the profitability of a particular course of action, and that the risks will not render them uncompetitive even in the short term, they are quick to respond.

A Textiles

1 Quality Requirements

Thai textiles are generally preferred for the quality-to-price ratio that Thai producers are able to maintain. This remains the most important criterion for most buyers from overseas markets. Most Thai manufacturers of textiles products for export see no major difficulty in achieving the quality guidelines required for the eco-label, even if they are not currently doing so.

2 Chemical Inputs

Dyes German buyers note that Thai producers are currently unwilling to change production inputs or processes to satisfy the requirements of the German Ecotextile label. Given evidence of larger "green" markets than present, and the increase in the number of eco-labels applying to textiles, this attitude may change.

Most textile dyes used in the Kingdom are imported. Thai producers currently use a range of reactive, disperse and direct dyes. Very few natural dyes are still in use, and they account only for a minute percentage of all garments/fabrics produced each year, their use being generally confined to traditional cloths and garments. The import of azo-dyes has been prohibited by law within the Kingdom for some time. The use of azo-dyes is also illegal (data on the use of these dyes are therefore very difficult to obtain). Unfortunately, this has raised some problems in relation to testing, because public and private laboratories have not had the necessary equipment in place to test for the presence or use of azo-dyes. With respect to the use of heavy metals, the quality of the dyes used and the content of heavy metals would depend on the manufacturer of the dye. Exported garments generally require the use of high-quality dyes. Many of these dyes are produced by dye manufactures that are already responding to "environmental imperatives" in OECD markets by offering a range of non-carcinogenic dyes with low to negligible content of heavy metals.

Oils used in spinning, knitting and weaving Given that even those producers who are making concerted effort to switch to more environmentally friendly processes and employ waste minimization approaches do not use oils of the fine grades required by the label, it is unlikely that many producers would currently satisfy this requirement of the label. No information is available on the cost difference that a switch to these oils would entail.

Detergents or complexing agents Producers use a range of detergents. No information is available on the relative cost of different detergents.

Bleaching agents Some producers are using hydrogen peroxide as a bleaching agent.

Flame retardants Use of flame retardants is dependent on the product and the market.

Crease-resistant finishes Use of crease-resistant finishes is dependent on the product and the market.

B Footwear

The Thai footwear market for export responds directly to buyer requests. Thus, if there is sufficient demand, the producers will attempt to produce footwear that meets the labelling requirements. Producers and trade associations approached saw no likely obstacles to trade in the labelling requirements. However, this may be because of lack of understanding of the scope of life-cycle analysis in the Netherlands label specifications. No information was available on the cost of compliance with the requirements.

1 Inputs to Footwear Production

The greatest possible limitation on the ability of footwear producers to respond to the labelling requirements is likely to be the availability of inputs in terms of more environmentally friendly leather products.

2 Chromium Emissions, PCP and Volatile Organic Substances

The majority of footwear producers who produce for export markets have already responded to requests to stop using PCPs. They are also prepared to respond to buyer demands that request changes in other chemical inputs.

C Footwear and Textiles

1 Energy Requirements

Very few producers have undertaken an environmental review. Few producers can assess energy use per unit product. Energy calculations would most likely have to be "back-of-the-envelope" calculations of number of units produced over total energy use. Given that energy prices are currently low in the Kingdom, there has been little incentive to invest in energy-saving machinery and processes. Energy use is thus unlikely to be very efficient. However, as energy demands increase rapidly, the Electricity Generating Authority of Thailand is currently promoting energy-saving equipment and techniques, and trying to raise the level of awareness on these issues.

2 Water Requirements

Where environmental reviews have been carried out, water has generally featured more in terms of reducing emissions of effluent, and improving water re-use. Water prices are currently low and until recently, there have been few incentives to conserve water. However, as the textiles industry depends to a large extent on access to water of a reasonable quality, and both the water quality and quantity in the Kingdom are deteriorating, this is likely to change in the near future.

3 Dust in Factories

As with noise pollution, it is difficult to determine the levels of dust in factories as this is not a high profile issue. Producers tend to disregard this as a problem.

4 Noise in Factories

Although health and safety regulations in the Kingdom cover noise in the workplace, it is difficult to determine whether producers would abide by the requirements of the legislation or the labels as noise pollution has not attracted a great deal of concern anywhere in Thailand.

5 Health and Safety in the Workplace in General

This is a difficult issue. The legislation to protect workers does exist. Multinationals and some large- and middle-scale producers have good records where the health and safety of workers is concerned. Where buyers regularly visit the production site it is possible that standards may be higher than in other cases. But in general, it would seem to depend on the attitude of the manager/owner of the factory. Reports of infractions are rarely publicized except in the cases of disasters such as the Kader Toy Factory fire.

6 *Waste-water Treatment Facilities*

A range of waste-water treatment facilities are in use in the Kingdom. In general, it would seem ill-advised to insist on one particular technology as this has been shown to discourage innovation that may lead to improvement in the efficiency of environmental protection technologies. In addition, the environmental situation of different countries may necessitate different approaches towards achieving the same goal. Large factories are almost invariably required to install waste-water treatment facilities of their own. It should be noted, however, that textiles factories are one of the largest contributors of biochemical oxygen demand in the Kingdom, and that it is the largest factories that contribute the greatest amount of pollution. On industrial estates a central waste-water treatment plant may be the more appropriate means of waste disposal.

7 *Clean Technologies*

Currently most producers focus on end-of-pipe technologies to address environmental concerns. With low energy and water prices, there are few economic incentives to adopt waste minimization technologies. Clean technologies are regarded as expensive both to buy and to maintain.

Even with stronger enforcement and economic incentives (including a growth in domestic and international green markets) to adopt waste-minimization technologies, there are still some problems facing Thai producers. First, the cost of such technologies may be prohibitive. The information on government assistance for environmental protection is not widely available, and the slowness of the bureaucratic process deters applicants. Second, there have been several complaints that companies marketing technologies from overseas are not willing to sell the know-how except at very high prices. The area of technology cooperation with regard to environmentally sound technologies is one which requires strengthening if developing-country producers are not to be discriminated against. There is also a pronounced need for the Government to place stronger emphasis on education at the secondary and tertiary levels, and encourage the development of technical skills in the workforce.

8 Testing

Both the Government and the private sector offer laboratory services which could be used to certify compliance with labelling requirements. The availability of all the necessary services from the private sector laboratories depends on whether a market for these services exists, and is thus determined by both the market overseas and the attitude of producers in the Kingdom.

The German Ecotextiles label has presented challenges in terms of the number as well as the types of chemicals permitted, especially with respect to testing for azo-dyes. Private laboratory services were at first unwilling to install new equipment specifically for the Ecotextiles label as it appeared that there might not be sufficient demand to make the tests profitable. This has changed partly because of the pressure exerted by the buyers of textiles products, and partly because it has been observed that the demand for such testing of textiles is likely to increase with the introduction of other labels for textiles in other markets. Multinational environmental services are at a particular advantage here, in that they have easier access to market information and trends in the countries in which they operate.

The cost for testing is unlikely to present a significant barrier unless a number of labels with a variety of testing requirements are brought out under different schemes. If buyers/importers can absorb some of the testing cost then this would obviously assist producers in non-OECD countries. If local standards institutes are accepted as arbitrators of label requirements, then this would also reduce the costs of applying for a label.

The textile industry, in particular, has a poor reputation with regard to environmental protection standards and attitudes towards environmental protection. This may be in part because of the highly obvious nature of some of the emissions from the textiles industry, e.g. colour. In addition, many producers in this highly labour-intensive industry in Thailand currently find themselves under pressure from competitors from countries with lower labour costs, and feel that environmental protection efforts are too expensive when they are unsure of their competitiveness.

Given that Thailand is losing its competitive advantage with regard to labour costs, a movement towards "green" markets may offer an alternative growth strategy for the textiles industry, in so far as textile producers are prepared to make the appropriate capital investment. At present, it is unlikely that many producers will be able to apply successfully for the European label. In addition, due to the fact Thai manufacturers produce a wide range of textile products for different markets, the industry feels that they can export to markets with lower levels of requirements. However, given adjustments within the industry, over the next two or three years, in response to these and other external demands to "go green",[20] there are no obvious requirements for the label that Thai textiles producers could not comply with.

In general, the footwear industry is quite new and uses high technology in comparison with the textile industry. The processes and products are usually under strict supervision by the buyer. Thus, the attitude of footwear producers towards eco-labelling was far more positive than that of textile producers. This reflects the nature of the footwear industry in Thailand which is strongly oriented towards satisfying demands from overseas buyers. At the same time, this may also reflect a lack of understanding of the nature of life-cycle analysis. For example, few producers seem to have given much thought to the issue of compliance costs or to that of the availability of stipulated inputs. The Thai Government and relevant organizations in the OECD countries could assist Thai producers in making the switch to "greener" production processes by:

- improving market research and disseminating this information to producers and trade associations;
- conducting workshops to inform producers about eco-labelling schemes – their aims, and the means by which products are assessed and labels are awarded, especially the concept of life-cycle analysis;
- improving understanding and acceptance of environmental management systems – in particular, highlighting their use in assisting with a cost–benefit analysis of implementation of clean technologies, and in providing a basis for accurate life-cycle analysis of production technologies;
- improving educational standards in the Thai workforce notably with regard to technical skills; and
- improving access to the technological know-how of clean technologies so that they can be adapted to the Thai context.

Eco-labelling schemes in developed countries could assist in minimizing the adverse impact of their schemes on Thai producers, *inter alia*, through:

- actively seeking inputs from industry and environmental expert representatives in producing countries in the consideration of life-cycle effects in a variety of environments, and in the publication of specifications that take environmental differences into account;
- actively disseminating information on the schemes and market research on particular product groups to Thai government and key industrial associations;
- actively pursuing ISO subcommittee 3 (TC207/SC3) on eco-labelling, and disseminating information to Thai Government and key industrial associations;
- collaboration with Thai government and industrial associations to provide training with respect to key concepts such as the life-cycle analysis and environmental management systems;
- recognition of the competence of local standards institutes in verifying and checking producers; and
- ensuring that a given product to be assigned a label has all its component parts produced by companies with an approved environmental management system in place.

This last element may provide a means by which local differences in environmental effects and in environmental concerns could be reflected, while still ensuring that producers have an incentive to take the environmental impact of their production processes into account.

Notes

1. This chapter is an abridged version of the study conducted for the Thailand Environment Institute, Bangkok, and presented at the UNCTAD Workshop on Ecolabelling and International Trade, Geneva, June 1994.
2. National Economic and Social Development Board, *National Income of Thailand* (Bangkok: NESDB, 1993).
3. Narongchai Akrasanee, David Dapice, and Frank Flatters, *Thailand's Export-Led Growth: Retrospect and Prospects* (Bangkok: Thailand Development Research Institute, 1991).
4. The majority of production for export is undertaken by the larger producers. Small-scale and household industries produce mostly for the domestic markets as they are unable to maintain the quality standards required by overseas markets.
5. Thailand Environment Institute, *Draft Report: Policy to Promote Business and Environment in Thailand*, vol. I: "Application of Polluter-Pays-Principle

for Environmental Quality Management at the National Level", and vol. II: "Policy to Promote Private Sector Participation in Environmental Monitoring and Analysis" submitted to the Canadian International Development Agency (CIDA), 29 April 1994.

6. On 14 August 1995, the Minister of Industry announced an initiative which aims to relocate factories in the Bangkok metropolitan area and to cluster some industry types so that appropriate waste treatment facilities can be provided.
7. Aswin Kongsiri, paper presented at the seminar on "Merging Business and the Environment: Asia and the Pacific", Bangkok, 2–3 December 1993.
8. While these densely industrialized provinces have the most persistent water and air pollution, industrial decentralization into the Northern and North-Eastern regions has also resulted in severe pollution incidents.
9. Prinya Deepadung, *Legal Liabilities of Industries under Specific Laws Concerning Wastewater Pollution Control* (Bangkok: Ministry of Justice, 1993).
10. Although enacted in 1992, there are several aspects of this legislation that have yet to be implemented let alone enforced.
11. See, for example, Thailand Environment Institute, *Draft Report*, op. cit.
12. See Deepadung, op. cit.
13. Ministerial Notifications of the Ministry of Industry announced in 1995 are addressing this problem. In notifications prescribing building types which are forbidden to relase waste-water into public water sources without treating the water, the definition of waste-water treatment specifically excludes dilution as a means to achieve government specified emissions standards.
14. That said, some manufacturers in industries where water of a reasonable quality is a key input to the production process (for example, the pulp and paper industry) have introduced more efficient production technologies based on water recycling and reuse. See Sarawoot Chayovan and D. Dacera, "Pollution Control and Waste Reclamation in Agro-based Industry: Practical Experiences", paper presented at the "Seminar/Workshop on Agro-based Waste Water Treatment and Recovery Systems", Bangkok, 15 November 1991.
15. The Pollution Control Department is currently making progress towards establishing monitoring stations that would collect this sort of base-line data.
16. Under *NEQA 1992* provision was made to remove import tariffs (up to 40 per cent in some cases) on equipment that would contribute to cleaner production or environmental research (on application to the Ministry of Science, Technology and Environment). This was challenged by the Ministry of Finance, and the compromise reached specified that such equipment must be used exclusively for the purposes of environmental protection or research. Any equipment that could be used in any other way may not therefore be eligible for a tariff reduction. In addition, tariff reduction is only granted after the equipment has been bought and used for a period of one year, after which it must be proved that it has contributed to environmental protection. These conditions tend to favour end-of-pipe technologies, and are a disincentive to apply for tariff reduction. In addition, the slowness of the bureaucratic process deters applicants.

17. However, at present only a few Thai producers are in a position to qualify for entering "green markets" in the OECD countries, especially where environmental criteria are to be based on process standards.
18. Modelled on the global Business Council for Sustainable Development (BCSD), TBCSD comprises a group of corporate business leaders from various business sectors interested and engaged in environment and development issues. The secretariat to TBCSD (the Thailand Environment Institute) is responsible for project management, coordination and information services. TBCSD focuses on enhancing the role of business in environmental policy formulation and on promoting the concept of "sustainable development" amongst business leaders. Unlike BCSD, TBCSD is more action-oriented than research-oriented, thus responding to the needs of the Thai context where active leadership by example is currently required in order to address both industrial and more general environmental problems.
19. The majority of producers approached were ill-informed about eco-labelling in general, the concept of life-cycle analysis and the schemes in place in OECD countries. For example, many regarded labels as equivalent to legislation, and not as voluntary schemes.
20. The response to labels overseas is likely to hinge on how rapidly the demand for "green" products grows.

9 Eco-Labelling Schemes in Poland

Zbigniew Jakubczyk

Higher levels of stringency of environmental standards and regulations in the European Union (EU) make it difficult for Polish exporters to meet EU eco-labelling criteria at present. Current environmental initiatives in Poland may be seen as part of an attempt to bring Polish standards to conformity with those in the EU. This chapter briefly discusses the state of environmental legislation in Poland and the eco-labelling initiatives under way, and goes on to focus on the problems and possibilities presented by European eco-labelling schemes for Polish exporters of wood, footwear and textile products to EU.

I POLAND AND ECO-LABELLING

It was only in 1993 that eco-labelling efforts began in Poland, and the first draft of the Eco-labelling Act was prepared that year. However, the eco-labelling project is still in its early stages of planning (see Box 9.1).

In 1993, there were approximately 13 000 Polish standards in force in the country, in addition to approximately 14 000 branch standards and 150 000 plant standards. The establishment of these standards was not centrally coordinated. Since 1994, Polish standards have become national standards; plant standards have been abolished and branch standards are being phased out. Polish standards also ceased to be obligatory in 1994, except those for the protection of the human life, for the health, safety and the hygiene of workers, and those for environmental protection.

The problem of standards is investigated by the Polish Committee on Standards, the Polish Centre for Products Testing and Certificates, and the Head Office of Measures. At present, there are ten teams carrying

Box 9.1 The project for a Polish eco-labelling scheme

The project to introduce an eco-labelling scheme in Poland is now under discussion in the Ministries of Environmental Protection, Natural Resources, Forestry, Industry and Trade, and in the consumers' federation. Decisions on awarding the eco-label are to be made by the Eco-labelling Council. This institution will have 17 members representing the relevant Ministries, as well as the consumers' federation, societies of producers and traders, environmental organizations and scientific institutions.

The procedure for awarding the label will include an assessment of the ecological impact of a product during its life cycle. For selected groups of products, assessment will be made by appointed scientific institutions. The criteria for eco-labelling will eventually conform to those in the EU, but some industries may have less stringent standards initially.

The award procedure will have two stages, as in the case of the Blue Angel scheme. Firstly, producers and exporters will apply for the label for a specific product. In this phase, they pay a fee equal to the cost of assessment. This cost is usually quite high. During the second phase, manufacturers or exporters will submit their application for the label to the Council. At this stage, it will be necessary for the product to obtain a positive recommendation from the Jury. The Council will examine whether the product fulfils the stipulated criteria. The Minister of Environmental Protection, Natural Resources and Forestry can veto the Council's decision. In case of a veto, the application will be re-examined by the Council. If the decision of the Council is positive and if it is approved by the Minister, the applicant will receive a certificate awarding the label and the conditions for its use. The applicant will pay a fee for using the label, depending on the sales volume of the product. All decisions of the Council will be published in the "Eco-labelling Bulletin". If the decision by the Council is negative, an appeal can be made.

The Polish system of eco-labelling will be self-financing. The fees collected will constitute a special fund to support the promotion of the eco-labelling system, research on new eco-products, and the publication of the "Eco-labelling Bulletin".

In October 1994, the Polish Ministry of Environmental Protection prepared a list of changes to the 1980 Law on Protecting and Shaping the Natural Environment. Two of the articles of this project introduced an eco-label named "Ecologically Safe", awarded to products that meet domestic requirements with respect to health protection, and are ecologically friendly in their transport, production, storage, use and waste disposal phases. A full life-cycle analysis is not a condition for awarding this label.

An attempt to develop a private eco-label has been undertaken by the Gliwice Plastics and Dye-stuffs. Their label – "Ekologicznie bezpieczny" – is based on Polish standards and on international regulations on the railway transport of dangerous materials. A full life-cycle analysis is not included in the assessment procedures. The project focuses on the chemical composition of dye-stuffs and varnishes. Unofficial eco-labels in the Polish market include those on energy-saving electric bulbs, fluorescent lamps and thermo-isolation two-pane sets.

out research on specific topics in the field of standardization. There are plans to create up to 250 such teams in the future. The Polish Committee on Standards disseminates information on ISO and IEC standards, as well as on certain regional and national standards. Among the 13 000 Polish standards, only 2000 fulfil criteria specified by the ISO and IEC, and only 200 are consistent with EU standards.

Harmonization of Polish standards with those in the EU began in 1991, focusing on 1700 building-industry and construction-material standards, 60 per cent of which meet ISO requirements. Polish standards on health protection are often more stringent than those in the EU. On the other hand, in the field of environmental protection and work safety, Polish standards are considerably more liberal. For instance, only 60 among the 1000 EU safety standards are fulfilled in Poland.

The Polish Centre for Products Testing and Certificates was established in 1993. Although from a formal point of view Polish systems of product assessment and certification have already been made consistent with EU procedures, it is still impossible to issue certificates that would be accepted in the Single European Market. Twenty Polish laboratories have been given the right to issue certificates that will be sanctioned within the EU in the near future, and some Polish enterprises received ISO 9001 certificates in 1994. However, applying for and obtaining an eco-label remains very expensive for Polish producers.

The first eco-labelling initiative in Poland was that of the logo for electrical goods, "E GIGE".[1] Currently, a Waste Act is being prepared by the Parliamentary Commission of Environmental Protection and Natural Resources. The Act regulates, *inter alia*, the import of one-use wrappings, especially produced from polyvinylchloride (PVC) and polytereflamimium. The Commission also plans to implement a deposit system for toxic waste. In addition, there are plans to introduce compulsory certification for imported cosmetics and household chemical products. Approximately 7000 such products are currently sold in the Polish market. However, a number of attest rules are violated, particularly by small firms.

II WOOD PRODUCTS

A Forest Economy in Poland

The introduction of ecological criteria in the Polish wood industry is in its early stages. Ideas on sustainably managed forestry, such as those included in "Project Tropenwald" or the Forest Stewardship Council, have not been implemented in Poland.

In state-owned forests, harvesting is usually kept lower than the forest growth rate. The ratio of harvest rate to forest growth rate is estimated at about 70 per cent,[2] a figure similar to those in other European countries. However, trees cut in Poland are often young, as the older trees are located away from transport roads. Private forests are harvested at a rate higher than the forest growth rate, as the Forest Act allows private owners to fell trees without permits.[3] Lack of adequate finance makes it difficult for state-owned forests to implement rational and sustainable exploitation of forestry resources.

Polish forests are facing the dangers of air pollution, especially from sulphur dioxide and nitrogen oxides, and of forest fires. Concerted regional efforts can help the conservation of forest ecosystems. An example of this would be the "Black Triangle" region (neighbouring territories of Poland, Czech Republic and Germany), where forests face very high emissions of SO_2. The cooperation among the "Black Triangle" countries is based on a 1991 agreement signed by Poland, Germany and the former Czechoslovakia and the European Community. The main objective of the agreement is to reduce SO_2 emissions from the power sector. The World Bank and the European Bank for Reconstruction and Development (EBRD) are also involved in the implementation of the "Black Triangle" programme. However, significant reductions in the levels of SO_2 will depend on the reduction of electricity generation in the lignite-fired power plants located in the area or on the installation of expensive flue gas desulphurisation (FGD) facilities in these plants.

B Environmental Measures on Wood Products

In response to requirements made by importers in the EU, efforts are being made in the Polish furniture sector to take account of environmental parameters. The Institute of Wood Technology in Poznań carries out the necessary tests. The first step in examining ecological characteristics of wood products is in monitoring the selection of type of wood, as some species contain toxic substances, especially formaldehyde. Many Polish producers have stopped using wood from alder, European olive-tree, yew, cypress, juniper, box-tree and mezereon, as these types of wood generate toxic dust during the process of hydrothermic machining. Besides formaldehyde, the dust contains carcinogenic and allergic chemical compounds.[4]

The second step in testing ecological characteristics of furniture consists in examining the emission of toxic substances. The attests are made according to criteria specified in *Gefahrstoffverordnung*. The main toxic substance is formaldehyde. The ambient standard set by German importers is 0.1 ppm. At times, other parameters such as VOS are also tested. The Institute has been trying to obtain authorization for awarding the European certificates for furniture clays, fibreboards and lacquers in Poland.[5] Certificates based on German standards are awarded to exporters of wood products at their own request, and so far this has not been connected with the award of eco-labels.

It is extremely difficult to make a reliable overall assessment of the performance of the Polish furniture industry from an ecological point of view due to the lack of reliable information. The available information relates to firms that have applied for certification. *Gefahrstoffverordnung* requirements are fulfilled by 80 per cent of the applicants, whereas Polish ambient air standards for living quarters are met only by 43 per cent of them, as the latter tend to be more stringent than their German counterparts. There has been an increase in the production of ecologically friendly furniture in Poland. This is linked, among other things, to the pressure exerted by the IKEA company which promotes ecological furniture in the Polish market. However, according to estimates by the Institute of Wood Technology, only 1 per cent of the IKEA customers can be regarded as ecologically conscious, in terms of taking ecological considerations into account while buying furniture. There is also a growth in the share of products covered with thermosetting lacquers which almost eliminate formaldehyde emission. However, no life-cycle analysis for furniture has been developed in Poland until now.

Some important ecological consequences are linked to the decrease in the export of Polish wood products. In 1984–5, Poland exported about two million cubic metres of wood per annum. In the years 1987–91, this figure declined to 500 000–900 000 cubic metres per annum. In 1992, the export figure was 1.3 million cubic metres and in 1993, one million. Pulpwood accounts for about 80 per cent of total wood exports. From an ecological point of view, the growing domestic demand for wood has to be considered disadvantageous in the long run since it delays the implementation of eco-labelling standards in the wood industry, as domestic producers pay less attention to these standards than European importers.

III TEXTILE INDUSTRY

The Polish textile industry is slowly beginning to adapt itself to eco-labelling schemes in some of the other European countries. The major ecological parameters of textiles concern the following:

- raw materials used for production;
- production processes;
- utilization of waste materials; and
- harmfulness for human health.

Advanced research is being carried out on raw materials and on human-health-related aspects. The Central Institute of Textile Research is currently carrying out research on the pH of products, contents of free formaldehyde, contents of heavy metals, contents of pesticides, especially pentachlorophenol, and chemical characteristics of dyes used. The Institute does not award any logo or label, but only a certificate containing the findings of investigations.

A resolution of the Polish Ministry of Health in 1986 regulates concentration standards for: organic compounds such as formaldehyde; halogenated carriers; chlorine bleaching; benzene; and naphthalene in habitable rooms in houses. These standards are essentially weaker than those prepared by *Markenzeichen schadstoffgeprufte Textilien*, but are close to Steilman standards (e.g. 500 ppm for formaldehyde).

The proposals made by Denmark on eco-labelling in textiles in the context of the EU are not widely known in Poland. Polish enterprises that export textile products apply parameters worked out by ÖKO-TEX,[6] particularly with respect to:

- free formaldehyde – for close to the skin 75 ppm and for other situations 300 ppm;
- heavy metals – As, 0.2 ppm; Pb, 0.8 ppm (new rule 0.000); Hg, 0.002 ppm for baby clothing and 0.1 ppm for others; CrIII, 2.0 ppm (new rule 1.0 ppm); and CrV, prohibited.
- residuum of pesticides – 1.0 ppm, thereof pentachlorophenol 0.5 ppm;
- aromatic amines – prohibited.

German importers of textile products have so far regarded the ÖKO-TEX requirements as sufficient. Polish textile producers may not fulfil the Danish proposals without pressure from EU importers and EU institutions.

The Polish system of environmental protection is based on emission standards and on environmental fees and fines. If the emission is lower than that allowed in an administrative permit, manufacturers pay a fee. If, however, enterprises violate the stipulations of the permit, they have to pay high fines. For example, there are two kinds of permits and fees to be paid by enterprises for using water resources: (a) for water intake, and (b) for waste-water discharge. The Polish system does not contain standards for consumption of water during fabric production. Waste-water discharge from manufacturing processes must be in compliance with the directive of the Ministry of the Environmental Protection, Natural Resources and Forestry on water standards. The case of air pollution is treated in a similar way. The established universal norms for noise and dust are based on parameters of Order of the Polish Ministry of Labour and Social Affairs of 1989.

Recently, some textile producers have attempted to implement environmentally friendly production processes. So far, they have been mainly focused on

- the selection of dyes and auxiliary chemicals;
- the improvement in chemicals bathing – instead of manual bathing, firms implement computer operated controls;
- the reduction or elimination of some chemicals through processing at high temperature, increased pressure, magnetic fields and low-temperature plasma processes.

Managers of several Polish textile plants fear that the introduction of eco-labelling criteria may result in eliminating Poland and countries such as Hungary and the Czech Republic from the EU market. It may take considerable time before domestic textile products in Poland will be able to fulfil eco-labelling criteria developed in the EU. Inadequate financial resources pose the most important constraint to the modernization of the Polish textile industry, and such modernization will be essential for Polish products to meet labelling requirements.

IV FOOTWEAR INDUSTRY

In the footwear industry, only the production of soles is currently subject to environmental regulation. The production of other parts of shoes, as well as the use of raw materials in their manufacturing, are not subject to regulation. More importantly, there are no restrictions at present on the use of chemicals and dyestuffs.

Environmental regulations for existing production facilities in the footwear industry have been specified by an Order of the Polish Ministry of Labour and Social Affairs in 1989. This Order, obligatory for all industrial branches,[7] regulates aspects such as permissible concentration of air pollutants in the work-place, maximum noise level, vibrations influencing the human body, exposure to low and high temperatures, humidity level, and infrared, ultraviolet and laser radiation.

One major difference between the Order and EU standards is that the Order does not specify any VOC parameter. Instead, there are about 250 standards in Poland for organic and non-organic chemical compounds.[8] Other main differences between the EU eco-labelling programme and the Polish regulations relate to the absence of a standard for total energy consumption during the manufacturing of shoes, the lack of emission standards for production, and the lack of standards for wrappings.

Currently, Polish footwear manufacturers use chlorine-bleached cotton in the production of canvas shoes. Chlorine-based solvents as well as plastic foam are used for making soles, and chlorine-based polymers, especially PVC, are commonly applied in manufacturing soles.[9]

In short, the eco-labelling criteria developed in the EU are currently not fulfilled by the Polish footwear industry. However, an important opportunity to eliminate PVC from soles made in Poland may be provided by a new polymer called Microeva, which does not contain chorine. For the production of ten pairs of soles, only three kilograms of Microeva are required,[10] while the corresponding amount for PVC exceeds ten kilograms. Microeva soles are lighter, and the overall energy consumption in producing a pair of shoes diminishes with the use of this new polymer. Microeva is being produced by the Central Laboratory of Footwear Industry in Cracow, but only in a limited scale so far.

In 1992, shoe-producing enterprises generated 2.9 cubic hectometres of industrial sewage.[11] However, the share of the footwear industry in the total industrial sewage discharged is small. Apart from sewage directly discharged into rivers, 0.9 cubic hectometres is treatment-requiring sewage. This has been subject only to mechanical treatment. The approximate cost of constructing a sewage-treatment plant with biological installations for one firm is about 40 billion zl (over US$2 million).

Notes

1. Head Inspectorate of Energy Industry (Glowny Inspektorat Gospodarki Energetycznej).
2. Unpublished information from the Institute of Wood Technology.
3. According to the Polish Ministry of Environmental Protection, about 15 000 private forests have been cut since 1992. See *Aura*, no. 4 (1994), p. 4.
4. On the selection of wood species, see W. Sandermann and A. W. Barghoorn, "HOLZ als Roh- und Werkstoff", *Gesundheitsschadigende Nutzholzer*, Jahrg. 14 (1956), pp. 37–40.
5. In 1994, four standardization committees for the wood industry, including a furniture team and a fibreboard team, were established at the Institute of Wood Technology.
6. These parameters are only slightly less stringent than those suggested in the Danish proposals, especially in the case of heavy metals.
7. The Order was amended on 21 October 1991. The paper refers to the present version.
8. For example, for formaldehyde, the standard is 0.5 mg/m^3.
9. The Research Institute of Footwear estimates the share of PVC in production of shoe soles at about 50 per cent.
10. K. P. Gasiorski, *Analiza mozliwosci rozwoju stosowania MIKROEVA* [Analysis of Possible Uses of MICROEVA], Cracow, 1994.
11. *Ochrona srodowiska i gospodarka wodna* [Environmental Protection and Water Economy], 1993, p. 143.

10 Eco-Labelling and the Developing Countries: The Dutch Horticultural Sector

Harmen Verbruggen, Saskia Jongma and Frans van der Woerd

This chapter discusses the proliferation of eco-labelling schemes in the horticultural sector in the Netherlands, with special reference to the implications of these schemes for developing-country exporters of horticultural products. Section I places the Dutch horticultural sector in perspective, and touches upon the economic and the environmental problems that have confronted the sector in recent years. Section II discusses four eco-labelling schemes that are either currently operational in this sector or are expected to be introduced in the near future. Section III identifies how the labelling schemes may prejudice the export interests of developing countries, and how the latter may respond to this, including through the introduction of eco-labelling schemes for their own products. The chapter attempts to spell out a number of principles on which international consensus needs to be sought in order to establish an international system for the mutual recognition of eco-labels.

I THE HORTICULTURAL SECTOR IN THE NETHERLANDS

The Netherlands has a long-standing tradition in the production and the export of horticultural products such as vegetables, fruit, cut flowers, bulbs, pot plants, mushrooms and trees. Horticultural products are grown on bare soil, in greenhouses and, increasingly, on artificial substrates. In 1991, the total production of the horticultural sector amounted to Dfl 12 000 million, of which 80 per cent was exported. Horticultural exports constitute 4–5 per cent of total Dutch exports.

As can be seen from Table 10.1, more than 60 per cent of the

Table 10.1 Producer value of Dutch horticulture, 1991 (million Dfl)

Greenhouse vegetables	2600
Greenhouse cut flowers	3200
Greenhouse pot plants	1900
Total greenhouse	7700
Other cultures	4300
Total horticulture	12 000

Source: LEI/CBS, *Tuinbouwcijfers 1992* (Den Haag, 1993).

Table 10.2 Production factors in Dutch horticulture, 1991

Sector	*Area (hectare)*	*Substrate (hectare)*	*Farms*	*Employment*
Greenhouse vegetables	4500	2900	4000	22 000
Greenhouse cut flowers	4000	600[a]	5600[a]	24 000[a]
Greenhouse pot plants	1300			
Greenhouse total	9800	3500	9600	46 000
Other cultures	98 800	–	6500	27 000
Total horticulture	108 600	–	16 100	73 000

Source: LEI/CBS, *Tuinbouwcijfers 1992* (The Hague, 1993).

Note: [a] This figure covers both greenhouse cut flowers and greenhouse pot plants.

production takes place under artificial, non-natural conditions in greenhouses. The value-added generated by greenhouse gardening amounts to 1 per cent of the Dutch GDP. Horticulture in Dutch greenhouses can be subdivided into three sectors:

- vegetables and fruit – specialized in tomatoes, cucumber and paprika;
- cut flowers – specialized in rose and chrysanthemum; and
- pot plants – variety of species.

The market situation at the beginning of the 1990s showed stagnation in the vegetable and fruit sector, slow growth in the cut flowers market, and rapid growth in trade in pot plants. This meant that the prospects for greenhouse vegetables have been bleak, and those for the pot plants sector have been the most promising.

Table 10.3 Input costs as percentage of production costs in Dutch horticulture, 1990

Sector	*Labour*	*Depreciation*	*Energy*
Greenhouse vegetables	32	12	17
Greenhouse cut flowers	30	17	12
Greenhouse pot plants	24	12	11
Greenhouse total	30	14	13

Source: LEI/CBS, *Tuinbouwcijfers 1992* (The Hague, 1993).

Note: In 1990, energy use in the horticultural sector constituted 75 per cent of the total energy use in agriculture in the Netherlands.

Table 10.4 Exports of Dutch horticulture, 1991 (percentage of production)

Sector	*Export as percentage of production*	*Imports as percentage of exports*
Greenhouse vegetables	85	17
Greenhouse cut flowers	70	
Greenhouse pot plants	70	12[a]
Greenhouse total	78	14
Total horticulture	80	77

Source: LEI/CBS, *Tuinbouwcijfers 1992* (Den Haag, 1993); and M. Hack and A. M. A. Haybroeck, *Visie op de internationale concurrentiekracht in de bloemisterij* (Utrecht: Rabobank, 1992).

Note: [a]This figure covers both and green house cut flowers and greenhouse pot plants.

Table 10.2 presents information on some basic inputs in Dutch horticulture: area of cultivation and labour. The area with greenhouses is relatively limited, but this area is used very intensively. In greenhouse vegetable growing, substrate cultivation has replaced soil cultivation for more than 50 per cent.[1] This share is steadily increasing. Substrate cultivation has also been introduced in flower gardening in recent years.

Not only labour, but capital and energy are also used intensively in Dutch greenhouse gardening, as indicated in Table 10.3. In comparison with almost all other industries, the share of energy costs in total production costs is the highest in the greenhouse sector. The pot plants sector shows lower demands on labour, capital and energy than the two other subsectors of greenhouse gardening.

Like all horticulture in the Netherlands, greenhouse gardening is extremely export-oriented, and the vegetable sector even more so (see Table 10.4). Dutch horticultural products dominate world export markets for cut flowers and pot plants with a remarkable 60 per cent share.[2] In fact, Dutch auctions set the prices for these products in the world market. More than 85 per cent of the Dutch horticultural exports are directed towards other countries in the European Union (EU), Germany being the largest consumer.

In recent years, however, the Dutch greenhouse horticultural sector has come under increasing threat from foreign exports. Most of the competing imports are sold in Dutch horticultural auctions and then re-exported to other EU countries. Most pronounced among these are the imports of tomatoes from the Canary Islands, Spain and Morocco (22 per cent of the auction turnover in 1992) and cut flower imports from Israel (9 per cent of auction turnover).[3] The emerging competitors are Spain (paprika, cucumber), Colombia, Thailand, Zimbabwe, Kenya and Ecuador (all cut flowers), and Denmark (pot plants).

As mentioned earlier, auctions play a prominent role in the production and trade of horticultural products. The Dutch auction system for horticultural products is still, in essence, the traditional public sale at which goods are sold to persons making the highest bid. Nowadays, the bidding procedure is fully computerized. Growers are registered with specialized auctions, which are also involved in quality control, marketing and the logistics of export trade. Two flower auctions dominate trade in cut flowers and pot plants, namely Flower Auction Aalsmeer (FAA) and Flower Auction Holland (FAH). Together, these two auctions control more than 80 per cent of the trade in cut flowers and more than 90 per cent of the trade in pot plants. Only a minor share of total trade in cut flowers and pot plants is traded without the intervention of auctions. Foreign suppliers can offer their produce for auction at the Dutch flower auctions. Production and trade in fruit and vegetables are less dominated by the auction system. In particular, imported products are traded without the intervention of the fruit and vegetable auctions. At present, the greenhouse horticultural sector in the Netherlands faces threats on three different fronts:

- First, with the exception of pot plants, the market prospects are generally poor, and competition from foreign owners is steadily increasing. Further efficiency gains are difficult to realize. Especially, the relatively high costs of low-skilled labour and the relatively high energy costs lay a heavy burden on firms.

- Second, the reputation of some of the greenhouse products has also come under threat in recent years, especially in the German export market. For example, vegetables have been suffering from a poor quality image, and cut flowers have received negative attention for environmental reasons.
- Third, after years of delay and poor enforcement, environmental standards are now being tightened in the horticultural (greenhouse) sector. Clear environmental objectives, including improvement in the use of energy, pesticides and chemical fertilizers, are being enforced. Substantial investments in alternative growing methods and capital equipment are often required for complying with the new standards. It is expected that 20–30 per cent of the greenhouse growers, especially the small-scale firms growing vegetables and cut flowers, will face serious economic difficulties.[4]

II ECO-LABELLING INITIATIVES IN THE DUTCH GREENHOUSE SECTOR

The Dutch greenhouse horticultural sector has responded to the challenges discussed so far by taking a variety of counter-initiatives. Environmental management systems have been introduced at the firm level, environmentally sound technological developments have been stimulated and instruments for communication have been strengthened. Various eco-labelling schemes have also been envisaged, with a view to fulfilling three interrelated objectives:

- improvement of the international competitive position of the sector, through the creation of segmented markets for horticultural (greenhouse) products; or
- improvement of the overall product quality; and/or
- improvement of the environmental performance of the horticultural (greenhouse) produce.

Thus, the eco-labelling initiatives in the Dutch horticultural sector are primarily a response to problems internal to the sector. They need to be considered as the offensive response of a sector under economic stress and severe criticism on grounds of quality as well as environmental aspects. It should be borne in mind, however, that the predominant reaction of the sector is defensive, as can be seen in strategies such as lobbying for lower environmental standards or longer compliance periods, negotiating relatively low natural gas prices, and denying the quality issue. Elements of this defensive, protectionist strategy also enter the eco-labelling initiatives at times.

The following paragraphs deal with four eco-labelling initiatives in the Dutch horticultural sector, namely "Milieukeur" cut flowers, the eco-labelling scheme of FAH, the fruit and vegetable label "Butterfly", and organic cultivation labels.

A "Milieukeur" Cut Flowers

The competent body for the award of the Dutch eco-label scheme is an independent foundation called "Milieukeur". The foundation is also responsible for the implementation of the eco-label of the European Community in the Netherlands. Since September 1993, Milieukeur has awarded eco-labels to notebooks and cat litter. Labels for shower heads, refrigerators, electric coffee machines, shoes, sitting chairs, toilet paper and paints are expected in the near future. The criteria for the award of the Dutch eco-label have already been formulated for these product groups. Recent activities of the Foundation include the initiation of a procedure for the development of a "Milieukeur" label for cut flowers. The first labels are expected to be awarded in 1995 or early 1996. This procedure conforms to the standard "Milieukeur" procedure of the Foundation.[5]

The procedure for the award of a "Milieukeur" label takes place in two successive rounds. In the first, a group of functionally related products is defined (in this case, cut flowers), and a set of environmental criteria to be met by products eligible for the label formulated. For each product group, a different set of criteria is formulated, as each group has its own environmental characteristics. The criteria are formulated on the basis of a practical life-cycle analysis, taking into account five separate product stages and eight categories of environmental aspects. These product stages are raw materials extraction, production of intermediates, product manufacturing, product use and removal. The categories of environmental aspects are resource use, energy, emissions, nuisance, waste, reusability, reparability and life span. On the basis of subcontracted research, a panel of experts of the Foundation formulates a set of criteria, These are discussed at a public hearing, and finally the panel decides on the criteria.

In the second round, individual producers and importers can apply for an eco-label for their product, which is awarded if the product meets the relevant criteria set by the Foundation. The producer or importer will be informed if the product does not meet all the criteria, so that steps can be taken to improve the environmental aspects of the product, and another request for certification can be submitted. Under the Dutch scheme, the eco-label is awarded for a limited period that varies between two and five years. If a shift to cleaner products takes place during that period, the label loses its significance and can be withdrawn. Alternatively, if still cleaner products become feasible in time, the criteria for the award of the label have to be reviewed.

In principle, all products – domestically produced as well as imported – available in the Dutch market are eligible for the Dutch labelling scheme. This, however, does not mean that the domestic and foreign producers are treated equally in practice. Firstly, foreign producers are not directly represented in the panel of experts that decides on the criteria. The panel is composed of environmental experts from various interest groups and the Government. The interest groups represented in the panel are producers, consumers, trade (wholesale and retail trade, importers) and environmental organizations. Thus, foreign producers in developing countries are not represented on the panel, and hence their export interests are not directly taken into account. Their positions can be voiced only through their trade representatives. Secondly, the Dutch eco-labelling scheme is clear that the product group criteria should take relatively high environmental standards as their point of departure. This is because the labelling scheme caters to the already high but still growing environmental awareness of Dutch consumers and because it aims to produce a clear innovative effect. Combined with the fact that foreign producers are not directly represented in the criteria-formulating panel, this implies that the strict standards of the scheme will also be applied to foreign products and production processes, without taking into account the environmental circumstances and preferences in foreign countries. Consequently, the Dutch eco-labelling scheme may have an extraterritorial impact, which can be disadvantageous for developing-country exporters. This may become particularly relevant for the product group, cut flowers. As mentioned earlier, the relatively high energy intensity of Dutch greenhouse produce has been criticized on environmental grounds. However, energy use is a crucial factor for the sector's competitive position in international trade. Undoubtedly, energy use will have an important place in the product group criteria for cut flowers, and low energy use or the use of sustainable energy sources will be strongly favoured. If domestic and foreign suppliers are treated equally, developing-country exports of cut flowers will obtain a new comparative advantage in so far as these are grown under more favourable climate conditions, i.e. with sunlight. However, it is unlikely that these two different production methods, i.e. artificially and naturally heated greenhouses, will be placed on an equal footing. Given the deteriorating competitive position of the Dutch greenhouse sector, developing countries may not be allowed to make use of a new comparative advantage in the Dutch market through an eco-labelling scheme. Therefore, energy use associated with the international transport of imported cut flowers may also be included in the product group criteria. The Dutch greenhouse sector views this as "fair" for levelling the playing field. A study on the energy intensity of domestic and imported greenhouse products has already revealed that, for instance, it does not make any difference from an environmental point of view whether roses are grown domestically in greenhouses or imported and transported by air from Colombia or Morocco. Both roses show the same energy content of about 6–7 Guilder cents.[6] It has also been argued that energy use in air transport is exempt from excise duties and taxes.

Although ideally the environmental externalities of international transport should constitute an integral part of a product's environmental profile, its present use seems directed at preventing developing countries from benefiting from a Dutch eco-label for cut flowers. Better-suited climate conditions in developing countries are not being considered as a trade-creating factor.

B Eco-Labelling Scheme of Flower Auction Holland

As described in section I above, auctions play a crucial marketing and logistic role for the horticultural sector in the Netherlands. Until recently, however, auctions did not consider themselves accountable for the environmental consequence of horticultural production. This attitude changed in the early 1990s, when it became evident that the public image of the horticultural sector and, as a result, the auction's future prospects were affected. Flower Auction Holland (FAH), one of the two largest auctions in the Netherlands, developed a classification scheme for cut flowers and pot plants that provides information on the environmental behaviour of firms and on various environmental effects of production processes. The FAH classification scheme is directed towards firms that grow cut flowers and pot plants, and are registered with FAH. The objective of the scheme is to improve the national and international market position of cut flowers and pot plants sold through FAH by improving both their environmental and their quality images. The classification scheme should induce firms to perform better in these respects, because the scheme classifies firms in environmental classes, keeps track of the environmental efforts of firms, and provides financial incentives – i.e. higher auction prices – for products from higher classified firms. The FAH classification scheme can be considered as an auction label: the label provides information to the flower trade on the environmental classes.

The FAH classification scheme takes as its staring point the concept of integrated environmental management. It takes four environmental themes into account, namely crop protection remedies, fertilizers, energy use, and waste. For each of these environmental themes, FAH has formulated three levels of stringency. Standards are set for each type of flower cultivation. These standards, of course, are closely related to the environmental objectives of the horticultural (greenhouse) sector, laid down in various national environmental policy plans. They typically reflect the environmental circumstances and societal preferences of the Netherlands. On the basis of these three standard levels, the firm's environmental performance on each of the environmental themes is determined. Points are awarded for each theme and, depending on the total points and the relative weights of themes, the overall environmental record of the product is indicated in classes A, B and C. There is a provisional agreement on the relative weights of themes, as indicated in Box 10.1.

Box 10.1 Relative weights of environmental themes in the FAH classification scheme

Level	*Crop protection remedies*	*Fertilizers*	*Energy use*	*Waste*	*Points*
Level 3	1	1	1	1	
Level 2	4	2	2	1	
Level 1	6	3	3	1	

Total points for firm X:

Environmental Class A: 10–13 points
Environmental Class B: 5–9 points
Environmental Class C: minimal requirement is to register for all themes

For instance, if a firm, for the cultivation of a certain flower, uses crop protection remedies according to level 1, fertilizers according to level 3, energy according to level 1, and produces waste according to level 2, the firm receives 6 + 1 + 3 + 1 = 11 points. For the cultivation of that flower, the firm's produce is classified in class A.

The FAH classification scheme has been in operation since 1993, and firms have been invited to register. Firms have to sign an agreement with FAH, and they are obliged to provide the necessary data on all four environmental themes on a fortnightly basis. The auction is entitled to scrutinize the reliability of the data with the help of experts and through firm inspections. Firms are excluded from participation if their data prove to be incorrect.

FAH tries to ensure full participation from its member firms. Efforts are made to extend the classification to all flower auctions in the Netherlands, and the reactions of other auctions have been positive. Ultimately, the goal is to introduce the scheme in all markets in the EU within a few years.

There are discussions on the possibility of opening the FAH classification scheme to foreign owners who sell their products through Dutch auctions, either via importers or as foreign members of the auction. As indicated in section I, the share of foreign-grown flowers in the auction's turnover varies from 6 to 15 per cent, and is steadily increasing. These imports originate in about 45 countries. The two largest flower auctions in the Netherlands receive ever more requests for membership from foreign suppliers. However, foreign participation in the classification scheme proves to be rather complicated.

Firstly, to become eligible for participation, foreign firms would need to keep a reliable environmental accounting system to be able to provide the necessary data per environmental theme of the classification scheme. In addition, there would be the problem of monitoring and checks on data reliability. Both conditions are very hard to meet for foreign suppliers, and the cost involved can be very high.

Secondly, foreign producers have to meet the standards, levels and weights of the FAH classification scheme. Otherwise, the scheme would lose its credibility in consumer markets. In order to keep up credibility, it seems inevitable that an additional environmental theme related to the environmental effects of international air transport, specially geared towards foreign suppliers, will be included in the classification scheme. According to the designers of the FAH classification scheme, an energy equivalent for international transport from the exporting country to Europe or the Netherlands has to be taken into account, although it is not yet clear in what way and with what weight. As has been argued with respect to the eco-label for cut flowers in section II.A, the inclusion of international transport in the classification criteria puts distant exporting countries at a disadvantage. As no reference has been made in these arguments to the environmental impact of export-related transport, one may suspect them of protectionist sentiments.

It will thus be very difficult for developing-country exporters of cut flowers to qualify for the FAH classification label. Consequently, flowers from developing countries will have a no-label status at the Dutch auctions. It is also possible for developing countries to circumvent the auctions and sell directly to wholesale and retail traders in the Netherlands and Europe. In both cases, however, foreign suppliers are deprived of the label that is supposed to improve their market position as well as of the financial returns on a more environmentally sound growing method. This worsens the competitive position of developing-country exporters of cut flowers to the European market.

C "Butterfly": The Fruit and Vegetable Label

At the initiative of the two large auctions, a labelling scheme has been developed for fruit and vegetables. Since 1992, this labelling scheme has been in operation for tomatoes, cucumber, paprika, apples and pears. In 1993, a label was also introduced for melon. Labels are expected in the near future for mushrooms, leek, fennel, varieties of cabbage, salad, carrots and strawberries. Other fruit and vegetable auctions in the Netherlands are increasingly joining this initiative. The label is visualized by a stylized butterfly, and is primarily meant to inform the buyer at the auction about the environmental performance of the product. The "Butterfly" label closely resembles the point system of the FAH classification scheme for cut flowers and pot plants, discussed in section II.B. However, while the FAH classification scheme introduced an integrated approach with four environmental themes, the "Butterfly" label has started with just one theme, i.e. integrated pest management, with other environmental themes proposed to be included in future. Integrated pest management involves the minimization of the use of broad-spectrum chemical pesticides and the introduction of natural, organic cultivation methods.

An important motive for the introduction of a classification scheme based on a points system is to get on board as many firms as possible: better a large number of firms improving their environmental behaviour a little than a few firms doing a lot. Moreover, it would result in wider dissemination of and publicity for the "Butterfly" label in sales markets, and hence a stronger market position for labelled products. This is why more than 95 per cent of the growers that applied for a "Butterfly" label for cucumber, tomato and paprika, and for pears and melon have been awarded the label. For apples, this share is approximately 75 per cent.

The "Butterfly" label is awarded only to growers and traders registered with a Dutch fruit and vegetable auction, and only Dutch growers and traders have been eligible for registration so far. In other words, the "Butterfly" label excludes foreign suppliers, and has been discriminatory in that respect. However, there have been some initiatives to discuss the possibility of opening the Dutch fruit and vegetable auctions to foreign growers and traders. This would make them also eligible for the "Butterfly" label. However, two conditions would have to be fulfilled. Firstly, foreign growers and traders have to be able to offer an assortment of fruit and vegetables, not only a single product. Although this condition is obligatory for Dutch growers and traders too, from a trade point of view, this anti-specialization requirement seems rather inefficient and discriminatory against foreign suppliers. Second, to guarantee the quality and reliability of the label, production methods of products offered by foreign growers and traders should be monitored and checked in the same way as in the case of their Dutch counterparts. This too seems rather complicated and costly to implement.

Exporters of fruit and vegetables can, of course, sell their products directly to wholesale and large retail traders, without the interference of auctions. As indicated in section I, fruit and vegetable markets – unlike the cut flowers market – are not monopolized by auctions. However, this would mean that imported fruit and vegetables are deprived of a unique selling point in the Dutch and the European markets, as the "Butterfly" label is expected to become.

D Organic Cultivation Labels

Since 1993, Flower Auction Aalsmeer (FAA), the largest flower auction in the Netherlands, has introduced a special eco-label for organically cultivated cut flowers, bulbs and pot plants. In organic cultivation, no use is made of artificial fertilizers and pesticides, and natural growing seasons are followed. The label is being introduced under the competence of a foundation for organic cultivation (SKAL), which issues the EKO-label. This is done on the condition that the SKAL products sold through the FAA also have to meet specific quality criteria, e.g.

with respect to the durability of the products. Products that meet both the SKAL and the FAA quality standards are awarded the GEA-label, which is specifically directed towards the consumer markets. The labelled products are sold thorough selected high-quality florists and natural food stores. Consumer prices for GEA-labelled products are about 30 per cent higher than those for regular supply. The share of GEA-labelled products in the turnover of FAA is about 1 per cent, and is expected to increase to about 3–4 per cent. The GEA-labelled products have been received very well by the Dutch and other European consumers. FAA considers the GEA-label as an important instrument to build a greener image.

SKAL also issues EKO-labels for fruit and vegetables sold directly to consumers or through natural food stores. Nowadays, EKO-labelled fruit and vegetables are increasingly offered in supermarkets. Their share in the Dutch market is about 5 per cent at present, and is expected to increase to 10 per cent. These organic cultivation labels are not open to foreign suppliers. One of the major problems, of course, is the inspection of foreign cultivation methods. But, in general, organically cultivated products are hardly traded internationally. These products face the additional problem of meeting the stringent phytosanitary standards in importing developed countries.

III FEASIBILITY OF ECO-LABELS FOR DEVELOPING-COUNTRY EXPORTS

The proliferation of eco-labelling schemes in the horticultural sector in the Netherlands primarily serves the sector's own objective of improving its competitive position through better environmental and quality image. These labelling schemes are wholly or partly based on the concept of life-cycle analysis or integrated chain management. This poses two problems for exporters from developing countries. First, all eco-labelling schemes in the horticultural sector emanate from relatively high environmental standards that are derived from the specific environmental and economic circumstances in the Netherlands, i.e. relatively capital- and technology-intensive growing methods which make intensive use of energy as well as of artificial fertilizers and pesticides, and take place in concentrated areas with a relatively high firm density. Implicitly, eco-labelling schemes apply these circumstances and the derived environmental standards to foreign growers, without taking into account the environmental circumstances and preferences in exporting countries. This may lead to serious trade distortion since, especially in the horticultural sector, different environmental and climate conditions across countries create country-specific comparative advantages in production and trade. Undoing a comparative disadvantage by relatively low energy prices, as in the greenhouse horticulture in the Netherlands, can already be considered such a trade distortion. It would be unfair towards developing-country exporters of horticultural products if the energy component related to international transport from foreign growers to the European markets is included in the eco-labelling scheme criteria, while the environmental effects associated with the international transport of exported goods are disregarded. Thus, in the case of trade in horticultural production, the cradle-to-import border approach adhered to in the Netherlands neutralizes revealed comparative advantages for developing countries in horticultural products.

This is not to say that, ideally, the externalities of transport should not constitute an integral part of the overall assessment of the environmental impact of a product. However, the present eco-labelling schemes do not include transport *per se* as an environment aspect, nationally or internationally. Besides, the transport-related externalities of a product are very hard to establish on account of varying distances and means of transport between producers, intermediate producers and consumers. Therefore, the inclusion of energy use related to international transport in the Dutch eco-labelling schemes for cut flowers, for instance, appears to display protectionist motives.

Furthermore, foreign producers are not represented in the institutions that design and implement eco-labelling schemes. While this is partly due to inattention and to reluctance with respect to the practical problems of monitoring and testing foreign growers, protectionist sentiments also seem to be involved. If these developments continue, imported products will be the only supply in the horticultural market that will have no label of any kind.

It is therefore of crucial importance for the prospects of developing-country exporters of horticultural products to respond to these developments by introducing comparable eco-labelling schemes for their products. However, to establish an international system of mutual recognition of eco-labels, consensus should be sought on a number of principles. The following principles may be considered:

- It should be recognized that each country can legitimately formulate its own eco-labelling criteria, taking into account its own environmental circumstances and preferences of environmental quality.

- It should be sufficient for the international recognition of labels that the country-specific criteria may concern local and national environmental problems only. This would boil down to a cradle-to-export border approach.
- Criteria that reflect concern about transborder and global environmental problems should be agreed on internationally. While each country should be free to include such criteria in its own labelling scheme, this should not be forced on countries, nor allowed to impede the process of mutual recognition.
- Although environmental criteria with respect to international transport of traded products should ideally be included in a comprehensive life-cycle approach that underlies eco-labelling schemes, they cannot in practice be included at present unless all trade flows are treated equally. This can only be realized through an international agreement.
- Most eco-labelling schemes take as their point of departure relatively high environmental standards, since they cater to the growing environmental awareness of consumers in developed countries, and as they wish to produce a clear innovative effect. For that reason, only a limited number of products within a product group is awarded a label. However, this certification of only the most environmentally sound products on the basis of a yes/no decision is not very attractive for developing countries. It is probably more in their interests to apply certification schemes based on a continuous scale, like, for example, the points system with three environmental classes used by FAH. The clear advantages of such a system are lower barriers of entry into the labelling scheme, higher participation rates, and the incentive to move up to higher environmental classes. Such a system does not pursue selection and exclusion, but promotes participation and stimulation. This serves the interests of developing countries more effectively, and perhaps better facilitates a system of mutual recognition of eco-labels.

Notes

1. Substrate cultivation takes place on artificial culture mediums, e.g. rockwool.
2. M. Hack and A. M. A. Haybroeck, *Visie op de internationale concurrentiekracht in de bloemisterij* (Utrecht: Rabobank, 1992).
3. LEI, *Landbouw-Economisch Bericht 1992* (The Hague, 1992).

4. See K. F. van der Woerd and S. Rosdorff, *Miow-Analyse voor de Gastuinbouw*, IES report 93/284, 1993.
5. See H. Verbruggen and S. Jongma, "Environment and Trade Policies in the Netherlands and the European Communities", paper presented at the SELA/UNCTAD/ECLAC Regional Seminar on Environmental Policies and Market Access. Santafé de Bogota, 19–20 October 1993. See also, Stichting Milieukeur, "The Dutch Ecolabel", Box 13.3 in I. Giezeman and F. Verhees, "Eco-labelling: Practical Use of the Cradle-to-Grave Approach", in this volume.
6. LEI, op. cit.

11 Canada's Environmental Choice Program and its Impact on Developing-Country Trade

Maria Isolda P. Guevara, Ramesh Chaitoo and Murray G. Smith

INTRODUCTION

This chapter presents a case study of Canada's Environmental Choice Program (ECP) and its impact on developing-country trade.[1] Section I introduces the Canadian eco-labelling programme with a discussion of ECP's objectives and features. Section II focuses on the nature and extent of the trade impact of the ECP on developing countries. The concerns of developing countries regarding the impact of eco-labelling programmes on market entry and competitiveness are assessed against eco-labelling and ECP. In addition, this section includes an evaluation of the programme's impact on the behaviour of both consumers and producers, some of the key findings of the market analysis and programme evaluation undertaken by external consultants, and a summary of the new initiatives and priorities adopted by ECP following its own programme evaluation. Based on this information, an appraisal may be made of how developing-country trade is presently affected by the programme and how it may prospectively be affected by changes in ECP. Section III pinpoints how ECP and Canada can be of assistance to developing countries intending to apply for the EcoLogo and/or intending to establish a national labelling system of their own. Section IV summarizes the major findings of the study and presents a scenario of where eco-labelling is headed and how it may be transformed as an instrument of environmental policy.

I THE CANADIAN ENVIRONMENTAL CHOICE PROGRAM

A Background

The Canadian Environmental Choice Program represents one of the initiatives designed by Canada to support its commitment to the principle and practice of sustainable development. It recognizes that the state of the environment is attributable to the environmental impact not only of production but also of consumption of products and services. By designing a programme which certifies that a product or service, bearing its label, has a reduced burden on the environment, the Government provides Canadian consumers the benefit of informed environmental choice. In turn, producers and suppliers are encouraged to contribute to the protection and improvement of the environment by developing new products and services or instituting changes in either the product, process or method of production/provision of service.

The programme traces its beginnings to several legislative initiatives, programmes and strategies introduced in Canada subsequent to the release of the Brundtland Report in 1987 after the conclusion of the United Nations Conference on Environment and Development. One of these initiatives was the *Canadian Environmental Protection Act* (*CEPA*). Also known as Chapter 16, this federal legislation gives the Government the power to protect human health and the environment from the risks associated with the use of chemicals and from exposure to toxic substances. It empowered the Minister of the Environment "to formulate environmental quality guidelines specifying recommendations in quantitative or qualitative terms to support and maintain particular uses of the environment". The Minister is also given the authority "to release guidelines and environmental codes of practice specifying procedures, practices or release limits for environmental control".[2] Operating under the *CEPA*, ECP was formally established in 1988. In 1992, the programme was eventually integrated under the Environmental Citizenship Initiative of the Green Plan.[3] See Box 11.1 for information on the structure of ECP.

Box 11.1 Environmental Choice Program: structure

Advisory Board

Responsibility It provides ECP and Minister of Environment with advice on and recommendations on formulation of guidelines
Remarks The 16-member Board is appointed by the Minister. It is comprised of volunteers from manufacturing (40 per cent) and the rest from retail, health care, environmental and consumer groups and academic institutions

Environment Canada

Responsibility It undertakes programme management and guideline development

ECP

Responsibility It handles day-to-day operations of programme. It drafts initial guidelines. It sets up Review Committees. It implements the guidelines
Remarks Its 18-member staff work in Strategic Planning and Marketing, Technical Unit, and Customer Relations, Policy and Administration

Review Committee

Responsibility It examines draft guidelines and ensures that these are defensible, both technically and scientifically
Remarks It is made up of 12–18 members of which five are from industry*

Technical Agent

Responsibility It inspects, certifies and validates compliance of applicants and licensees with criteria and guidelines, through product tests and plant visits
Remarks Calian Communications Systems of Ottawa was contracted in 1992 for a three-year period. The first technical agent was Canadian Standards Association

In-house or External Experts

Responsibility It advises ECP in preparation of the Technical Briefing Note (TBN).
Remarks TBN provides comprehensive assessment of environmental, technical and market status of product category.

---

* In exceptional cases, there are also provisions for the Minister to appoint a panel of independent experts to review proposed final guidelines which, in the Minister's view, have caused significant controversy.

B The Objectives and Rationale of ECP

Environmental Choice Program is the official name for Canada's national eco-labelling program. It also refers to the organization (popularly known as "Environmental Choice") responsible for the programme's implementation. As a program, ECP is voluntary in nature. It constitutes a market-based instrument of environmental policy that complements regulations, protocols and other economic instruments. Its official mark or label is called the EcoLogo,[4] which consists of three doves intertwined to form a maple leaf, and encircled by the words "Environmental Choice – Choix environnemental". The stylized maple leaf embodying the EcoLogo symbolizes the cooperation between government, business and consumers. By working on all three levels, Environmental Choice intends to strike a balance between attaining environmental objectives through consumer awareness and purchase, and ensuring that industry is willing and able to meet its criteria. The EcoLogo is granted to products and services which have been tested and verified by Environmental Choice as being less harmful to, or which have a reduced burden on, the environment.

ECP was developed "to reduce the stress on the environment by encouraging the demand for and supply of environmentally responsible products and services". In support of this mandate and in order to be an effective market instrument, ECP recognizes that there must be public awareness for both the programme and the EcoLogo, that there must be a sufficient number of certified products and services in different categories available in the marketplace, and that its processes must be transparent, accessible and credible. The programme adopted three interdependent principles to guide its operation – credibility, relevance and responsiveness. The programme emphasizes environmental, scientific and technical credibility in the development of its criteria. In order to remain relevant, the programme must be able to meet its mandate. Finally, noting that its clients are consumers (household and institutional) and industry, the programme must be sensitive to their concerns and needs.[5]

C ECP Procedures

The process of eco-labelling in Canada can be broadly divided into four stages. These include:

- selection of a product category for eco-labelling;

- development of product/service guidelines;
- granting of licences to use the EcoLogo; and
- monitoring of licensee operations to ensure compliance with the guidelines.

1 Selection of Product Categories and Technical Briefing Note Preparation

Although anyone may propose a product category to be considered for eco-labelling, in practice, the majority of the suggestions generally come from industry. From the proposals, an issues paper is prepared for consideration by the Board. This paper explores the market and environmental impact of the product or service. Categories recommended to the Board for inclusion in the programme are those found to have the greatest potential for environmental improvement, those with sufficient volume of sales (i.e. the product is marketable) and those which enjoy a high level of interest from the industry sector (i.e. companies are willing and able to apply for the EcoLogo, thereby signifying the marketability of the guideline). After the Board has conducted its review, the categories may be accepted or rejected or further information may be requested.

Once a product category has been selected and appropriate Government departments have been consulted, a Technical Briefing Note (TBN) is prepared. The TBN examines variables which include the following: energy consumption and resource use; release of toxic chemicals during production, use and disposal of the product; the reduction of volume, weight and/or toxicity of packaging material; and other features which affect the product's recycling potential. It identifies the potential areas for reduction of the environmental burden. It also addresses the possible market shifts and other market impact expected as a result of increased production of, and demand for, ECP certified products and services.

2 Development of a Product/Service Guidelines

After the TBN is reviewed, the next step is the development of a guideline by ECP, with the assistance of the Review Committee. The guideline includes the following components.

(a) An impact assessment of the product or service Instead of a thorough life-cycle analysis (LCA) as a basis for developing a guideline, ECP conducts only a life-cycle review. It pinpoints the stage or

stages of production where the environmental burden is most obvious and significant, and then develops criteria around that stage(s) which will eliminate or reduce the burden. While a market analysis is also conducted to determine the volume of sales affected by the product or service and the degree to which there is industry acceptance, the environmental impact is given more emphasis.

(b) Definition or interpretation of terms Terms that are generally technical in nature are described or clarified. For example, in the guideline for water-based paints, the following terms are defined: "flash point", "aromatic hydrocarbons", "halogenated solvents", "volatile organic compounds", and "water-based".

(c) Coverage of the category This itemizes the types of products included in the category. For example, water-conserving products include water-conserving showerheads, toilets, toilet retrofit devices, faucets and aerators, and trickle valves.

(d) Product/service-specific requirements ECP establishes product/service-specific guidelines that generally pertain to product content, technical, safety and performance standards. ECP utilizes both product standards and process and production method (PPM) standards, both of which may or may not affect product characteristics. As its main objective remains environmental, ECP ensures that its standards address both consumption and production externalities. Depending on the product category, recycled and post-consumer fibre content may be specified.[6] As well, there are requirements on the packaging content when the package is part of the final product, as in the case of laundry and automatic dishwashing detergents. It prescribes that certain products must not be formulated or manufactured with a certain input.

For production externalities that take place in the country of origin, ECP does not require compliance with its product-related PPMs. Compliance with applicable local environmental standards is sufficient. However, once the good is imported into Canada, and if it is to qualify for the EcoLogo, it must meet ECP's environmental criteria with respect to the product's consumption and disposal.

The criteria that ECP establishes are intended to allow a leadership component of industry to qualify for the EcoLogo. It is currently expected that the product/service-specific guidelines would be met by only 20 per cent of products in a given category. The objective is to get the industry leaders to set the example of environmental leadership which other companies are expected to follow if they want to compete successfully. This threshold level of 20 per cent has been graphically illustrated as that "notional" level where at a given level of stringency in criteria, a specific percentage of the market is willing and able to meet the criteria and have their products or services licensed, resulting in environmental benefits. If the criteria are too stringent, no company will be able to qualify for a label. Consequently, no licenses are awarded, no eco-labelled products or services become available, and no environmental benefits are realized. On the other extreme, if the criteria are too lax, there is neither incentive nor pressure for companies to apply for a license. Therefore, no eco-labelled products or services become available, and no environmental benefits are realized.

The criteria chosen for each category are based on the best information available, on standards that are extensively utilized (that is, close to international standards), and which do not run contrary to existing standards set by Canada's standardization bodies, as well as existing national laws, initiatives and regulations, both in Canada and other countries.

(e) General Requirements Common to all guidelines are the following general requirements which state that:

- The product must meet or exceed all applicable governmental and industrial safety and performance standards; and
- The product must be collected, transported and manufactured in such a manner that all steps of the process including the disposal of waste products arising therefrom will meet the requirements of the Canadian Environmental Protection Act (CEPA) and all applicable government regulations.

ECP clearly recognizes as sufficient, compliance with local standards on industrial safety and performance required in the production or processing of the product. Exporters to Canada need to comply only with their local standards. As it does not consider itself in the enforcement business, ECP relies solely on the attestation of the company's chief executive officer that all pertinent standards have been met.

(f) Notices This section refers more to the programme's requirement that manufacturers or importers adhere to the policies and targets stated in the National Packaging Protocol (NPP)[7] and to adopt and follow the Code of Preferred Packaging Practices.[8] Any reference to a

standard means its latest edition. Depending on the product, this portion of the guideline also apprises producers and importers that some criteria may be evaluated or new requirements added from time to time.

(g) Verification Procedure With respect to verification requirements, companies ensure that ECP's technical agent has access to "relevant quality control and production records and production facilities on an unannounced basis". The company is also required to provide ECP with the required attestation from the chief executive officer, as well as advise ECP, in writing, in the event of a violation.

(h) Licensing Conditions ECP specifies where the EcoLogo will appear, what words or phrases should accompany it, that the wordings be in accordance with its Graphic Standards Manual (GSM), and that any accompanying advertising complies with the requirements of the guideline, the license agreement and the GSM.

Once the initial guidelines are prepared, the Advisory Board scrutinizes the draft and the supporting documentation (i.e. the TBN and comments from the Review Committee). If satisfied, the Board recommends that the guideline be released for public review and comment. The notice on the ongoing formulation of a guideline is then announced in the *Canada Gazette*, two national newspapers (currently *The Globe and Mail* and *La Presse*), and a Ministerial press release. Written public comments are invited.

The comments received during the public review period may cause ECP to modify the guideline. Members of the Review Committee are then provided with a final opportunity to examine any proposed revisions to the guideline. The ECP Advisory Board reviews the guideline with the relevant documentation from the public review comments and the Review Committee. When the Board is satisfied that all relevant issues have been appropriately addressed, and all interested parties have had an opportunity to comment, the draft guideline is recommended to the Minister of the Environment. The final guideline is issued by the Minister, under the Canadian Environmental Protection Act, and announcements are made in the official Government publication, *Canada Gazette*, as well as national media and press releases.[9]

After the guidelines are established, they may, in due course, be formally reviewed by ECP as new information and technology become available and as more companies are able to meet the standards. This is to guarantee that environmental leadership continues to be achieved while ensuring that companies are able to qualify for the label in order to increase the number of EcoLogoed products and services in the marketplace.

3 Applying for the EcoLogo and Awarding of Licenses

Once product guidelines have been published, any manufacturer/supplier or importer of a product in this category may apply for the EcoLogo. All ECP guidelines are made available upon request. Enquiries about the programme or applications for the EcoLogo should be addressed to ECP.

The applicant is sent an application form, a copy of the standard license agreement, information on fees payable and a copy of the relevant product guideline. After an official application for the EcoLogo has been received, the ECP's technical agent provides the applicant with an estimate of the costs relating to verification and testing of the company's product for compliance with ECP standards and guidelines. These procedures also involve initial plant visits by the agent, and related expenses such as travel and per diem, which are paid for by the applicant. The one-time certification fee may vary with the product and the manufacturer, depending on the extent and complexity of the product testing, the number of products and plant sites involved. As well, there are additional costs borne when additional visits and product testings are undertaken to re-establish compliance.

If the product or service meets the ECP guideline, a license, granting the use of the EcoLogo, is issued to the company for a three-year period. Once the license to use the EcoLogo registered mark is granted, the licensee pays an annual fee based on estimated gross annual sales of the certified product. For sales up to \$100 000, the fee is \$300; for sales up to \$250 000 it is \$750; for sales up to \$500 000, the fee is \$1500; for sales up to \$1 million it is \$2500; and for sales in excess of \$1 million the fee is \$5000.[10]

4 Monitoring of Licensees

Over the term of the license, licensees must submit annual attestations confirming their compliance with the terms of the contract. As well, the technical agent verifies continuing compliance with the guideline. Under the terms of the contract, representatives of Environmental Choice may visit the contracting party's factory or other premises at any time. Costs relating to inspections are covered by the license fees.[11]

In principle, if non-compliance is found after the licensing agreement is in place, the ECP may choose to terminate or suspend the agreement. They may also require that the firm try its best to remove the EcoLogo from the particular product. ECP staff indicated that there have been a few violations of the guidelines by licensees, but these were not deliberate or malicious.[12]

D Current Status of the Program

At the time this case study was completed in June 1994, ECP had final guidelines for 29 products and categories, with four under review. Four had drafts under discussion while eleven had guidelines under development. (See Box 11.2 for a detailed listing of the categories by stage of guideline development.) Of those products with final guidelines, only sixteen guidelines have licensees, most of which are concentrated in the paints and fine paper categories. This represents 150 companies covering a total of 65 products.[13]

The current licensees under ECP include domestic and foreign manufacturers, as well as Canadian distributors and importers of such foreign-made products as paints, fine paper and shopping bags. There are presently fourteen foreign companies with licenses to use the EcoLogo. They are all from the United States. There are no licensees from developing countries. Instead, there are suppliers, for example, from China, Pakistan, Taiwan and India which presently supply either the raw material or the finished product to Canadian distributors and manufacturers of shopping bags who are licensed to use the EcoLogo.

These statistics are bound to change significantly over the years as ECP implements its action plan. ECP is aware that it must enhance public awareness for both the programme and the EcoLogo by expanding its product base and increasing its visibility in the retail sector (food stores, general merchandise stores, pharmacies and gasoline stations). It recognizes that it must conduct itself as a business – with products to develop and sell and targets to achieve. Therefore, product labelling and procurement (corporate and institutional purchasing) are now its two main business lines. To help identify and assign priorities to product and service categories for the next two years, ECP will be guided by a number of parameters: environmental benefits to be derived from programme coverage, the volume of sales in Canada and industry reception.[14] Therefore, ECP expects to expand its current base of operating guidelines to 60 guidelines. It will look into developing generic guidelines which will allow ECP to license products for which there is no licensee base and/or market size to warrant a formal guideline.

Box 11.2 ECP product categories (as of March 1994)

Finalized guidelines				*Discussion drafts*	*Draft guidelines under development*
Automotive engine oil*	Residential waste composting systems	Automatic dishwashing detergents	Diapers	Sanitary paper from recycled paper	• Vegetable-oil-based lubricants • Water heater • Retrofit devices • Residential heating system • Office and home printing equipment • Inks • Wallboards • Windows • Driveway sealers • Photofinishing services • Industrial cleaners degreasers • Printing services
Products from recycled plastic	Automotive fuels	Batteries: non-rechargeable	Laundry detergents	Unbleached paper products	
Batteries	Reusable utility bags	Domestic water heaters	Adhesives	Bleached paper products	
Fine paper from recycled paper	Major household appliances	Building materials: acoustical products	Sealants and caulking compound	General purpose cleaners	
Miscellaneous products from recycled paper	Energy-efficient lamps	Dry cleaning services	Paints: water-based*		
Newsprint from recycled paper	Diaper services	Building materials: thermal insulation			
Paints: reduced pollution solvent-based*	Water conserving products*	Toner cartridges			
Heat recovery ventilators	Compost	Engine coolant concentrate			

* Final guidelines under review.

ECP is also working towards the recognition of, and preference for, EcoLogoed products and services in the procurement practices of both corporate institutions and the Government. Federal procurement alone is considered to substantially help increase the visibility of and acceptance of the programme and the label.[15] Therefore, ECP is examining the possibility of having its certified products and services listed in the catalogues of procurement agencies, school boards, as well as municipal and provincial Governments. The concept of authorized use is also being studied whereby purchasers of EcoLogoed papers will be allowed to display the logo on their printed materials.

II ECP AND ITS IMPACT ON DEVELOPING COUNTRIES

Although eco-labelling programmes are voluntary, their trade impact remains a major issue because eco-labelled products are tradeable and guidelines incorporate standards and administrative procedures which may have a trade impact upon their application. The actual trade impact may be favourable in terms of market opportunities, or unfavourable if trade barriers are created.

A Eco-Labelling and Trade Barriers

At meetings of the UNCTAD and the GATT Group on Environmental Measures and International Trade, developing countries raised their concerns that the implementation of eco-labelling programmes can restrict market entry and undermine competitiveness. As eco-labelling, in its present form, is neither a law, regulation nor mandatory practice, it cannot be considered a trade barrier – i.e. a constraint that grants any advantage, favour, privilege, or immunity to one country but not another, or solely to domestic production. As long as eco-labelling is voluntary, it cannot be considered a discriminatory trade measure either, like customs duties charges, or discriminatory taxes or regulations. However, eco-labelling does affect production patterns by influencing the behaviour of consumers, producers and service providers. By certifying that an eco-labelled product or service is environmentally responsible, eco-labelling programmes assure environmentally conscious consumers of the credibility and soundness of the environmental claim behind the label. Producers who manufacture products and provide services that have a reduced burden on the environment are able to supply what consumers want, and they can expect increased sales and profits, as well as an improved environmental image which helps solidify and expand their captive market. While eco-labelling has an impact on production patterns, its impact on trade patterns is not significant since eco-labelling is voluntary and therefore does not have the same impact as regulations, taxes and fees which are mandatory in nature. Market entry is not dictated by the presence of an eco-label on a product.

While the foregoing observations confirm that eco-labelling is not a trade barrier *de jure* and does not have the purpose of a trade barrier, it is not precluded from having the effect of a trade barrier. Eco-labelling guidelines embody testing, labelling, packaging and certification requirements, which upon application may have the effect of technical barriers to trade. The concerns of developing countries which were raised at UNCTAD and GATT meetings[16] pertain specifically to this issue. Following is a summary of their views.

- First, the selection of products and services for coverage in an eco-labelling programme is principally dictated by domestic *environmental interests*. As such, this may limit, if not entirely exclude, participation of foreign producers whose national environmental interests are different and whose *economic interests* provide much of the impetus behind efforts to sustain market access in developed countries which are environmentally conscious and active.

  There is also the question of transparency. Concern has been raised about the opportunities for foreign producers to be made aware of existing and emerging eco-labelling programmes, and their product selection and guidelines.
- Second, eco-labelling programmes generally rely on some approach to LCA. The concern of developing countries arises when an LCA determines that the environmental burden, for which criteria are established, takes place in the early stages of the product's life cycle – raw material extraction and/or production. Should these phases take place outside the country's own territory, imports are bound to be affected.

  While the environmental impetus behind such criteria may be justified, the standards-based criteria established may be inappropriate and difficult for developing country producers to meet. Such difficulties may be associated with their level of economic development, resource endowments, technological capacity and financial resources. Some developing countries may face discrimination if their economies rely on a specific raw material which is excluded by a standard on PPM. A change in product technology or the adoption of a new technology may be costly to undertake. The goods, services and technology may be available on favourable terms only to domestic producers. In some cases, exporters may be compelled to source their inputs from importing countries, as may be the case with manufacturers who must meet recycled content or post-consumer fibre content, but are limited by the absence or lack of recycling facilities. Thus, the risk of losing markets is both real and potential.

- Third, concern has also been raised over the loss of international competitiveness as a result of higher costs of production or operation associated with compliance with eco-labelling criteria. This is particularly the case when price is the basis for competitive advantage. Costs incurred in applying for an eco-label include those resulting from required testing, verification, certification and licensing. Costs tend to increase if standards are differentiated at national, regional, provincial and local levels. Furthermore, if a manufacturer supplies the same product to different countries with their respective eco-labelling programmes, compliance with eco-labelling guidelines becomes more cumbersome and costly for foreign producers. This may sometimes result in the same product having to undergo different adjustments, in terms of product content, production and process methods, just to accommodate the various requirements of different markets. Opportunity costs may also be incurred when delays in obtaining a license due to a complicated or rigorous licensing procedure result in the failure of producers to meet the market launching of a product.

Regardless of their country of origin, all producers must meet the same criteria. Yet, it is clear that their ability to cover the costs will vary significantly across countries. Producers from developing countries may be disadvantaged by their size, relatively smaller market shares and limited financial resources (in addition to competition for the usage of existing resources). On top of the costs associated with testing, certification and licensing, manufacturers may be compelled to adjust their production runs to meet required changes in input or technology. Unless they are assured of a market base and an ability to pass on costs to the consumers, such producers risk weakening their overall competitiveness.

Although there may be negative effects on the competitiveness of developing-country exports because of the costs of compliance, there also may be greater relative benefits in certain circumstances. If consumers have a negative image of particular products from particular countries, then an EcoLogo may help overcome that negative image.

B ECP and its Trade Impact

As described above, developing countries have pointed to specific features of and procedures in eco-labelling which may have the effect of a *de facto* trade barrier. This segment of the report ascertains if such concerns are legitimate in the context of the Canadian programme.

1 Product Selection

As the programme currently stands, ECP's product and service categories do not affect developing countries since they are not of export interest or advantage to them. In the first two years of its operation, ECP focused on the environmental benefits of recycling and pollution reduction. This was evident in the categories it selected during the period – automotive engine oil, fine paper from recycled paper, paints, composting systems for residential waste, reusable utility bags and products from recycled plastic.

Over the next few years however, ECP is expanding its product base to ensure that certified products and services become available in the market. To create and expand consumer awareness of the programme and the EcoLogo, focus will be given on products and services used often, and in large quantities, by households, corporations, government and institutions. Product selection will also continue to be guided by Canadian environmental priorities, even if there is no deliberate policy to exclude developing-country concerns.

Although the products under consideration have not been made public pending submission of the proposals to the Board, ECP has confirmed that they are not considering the inclusion of textiles, clothing, footwear and tropical timber as is the case with the European Union. Instead, they are looking into the eco-labelling of processed food. Since Canada already imports from developing countries, eco-labelling of food products may have a potentially significant impact on developing-country trade.

Nevertheless, it should be made clear that even if more product categories are brought on stream and their coverage expanded, the impact on developing countries will depend on whether or not these new products or services constitute their major foreign-exchange earners. If they do, their export to Canada should not be hampered if they fail to qualify for the EcoLogo. However, the opposite holds true if eco-labelling in Canada becomes widespread as a result of enhanced consumer awareness and preference for EcoLogoed products and services. Inevitably, both domestic and foreign producers and suppliers may find it in their best economic interests to have their products or services display the EcoLogo.

On the issue of participation in the product selection process, the ECP is open to the public. While it does not actively solicit input from overseas due to cost considerations, it does not exclude developing countries from participating. In practice, however, the products suggested for consideration come from several groups, with the bulk originating from local industry. Unless foreign producers operate in Canada or are represented by their subsidiaries or affiliates in Canada, it will not be possible for the former to be represented at all times when deliberations on product selection take place.

2 *Criteria Development*

Use of product life-cycle analysis In the absence of a uniform approach to LCA and on account of cost considerations, ECP conducts only a very rough life-cycle review on its selected products, effectively reducing the number and types of criteria being developed for each stage, as well as the cost and the time associated with compliance. A review of the current set of final guidelines of the programme reveals that environmental criteria have focused on waste management and pollution reduction, as well as energy and water conservation. Major concerns arise however, if the LCA evolves into a customary practice with an international methodology that is exhaustive. If it becomes comprehensive according to the SETAC (Society of Environmental Toxicology and Chemistry) definition, the use of the LCA may become more problematic for developing-country producers, especially if in-depth assessments result in the identification of the environmental burdens at the initial stages of the product life cycle. Yet, under present circumstances, the use of any form of the LCA does not affect developing-country trade because the inability of a foreign product to meet ECP guidelines developed from such an analysis does not restrict its market entry into Canada.

Use of standards The standards utilized by ECP are generally close to international standards or reflect what are generally used. It also ensures that the standards it uses do not run contrary to or duplicate existing standards on performance, quality and safety. A scrutiny of existing guidelines discloses that international, American, Canadian or provincial standards are used. While ECP utilizes production method standards, it does not require compliance with these PPMs as long as the process takes place outside Canada. Attestation to the exporting company's compliance with own national environmental laws and regulations is sufficient. It is only when the product is to be consumed and disposed of within Canadian soil, and only if it is to qualify for the EcoLogo, that it must meet pertinent ECP environmental criteria.

Another issue that deserves examination is whether the standards are absolute or relative in nature. Absolute standards are more stable and are clearly known and disseminated internationally, whereas relative standards tend to be dictated by domestic industry and what they have been able to achieve as a result of technological progress or innovation. ECP uses absolute standards where applicable. Additional product-specific standards are developed locally, and relative standards are also used when criteria are upgraded to reflect technological and market developments.

Threshold level Since ECP guidelines will tend to reflect Canadian conditions and priorities, only Canadian companies may be expected to meet the criteria and, therefore, account for the 20 per cent of the market that is able to pass the threshold. Over time, however, as a higher percentage of the market is able to meet the criteria, and as technological progress is achieved on an industry scale, ECP will upgrade the criteria in order to maintain the same threshold.

The 20 per cent level has not been established deliberately to exclude foreign suppliers, especially those from developing countries, and cannot be seen as a barrier to trade, since obtaining the EcoLogo is not a condition for market entry.

Transparency of criteria All the procedures of ECP are transparent. In fact, its Design Statement was prepared to present a "clear and public record" of what the programme is all about.[17] While the detailed guidelines are not printed in their entirety in the *Canada Gazette*, announcements on the guidelines' final release and availability are made in this official publication. The *Canada Gazette* is circulated to all embassies and it is standard operation for trade offices to scan them. Exporters may deal directly with the Canadian embassies and consulates to obtain information about products and services with operating guidelines.

As well, ECP information kits can be obtained readily from ECP and overseas enquiries about the programme are actively entertained.

Participation in criteria development The entire ECP process is open to public participation. While there may be limits to the number of persons involved in the Advisory Board and review panels, representation of various interest groups is at least ensured. It is in the public review process of the draft product guidelines where public participation is encouraged. The 60-day review process enables anyone to consult with ECP and present their views on the guidelines under review. While foreign producers may not be able to actively and regularly participate at the stages of product selection and formulation of the criteria, they have the opportunity to present their views and concerns during the public review. This ability rests critically on their physical presence and their ability to devote time to the process. Otherwise, the tendency will be for foreign exporters to become aware of the guidelines after all the details have been finalized.

While the process is open to the public, the content and direction of eco-labelling remain tied to domestic environmental interests. It has been suggested that there is a need to draw the line with respect to involving foreign producers in the establishment of product criteria. But if developing-country producers are not allowed to participate, this will raise the issue of discrimination.[18] To avoid this, a possible solution is for foreign producers from developing countries to work closely with (green) Canadian consumer groups and environmental organizations. Such a cooperation may be facilitated if the foreign producer demonstrates that its products are environmentally less harmful and therefore deserve the EcoLogo. Given the increasing environmental consciousness and activism of Canadian consumers and environmental groups, some support may be expected.

Compliance testing and verification Competitiveness can be undermined if administration-related costs become prohibitive. Companies that operate plants located outside Ottawa, where the technical agent is located, can incur higher costs because of the travel-related expenses involved. If plants are located overseas, the costs may be further magnified as was the experience of small licensees.[19] Costs can also increase, the longer it takes for the technical agent to complete testing and verification. This happens when more products are involved, when processes are complex, and when more plants have to be inspected. In order to reduce costs, ECP has advised its licensees that site visits will be coordinated.[20] Moreover, as ECP's technical agency has eighteen inspectors operating across the country, testing and certification of applicants may be facilitated and made cost-effective.

C Impact of ECP on Consumers and Producers

Changes in the behaviour of both consumers and producers as a result of the ECP explain the conditions under which domestic and foreign suppliers compete within the Canadian market. In particular, would help ascertain if overseas suppliers face pressure when their products or services do not bear the EcoLogo or fail to qualify for the EcoLogo.

1 ECP and the Consumer

According to the Environmental Monitor, awareness for the EcoLogo increased to 51 per cent in 1993 from 19 per cent in 1990.[21] While such ratios seem encouraging, they should not be taken at face value. It is important to know whether such awareness was aided (with leading questions or explanations) or unaided (requiring no prompting). ECP noted that while specifically designed polls over the last three years found that awareness has increased and was over 50 per cent in July 1993, the level of awareness which was not prompted remained below 10 per cent. In a public survey conducted for Hickling Corporation in 1993, it was also revealed that 64 per cent of the respondents expressed willingness to pay 10 per cent more for a product bearing the EcoLogo compared with 81 per cent in 1990.

There is a disparity between the expressed willingness and the actual purchasing behaviour, which has been ascribed to the following factors: real or expected higher prices of environmentally oriented products; additional actions required to realize advertised environmental benefits (need to separate and return recyclables); limited availability of labelled products; availability or lack of infrastructure needed for such activities as recycling or composting; and continued scepticism regarding environmental claims and brand loyalty.[22] As is currently the case in Canada, this willingness is quickly tempered during periods of economic recession when price becomes the major determinant in consumer choice.

The poor visibility of the programme has been attributed to both the types of products and services covered by the programme and the limited number of products with operating guidelines. ECP has acknowledged that poor attention has been paid to the consumer market in the selection of products and services. The retail sector which serves as the outlet for close to 40 per cent of all economic activity in Canada has not been significantly touched nor targeted by ECP. Another segment of the Canadian market in which ECP has not successfully made any inroads is in the federal, provincial and municipal levels of government. Although the federal Government started to promote better environmental choices in is procurement policies, the Code of Environmental Stewardship recommends neither preferential treatment for the EcoLogoed products nor environmentally labelled products in general. On the other hand, municipal Governments across Canada are now being forced to pay close attention to environmental issues. Several municipalities in Ontario and British Columbia already require that their purchasing officers buy products which carry the EcoLogo, in preference to other substitutes. The main thrust of this environmental consciousness can be traced to pollution and solid waste management problems at landfills.

In summary, developing-country trade has not been seriously affected by eco-labelling in Canada because of the programme's limited coverage and consequent limited visibility, especially in the retail sector. The extent of consumer demand for eco-labelled products and services has not been significant enough to affect marketability of imports. In the long run, however, suppliers from developing countries may be affected as ECP increases its presence in the consumer market.

2 *ECP and the Producer*

Another approach to determining if developing-country trade is affected by the Canadian programme is to gauge ECP's impact on producers and suppliers of products and services for which guidelines and/or licenses have been issued. One of the reasons why companies may not be willing to apply for the Logo is the difficulty associated with meeting the required threshold of 20 per cent. Another factor is its inability to discern any advantage in having its products or services certified by the program. On account of the programme's limited production selection, the level of consumer awareness is correspondingly insignificant. Therefore, it creates the perception that there are no significant widespread commercial benefits to be derived from displaying the EcoLogo. Moreover, while a percentage has expressed a preference for environmentally responsible products and services, there is still a general reluctance to pay a premium for them. Therefore, under present conditions, manufacturers and suppliers face no pressure or incentive to apply for the EcoLogo in order to enhance their products' marketability.

In recapitulation, the foregoing investigation concludes that the ECP is not a significant barrier to developing country trade. The ability of developing countries to supply the Canadian market is not restricted if their products or services do not apply for the EcoLogo or are unable to qualify for a license. Moreover, overseas suppliers do not face stiff competition from eco-labelled like products and services because of the limited number of EcoLogoed goods and services available in the market. The subsequent low levels of consumer awareness of the programme and its label has not given industry the incentive to apply for the EcoLogo as a means to market its products and services. In addition, for overseas suppliers intending to apply for the EcoLogo, the program, as it is designed, ensures that its production selection, guideline development and administrative procedures do not deliberately discriminate against any country.

At the same time, it is interesting to note that unless Canada's trade structure changes, developing countries will not be affected significantly by developments in the Canadian market. The bulk of Canada's trade is with the United States. In 1993, total Canadian imports from all sources amounted to C$166.2 billion.[23] Of this amount, 67 per cent came from the United States alone,[24] and this is expected to increase due to further economic integration with the United States.[25] On the other hand, while trade with developing countries in Asia, Africa, and Latin America have reflected some considerable growth last year on an aggregate basis, these could be attributed to a few and large countries. Comparatively, total imports from developing countries, with the exception of China and the newly industrializing countries (NICs), are still insignificant against those from other developed-country trade partners. In terms of products, Canada's major imports are technology-intensive manufactured goods and services, while its imports from developing countries are generally low-cost consumer goods. Excluding consumer electronics from the NICs, the main product groups of export interest to developing countries are foodstuffs, textiles and clothing.

Over the long run, however, conditions in the Canadian market are expected to change. The impact on developing-country trade will become more relevant when Canada increases its trade volume with developing countries and when the eco-labelling programme increases its product coverage to include products of export importance to developing countries. More importantly, the impact will be critical if eco-labelling in Canada develops into an industry norm. Foreign suppliers may find in eco-labelling a useful strategy for competition, and developing-country suppliers may use eco-labelling to build up an environment-friendly image in the Canadian market. The nature and stringency of prospective ECP guidelines will be crucial to determining its impact in the future. In this case, developing countries in particular will need technical and financial assistance to enable them to comply with the criteria and guidelines that may increasingly become rigid as environmental protection is stepped up in Canada.

III ECO-LABELLING AND DEVELOPING COUNTRIES: HOW ECP CAN BE OF ASSISTANCE

The knowledge of how ECP has fared these past five years and what its new initiatives and priorities are, can provide a picture of the likely evolution of the Canadian programme and how developing country trade can prospectively be affected. As earlier cited, three situations must concur if developing country trade is expected to be affected in a significant way: Canada expands its trade with developing countries; the programme coverage is enlarged to cover products of export interest to developing countries; and eco-labelling in Canada develops into an industry norm. Under the condition that the Canadian consumer becomes increasingly discerning in his/her purchases on the basis of environmental considerations, it would be vitally important for foreign suppliers to project an image of environmental quality. Therefore, developing countries are faced with two options: (1) to have their products and services certified by ECP, or (2) to develop their own labelling programmes. For each of these options, Canada can be of assistance to developing countries.

A Apply for the EcoLogo

As the criteria established by ECP will be dictated by local environmental imperatives, adjustments to accommodate developing country trade concerns and different environmental conditions may not be feasible. Therefore, all that the ECP can do is ensure that in the programme's implementation, like products and services are not discriminated against on the basis of their origin, that its criteria continue to have scientific bases and rely on international standards as much as possible, and that its process remain transparent and open to public participation.

On the question of complying with ECP criteria and guidelines, developing countries may need either or both financial and technological assistance in order to adapt their product/services and processes accordingly. The transfer of affordable and appropriate technology for "greener" products and services and/or cleaner production technologies would significantly contribute to the reduction of environmental burdens at the stages of production and processing which would be a preventive rather than just an end-of-pipe solution such as waste minimization and pollution prevention at the stages of consumption and final disposal. In addition to technological transfers, Canada can provide financial support to help cover the substantial capital investments that developing country exporters (especially small-sized companies) will incur if they are to comply with Canada's eco-labelling criteria and guidelines.

B Developing Own Labelling System

Even as a voluntary program, eco-labelling has been emerging as a popular instrument of environmental policy. At present, such programmes exist in 21 countries, some of which are trading partners and competitors.[26] However, as new programmes are introduced worldwide, trade barriers may arise if the programmes are highly diverse in form and substance. To address this potential, a number of approaches have been introduced in which Canada can play a leadership or collaborative role. This is relevant for developing countries who wish to develop their own eco-labelling programmes.

1 Adoption of Part or All of an Existing Program

When developing a programme, developing countries can refer to an existing programme, particularly the pioneering German Blue Angel Programme and Canada's ECP. Or, they can design their own programmes. Several inquiries have been made of the ECP from both developed and developing countries, and many country programmes have been based on it such as India's Ecomark, Singapore's Green Label and New Zealand's Environmental Choice Programme. A survey revealed that some of the ECP features such as the public review process, some guidelines (which some countries have adopted in their entirety) and fee structure were found appealing by developing countries.

While ECP is quite open to discussing its programme with other countries interested in developing their own programmes, it clearly stresses that ECP has been designed to address Canadian environmental imperatives, conditions, priorities and preferences. Therefore, in its current form, it may not be replicable, transferable and appropriate to meet developing-country needs. It advises that when designing a programme, several elements should be looked into. Prior to designing a programme, it must identify and prioritize the environmental problems it wants addressed by the programme, its resources and institutional support. When designing the programme it should include time frames, management and staffing requirements, an initial focus on product or service categories given its environmental objectives, costing, dialogue and coordination between industry groups, public sector and government, whether the certifying body is government or private, who will be the technical agent, procedural fairness, the establishment of an advisory board to lend credibility, availability and access to information, public participation, as well as the processes of selection, guideline development, verification and licensing.[27]

Based on its own experience, ECP has a lot to offer developing countries. As one of the pioneers in eco-labelling, ECP developed its own processes of market analysis, guideline development, certification, audit and licensing procedures. Therefore, ECP can assist developing countries in a number of specific areas: conduct of market research and analysis as a basis for the national programme's product selection and scope; life-cycle analysis and environmental impact assessment as the basis for selecting standards and developing overall product guidelines; design of management, marketing and administrative procedures behind the operation of a national eco-labelling programme; and the development of procedures and related training of certification and testing bodies.[28]

2 *Mutual Recognition*

As new programmes emerge, barriers to trade may be expected if there is considerable diversity in the programmes which translates to different criteria for the same types of products and services that an exporter may supply to different markets. The matter of standardization had been raised as a solution. However, this approach has been found to be neither practical nor desirable because it would negate the legitimate differences which exist across countries with respect to environmental conditions, preferences and priorities. Therefore, the only way to reduce barriers that may arise from diversity is through harmonization or mutual recognition.

Mutual recognition is defined as the acceptance that the criteria used for awarding labels or the labels themselves, although not the same, are equivalent to that used or awarded by another.[29] In this way, technical barriers to trade are reduced and market fragmentation resulting from diversity of national standards is averted.[30] Mutual recognition can also be in the form of exchange of information, exchange of guidelines, exchange of licenses, use of internationally acceptable certification systems, and training of local standardization entities. Mutual recognition is further facilitated by the evolution of national programmes based on existing ones. Another factor is the adoption of an internationally agreed set of terms and definitions, as well as principles pertaining to the use of international standards, the development of standards which are scientifically and technically defensible, the adoption of an approach or methodology for LCA, transparency of process, as well as public access and participation.

3 International Labels

The introduction of internationally based labels in place of individual national labels has been suggested as a means to avert the confusion resulting from the presence of different national labels for the same product or service category. An example (although on a regional scale) is the European Flower which is the single eco-label used by the member countries of the European Union on different products for which they have been responsible for developing criteria. Other examples include *Projekt Tropenwald* and the Forest Stewardship Council.

IV CONCLUSIONS

This chapter has argued that under the status quo, developing-country trade is not significantly affected by Canada's Environmental Choice Programme. The reasons include the following.

- Canada's eco-labelling programme is voluntary. Developing countries wishing to export to Canada can sell their products and services in the Canadian market, even if they do not apply for the EcoLogo, or are unable to qualify for the EcoLogo.
- Canada's eco-labelling programme does not have the effect of a trade barrier, even if it incorporates standards and conformity assessment procedures in its guidelines. Product selection and guideline development are open to public review and comment. Its criteria are based on existing standards.
- Focusing on the programme alone, ECP's current selection of products and services are not of export interest or advantage to developing countries.

However, with the new initiatives and priorities set out by ECP, market conditions are expected to change. Both visibility and public acceptance of the programme and the EcoLogo may significantly increase over the years. While its selection of categories will continue to be influenced by Canadian environmental conditions and imperatives, marketing factors will also be taken into consideration to ensure that the products are marketable and that the guidelines developed for the categories are marketable as well. As both households and corporate/institutional sectors continue to be targeted by ECP's marketing efforts, Canadian consumers may be expected to increasingly demand EcoLogoed products and services.

Against this scenario, eco-labelling in Canada can develop into an industry norm where manufacturers and suppliers realize that it would be to their economic advantage if their products and services bear the EcoLogo. Consequently, foreign suppliers will have to do the same if they are to compete effectively in the Canadian market. In this regard, the products and services eventually selected by ECP, the coverage of such categories, as well as the nature and stringency of ECP guidelines will be of material importance to developing countries. This also assumes, however, that developing countries are successful in increasing their market share in the Canadian market.

Assuming that Canadian manufacturers increasingly source their requirements outside North America, then ECP offers market opportunities for developing countries on the basis of both existing categories and those under consideration. Suppliers of alternative shopping bag materials such as jute, cloth and nylon can create market niches. Developing countries can supply cereal crops, sugar beets, waste agricultural products, as well as wood and wood waste for fermentation by Canadian manufacturers of ethanol. Wood and wood-based materials can be supplied for the manufacture of fine paper. Now that agro-based food is under consideration by ECP with Agricultural Canada, another market opportunity is signalled for developing countries.

As more developing countries supply the Canadian market, they would need assistance in complying with the requirements of ECP. Therefore, technical and financial assistance in a variety of areas can be provided by Canada. They can also be assisted in developing their own labelling programmes as a market-based instrument of environmental policy. This would help facilitate the mutual recognition of eco-labelling programmes worldwide.

Meanwhile, one area which needs further study is the issue of packaging and its impact on exports from developing countries. The *Na-*

tional Packaging Protocol which has set specific targets for diversion of packaging from the waste stream, will be applied to both domestic and imported packaging.[31] In addition, government policies and practices such as procurement will be developed and implemented to support the achievement of the objectives of the Protocol. Although the Protocol is not mandatory, it has had great impact. Canadian industry has accepted it in principle, and is working towards meeting the targets.[32]

There is also a fast increasing trend towards packaging that can be reused or recycled. Considering that recycling and reuse of packaging material is fast becoming the norm, there will be pressures on companies intending to market their products in Canada to arrange for the reuse or recycling of the packaging materials within Canada.[33] Alternatively, it may become necessary to return the packaging waste to the originating country. In any event, it will be costly or practically impossible to address this problem. However, domestic companies will not tolerate the fact that foreign competitors operate under less stringent conditions regarding their responsibility for the packaging waste generated by the transportation and consumption of their products. While waste reduction in Canada is not mandatory as in Denmark or Germany, ECP requires manufacturers to adhere to the targets of the National Packaging Protocol and to adopt and follow the Code of Preferred Packaging Practices.

On the whole, eco-labelling has emerged as a popular instrument of environmental policy which influences consumer and producer behaviour. Since eco-labelling is directed at products and services which are tradeable and eco-labelling programmes use standards and conformity assessment procedures, the instrument's trade impact remains a potential major concern, even if eco-labelling is voluntary in nature. In this regard, international cooperation, through consultation or international agreement, is fundamental if such programmes are to succeed in meeting their environmental objective while ensuring that they do not create or have the effect of restricting market entry or undermining competitiveness. Harmonization efforts at the international level are still at the discussion stage but its importance is underscored by the need to ensure that countries which supply the same products to different markets, do not face obstacles to trade in the course of complying with the respective guidelines of a number of eco-labelling programmes already in existence or in the process of development.

Notes

1. This paper is the abridged version of a study undertaken by the Centre for Trade Policy and Law for the International Development Research Centre (IDRC) as part of UNCTAD's larger study of the impact of environmental policy instruments, including eco-labelling, on developing-country trade. This case study was presented at both the preliminary and final workshops on "Eco-labelling and International Trade" which were held respectively in Ottawa on 14 September 1993 and Geneva on 28–29 June 1994.
2. This refers to Subsection 8(1). Meanwhile, subsection 8(2) stipulates that "the objectives, guidelines and codes of practice referred to shall relate to the environment; recycling, reusing, treating, storing or disposing of substances or reducing the release of substances into the environment; works, undertakings or activities that affect or may affect the environment; or conservation of natural resources and sustainable development".
3. The Green Plan is the national strategy and action plan for sustainable development which was launched by the Federal Government in December 1990. The Environmental Citizenship Initiative is a component of the Green Plan. It manages several government-funded programmes which focus on the voluntary action of all sectors of society in the pursuit of sustainable development. See Canada's *Green Plan – The Second Year* (published by the Ministry of Supply and Service, cat. no. En21–110/1993E) and Environmental Citizenship Initiative (ECI) information brochure.
4. The EcoLogo is an Official Mark of Environment Canada registered under the Trademarks Act, R.S.C. 1985, chapter T-13, section 9 (1)(n)(iii).
5. Briefing Note on the Environmental Choice Program, 31 March 1994.
6. ECP's support for the 3 Rs – Reduce, Reuse and Recycle – considering that Canada is the world's second largest generator of waste on a per capita basis, after the United States.
7. The NPP was introduced to reduce the amount of packaging sent for disposal by at least 50 per cent of 1988 levels by year 2000.
8. The Canadian Code of Preferred Packaging Practices was drafted by the Canadian Council of Ministers of the Environment to assist manufacturers, marketers and distributors of packaging in contributing to the minimization of waste from packaging.
9. Targeted announcements in trade publications are being looked into as a complement to the press releases and *Canada Gazette* announcements. See "The Environmental Choice Licensee Workshop Report" which is a collation of the results of three licensee workshops conducted in Toronto, Montreal and Vancouver. Representatives from 40 licensees discussed various issues with ECP officials in the technical, policy and marketing divisions. This report is a 7-page document received by the authors from the Environmental Choice Programme.
10. At the same time that some licensees and applicants have complained about the cost of certification, there are some licensees who find it unfair that companies, having different levels of sales, bear the same cost simply because their sales fall within a range specified in ECP's fee structure. ECP believes that the cost of utilizing the EcoLogo is modest. However, they are considering a change in the computation of the annual fee from

a fixed amount based on sales, to a percentage of product sales.

11. According to ECP, "if the guideline changes and a company has to re-certify its product to ensure compliance, this is not covered by the licensing fees".
12. Rather, they have been due to oversight or negligence. In the past, delinquent licensees have been given up to six months to rectify the problem.
13. Licenses are granted for each product and a company may have several product types (e.g. paint) for which it has been awarded separate licenses.
14. Environment Canada commissioned Ernst & Young to undertake a market analysis for this purpose. In the selection and prioritization of categories, Ernst & Young looked at two market variables – household expenditures (consumer spending) and federal procurement (institutional spending). As well, it looked at the environmental impact (natural resources, energy, contaminants and greenhouse gas). See *Environment Canada – Environmental Choice Market Analysis – Final Report*, prepared by Ernst & Young, January 1994.
15. The federal Government alone purchases about $10 billion worth of goods and services annually.
16. Extensive reference was made to deliberations of the GATT Working Group on Environmental Measures and International Trade (EMIT) and analysis of UNCTAD. GATT documents cover the period September and November 1992, March, May, June and July 1993 and February 1994. Also refer to UNCTAD reports TR/B/40(1)6 dated 6 August 1993 and TD/B/WG.4/6 dated 23 August 1993. The subject was the focus of various papers of UNCTAD's Trade and Environment Section. See Veena Jha, René Vossenaar and Simonetta Zarrilli, "Ecolabelling and International Trade", UNCTAD Discussion Paper, no. 70, October 1993, and Veena Jha and Simonetta Zarrilli, "Ecolabelling Initiatives as Potential Barriers to Trade – A Viewpoint from Developing Countries" in this volume.
17. If it is any indication, then Environment Minister Jean Charest declared at the June 1992 Rio Summit that Canada is committed to increasing recognition of the need for transparency, accountability and inclusion in the way decisions are made with respect to the environment.
18. Recent draft criteria for paper products in the European Union resulted in bitter complaints by the Brazilian Association of Pulp Exporters of discrimination against non-EU producers because the criteria take into account only EU production conditions and environmental impacts. The Brazilians were not allowed to participate in the drafting discussions. (*Environment Watch: Western Europe*, 5 March 1993, p. 13.) See also, ABECEL, "EU Eco-labelling of Tissue and Towel Paper Products: A Brazilian Perspective", in this volume.
19. This would not have been the case when the Canadian Standards Association (CSA) served as ECP's first technical agency. This is because CSA has branch offices in the Western, Prairie and Atlantic regions of the country, in addition to offices in Belgium, Japan, Taiwan and Hong Kong.
20. See "The Environmental Choice Licensee Workshop Report", op. cit.
21. Cited by US Environmental Protection Agency in *Determinants of Effectiveness for Environmental Certification and Labelling Programmes* (Washington, DC, Office of Pollution Prevention, US EPA, April 1994).

22. Ibid.
23. This figure excludes re-imports of Canada in the amount of $3.175 billion.
24. The majority of cross-border trade between the two countries consists of intra-industry and intra-firm trade and pertains largely to the automobile industry.
25. The reality that United States exports may, in fact, be made up of inputs from developing countries is not ignored. However, it is beyond the scope of this paper to scrutinize *entrepôt* issues or the impact of global production networks in detail.
26. These would include seal-of-approval, single-attribute certification and report card type labelling programmes which are all voluntary in nature. See US EPA study, op. cit.
27. See *Environmental Labelling in OECD Countries* (Paris: OECD, 1991) and "Speaking Notes [of Pat Delbridge, then Chair of ECP] from a Presentation of the Canadian Environmental Choice Program" during the International Conference on Environmental Labelling – State Affairs and Future Perspectives for Environment Related Product Labelling, Berlin, July 1990.
28. With respect to the development and training of local standardization institutions, the International Organization for Standardization (ISO)-trained or credited local standardization bodies can be used to conduct the tests and verification in the home countries which could replace the certification bodies of the foreign eco-labelling programme. Another recommendation is the use of ISO-standardization tests which will eliminate the need for foreign personnel.
29. A precedent was set by the International Convention on Mutual Recognition of Pharmaceutical Products as developed by the EFTA.
30. "Report of the GATT Secretariat to the Second Meeting of the Commission on Sustainable Development, 16–31 May 1994."
31. Between 1988 and 1990 imports of packaging amounted to 23 per cent of new packaging used.
32. In 1988, the total amount of packaging disposed was just over 5.3 million tonnes; in 1990 total packaging disposed was slightly more than 4.5 million tonnes. (*Results of the 1990 National Packaging Survey*. CCME, December 1992). The Canadian Council of Ministers of the Environment has stated its intent to establish packaging regulations at provincial and federal level if the 20 per cent target for 1992 is not met. However, it appears that the target has been exceeded.
33. A related point is the fact that the majority of bulk packaging from developing countries consists of wood, (pallets and crates), and these pose particular problems at landfills in Canada. There have been some trade concerns surrounding wood packaging for imported products, but it is really a phytosanitary, rather than a broader environmental issue. Since it is usually low quality untreated wood that is used for crates and pallets, pests and other living organisms which can invade local forests, may be present in the wood.

12 The German Eco-Label "Blue Angel" and International Trade

Kilian Delbrück[1]

I CONCEPT OF THE GERMAN ECO-LABELLING SCHEME

Chapter 4, paras 20 and 21 of Agenda 21[2] read as follows:

> The recent emergence in many countries of the more environmentally conscious consumer public, combined with increased interest on the part of some industries in providing environmentally sound consumer products, is a significant development that should be encouraged. Governments and international organisations, together with the private sector, should develop criteria and methodologies for the assessment of environmental impacts and resource requirements throughout the full life cycle of products and processes. Results of those assessments should be transformed into clear indicators in order to inform consumers and decision-makers.
>
> Governments, in cooperation with industry and other relevant groups, should encourage expansion of environmental labelling and other environmentally related product information programmes designed to assist consumers to make informed choices.

In July 1990, an international conference on environment-related product labelling was held in Berlin with participants from 26 countries. The conference agreed on the Berlin statement on environmental labelling. This statement stressed that the environmental label is a form of environmental policy eminently suitable for market conditions. It is not based on orders or bans but on information, motivation and the commitment felt by both producers and consumers alike. The German environmental label "Blue Angel" was introduced in 1977 by the Federal Minister and the Ministers for the Environment of the *Länder*. The "Blue Angel" may be awarded to products which, in comparison with other products serving the same purpose, are particularly acceptable in terms of environmental protection.

The particular environmental acceptability of a product may be due to a variety of factors. For instance, a product may have particularly low pollutant emissions, it may help to reduce waste generation or effluent discharges, it may serve to minimize the content, or preclude the addition, of harmful ingredients, or it may be conducive to the recycling of wastes. Products marked with the environmental label should not be less safe or less serviceable than other comparable products. All these aspects are considered in a balanced and comprehensive analysis that provides the basis for awarding the "Blue Angel" label.

The "Blue Angel" is jointly sponsored by:

- the *Umweltzeichen* jury, an independent panel made up of representatives from the scientific, business and environmental communities and from consumer organizations;
- the German Institute for Quality Assurance and Labelling (*Deutsches Institut für Gütesicherung und Kennzeichnung e.V. – RAL*); and
- the Federal Environmental Agency (*Umweltbundesamt*).

The process for the awarding of the "Blue Angel" has two stages. First, award criteria are developed for a certain product or product group in a publicly verifiable form by an independent jury, in consultation with experts. The second stage involves the submission of applications for the award of the label by individual manufacturers and the review of these applications, leading to the completion of a contract for the use of the label.

At the first stage, the Federal Environmental Agency collects suggestions for the development of label criteria for a new product or product group, and forwards them to the jury which, twice a year, makes a pre-selection of those product groups deserving closer scrutiny. RAL then organizes expert hearings for the preparation of the final decision of the jury. This decision is then announced to the media. The award criteria are also published.

At the second stage, manufacturers interested in the award of the label on the basis of established criteria submit their applications to RAL. The applications are reviewed by RAL with the participation of the Federal Environmental Agency and the *Länder*. Finally, contracts are signed between RAL and the manufacturers.

For each application, a specific catchword prescribed by the jury, pointing out the particular "environmental protection features" of the respective product or technique, is included in the bottom line of the environmental label. This special feature serves to avoid the impression that the product is absolutely environmentally sound. Besides, it provides additional information to the consumer.

All award criteria are valid only for a maximum period of three years. For product groups for which a more rapid further development from the present state of the art is expected, the jury may also determine shorter periods of validity. Thus, it is guaranteed that products with the "Blue Angel" are always of above-average standard.

The "Blue Angel" has become increasingly well-known over the nineteen years since its establishment. Polls have shown that the majority of the public considers that the "Blue Angel" is an objective and neutral eco-label.

II THE "BLUE ANGEL" AND FOREIGN MANUFACTURERS

The "Blue Angel" label is available to foreign manufacturers on the same conditions that apply to German companies. Foreign manufacturers may apply for the award of the label based on established criteria for the product, or they may make suggestions for establishing a new set of criteria. The costs for establishing new criteria are not borne by the applicant. The only costs for a manufacturer who is awarded the label are an administration fee and a contribution to an advertisement fund ranging at the moment from 420 DM to 4776 DM per year, depending on the annual turnover of the manufacturer.

The opportunity to apply for the "Blue Angel" has been intensively used by several foreign manufacturers. Around 10 per cent of all contracts completed with RAL on the use of the label have been signed by foreign firms. The list of foreign companies comprises 131 foreign contractors and 498 products. It is led by contractors from France, the Netherlands, Switzerland, Italy and the United Kingdom. These countries are among the major exporters to Germany in general (see Box 12.1).

Until now, manufacturers from developing countries have not featured on this list, mainly because the products involved have not been of great interest to them, but this situation may change. The organizations involved in the "Blue Angel" system would welcome such a development, as well as a greater role for manufacturers from developing countries in the "Blue Angel" system.

The institutions involved in the award of the label have not received

Box 12.1 Number of foreign companies using the "Blue Angel"

Austria	15
Belgium	5
Denmark	9
Finland	2
France	22
United Kingdom	16
Italy	15
Liechtenstein	2
Netherlands	19
Norway	1
Protugal	1
Spain	1
Sweden	3
Switzerland	17
Yugoslavia	3
Total	131

any complaint from developing countries to the effect that certification or transparency problems constitute a barrier to their participation in the system. For many products, the award criteria prescribe no specific certification procedure; it is expected that competitors and consumer associations will exercise enough pressure on the individual manufacturer who applies for the label for a particular product. If the award criteria prescribe certification procedures, they must be carried out under the auspices of RAL. However, there is no general bar on part of the procedure being carried out abroad. The criteria for the "Blue Angel" and the decision to develop new criteria have been published, and these are easily available.

The "Blue Angel" system is very cautious in establishing criteria linked to environmental problems caused during the production phase of a product. The reasons are both the practical difficulties in ensuring reliability of the label and the special sensitivity of these criteria for potential trade conflicts. Besides, there are several unresolved methodological problems. For example, how should the specific product-related damages to the environment be identified, when the product is manufactured in a factory with a wide range of other products. Another problem is that only the producer of the final product is legally responsible for the fulfilment of the labelling criteria. But this does not mean that life-cycle considerations are excluded in the "Blue Angel" system. On the contrary, they are systematically included in the first screening stage and they have consequences for the selection of product groups.

III MULTILATERAL APPROACHES TO ECO-LABELLING

All efforts aimed at establishing cooperation between the eco-labelling systems of different countries and markets need to be welcomed. Active steps in this direction have been taken by the institutions involved in the "Blue Angel" system, with the organization of the 1990 Berlin Conference, participation in the 1992 Lesbos Conference and, recently, active participation in the process of international standardization in the field of eco-labelling in the International Standardization Organization (ISO) technical committee 207 on environmental management. These efforts have led to some conclusions concerning further steps towards multilateral cooperation between different eco-labelling systems.

As a voluntary system, every eco-labelling scheme is based on acceptance and trust on the part of consumers. It is not possible to regulate or order consumer acceptance; it can only grow when the consumers are convinced that they can rely on the label and that the label criteria do not promise more than they actually deliver.

In any case, consumers expect the eco-label to help them in choosing products, following their own environmental concerns and priorities. These basic conditions can be fulfilled by one-country systems, by systems bringing together several countries, and by the coexistence of both approaches. If environmental problems and consumer concerns are similar, multilateral approaches can be followed more easily. This applies to a large extent to the European Union (EU) eco-label with its background of 20 years of common environmental policy. None the less, even in this context, there are certain differences, and the initial experiences with the EU label indicate that EU criteria will follow another approach and cannot substitute "Blue Angel" criteria. However, data do not exist so far on the acceptance of the EU label by consumers. Thus, for the time being, the coexistence and the competition of both systems seem to be the appropriate solution.

Efforts directed at harmonizing eco-labelling systems – either in the context of international standardization bodies or in the context of intergovernmental organizations – should first concentrate on the fundamental principles and structures for the exchange of information. The next step could be a consensus about test methods and verification procedures – again, with mutual confidence and with consumer confidence as their basis. The development of common criteria could – in appropriate cases – only be the last step, if the above-mentioned steps have already been fulfilled. Even in such cases, the independent decision-making processes of different systems (e.g. involvement of relevant communities in different countries) would need to be taken into account, as a prerequisite for success and acceptance.

In all the different cases, the alternatives of harmonization and mutual recognition exist. But although mutual recognition could in principle provide an alternative in some cases, it is in general not an easy solution, because every scheme of mutual recognition has to be based on some agreement on the equivalence of principles, test methods, verification procedures and criteria, as well as on mutual confidence. The discussion on equivalence is at its very early stages now, and it does not appear likely to lead to concrete results faster than the discussion on harmonization could be satisfactorily concluded. With respect to mutual recognition, it needs to be stressed that the avoidance of negative trade effects should not endanger the necessary confidence and acceptance of consumers.

Notes

1. The views expressed in this paper do not necessarily represent those of the German Federal Ministry for the Environment, Nature Conservation and Nuclear Safety.
2. Agenda 21 was adopted by the United Nations Conference on Environment and Development on 14 June 1994. It is a comprehensive programme of action to be implemented, until the twenty-first century, by governments, development agencies, United Nations organizations and independent sector groups in every area where human activity affects the environment.

13 Eco-Labelling: Practical Use of the Cradle-to-Grave Approach

Ineke Giezeman and Frits Verhees

After the German "Blue Angel" programme came into being, the Scandinavian countries, France and the Netherlands also developed their own environmental labels. European integration in this field has arisen through the regulation of the European Union (EU) concerning the European eco-label.[1]

One feature shared by all these labels is that they are offered to manufacturers as voluntary marketing instruments. This enables consumers to give weight to environmental aspects while making their purchasing decisions. The manufacturer shows that the product is less environmentally damaging and that his company seeks to create a better environment. Eco-labels serve the general interest by influencing demand and supply in such a way as to cause a shift to less environmentally damaging products and production methods. An environmental label on a product signifies that the product is less environmentally damaging than other products in the same category.

Evidently, the development and implementation of such an instrument has to be managed by an independent body. The Dutch environmental label is implemented by the Stichting Milieukeur (see Box 13.3). Stichting Milieukeur is also responsible for the implementation of the European eco-label in the Netherlands. The EU is frequently consulted on the development of requirements for different groups of products and the methods of certification by different member States.

A question strongly related to the independence and reliability of an environmental label and the body implementing the label is the question of to what extent the environmental label does effectively mean that the product is less environmentally damaging. In order to guarantee that, two conditions have to be fulfilled:

- The sets of requirements for the environmental label have to be based on an analysis of all the environmental aspects during the all stages of a product's life. Requirements should not focus only on one or several environmental aspects and stages, as this could result in merely shifting the environmental damage to other aspects and/or stages in the product's life. This would indeed reduce the effectiveness of the environmental label.
- The standard adopted should always be sufficiently high. Only a limited number of products should be able to receive the environmental label. This is to give sufficient content to the innovative effect of the environmental label and to ensure that the environmentally conscientious consumer can choose the best products available.

Drawing up the sets of requirements for the environmental label will therefore have to be based on research "from cradle to grave", from raw materials to waste, and will have to take into consideration all the environmental aspects involved. Doing that, the environmental label will have to deal with the current discussion on environment-directed life-cycle analyses (LCAs). There has been considerable discussion on the issue of LCAs. However, this has not been very promising, and may also have inadvertently restricted the possibility of effective action. It needs to be clearly recognized that LCAs do not provide an alternative to decision-making; LCAs can only supply information and thereby support the decision-making process.

Some experts are of the opinion that certain standards have to be fulfilled before research can be qualified as "life-cycle analysis".[2] In our view, different interpretations of LCA are possible, depending on the context. However, the concept of life-cycle analysis always means that a cradle-to-grave approach has been adopted. In this paper, the concepts "life-cycle analysis" and "cradle-to-grave approach" will be used interchangeably.

This brings us to the very root of the argument. Instead of searching for one precise and comprehensive LCA method, it may be necessary to conduct cradle-to-grave studies within a more general framework in order to implement private and public measures and action. This may be an effective way to reduce environmental pollution, whereas an exclusive focus on refinement of methods may prove to be a hindrance to effective action. Stichting Milieukeur follows this pragmatic approach in drawing up sets of requirements for the various environmental labels for groups of products. This paper provides a description of this pragmatic approach and of the general framework from which Stichting Milieukeur functions.

I METHODS

Stichting Milieukeur believes in the need for a general framework within which the LCA may be conducted in order to guarantee equal treatment to every product group. The purpose of LCAs is to clarify options, e.g. for the drawing up of requirements for environmental labels, and to supply the necessary information.

Within a broad methodological framework, information is collected through research and through consultations with experts and other concerned parties, *inter alia,* through hearings. Decisions are made by a broadly composed panel that includes experts from the government as well as from organizations of environmentalists, manufacturers, consumers and retailers. Research facilitates the decision-making process within the panel of experts.

The core of the general framework within which studies are conducted is a matrix with all the items that have to be dealt with. Combining five product stages (raw materials, production of materials, production of products, use of products and processing of waste) with 25 environmental aspects (mainly raw materials, energy, emission, nuisance, waste, recyclability, reparability and life span) yields 125 items (see Box 13.1).

Research is divided into two parts. In the first, emphasis is laid on making an inventory and on selecting the relevant environmental aspects for the product group concerned. This is guided by the following basic assumptions:

- the basis for the evaluation is the entire product life chain and all the environmental aspects;
- a "complete" analysis is not the issue while filling in the matrix – after the inventory has been made, only those cells that provide environmental benefit are selected;
- a product group is a group of products which, according to the consumer, have the same practical purpose and belong to the same market sector;
- an environmental label can only be set up for a product within which products distinctly differ in degrees of environmental damage; and

Box 13.1 Matrix for light sources

Main aspects		Environmental aspects	Production of raw materials	Production	Transport	Use	Waste phase
Resources	1.	Use of renewable resources	+				
	2.	Use of scarce renewable resources	+				
Energy	3.	Total amount of used resources					
	4.	Use of non-renewable energy				+	
Emissions	5.	Use of renewable energy				+	
	6.	Emission of acidifying compounds				+	
	7.	Emission of nutruficating compounds				+	+
	8.	Emission of greenhouse gases				+	+
Nuisance	9.	Emission of compounds harmful to the ozone layer				+	
	10.	Emission of compound toxic to flora and fauna					
	11.	Emission of compounds toxic to man					
Waste	12.	Emission of waste heat					+
	13.	Emission of radiation				+	+
Reusability	14.	Emission of odouring compounds					+
	15.	Noise nuisance for user/surroundings					
Reparability	16.	Risk of calamity					+
Lifespan	17.	Damage to nature/countryside/spatial quality					
	18.	Amount of waste before processing				+	
	19.	Amount of waste after processing (final waste)					
	20.	Amount of chemical waste					
	21.	Reusability of the total product					
	22.	Reusability of parts of the product					
	23.	Recyclability of materials					
	24.	Reparability of the product					
	25.	Technical product life					

- the point is to determine whether a product as a whole causes significantly less environmental damage, although this does not mean that the product has to score more favourably in each stage and with regard to every environmental aspect.

In the second part of the study, requirements and measuring methods are devised for the selected environmental aspects. Attention is paid to functional requirements that can be made on products. These are examined in order to determine the extent of their influence on the level of environmental standards. They are also taken into account in the formulation of requirements, so that inferior products can be prevented from being awarded an environmental label and from affecting the image of the label. Also important for drawing up the requirements are the statutory requirements which could be used or which could make it unnecessary to draw up requirements for certain environmental aspects. Usually the requirements of the environmental label exceed those set by legal standards.

For the second part, the following basic assumptions apply:

- environmental requirements aim at the largest possible reduction of environmental damage;
- environmental requirements have to be within the reach of the manufacturer;
- environmental requirements are higher than those of the statutory requirements;
- at least one product or brand for sale has to be able to meet the requirements or has to be able to be awarded the environmental label within the foreseeable future;
- the formulation of environmental requirements has to be done as accurately as possible;
- the functional quality has to be sufficient;
- requirements can be set for information and packaging; and
- the period for which the environmental label applies has to be determined.

The study conducted by Stichting Milieukeur into the product group of light sources can be sited here to illustrate the procedure. In the first part of the study, environmentally important aspects for this product group were selected by means of a matrix (marked with a plus sign in Box 13.1).

This study concluded that a number of environmental effects (e.g. energy and emissions) cohere with the energy consumption of the lamp in the operational stage. Also relevant are the use of heavy metals and in particular the use of mercury, the radioactivity of the lamp and the technical life span. These aspects have to be taken into consideration because they bring about environmental effects other than the energy consumption. The environmental label should concern itself not only with questions of quantity but also with quality, especially in areas where environmental damage can be reduced this way. In the second part of the study, environmental and operational requirements are formulated. Because of the importance of energy consumption during the operational stage, high requirements have to be met concerning the energy efficiency of the lamp. Initially the line was drawn at 60 lumen per watt. Only high powered lamps were able to meet these requirements, and therefore a power-dependent standard was chosen. In addition, maximum values were determined for the other aspects mentioned, at times in combination with requirements in the field of product information. For example, negative effects on the environment caused by heavy metals in lamps can be reduced further by informing the consumer that the Netherlands have a system for collecting small chemical waste, including lamps.

II PROBLEMS AND SOLUTIONS

This section will focus on the most important problems connected to LCA and illustrate the pragmatic approach adopted by Stichting Milieukeur to resolve them. These problems concern (a) the common basis for comparison, (b) pitfalls in the comparison of products, (c) the relevance of certain environmental aspects, and (d) insufficient information.

A Common Basis for Comparison

Stichting Milieukeur uses the concept of the functional unit in its studies. According to the Dutch standard for LCAs, a good functional unit has to indicate the central function of the product as well as how much of this function is taken into consideration.

Stichting Milieukeur's study of coffee-makers could serve as an example. In this case, not all the elements of the functional unit have been based on scientific data, and some motivated assumptions have been made. The functional unit in this case is the environmental damage in the life cycle of a coffee-maker per 1000 cups with a life span of five years, assuming that the consumer utilizes half the capacity twice a day to keep the coffee hot for half an hour.

B Pitfalls in the Comparison of Products

LCAs are often directly associated with comparison between products with a view to pronouncing preference for one of the products from an environmental perspective. However, this is not the objective of the environmental label. The environmental label is concerned with determining the most important environmental aspects and subsequently linking requirements to those aspects. This means that sample products are worked with whose structure does not necessarily correspond to the actual structure of the products. This also means that not every environmental aspect needs to be filled in order to come to a conclusion, and that a less detailed approach can be pursued. The selection of environmental aspects is not directly linked to a certain product or brand. For instance, the Dutch standard of the CML gives the outcome of an LCA study according to the first approach (comparison of products) (Box 13.2).

Box 13.2 Two office chairs compared

Effect	Chair 1	Chair 2
Abiotic exhaustion	0.10	0.11
Biotic exhaustion (jr^{-1})	0	0
Greenhouse effect (kg)	12	17
Effect on the ozone layer	0	0.002
Human toxicity (kg)	13.2	9.2
Ecotoxicity ("water") (m^3)	0.03	0.01
Ecotoxicity ("land") (kg)	0.02	0.03
Photochemical ozone creation (kg)	1.10^{-7}	3.10^{-8}
Acidification (kg)	1.1	2.7
Nutrufication (kg)	2.3	3
Odour (m^3)	3.10^{-5}	1.10^{-5}
Noise ($Pa^2.s$)	?	?
Damage ($m^2.s$)	?	?
Victims	?	?

Within the framework of the environmental label, it would be very difficult to prefer one product to the other in this case, since Chair 1 scores better on environmental aspects such as abiotic exhaustion and greenhouse effect, while Chair 2 shows a more favourable picture on other aspects (human toxicity). What is more, quantitative information is lacking on aspects such as noise so that the conclusions are never entirely reliable. Stichting Milieukeur is at present working on an environmental label for chairs, and studies have been carried out for this. These studies followed a different approach, the basic assumption being that chairs can consist of different materials. A large number and wide range of materials apparently causes a chair to be relatively more environmentally damaging in all stages. This applies to nearly all the product life stages from the environmental matrix. Research proves that five different options can be suggested:

- reduction of the total use of energy in the manufacture of parts (e.g. by limiting the energy consumption for materials per chair, which the designer can direct by his or her choice of materials);
- limiting the most environmentally damaging raw materials;
- adjustment to the process of surface treatments;
- advancement of the life span of the chair; and
- advancement of the recycling of waste by dismantlability of the chair and limitation of environmentally damaging raw materials and impracticable materials.

Requirements can be set for every option. Subsequently, it can be determined whether there are chairs that can meet these requirements. This way, discussions and choices concerning environmental aspects and requirements are not directly related to specific products.

Box 13.3 The Dutch eco-label: added value for product and environment
(*Stichting Milieukeur**)

The Dutch environmental labelling system was developed at the instigation of the Dutch Ministry of Housing, Physical Planning and Environment, and the Ministry of Environmental Affairs. There was close consultation with all parties involved – manufacturers, retailers, consumers, certification authorities, and environmental groups. The *Stichting Milieukeur* (Eco-labelling Organization) is responsible for organizing the Dutch eco-labelling system. The Government set up this independent body in April 1992, in close consultation with all the interest groups involved. The organization owns the eco-label, sets the environmental standards for the system and monitors the use of the label. The organization's panel of experts plays an important role in its work. The panel includes representatives of the Government, alongside those of manufacturers, consumers, retailers and environmental organizations. The organization is to conduct an advertising campaign to inform the public about the eco-label. It will also keep manufacturers, consumers and retailers regularly informed of the latest developments concerning the environmental labelling system. In order to qualify for the eco-label, a product must meet the requirements set by the Stichting Milieukeur. Since each group of products has its own specific environmental impact, different standards are set for each group. It might be that only one product within a group is eligible for the eco-label, but there might equally be several which qualify. However, the environmental label cannot be requested for all consumer goods. Food and pharmaceuticals are not covered by the system, since regulations on product information already exist for these groups.

The main priority in deciding whether the environmental labelling system should be applied to a particular group of products is to establish whether the environment will benefit from this. If all the products within a particular group are equally environmentally damaging or benign, there is no point in awarding an environmental label to any of them. After all, it is of little consequence to the environment whether the consumer buys one product or another. Environmental labels are therefore only developed for product groups in which there are clear differences in environmental quality.

When environmental standards are set, account is taken not only of the product as it is sold, but of the entire product life cycle, from the use of raw materials and energy during the production process, via the packaging, to the processing of the product at the waste stage. The damage caused to the environment at each stage of a product's life is examined. Products are therefore assessed on the basis of all the requirements set by the Stichting Milieukeur, which looks at everything to do with the product, from cradle to grave. Needless to say, the products also have to fulfil the usual quality requirements. The Stichting Milieukeur's standards are therefore high – generally a little higher than the statutory requirements – but they are based on existing products, and are in all respects technically feasible. The organization takes as its basis the very latest environmentally friendly know-how and technologies. Science and technology are constantly developing, and therefore the standards are reviewed regularly, every three years on average.

---

* Based on a brochure published by Stichting Milieukeur, entitled "The Dutch Eco-Label: Added Value for Your Product and Environment".

C Relevance of Certain Environmental Aspects

Sometimes it is useful to determine which environmental aspects are especially important in a product's total environmental damage. This aspect can then be paid special attention while formulating requirements for labelling. Methods and techniques developed within the scope of the LCAs can facilitate the decision-making process in this way. Stichting Milieukeur's study on coffee-makers assessed which parts of the machine significantly cause many of the product's environmental effects. In this case, the consumption of electricity during the consumer stage had more influence than packaging, filters or materials.

D Insufficient Information

In LCAs, it is common to pursue complete and quantitative data. If quantitative data, in relation to the functional unit, cannot be presented, the aspect concerned is no longer used or, more commonly, time-consuming and expensive quantitative studies are proposed.

The key principle in the pragmatic approach of the Stichting Milieukeur is that research has to be in line with the level of knowledge. If a "cell" in the matrix cannot be filled in quantitatively, the approach of the Stichting Milieukeur is to consider the matter in qualitative terms. The label is not seen as absolute, and the requirements are reviewed every three years on average.

In Stichting Milieukeur's study of cat litter effects on nature and landscape, raw material collection proved unquantifiable. It was found, however, that clay minerals are collected as raw materials for certain kinds of cat litter. This has a negative effect on the landscape, as large areas are excavated without attempts to repair the damage. This piece of qualitative information can result in a decision to prefer certain kinds of raw materials for this group of products within the framework of the environmental label.

III CONCLUSION

A cradle-to-grave approach is necessary in setting up requirements for the environmental label. Such an approach will help this voluntary marketing instrument to contribute effectively to integral chain management. However, LCAs will never be able to replace the decision-making process. They are only a means to facilitate well-founded decisions. The environmental label is an instrument that cannot wait for the results of new, time-consuming studies. Therefore, efforts at labelling will have to begin with the means at our disposal now. Only in this way can environmental damage be reduced.

Notes

1. EC regulation no. 880/92 of the Council of 23 March 1992 on a community eco-label award scheme.
2. For example, in the Netherlands, see "Instructions for Environment-Directed LCAs of Products of the CML". See also R. Heijungs (ed.), *Milieugerichte levenscyclusanalyses van produkten* (1992).

14 Timber Certification Initiatives and their Implications for Developing Countries

Markku Simula

There are two main global environmental concerns related to forestry:

- climate change on account of the role of trees and forests in the carbon cycle; and
- biodiversity conservation, as the bulk of the world's genetic resources are found in forest ecosystems, mainly in the tropics.

The fundamental role of forests in maintaining life-supporting systems is gradually being understood now. Since this role is partly indirect (through upland soil and water conservation and through the impact on climate), forestry continues to have a low priority in political decision-making. Furthermore, it is often perceived as a marginal sector on account of its limited direct contribution to GDP in most countries.

Deforestation (loss of forest area or forest quality) is the key issue regarding forestry in tropical countries. This is a social problem related to inadequately defined or conflicting territorial rights of people living in and around forest areas. In this context, the rights of indigenous or autochthonous people pose a specific issue. Industry and trade are often naïvely depicted as key agents of forest destruction and tropical countries are readily blamed as the main culprits. However, these perceptions are often the result of a simplistic understanding of the complex problems of forestry and of hasty searches for quick solutions. In fact, tropical countries are not alone with the problems of forest degradation.

In the temperate and boreal forest zone, the forest areas are largely stabilized, and the key issue is how they should be managed for a variety of purposes. Past management practices have been criticized for giving too much emphasis to timber production with inadequate consideration to the environmental and social roles of forests (biodiversity, soil and water conservation, recreation, aesthetic values, etc.). We should also recall that forests have intense emotional import for many.

Discussions on the world's forests have recently focused on the possible role of international trade in resource management.[1] There is an increasing recognition that trade itself is rarely the main cause of environmental degradation.[2] On the contrary, trade is seen as a potential instrument which may contribute to environmental conservation through the promotion of trade in "environmentally friendly" products.

Although concern about the long-term availability of wood to world markets is shared by both the producers and the importers of timber, consumer demand for sustainably produced timber has not been significant enough to influence sources of supply so far. Environmental groups have used a two-pronged strategy to influence trade in forest products so as to enhance its role in resource conservation. The purpose is to bring about a change in trading patterns through the certification of timber products imported by the developed countries. In addition to providing information to the public and the mass media on the gravity of the impact of forest degradation, some of the more radical groups have exerted direct pressure upon selected traders, particularly DIY (do-it-yourself) chains, that have a high visibility among consumers, with harassing tactics such as barricades and demonstrations. The main concern of traders in this situation is to safeguard their market shares and image, and several of them, anxious to be seen as green, have started taking action to prove through third-party certification that the sources of their timber products are sustainably managed.[3]

This paper reviews the current situation (mid-1994) in timber certification and explores the potential role of this trade instrument in resource management and conservation, with particular reference to the implications of these issues for developing countries.

I CONCEPTUAL FRAMEWORK

A Issue

The main environmental concern that underlies timber certification is the quality (sustainability) of management of forests from which timber and timber products are sourced, and not emissions or waste disposal in the course of processing, manufacturing and utilization of timber.

Thus, timber certification focuses on a single aspect of the processes and production methods (PPMs) related to the source of raw material, i.e. how the forest is being managed.

Existing international agreements related to forests and timber (i.e. international conventions on climate change and biodiversity conservation, the International Tropical Timber Agreement, Convention on International Trade in Endangered Species of World Flora and Fauna (CITES), and the forestry principles formulated by the United Nations Conference on Environment and Development (UNCED)) imply that trade measures could function as an appropriate tool for achieving sustainability under certain conditions. Product differentiation would be a prerequisite for the use of selective trade measures, while it could also guide consumer behaviour.[4] Environmental labelling, based on the certification of forest management and the chain-of-custody until final end-use/consumer, can be considered an appropriate mechanism for such differentiation.

B Definitions

1 Timber Certification

Timber certification is a process which results in a written statement (a certificate) attesting the origin of wood raw material, and its status and/or qualifications following validation by an independent third party.[5] It is, however, noted that certification may be used in order to validate any type of environmental claim made by a producer, or to provide objective, neutral information disclosing facts about a product that would not necessarily be disclosed by the manufacturers.

In order to provide the necessary information to the final user, timber certification has to include two main components:

- certification of (sustainability of) forest management; and
- product certification (chain-of-custody) (see Figure 14.1).

Certification of forest management takes place in the country of origin, while product certification covers the supply chain both in domestic and export markets.

2 Certification of Forest Management

Certification of forest management involves an assessment of relevant aspects such as forest inventory, management planning, silviculture, harvesting, road construction and other related activities, as well as

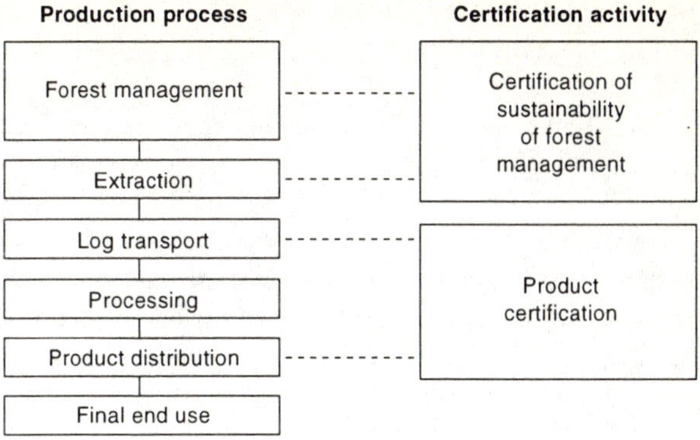

Figure 14.1 Summary framework for timber certification

the environmental and economic impact of forest activities. Inspection of forest management includes a review of relevant documentation and field checks before, during and after harvesting. Assessment is based on a set of predetermined principles and criteria, specific to the operating area.

3 Product Certification

In product certification, roundwood and processed timber products from certified forests are traced through successive phases of the supply chain (chain-of-custody). These phases include log transportation, log storage, primary processing, intermediate product storage, transport of intermediate products, various phases of further processing, as well as product transport and distribution up to the final consumer. The supply chain tends to be a rather complex network among a large number of operators, ranging from individual entrepreneurs to large transnational corporations. Ownership and custody of raw materials, semi-finished products and finished goods typically change several times in the supply chain.

Certification of forest management can be carried out at different levels: (a) country; (b) district or region; (c) company or forest owner; or (d) forest management unit. The level selected has implications for the way in which product certification is instituted.

C Objectives of Timber Certification

The fundamental objectives of certification of timber and timber products are:

- to improve forest management; and
- to ensure market access.

Certification is not considered a sufficient condition for achieving either of these objectives. However, with respect to market access, it may prove to be, at least partly, a necessary condition in certain markets.[6]

A set of ancillary objectives can also be attached to timber certification, and these may be achieved through improved internal and external transparency of operations. Such objectives can be set at the sectoral level (e.g. better control of forestry operations and land use change, higher recovery of collection of forest fees and taxes) or at the firm level (e.g. improved total productivity, cost savings).

Certification has a potential role in contributing to the internalization of environmental effects in the production costs of timber and timber products. This should involve a broader-based valuation of forest products than is reflected in the current market prices. This process should result in increased revenue to forest managers for improving their production systems so that requirements of sustainable forest management can be met. It is, however, noted that certification would need to be part of a sufficient policy mix for internalization to be effective.[7]

The wider the objectives, the more complex and costly the certification system tends to become. None the less, marginal benefits through expanded objectives may outweigh additional costs in the design of certification systems.[8]

D Sustainability of Forest Management

Several attempts have been made to define the principles and criteria of sustainable management both in the tropics[9] and in the temperate and boreal zones.[10] Sustainability has to be perceived in a broad context, taking into account the economic, social and environmental roles of forests. Sustainability is achieved through multipurpose management of forests so that their overall capacity to provide goods and services is not diminished. Such goods and services include timber, fuel wood, food and a large number of other non-wood goods, environmental services to soil and water conservation, habitats for the preservation of genetic resources and biological diversity, as well as the amenity value of forests.[11]

It needs to be recognized that "sustainability of forest management" is an evolving notion. The emphasis put on particular forest goods and services has shifted over time due to the changing needs and values of society. Needless to say, this process will continue in the future.

Recognizing the difficulties in defining sustainability for operational purposes, some certification schemes attempt to establish whether the current management is "good" or "acceptable". Behind this move, there is also a recognition that it may take a long time before such comprehensive forest management that could qualify as "sustainable" is likely to be practised in most parts of the world, particularly in areas where forests are under the greatest threat now.[12] For example, it was found in 1989 that no more than 1 per cent of natural tropical forests could qualify for sustainable management according to a set of specific criteria.[13]

In spite of the practical difficulties in definition, the concept of sustainability of forest management provides an overall goal. The producing member countries of the International Tropical Timber Organization (ITTO), for example, have committed themselves to achieving this objective by the year 2000, while the consuming member countries have also made a similar commitment with respect to their own forests.[14]

II CERTIFICATION INITIATIVES

A Regional and National Initiatives

In a number of timber importing and exporting countries, initiatives that would lead to timber certification have been taken. These measures are taken by the market in response to pressures for bans and boycotts concerning tropical timber (e.g. in Germany, the Netherlands, the United Kingdom), or as a proactive move by exporters (e.g. Indonesia and Brazil). Legal provisions for certification exist at the national level in Austria and at the level of state and local governments, e.g. in Germany, the Netherlands and the United States. In many other countries, timber certification is being studied in order to define appropriate modalities for practical application. This work is generally carried out by the private sector, with direct or indirect participation by governments.

In three importing countries, commitments have been made to import tropical timber from sustainably managed forests from 1995 onwards. In the Netherlands and Germany this commitment is made on a sectoral level, but may not be achieved due to the limited availability of acceptable supplies and to the slow progress in setting up the necessary implementation mechanisms, particularly in the countries of origin. In the United Kingdom, a group of traders (WWF 1995 Group) have declared their commitment to sustainable supplies.

The status of the more advanced regional and national-level initiatives in mid-1994 is summarized in Box 14.1. Governments appear to play an active role in Austria, Indonesia, the Netherlands and Switzerland. The European initiatives have started with tropical timber, but they are expected to address all types of timber in due course.

A regional approach has been adopted by the member countries of the African Timber Organization (ATO). The Central American countries too have decided to explore the feasibility of a regional scheme. Such an approach may also emerge in the Andean countries.

Due to the paucity of available information, only a few governments have been able to define their positions on timber certification. Even in cases where positions have been adopted, they are still evolving. In general, governments fall into three groups: (a) supporters; (b) those who have reservations; and (c) those who are against. The views of governments are not necessarily unified in individual countries, as the departments of economic and trade affairs, forestry and environment may have different opinions on the subject.

Timber certification no longer appears to be a North–South issue, but an issue between importers and exporters. Supporters of certification tend to be those countries that (a) largely depend on imports in their timber supplies, (b) have taken action as a response to possible market pressure, or (c) may see certification as a major tool for improving control and supervision of forestry activities.

There appears to be a consensus that certification, if applied, should cover all types of timber. However, some importing countries would like to see the work start with tropical timber because of strong domestic pressures to boycott the use of products made thereof. Governments generally prefer intergovernmental arrangements as a multilateral solution to the problem of harmonization of different certification schemes. However, a global process has been difficult to launch. Various stakeholders, often for different reasons, consider credibility a key problem. A majority of the governments agree that a credible certification scheme may not be set up with government participation alone. Views differ regarding the desirability and the extent of external monitoring, and the control of national certification procedures (the sovereignty issue).

Box 14.1 Timber certification initiatives (June 1994)

Africa

Green Label for African timber is an intergovernmental scheme which is still in the planning phase. African Timber Organization (ATO) will be the governing body for the label. Green Label will be based on regional criteria and guidelines.

Austria

A federal law (1993) provides for the creation of a quality mark for timber and timber products from sustainable exploitation. The advisory board would include representatives from the Government, industry, social and economic partners and non-governmental organizations (NGOs). Details of the system are being worked out.

Brazil

CERFLOR is a private sector initiative that seeks to ensure market access for Brazilian forest-based products. Detailed planning is under way.

Germany

Initiative Tropenwald, funded by timber trade union, timber industry and timber importers, focuses on the certification of tropical timber. The scheme is in an advanced planning phase.

Netherlands

Within the Netherlands Framework Agreement on Tropical Timber, signed by the Government and the main stakeholders, a certification scheme is being developed for implementation through bilateral cooperation.

Switzerland

A proposal for the establishment of a certification scheme for domestic and imported timber is being discussed by the main stakeholders.

United Kingdom

The 1995 Group of timber merchants led by the World Wildlife Fund (WWF) have set 1995 as the target for sourcing wood products from only sustainably managed forests. The status of forest management in the present supply sources is being reviewed by the buyers. Another recent initiative is the Woodmark scheme of the industry. It provides point-of-sale information on origin and on compliance with felling regulations.

Views of the trade and industry on certification vary from outright opposition to strong support. Importers who directly face strong local environmentalist pressures or traders who see certification opening a market niche or offering them a comparative advantage often support certification. In most countries a wait-and-see attitude is adopted for the time being. Trade is concerned about the possible impact of certification on production and distribution costs, as this may reduce the competitiveness of timber and timber products in the marketplace *vis-à-vis* their substitutes, while the results achieved in the improvement of forest management through certification may be rather limited. On the other hand, it is also apparent that some traders view such developments as good business opportunities. They use environmental arguments as part of their long-term strategy, a tendency which is clearly on the increase.[15]

B NGO and Private Sector Initiatives

While certification schemes and initiatives at international, regional and national levels are still in their nascent phase, a few NGOs and private companies in two countries (the United Kingdom and the United States) have been active in developing and implementing their own schemes. In mid-1994, five schemes were considered fully operational, while about ten were in the planning phase.

NGO schemes stress the improvement of forest management, while also providing tools for market promotion and consumer assurance. Some systems include development objectives as well, and attempt to provide assistance to community-based operations. Private schemes emphasize the marketing aspect of certification and the verification of claims that can be used in promoting the product.

The following common features can be observed in the existing and planned certification schemes: (a) there are varying levels of clarity in the definition of principles and criteria; (b) the systems tend to be general, referring to all types of forests and timber products; (c) the systems include both forest inspection and chain-of-custody verification; (d) multidisciplinary teams (forestry, ecology, sociology/social anthropology) with local expertise are often used in evaluation; (e) there is standardized reporting; and (f) there are rules on the use of labels.

There are also differences between individual systems especially with respect to (a) the role of the company to be certified in the process; (b) the objectives of the systems; (c) organizational arrangements, particularly decision-making on certification and accountability; (d) operational procedures; and (e) costs of certification.[16]

The result of certification can be a simple pass or fail for the award of the certificate, or qualifications such as "well-managed" or "sustainable". Some schemes are aimed at certifying domestic forest products while most attempt to cover timber and timber products from all types of forests.

The organizational set-up of NGO schemes involve advisory boards and various committees. A certification committee may decide or make a recommendation on certification. Peer reviewers are typically used. In private schemes, it is the programme director or the team leader who takes the decision on certification.

Detailed data on certification costs are not available. It appears that the cost of using private certifiers is generally higher than that of schemes run by NGOs. The validity period of certification varies. It may be up to six years, or it may cover the management planning cycle. Some certificates are valid for a year, but are renewable. Annual monitoring is provided if the validity period is longer than a year.

A licence agreement or similar contract is usually made between the client and the certifier to specify the duties and rights of both parties. The rules of the use of the label tend to vary, and they may be strict or flexible. The label may also be authorized for use at (a) "point-of-purchase" when certification of the chain-of-custody has been included, (b) "non-point-of-sale" which means that the label can be used in promotional literature or banners, or (c) both. Product certification may be on an exclusive or on a non-exclusive basis. Some schemes require that products are made entirely of certified wood before a certificate can be awarded.

Falsification is considered a potential problem, and anecdotal evidence suggests that labels have sometimes been used by unauthorized sources. A more common problem is that the client – sometimes perhaps due to ignorance of the rules – overextends the use rights of the label, giving in promotional literature an impression that certification applies to all his products, even though only a part of them may have been certified.

It is estimated that in 1993, about 1.5 million cubic metres of timber and timber products were produced world-wide from forests certified through the existing schemes. A total of about 35 suppliers was certified. Most of the certified timber was of tropical origin and sold in the United States market. The volume is clearly marginal, accounting for less than 0.5 per cent of the world timber trade.[17]

Box 14.2 Forest Stewardship Council

Objectives

The goal of the Forest Stewardship Council (FSC) is to set a common standard for forest management by promoting widely recognized principles and criteria of forest management. The purpose is to provide a consistent framework mechanism for measuring, monitoring and evaluating the attainment of continual improvements in forest practices in all types of forested regions of the world (boreal, temperate and tropical). FSC intends to oversee the international application of their principles and criteria through an accreditation programme, while national groups ensure implementation in the field. The FSC programme is expected to help decrease consumer confusion arising from multiple and, at times, conflicting claims.

Accreditation

Certification programmes can apply voluntarily to the FSC for accreditation in order to gain the right to use the FSC's name in their labels. In fact, all the existing private and NGO schemes have been involved in setting up the FSC. The Council will assess these requests, on the basis of the certifier's adherence both to FSC principles and criteria and to specific local standards evaluated and approved by the Council. The accredited certification organizations will be monitored, but the FSC will not itself certify products.

Organizational structure

The organization of the FSC consists of a general assembly, a board of directors, a secretariat, technical and accreditation committees, and regional representatives. The board makes the decisions on accreditation. It has a minority participation of economic interests, while the rest represents social and ecological interests (NGOs). There is an attempt to maintain a balance in North–South representation, as well as in representation among regions and between genders.

C Forest Stewardship Council

The creation of the Forest Stewardship Council (FSC) as an international body to encourage good stewardship of forests world-wide was first proposed in 1989. Details of the FSC are summarized in Box 14.2.

FSC seeks to take the lead in timber certification efforts, since there is no other international mechanism at the moment that can harmonize and coordinate timber certification schemes. The advantage of this is to have world-wide coverage of all types of forests that can be evaluated against a common set of principles and criteria. On the other hand, the FSC initiative has been criticized on a variety of accounts, including lack of participation of governments. There is also a risk that two types of standards may be used for regulating forestry, i.e. the national rules and regulations of the respective forest administration, and those of the FSC used by certifiers. Such parallel standards and varying interpretations can lead to confusion and unnecessary and costly overlaps in supervision and monitoring, particularly when interpretation tends to change over time. It has also been argued that the limited participation of industry and trade in the process of preparation of principles and criteria is another drawback. This would need to be rectified when national systems are established, as it is known from experience that labelling schemes without industry participation and support have tended to fail. Furthermore, the FSC has been criticized for designing its criteria to meet the needs of trade and industry primarily in developed countries and for not paying adequate attention to the specific requirements of the forest industry in tropical countries.

III TIMBER CERTIFICATION AS A TRADE POLICY INSTRUMENT

A GATT Compatibility

The basic principle of non-discrimination, central to the General Agreement on Tariffs and Trade (GATT), has implications on how timber certification should be applied. Voluntary certification of the environmental aspects of PPMs appears to be compatible with the General Agreement, so long as it does not lead to discrimination among countries or to trade restrictions. In the context of the General Agreement, an environmental label would count among the least distortive measures, since it leaves the choice to the consumer.

The Agreement on Technical Barriers to Trade (TBT) of the Uruguay Round requires transparency in the design and preparation of measures, taking trade interests into account. International standardization or harmonization and mutual recognition would be desirable for reducing the TBT nature of certification/eco-labelling.[19]

B Certification as a Complementary Trade Instrument

Two types of trade policy options have been identified to encourage the sustainable use of forests:

- those related to altering the pattern of trade; and
- those related to raising revenue for sustainable forest management.

Certification may not strictly be considered a policy option, as it is basically a means for providing information on the traded timber products to consumers.[20] However, differentiation of traded products through certification is an important prerequisite for many selective policy instruments, such as selective bans, quotas and tariffs for unsustainably produced timber, or selective reduced tariffs, elimination of quotas targeted subsidies and other trade-stimulating measures used for promoting sustainable forest management (see section I. C above).

In the assessment of policy options, the focus should in general be on the effectiveness in attaining objectives and on the efficiency in the use of resources, while taking social, economic and environmental effects into account. Political, institutional and commercial feasibility also need to be assessed, and the sufficient and necessary conditions identified. Furthermore, the effectiveness of certification as a policy instrument itself should in principle be assessed in the context of a policy package of which certification is a component. There is, however, a lack of definition of such commonly agreed packages.

The principal objectives of timber certification are improved forest management and ensured market access. The effectiveness of a certification scheme in meeting these objectives will depend on several factors, as indicated below.

Improved forest management:

- *trade significance* – the share of internationally traded timber in total production; and
- *rent capture* – the amount of additional resources which may be captured by forest managers through higher prices.

Market access:

- *market share* – the existence of demand for certified timber; and
- *price* – the willingness to pay a premium for certified timber.

Other:

- *short run* – the existing degree of certifiability of forest management; and
- *long run* – the cost implications of certification, including incremental costs due to the improvement of forest management and to the certification process.

C Trade Significance

About 80 per cent of the total roundwood production in developing countries is used for fuel and other non-industrial uses. Out of the industrial roundwood production, about 30 per cent enters international trade in various forms. In developed countries, industrial wood accounts for 83 per cent of the total roundwood production, and about 50 per cent is traded in various forms.

The developing countries accounted for only 16 per cent of the world exports of wood-based products in 1992 in value terms. This indicates that timber certification would have more impact in the developed countries. Furthermore, due to lower dependence on trade, forest management is likely to be less influenced by certification in developing countries. If certification is also applied to timber products consumed locally (as planned in Indonesia, for example), the effectiveness of this trade instrument could be significantly increased.

D Rent Capture

The division of gross revenue generated by tropical timber exports in the form of logs, sawnwood/plywood and further processed products between exporters and importers in a "typical" case is given in Figure 14.2. The share of the producing country varies by products from 10 to 35 per cent, the high level being achieved by exports of further processed products.[21]

The rent elements of gross revenue are reaped in the form of items such as licence fees, royalties, other levies, taxes and profits, after the various production factors (labour, capital, energy, etc., but excluding land) have been paid for. The share of these items in the border price in a "typical" case is estimated approximately at 25–40 per cent in logs and primary processed products and at 35–50 per cent in further processed products such as joinery, furniture, etc.[22] It goes without saying that these percentages vary extensively by country and by local conditions within countries.

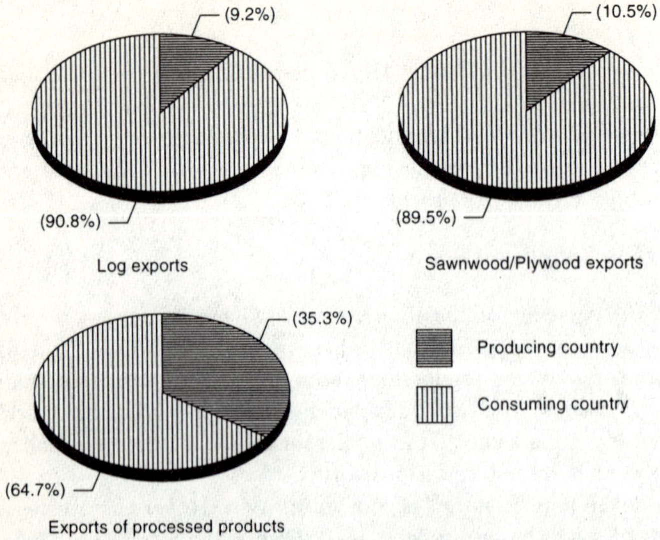

Figure 14.2 Division of gross revenue from tropical timber.

The costs and taxes of the processing and distribution chain in consuming countries are often proportional to the value of the product. Therefore, only a small share of a possible premium of sustainably produced timber products would in effect be reaped by the producing countries. Furthermore, only an even smaller share would actually be channelled to forest management.

In sum, without special measures, certification is not likely to result in a significant increase in rent capture by forest managers, even if the consumer is willing to pay a premium for such products.

E Price Premium and Market Share

Two questions are relevant for assessing how large the possible price premium for certified timber could be:

- is there willingness to pay; and
- does this willingness materialize in actual purchasing decisions?

In the United States, Winterhalter and Cassels have recently studied the willingness to pay for assurances of sustainability.[23] In their sample of 12 000 consumers having annual household incomes greater than $50 000 (which may not be representative of the mass market), 68 per cent of consumers were "willing to pay more for furniture whose construction material originated from a sustainably managed North American forest" while the rest (32 per cent) would not pay a premium. The views on the extent of the premium varied from 1 to 15 per cent.

In the United Kingdom, a survey was carried out by MORI and WWF in 1991 on public attitudes towards tropical rain forests. It concluded that:

- the main factors in buying wood products are quality, price and style of product;
- 33 per cent would accept higher prices for wood products if it would guarantee that the raw material comes from countries protecting their forests;
- 50 per cent found labelling of wood products (origin, content) very or fairly important; and
- 33 per cent would be prepared to pay an average 13 per cent extra for sustainably produced timber.

In 1993, a survey of timber merchants in the United Kingdom revealed that the most important criteria of their purchasing decisions were the following (in order of priority): price, quality, ease of supply, timber sourced from well-managed/sustainable supplies, customer pressure to stock environmentally friendly products, and environmental lobbying.[24] The first three criteria were clearly more important than the others.

As yet, there is no convincing evidence on a general price premium for sustainably produced, certified timber and timber products in the marketplace. The increased production costs are not, therefore, likely to be readily passed to the consumer without a reduction in consumption. There are, however, some market segments where willingness to pay a price premium can be expected and could be exploited by trade. The importance of this segment apparently varies by country. It would appear justified at this stage to refrain from using the willingness-to-pay argument as a general policy guideline until more information becomes available. The objective of ensured market access should therefore be perceived from the point of view of market shares rather than from that of additional prices. Increase in the market share of certified products will have to compensate for cost increases that may have been incurred in the process of obtaining a certificate.[25]

The demand for certified timber is observed at least at four levels: (a) consumers, (b) retailers, (c) architects and other specifiers, and (d) public sector projects. Consumer demand appears to vary extensively between countries, but it is expected to correlate with income levels (within a country) and with environmental awareness. As for type of product, there appears to be proportionally more demand for certified timber in high-value-added consumer products like furniture than in building products and in commodity timber.

F Trade Diversion and Substitution

Due to differences in export patterns, some suppliers depend more on environmentally sensitive markets. Africa and the Nordic producers, who primarily depend on the European market, would possibly be at a disadvantage from the potential negative impact of certification on competitiveness, since a higher share of their total exports would have to comply with certification requirements than that of other exporters. This assumes that certification will spread in Europe faster than elsewhere.

Some trade diversion could also occur when exporters redirect their timber from environmentally sensitive markets to those where certification would not be required. Indications of such changes in trade patterns (e.g. increased exports from African and Nordic countries to Asia) can already be observed, although at present they appear to be motivated less by environmental considerations than by demand and supply factors. In the long run, if certification is applied in all importing countries, such trade diversions can be avoided.

The only conclusion possible at this stage is that if certification costs are passed over to consumer prices, even small changes could induce large changes in trade patterns due to high elasticities of substitution between sources/destination. Therefore, certification schemes limited to exports may result in changes in trade patterns, but they may not necessarily influence management practices.[26]

Substitution elasticities of timber products in relation to competing materials are moderate.[27] A timber price increase induced by costs of sustainable management and certification will contribute to substitution, if similar relative price increases do not take place in competing materials. Possible impacts cannot be estimated here due to uncertainty about the magnitude and nature of cost increases.

However, if life-cycle analyses were carried out on timber and its substitute materials, timber is likely to show a competitive advantage, thanks to the renewability of its raw material source. There is a need to encourage such comparative studies rather than analyses that focus only on the assessment of a single issue of the production process, i.e. forest management.

G Cost Competitiveness

The implementation of timber certification involves two types of costs:

- costs of sustainable management; and
- costs of certification.

The costs of sustainable management vary extensively. Available information on this aspect, crucial for policy decision-making, is scanty. Very few reliable estimates seem to exist, partly due to lack of operational definitions of sustainability. As a rule, sustainability as a management objective can be expected to increase production costs of all types of timber. However, in some cases, the resulting less intensive management of timber production and more detailed planning may also reduce costs (depending on how the time factor is included in calculations). The relative impact on production costs is expected to be higher in the natural forests in developing countries than elsewhere. Further studies in this field would need to be based on common approaches to allow comparability. Such studies should include both silvicultural and harvesting costs in their analyses, and cover both direct and indirect costs related to the internalization of all aspects of sustainable forest management.

There is a similar lack of information on the costs of certification. This is due to three main reasons:

- the unit costs vary extensively between situations (size, type and location of operation), certifiers (non-profit organizations and private companies), teams and methods used (composition of teams, use of local staff, extent of fieldwork, etc.);
- most would-be certifiers do not yet know what the costs will be; and
- this kind of information is often considered highly confidential.

Certification would be easier and less expensive to implement by the processing industry when they own their forest land, or when they possess long-term concessions. One may expect this to be true in the case of land managed by governments too.

As the cost of certification is essentially a fixed cost, large-scale forest owners or concession holders could absorb the additional cost more easily than small forest owners because of economies of scale. Special arrangements (e.g. regional or district-level assessments) might be required for communal lands and small forest owners, so that they do not get unduly penalized through certification.

At present, many small-scale producers of timber or chain-sawn lumber (both private entrepreneurs and communities) in developing countries do not operate in conditions and using methods which would qualify for certification of sustainability. In some countries, these operators may account for the bulk of the total timber production. Often the institutional prerequisites, such as long-term land tenure, are not in place. This very large group of operators, particularly in Africa and Latin America, would be forced into a socially intolerable situation if their source of living disappears. Possible negative effects should be considered and mitigating measures taken, before certification can have a positive impact on forest management on a national scale.

In general, it appears that certification may promote plantation timber-based products and, therefore, give a boost to the plantation establishment. It is also likely to increase vertical and horizontal integration of timber industries. Certification may provide a competitive advantage to large-scale producers who can more easily comply with the various requirements of product certification (e.g. documentation, internal control systems) and who can more easily absorb the costs due their economies of scale. It may place suppliers from developing countries at a disadvantage, as they may find it more difficult than their competitors from developed countries to meet the information requirements of certification.

IV TOWARDS VIABLE CERTIFICATION SCHEMES

The general requirements or principles for a viable timber certification system are (a) credibility, (b) coverage of all types of timbers, (c) objective and measurable criteria, (d) reliability, (e) independence, (f) voluntary nature, (g) non-discrimination, (h) acceptability to the parties involved, (i) adaptability to local conditions, (j) cost-effectiveness, (k) transparency, (l) goal-orientedness, and (m) practicability.[28] Credibility is one of the most important requirements, involving transparency, competence of certifiers and control and monitoring of certification systems.

The focus in certification should be at the country level. However, it is necessary to have a common international framework, straddling all the main types of forest ecosystems on which localized schemes can be developed. Mechanisms for mutual recognition and harmonization of certification systems are urgently needed in order to avoid confusion at the consumer level. By addressing the issue of certification at a multilateral level, countries may be able to minimize the problem of trade diversion. At the same time, standards would need to be agreed on in a cooperative manner so that the risk of trade diversion may be reduced.[29] While FSC has been involved in important pioneering work, in its present form it may not be able to provide for all the perceived requirements for adequate harmonization and mutual recognition of various timber certification schemes.

There appears to be support for country or district-level certification, but the necessary preconditions for feasible arrangements have not been clearly defined.[30] Certification of forest management at the level of the management unit will rank highest in terms of credibility, but the costs will also be accordingly higher. It appears that the operation of several independent certifiers in a country is preferred so that monopolistic tendencies can be prevented.

V CONCLUSION

In spite of uncertainties related to the effectiveness of certification of timber and timber products as a policy tool for facilitating improved forest management and despite the lack of definition of feasible certification systems, certification will be inevitable at least in a number of major import markets. In view of the general preference given to this type of trade instrument, the prevailing trend towards environmental labelling is also expected to extend to timber and other forest-based products. Questions related to the demand for certified timber products, to possible price premium, and to the impact on production and distribution costs of certification may prove to be less relevant if there is general acceptance that an independent third party is necessary for verifying the status of forest management.

There is a need to continue the policy dialogue between producers/exporters and importers to reach an agreement on (a) the definition of sustainable forest management, (b) harmonization of timber certification schemes, and (c) the additional policy elements necessary for making certification effective and cost efficient in attaining its main objectives, with particular reference to developing countries.

Further studies would be needed on how certification could contribute to internalization of the environmental aspects in production costs and product prices. Life-cycle analyses on timber and timber products *vis-à-vis* their substitutes seem particularly important. There is also an urgent need to identify the kind of support developing countries may need in order to meet the emerging requirements of timber certification and to avoid possible adverse socio-economic and environmental impact.

Notes

1. For example, see Organisation for Economic Cooperation and Development (OECD), *The Environmental Effects of Trade* (Paris, OECD, 1994).
2. P. Low, ed., "International Trade and the Environment", World Bank Discussion Paper no. 159, Washington, DC, 1992.
3. See H. G. Baharuddin and M. Simula, *Certification Systems of All Timber and Timber Products* (Yokohama: ITTO, 1994).
4. For example, see London Environmental Economic Centre (LEEC), *The Economic Linkages between the International Trade in Tropical Timber and the Sustainable Management of Tropical Forests*, ITTO Activity PCM(XI)/4 (London: ITTO, 1993).
5. See H.G. Baharuddin and M. Simula, op. cit.
6. Ibid.
7. UNCTAD, "The Effects of the Internalization of External Costs on Sustainable Development", TD/B/40(2)/6, 1994.
8. M. Simula, "Consumer Initiatives on Eco-labelling of Tropical Timber and their Implications for Indonesia", Seminar Sehari Eco-labelling Produk Hasil Hutan, Jakarta, 1993.
9. See International Tropical Timber Organization (ITTO), *Guidelines for the Sustainable Management of Natural Tropical Forests*, ITTO Policy Development Series, no. 1 (Yokohama: ITTO, 1990); *Criteria for the Measurement of Sustainable Tropical Forest Management*, ITTO Policy Development Series, no. 3 (Yokohama: ITTO, 1992); *Guidelines for the Sustainable Management of Planted Tropical Forests*, ITTO Policy Development Series, no. 4 (Yokohama: ITTO, 1992); and *Guidelines for Biodiversity Conservation in Tropical Production Forests*, ITTO Policy Development Series, no. 5 (Yokohama: ITTO, 1993).
10. For example, Workshop on Environmental Criteria/Indicators for the Sustainable Development of Boreal and Temperate Forests, CSCE, 1993.
11. Food and Agricultural Organization (FAO), *The Challenge of Sustainable Management* (Rome: FAO, 1993).

12. Ibid.
13. D. Poore, *No Timber Without Trees* (London: Earthscan, 1989).
14. UNCTAD, "Draft International Tropical Timber Agreement", TD/Timber, 2/L.9, 1994.
15. See M.D. Eisen, "What Markets Want from Timber Certification: Implications for Tropical Timber Management", Conference on Timber Certification: Implications for Tropical Forest Management (New Haven, Conn.: Yale University, 1994) and Morgan-Grampian, *Timber and the Environment Survey 1993* (*Timber Trade Journal* in conjunction with *DIY Week*, 1993).
16. See H.G. Baharuddin and M. Simula, op. cit.
17. Ibid.
18. See Environmental Protection Agency (EPA), *Status Report on the Use of Environmental Labels Worldwide*, EPA 742-R-9-93-001 (Washington, DC: Office of Pollution Prevention and Toxics, 1993).
19. V. Jha, R. Vossenaar and S. Zarrilli, "Eco-Labelling and International Trade", UNCTAD Discussion Paper, no. 70, October 1993.
20. See LEEC, op. cit.
21. International Tropical Timber Organization (ITTO), *Pre-project Report on Incentives in Producer and Consumer Countries to Promote Sustainable Development of Tropical Forests*, PPR 22/91(M, F, I) (Oxford: Oxford Forestry Institute, 1991)
22. Ibid.
23. See D. Winterhalter and D.C. Cassels, *United States Hardwood Forests: Consumer Perceptions and Willingness to Pay* (West Lafayette, Ind.: Purdue University, 1993).
24. See Morgan-Grampian, op. cit.
25. See V. Jha *et al.*, op. cit.
26. See D.J. Brooks, "Tropical Timber Markets, Trade and Labelling", Conference on Timber Certification: Implications for Tropical Forest Management (New Haven, Conn.: Yale University, 1994).
27. Ibid.
28. See H.G. Baharuddin and M. Simula, op. cit.
29. See P.N. Varangis, C.A. Primo Braga and K. Takeuchi, "Tropical Timber Trade Policies: What Impact will Eco-labelling Have?", The World Bank Policy Research Working Papers 1156, Washington, DC, 1993.
30. See, for example, LEEC, op. cit.

15 Is there a Commercial Case for Tropical Timber Certification?

Rachel Crossley, Carlos A. Primo Braga and Panayotis N. Varangis[1]

INTRODUCTION

Environmental concerns in developed countries about the link between trade in tropical timber and deforestation have fueled demands for the use of trade measures as a way to influence production processes in exporting countries. Calls for bans of tropical timber and for consumer boycotts proliferated in developed countries in the 1980s, but were generally not successful and subject to controversy. More recently, however, timber certification (TC) has been identified as a potentially better instrument with which to promote sound forestry practices.

The TC approach is attracting considerable attention from government, multilateral institutions and non-governmental organizations (NGOs). One of its strengths is that it can be designed as a market-based (consumer-driven) instrument. Moreover, as discussed below, it is less likely to foster trade disputes at the level of the General Agreement on Tariffs and Trade (GATT) than unilaterally imposed discriminatory trade instruments (such as import prohibitions). Last, but not least, it is argued that it can reward timber-producing countries that adopt better forest-management practices.

TC involves awarding an eco-label or a certificate to companies whose wood and wood products have been produced according to "sound" environmental, social and economic criteria. According to its supporters, TC enables consumers to signal their preference for "responsibly produced" forest products to producers, contributing to better forest management (and possibly a reduced level of deforestation). Different levels of environmental awareness among the consumers within a country or across countries can provide incentives to producers to implement product differentiation or market-niche strategies.[2]

Most developed tropical timber importing countries are fully engaged in national and international debates on labelling of timber and its products. After some initial resentment towards what was perceived by producing countries as "eco-imperialism" on the part of developed countries, and an attempt to restrict timber market access, several timber producing countries have recognized that certification is a market reality and might even offer competitive advantages to those that pursue it. Moreover, the development of locally appropriate field-level criteria for TC can facilitate the achievement of "sustainable management", a concept that most timber producers made a commitment to by endorsing the International Tropical Timber Organization (ITTO) "Year 2000" program. Hence, many exporting countries are now seriously investigating the viability of creating or promoting national and international timber certification systems. However, there are many practical issues to be resolved before effective worldwide certification can be introduced. Currently, certified timber and timber products account for a very small share of world trade in all types of timber (approximately 0.5 per cent).[3]

One of the main determinants of whether timber certification will become a global reality is whether sufficient financial incentives exist to induce producers to become certified. The central objective of this paper is to provide basic, preliminary analysis of financial incentives of voluntary timber certification. Although certification is planned to apply to all types of timber, this paper focuses on certification of tropical rather than all types of timber. However, much of the analysis has implications for other timber producers and consumers.

In this chapter, financial incentives are considered in terms of increases in timber export revenues due to certification and do not include potential long-term financial, environmental and social benefits due to better forest management and maintenance of biodiversity. In addition, the financial incentives presented do not include cost estimates associated with implementing timber certification.

Section I analyses the size, type and direction of the global tropical timber trade and identifies those producing countries that are most likely to be affected by the demand for certified timber in developed countries. Section II constructs a scenario in an attempt to assess the financial implications of TC for producer countries. Special attention is given to: (i) the so-called "green premium"; (ii) the potential role of TC in recapturing timber markets lost to date and averting potential market share losses in the future; and (iii) the implications of TC becoming a condition for market access to developed economies. The paper concludes with a summary of its main findings and a brief discussion of broad policy changes necessary for supporting improved forest management worldwide.

I GLOBAL TIMBER RESOURCES AND TRADE

A The Tropical Timber Trade

Timber certification most likely will have its initial (and perhaps only impact) on that portion of the tropical timber produced that enters trade and that is imported by those countries that have been involved in developing norms and guidelines noted in the previous section. It is therefore crucial to understand the dynamics of the tropical timber trade and more specifically, the particular producing countries and quantity of timber that could potentially be affected by certification.

While TC is intended to apply to all types of timber, the focus of this paper is on tropical timber products, excluding fuelwood. Hence, the figures presented will focus on the tropical timber trade. The FAO timber statistics used do not distinguish between tropical and non-tropical timber, but use a distinction between non-coniferous (temperate and tropical together) and coniferous. With certain exceptions, the non-coniferous timber production of developing countries can be classified under tropical. Major exceptions are China, Argentina, Chile and the Near East, which are relatively large producers residing in the temperate zone. While some other developing countries located in temperate areas are still included in our data, their magnitude in both trade and production values and volumes are not significant to distort the analysis.

Trade in tropical timber products has frequently been blamed for the disappearance of tropical forests. However, as shown by Table 15.1, taken on aggregate, exports of industrial non-coniferous roundwood (logs and pulpwood), sawnwood and wood-based panels (plywood, veneers, particle board and fiberboard) from developing countries account for about 25 per cent of production. Thus, most of the timber produced in developing countries is consumed locally. If values are considered instead of volumes, the percentage of the value of trade in the value of production is higher than 25 per cent, since the more valuable logs and timber products tend to be exported. By valuing world production (industrial roundwood) on the price of logs in the Indonesian domestic market (around $100 per cubic metre in 1991),

Table 15.1 Production and export of timber products in developing countries, 1991

Product	*Export volume (1000 cubic metres)*	*Export value (million US$)*
Logs (NC)	25 868	2420
Sawnwood (NC)	8919	2285
Wood-based panels	12 652	4318
Total		9023

Source: World Bank, IECIT, calculations based on FAO, *Forest Products Yearbook, 1991.*

Notes: (i) NC signifies non-coniferous;
(ii) Wood-based panels are mainly veneer and plywood, but also include particle board and fibreboard.

the percentage of export value on the production value is at most around 33 per cent. This is an overestimate. (Note that the value of Indonesian logs in the domestic market is an underestimate of the "true" value because the export ban on logs in Indonesia has led to reduced domestic prices for logs.)

Table 15.1 also shows the timber revenues of timber-exporting developing countries (excluding China, Argentina, Chile and the Near East). The total exports for non-coniferous logs plus sawnwood plus wood-based panels is $9.02 billion. In addition, wood furniture and wood manufactures exports from developing countries (excluding the countries mentioned earlier) are estimated to account for around $1.64 billion. Thus the value of the total timber export revenues for logs, sawnwood, wood-based panels, wood furniture and wood manufactures from developing countries was around $10.66 billion in 1991.

In several countries, the forestry sector is one of the main pillars of the economy, and timber trade accounts for a much greater share of production; it is on these countries that TC will potentially have a greater impact. Table 15.2 illustrates that the two largest exporters of tropical timber non-manufactured products are Malaysia and Indonesia; trade accounts for a large part of their production. In 1990, exports of logs and timber products accounted for about 75 per cent of timber production for Malaysia and 60 per cent for Indonesia. Other countries with high export shares are: Congo (62 per cent), Côte d'Ivoire (57 per cent), Gabon (78 per cent), Ghana (49 per cent) Liberia (64 per cent) and Papua New Guinea (60 per cent).

Table 15.2 Shares of major exporters and importers in tropical timber trade

Major exporters country/regions	*Share of world exports (%) 1990*[b]	*Major importers countries/regions*	*Share of imports (%) 1987*
Countries			
Malaysia	41.5 (19.6)	Japan	28.1
Indonesia	23.8 (13.8)	China	9.2
Singapore[a]	4.6 –	USA	7.5
Brazil	3.3 (19.6)	South Korea	6.2
Côte d'Ivoire	2.1 (1.4)	Singapore	6.2
Papua New Guinea	1.7 (1.8)	United Kingdom	4.7
Cameroon	1.5 (1.8)	Hong Kong[a]	4.2
Congo	1.4 (0.8)		
Gabon	1.4 (0.6)		
Regions			
Asia	82.2 (52.6)	Asia	54.3
Latin America	5.4 (26.8)	EU	20.1
Africa	8.8 (17.9)		

Sources: World Bank, International Trade Division; German Bundestag (1990); Zarsky (1991).

Notes: Timber trade in sawnwood, wood-based panels (converted in roundwood equivalent) and logs.
[a] Transit country.
[b] Inside the parentheses are the world production shares of each of the exporters in 1990.

Eighty-two per cent of global exports of tropical timber originate from Asia, particularly Malaysia and Indonesia, which together account for about two-thirds of world tropical timber exports. Thus, while in aggregate, trade in tropical timber cannot be said to be the major contributor to tropical deforestation, for several countries it can be argued that it has been an important factor in the process. For this reason, better management of forests in these countries is crucial for sustaining the local timber industry and exports in the long run.

Figure 15.1 illustrates that 72.5 per cent of tropical timber is consumed by developing countries and Japan and not by Western developed countries where demand for certified timber appears to be strong. Imports by developed countries, excluding Japan, accounted for 27.5 per cent of all imports in 1987. The concern over environmental issues

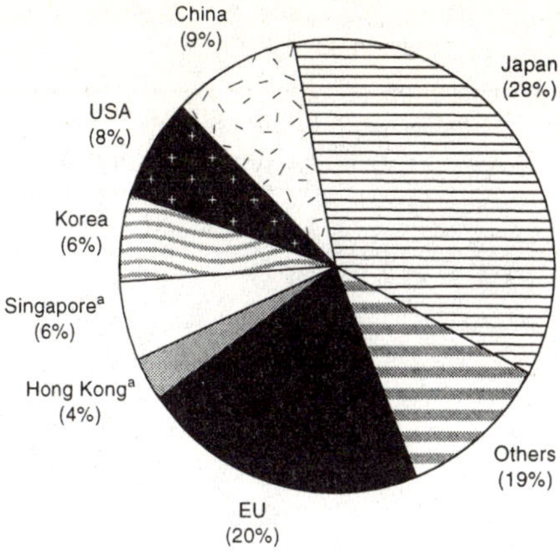

Figure 15.1 Major importers of tropical timber

Notes: Figures for 1987.
[a] Volume and value of tropical timber products exports in a transit country

has not reached the vast majority of consumers in developing countries and hence certified timber is not likely to be in high demand in those markets, at least in the short to medium run.

Developing countries also account for most of the increase in tropical timber consumption that has occurred recently and is forecasted in economic models.[4] Also noteworthy is the increasingly large quantity of imports of temperate hardwood and softwood (coniferous) timber products by developing countries. However, the markets that will drive the move towards certification are those of the United States and Europe. In order to assess the potential revenues available to producers selling certified products, the magnitude of the market likely to be affected (at least in the short to medium term) must be estimated. The following analysis, therefore, identifies those producing countries that rely on the markets of Europe and the United States, and quantifies the volume and value of timber products reaching those markets. It is assumed that certification will affect the following timber products: logs, sawnwood, panels, wood furniture and wood manufactures. It is also assumed that the affected timber trade from developing countries will include non-coniferous hardwoods.[5]

The principal trading partners of the major developing-country exporters for non-coniferous timber products (logs, sawnwood and panels) are broken down and presented in Table 15.3 (wood manufactures

Table 15.3 Trading partners of major exporters of tropical timber products, 1993

Exporter/importer	*Importing country share of total exporter exports (exports as a share of national production)*[b]			
	Japan	*Asia*[a]	*EU*	*USA*
Brazil	–	–	46.54	20.17
	–	–	(1.68)	(0.73)
Cameroon	3.16	–	67.72	–
	(1.26)	–	(27.10)	–
Congo	–	–	88.34	–
	–	–	(57.90)	–
Côte d'Ivoire	–	–	62.45	–
	–	–	(34.14)	–
Gabon	–	–	68.76	–
	–	–	(41.52)	–
Indonesia	33.80	37.73	9.10	8.54
	(24.04)	(26.83)	(6.47)	(6.07)
Malaysia	32.19	49.62	5.42	–
	(25.44)	(39.22)	(4.29)	–
Myanmar	1.62	92.85	–	–
	(0.30)	(16.58)	–	–
Papua New Guinea	56.31	39.35	–	–
	(30.49)	(21.31)	–	–

Source: World Bank, IECIT, calculations based on FAO, Forest Products direction of Trade.

Notes: [a] Asia excludes Japan. Major Asian importers are: Korea, China, Thailand, India, Hong Kong, Singapore, and the Philippines.
[b] denotes that data were not available. However, it is expected that the share, even if available, would be small.
Timber products include: sawlogs and veneer-logs, sawnwood and plywood.

and wood furniture are dealt with in the next section). Asia is the largest importer (54.3 per cent) of these timber products; China, Japan and South Korea account for a little less than half of the total of these tropical timber products[6] imports from Malaysia, Indonesia, Papua New Guinea and Myanmar. These statistics show that the dominant pattern in tropical timber trade is from South-East Asian producing regions to East Asian import markets.

The table also indicates countries that export large quantities of their production of non-manufactured tropical timber products that are most likely to be affected by any demand in European and, to a lesser de-

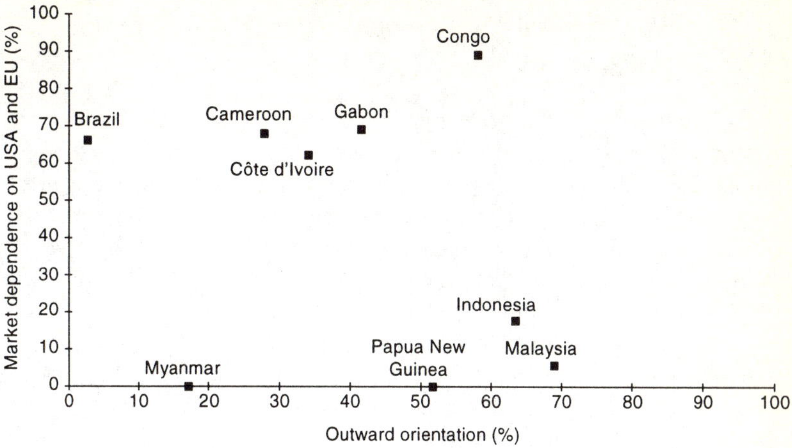

Figure 15.2 Exporting-country exposure to timber certification

gree, the United States markets for certified timber products. African producers will be most heavily affected, since they export a large percentage of their production to the European Union (EU). This is not the case for Indonesia and Malaysia however; they both export little of their overall production and only 12 per cent and 4 per cent of their total exports respectively go to the United States and the EU. Although the EU and United States account together for 66 per cent of Brazil's timber exports, only a little over 2 per cent of production is actually exported to these two destinations. To the extent that TC will be more likely to affect those producers that export their products to these markets, they will be a very small number of the total. Other Asian timber exporting countries, such as Myanmar and Papua New Guinea, may not be significantly affected by certification as these countries export to other markets in Asia in which there is little, if any, demand for certified timber.

These points are further illustrated by Figure 15.2. A developing country is more likely to be affected by TC, the higher the outward-orientation of its timber industry (as measured by exports as a share of national production) and the greater its market dependence on the EU and the United States (as measured by the exports to the EU and the United States combined, as a share of total timber exports). As Figure 15.2 shows, African countries are the ones typically clustered in the high-exposure corner of the box.

B The Role of Wood Furniture and Wood Manufactures in Timber Trade

Most statistics available on tropical timber products include few data about wood furniture and wood manufactures. In value terms, though, wood furniture and wood product exports from developing countries account for a significant and growing share of the total value of their timber and timber product exports to developed countries. It is worth noting that as a result of the Uruguay Round negotiations, tariff escalation (that is, a situation in which the tariff applied to imports of a product goes up as the level of processing increases) for wood products has decreased at the top of the processing chain.[7] In other words, these results create additional incentives for producers from developing countries to move towards higher-value-added products such as furniture and wood manufactures. Trade patterns of these products are particularly important to identify as they are most likely to be targets for certification, because they are high in value and most "visible" in the market place (much more so than plywood used in construction, for instance). It is important, therefore, to estimate the value of these products in the market place in order to assess more accurately the economic impact of certification.

For example, for the United States in 1992, the value of wood furniture imports accounted for about 68 per cent of the total value of hardwood imports from developing countries; up from 25 per cent in 1978. Also, for developing countries, the share of exports of wood manufactures and furniture going to developed countries is high. For 1991, the total value of wood furniture and wood manufactures exports from major developing-country exporters (the ones listed in Figure 15.3) was around $1.372 billion, with 80.5 per cent (or $1.1 billion) absorbed by developed countries.

Figure 15.3 clearly shows that the majority of developing-country exports of wood furniture and wood manufactures are absorbed by developed countries. An important implication of this is that the share of total timber exports from developing to developed countries could be higher than indicated earlier. For example, if the Republic of Korea imports logs from Malaysia, processes them and exports wood furniture to the United States, the statistics presented earlier do not capture the fact that Malaysian timber ultimately goes to the United States. Thus, those producing countries for which the United States and Europe were not important markets for logs, sawnwood and panels may in fact be more strongly affected by TC than first indicated, as a sig-

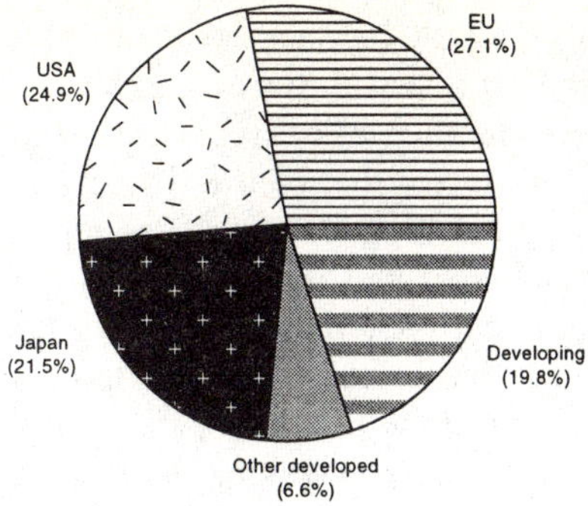

Figure 15.3 Major importers of wood furniture and wood manufactures from developing-country producers[a]

Notes: [a] Major wood furniture and wood manufactures developing-country exporters are: Brazil, Chile, Indonesia, Korea, Malaysia, Philippines, Singapore, and Thailand. Other major exporters not in the group due to data unavailability are: China and Hong Kong.
Source: Calculation from UN Trade Statistics.

nificant share of their raw timber may be exported to an intermediate country to be processed before being exported.

II LIKELY REVENUES AVAILABLE DUE TO TIMBER CERTIFICATION

This section assesses the potential financial benefits of timber certification to producers. In theory, certification could increase export revenues of producing countries through three mechanisms.

- First, certified timber sales may attract a "green premium", i.e. certified timber may be able to be sold at a higher price than uncertified timber. Surveys undertaken in the United Kingdom, other European countries and the United States found that consumers would be willing to pay moderate premiums for environmentally friendly timber. More specifically, Winterhalter and Cassens[8] reported that 34 per cent of consumers surveyed in the United States were willing to pay a 6–10 per cent price premium for sustainable wood, while Gerstman and Meyer's survey reported a willingness to pay a 1–5 per cent premium from 75 per cent of consumers surveyed. A Purdue University survey also indicated that among architects and designers surveyed, 57 per cent were willing to pay a premium of between 1 and 5 per cent and 36 per cent were willing to pay between 6–10 per cent. Results of two surveys in the United Kingdom have been reported by Haji Gazali and Simula,[9] and indicated that consumers were willing to pay around a 13 per cent premium for tropical timber products.[10]

- Second, certified timber may recapture those markets that have for some time banned the use of tropical timber. Such a ban is in effect in some 200 city councils in Germany and 51 per cent of Dutch municipalities. A number of states and cities in the United States, have banned, or proposed a ban, on the use of tropical timbers in public construction projects. Among them are the states of Arizona, California and New York, and the city of Minneapolis. If certified timber does become available, these markets may accept tropical timber again.
- Third, certified timber exporters may avert further losses of market share in those countries that are currently developing legislation or voluntary initiatives to exclude non-certified timber.

Table 15.4 presents the value of trade globally and by major consuming regions that will likely be affected by timber certification. The figures of Table 15.4 will be the basis for all further calculations.

In order to calculate the potential benefits due to timber certification, a scenario can be developed by addressing the following questions:

- What is the likely size of the market ("niche") to be affected by certification?
- How will the "green premium" affect tropical timber prices?
- What is the size of the market that could be potentially lost in the future and how much of that loss could be averted by certification?[11]

The assumptions made in answering these questions are analysed and explained below.

The Size of the "Niche" Market Affected by Certification

Timber certification will most likely affect developed countries and in particular tropical timber markets in Europe and the United States.[12] Concerns about the environmental impact of consuming tropical tim-

Table 15.4 Regional values of trade in tropical timber products

Region	*Estimated value of logs, sawn and panels*	*Value of wood furniture and wood manufacture imports*
World total	9023	1640
All developed countries	5414	1310
All developed, except Japan	2887	968
Europe (EU + EFTA)	2075	492
USA	677	408

Notes: (1) All figures are in millions of US dollars.
(2) Scenarios are based on 1991 values of trade.
(3) The following assumption were made:
(i) for logs + sawn + panels the shares of importers' values are the same as the shares of importers' volumes (see Table 15.2).
(ii) 60% of log + sawn + panel trade goes to developed countries. Japan's share is 28%, Europe's share is 23% and the US share is 7.5%.
(iii) 80% of wood furniture and wood manufactures trade goes to developed countries. Japan's share is 21.5%, Europe's (EC12 plus EFTA) share is 30% and the US share is 24.9%.

ber seems to be most significant in certain countries of Europe – the United Kingdom, Germany, the Netherlands and Austria. The first three countries are also among the six largest consumers of tropical timber products in Europe (the others are France, Italy and Spain). In the United States, there is also a significant degree of support within certain concerned groups.

Timber certification is expected to have most of its impact at the retail trade level, where the final consumers can directly exert their influence. So far, several retailers in Europe and the United States have shown interest in timber certification. The tropical timber that goes to final consumption and it is "visible" by the consumer is estimated to be around 50–60 per cent for Europe.[13] While there are no firm estimates available, the authors' discussions with NGOs, wholesalers, retailers and market exporters involved in the certification effort indicated that between 10 and 20 per cent of the timber in the European tropical timber market will potentially be affected by certification, while certification is likely to affect between 5 and 10 per cent of the United States tropical timber market. In short, the "niche" market for which TC may become a major factor in influencing consumer decisions is only a small part of the total market for tropical wood in developed economies.

The Size and the Distribution of the "Green Premium"

Price increases, due either to excess demand or to certification cost recovery, will be limited by the possibilities of substitution between tropical and other timbers or materials. However, price increases due to certification will be more prevalent in the "niche" market segments described earlier. The final impact on producer revenue will depend, as discussed before, on relevant price elasticities for these products and on the shift in demand for certified wood. For our calculations we consider the case of the "green premium" as described in Appendix 1.

Advocates of certification, however, claim that the main impact of certification will not be brought about through increased prices paid by the consumer. Rather, they argue that the consumer will pay the same price for certified timber; this will come about due to the introduction of improved inventory tracking systems under certification, enabling retailers to bypass a number of intermediaries in the trade, and buy more directly from the producer.[14] A larger share of the incremental revenue available would therefore be captured by the producer, as a result of reduced trade intermediation.[15] This would provide a greater incentive than a price increase on the final product (which would have been captured by wholesalers and/or retailers). Also, in this case, because the price to the consumer would not be affected, no substitution effects (away from tropical) would be likely. In this scenario, the "green premium" would take the form of an expansion of market share for certified producers without changes in prices. However, further empirical research is required for a proper evaluation of these claims.

A Potential Additional Revenue Gains through Averting Losses in Markets that will Require Certification

In view of the many countries that are considering introducing voluntary (and possibly) mandatory restrictions on import of non-certified timber, estimates can also be made of the quantity of timber that might be displaced in the future as a result of TC. It is assumed that the timber that is not accepted in the future in Europe (due to being non-certified) will be offered to other countries.[16] This, of course, will have a negative impact on non-certified tropical timber prices but positive impact on non-certified tropical timber revenues, assuming an elastic demand for tropical timber.

If certification is demanded by importing nations for tropical timber only, there is a strong possibility of trade diversion. As Varangis *et al.*

argued,[17] if Asian consumers (that absorb most of tropical timber trade) do not show preference for certified timber products, while consumers in Europe and North America do, tropical timber from uncertified (unsustainable) sources will flow to Asia while timber from sustainable sources will be diverted into North America and Europe. This assumes that not all tropical timber comes from unsustainable sources. Even in the extreme case of no tropical timber being able to qualify for certification, trade diversion is still likely to take place in the event that Asian consumers do not express preference for certified timber products. In this extreme case, the United States and Europe will probably consume very little or no tropical timber (because it will be rejected from their markets) while Asian importers may substitute tropical for temperate timber, absorbing almost all tropical timber exports. Indonesia, for example, has substantial opportunities for substituting Asian and Middle-Eastern markets for those of Europe and America. Furthermore, the rejection of tropical timber products due to eco-labelling in Europe and the United States would reduce the price of these products and make them more attractive to Asian importers.[18] As already noted, the adoption of eco-labelling programs in European countries is more likely to affect timber exports from African producers. However, Japan has been increasing imports of African timber, particularly from Gabon. Hence, some degree of trade diversion could take place even for African timber. This scenario could take place under these conditions, whether tropical timber certification is introduced on a voluntary basis or imposed unilaterally.[19]

Trade diversion can also take place even under the case where all timbers (tropical, temperate and softwoods) are covered by certification. It could be the case that softwoods and temperate hardwoods could much more easily meet the certification criteria and/or compliance of softwood and temperate timber producers is much broader than in tropical timbers. In this case, trade diversion will likely take place in a similar manner to the tropical timber certification case. That is, most tropical timber is likely to be absorbed within developing countries (producers and major importers) substituting for other timbers.

In order to give a rough estimate of the potential market loss that could be averted if certification is adopted, the following scenario was developed:

- First, it was assumed that if certification is not adopted, the whole market "niches" that are likely to be affected by certification will be lost. As stated earlier, certification is expected to affect 20 per cent of the European and 10 per cent of the United States market. Thus, in the absence of certification, we assumed that these markets will be lost. These lost markets were estimated to be worth approximately $622 million.

- Second, it was assumed that timber exports destined for the lost market segments above will be diverted to non-European/United States destinations. This would increase exports to these destinations by 8.9 per cent. Based on a price elasticity of demand of 1.7, the increase in exports will increase revenues in non-European/United States destinations by $256 million.[20]

Thus, the net future losses (gains) if certification is (not) applied for the market segments described above will be of the order of $366 million ($622–256 million).

Certification could increase revenues by recapturing lost markets. One of the potential benefits available to developing-country producers through certification is the recapture of market segments that have already been lost. Environmental concerns have already caused many Governments of European countries to ban (or consumers to discriminate against) tropical timber.[21] Because there are no sound estimates of the already lost market share for tropical timber we will not consider this potential effect in our calculations. However, the magnitude of this figure does not alter the thrust of the argument developed in this chapter. Even if we assume that all the reduction in the import value by European consumers was due to environmental concerns during the periods 1987–9 and 1991–2, it will result in a loss of $340 million. However, adjusting for the tropical timber price increase during the same period (about 13 per cent), and assuming a price elasticity of demand of 1.7 per cent, the decrease in the European value of imports becomes around $149 million. Including these $149 million to the potential benefits calculated in the following section will not significantly change the overall potential revenues available to developing countries due to TC.

B Estimation of Likely Commercial Benefits from Timber Certification

Based on the discussion above, the following is a rather optimistic scenario on how tropical timber certification will likely affect timber revenues from tropical timber producing countries. The assumptions underlying the scenario are that:

Table 15.5 A scenario for timber certification

Source of revenue	*Commercial benefits available (million US dollars)*
(i)–(iii): Incremental revenue from European and American market niches	62
(iv): Aversion of additional potential losses in the absence of certification minus additional revenues derived from related trade diversion	366
Total commercial benefits due to TC	428
Revenues as a percentage of export timber revenues of developing countries[a]	4%

Note: Figures are based on 1991 trade values and flows.
[a] The group of developing countries is defined as in FAO, and excludes China, Argentina, Chile and the countries of the Near East.

(i) 20 per cent of the European[22] market will be affected (market "niche" for certified timber);
(ii) 10 per cent of the American market will be affected (market "niche" for certified timber);
(iii) 10 per cent increment of revenues due to the "green premium" (affecting the market "niches" for certified timber (i) and (ii) above);
(iv) in the absence of certification, the whole market "niches" identified above, i.e. (i) and (ii), would be lost.

The figures for this scenario are shown in Table 15.5.

If it is assumed that there will be no further losses in market share if certification is not adopted, then the incremental revenues due to certification total $62 million – the equivalent of a 0.6 per cent increment of the total value of tropical timber product export revenues of developing countries.[23] If the market segments ("niches") affected by certification are totally lost in the absence of certification, the potential revenues associated with certification rise to $428 million; the equivalent of 4 per cent of export timber revenues of developing countries.

In these calculations we did not calculate the recapturing of the markets already lost due to environmental concerns. However, previously we calculated that the value of tropical timber imports in Europe has dropped by about $149 million (after adjusting for price increases).

Thus, even if we assume that all of it was due to environmental concerns and all of it could be recaptured with TC, the total potential revenues of Table 15.5 would increase to $577 million, or 5.4 per cent of the total timber export revenues of developing countries.

These figures indicate that the potential financial incentives of tropical timber certification from the perspective of producing countries are limited, at least for the short to medium term. However, individual producers that first become certified could establish themselves in a market niche and potentially receive significant financial benefits. In addition, producing countries may have other non-economic, long-term benefits accruing from the adoption of better forest-management practices and the maintenance of biodiversity.

C Costs Associated with Timber Certification[24]

The analysis proposed above has not addressed the costs associated with TC. In practice, a TC scheme entails two types of costs at the company level. The first is the cost for the company to operate in a sustainable manner, according to a set of agreed principles and criteria. The second is the cost of the certification process.

The cost of sustainable forest management, which is also referred to as compliance cost to the TC scheme, varies widely across types of forests (heterogenous versus homogenous, tropical versus temperate and boreal). As pointed out by Haji Gazali and Simula,[25] the lack of reliable estimates on the cost of sustainable forest management is mainly caused by the lack of commonly agreed operational definitions of sustainability. In Sarawak, an ITTO study reported that the cost of nearly zero impact logging would increase the cost of logging by 100 per cent or about $60 per cubic metre log. In the Philippines, Paris and Ruzicka[26] reported that sustainable forest management would cost an extra $38 per cubic metre log. An estimate by Dianasari for the externality costs of forest destruction due to logging in Indonesia, leads to additional cost of about $70 per cubic metre log.[27] Jaakko Pöyry estimated that the cost of compliance ranges between zero and $13 per cubic metre log.[28] Most of these estimates suggest that the cost of sustainable forest management per cubic metre log likely lies between 10 and 20 per cent of the current average international tropical log price of about $350. Application of common principles and criteria for sustainable forest management is expected to eventually lower the compliance cost over time.

For certification costs which will consist of inspection, timber tracking and monitoring costs, so far there are no reliable estimates. These costs will depend mainly on the availability of information on the forest inventory and adequacy of forest maps. In developed countries where expertise and information systems have been developed in the forestry field, the cost is estimated to range between $0.30 and $0.60 per hectare. In developing countries, rough estimates suggest that the certification cost will be in the range of 5–10 per cent of existing logging costs. A significantly different cost estimate was reported by Septiani and Elliot.[29] SGS/Indonesia estimated a $1.30 cost for tracking per cubic metre timber while SGS/New Zealand came up with $7 per cubic metre.

In the context of costs for TC schemes, international mutual recognition and harmonization of principles, standards and criteria becomes a central issue to developing countries that export timber products. If each developed country that imports timber products were to impose its own requirements, or if each of them were to subscribe to different certification or accreditation systems, it is conceivable that the costs would become prohibitively high for developing-country exporters to enter developed-country markets.

At the national level, the eco-labelling and timber certification initiatives may also involve significant costs, such as foregone export earnings and/or opportunity costs in terms of the resources committed to develop the eco-labelling schemes. For example, the Indonesian Government recently announced its commitment to reduce the sustainable log harvest from 31.4 to 22.5 million cubic metres per year to be reached over the next five years. If this is considered to be a means of implementing the sustainable forest management, it will cost the country at least $300 million per year in the form of foregone foreign-exchange revenue in terms of plywood exports.[30]

The rough estimates presented in this section indicate that the combined costs of compliance, the certification costs and the foregone export earnings could be significant. These costs further qualify the financial benefits of implementing TC.

III CONCLUSIONS

In trying to answer the question "is there a commercial case for timber certification?", we found that producers can benefit from TC even though the direct impact (that is the "green premium") is small in aggregate terms. If one assumes that eco-labelling will become a condition for market access in Europe and the United States, then the appeal of TC increases. But even in this scenario, under rather optimistic assumptions, the share of revenues from tropical timber exports affected by TC is unlikely to be large. In this context, one should not expect TC to provide significant financial benefits to developing countries in the near future.

On a more positive note, TC may provide competitive advantages to firms participating in credible certification schemes. On a country level, producing countries may enjoy long-term economic, social and environmental benefits due to better forest management practices. It remains true, however, that the implementation of such schemes on a broad basis continues to be a challenge not only from a technical perspective, but also in terms of the lack of accepted multilateral standards. Moreover, the costs of implementation of TC further qualify the dimensions of the economic benefits that can be appropriated by producer countries. Hopefully, TC will help in the development of appropriate criteria for forest management, that will be adopted not only by producers that export to sensitive markets, but all producers. There are, however, many complex factors that influence the decision-making process of the producer. Enabling producers to capture greater revenues will not ensure that improved forest management systems and decreased deforestation rates ensue. The policy environment in which most producers function is highly distorted. Market and policy failures in both the forest and related sectors are, in fact, the major causes of deforestation and forest degradation.[31] These failures must be addressed concurrently with the introduction of a certification system, to enable the market signals it creates effectively and properly to influence forestry in developing countries.

APPENDIX 1

The Market for Tropical Timber and Eco-Labelling

This annex summarizes the potential impact of eco-labelling in the market for tropical timber, following the analysis introduced by Mattoo and Singh.[32] Assume that we have two situations. One is the pre-label and the other the post-label situation. In the pre-label situation, there is a product that is undifferentiated

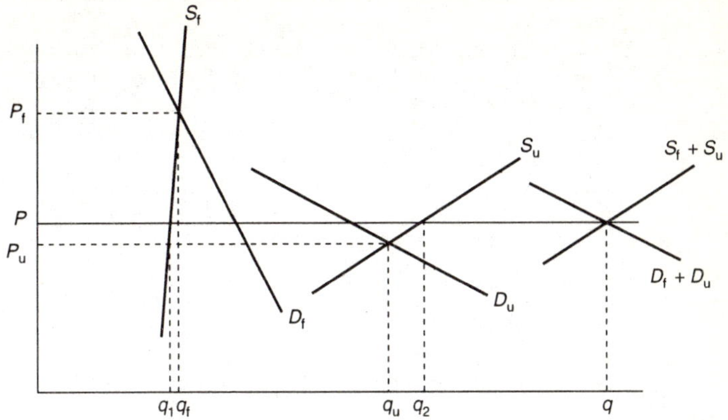

Figure 15.4 Price and quantity effects of timber certification

in the market and demanded both by consumers who are concerned about the environment and by consumers who are not. Now labelling is introduced and products are differentiated according to whether they are produced by environment friendly methods (f) or environment unfriendly methods (u). Let us also assume that consumers concerned about the environment buy exclusively environmentally friendly (f) goods when goods are differentiated, while the rest of the consumers buy the cheaper product, irrespective of its method of production. Consider the case where, after product differentiation, at the pre-labeling price (p) the demand for the friendly good is greater than the supply (and the demand for the unfriendly good is less than the supply): see Figure 15.4.

At the price prevailing at the pre-label case (p), the total quantity produced is q, being allocated as q_1 for the friendly and q_2 for the unfriendly goods. In the post-label case, the friendly good sells at a premium $p_f - p$ with quantity q_f clearing the market for the "friendly" good, while the unfriendly good sells at a discount $p - p_u$ and again the quantity is q_u.

Under the above scenario the production of the environmentally friendly good will increase ($q_f - q_1$) and that of the environmentally unfriendly good will decrease ($q_2 - q_u$). These descriptions seem appropriate for the tropical timber market, based on available estimates of supply and demand. Note that in the opposite case where at price p the supply of environmentally friendly good exceeds the demand (and the demand of the environmentally unfriendly good exceeds the supply) the production of both goods will be unaffected, given the arbitrage between the two goods by the environmentally non-concerned consumers. In this latter scenario, eco-labelling will not have an impact in encouraging (discouraging) the production of the environmentally friendly (unfriendly) good.

In calculating the additional revenues resulting from eco-labelling we assume very elastic demand and supply curves for the unfriendly good and rather inelastic schedules (curves) for the friendly good. A very elastic demand curve for non-certified (unfriendly) timber is possible given the existence of many substitutes. By doing so, the price discount $p - p_u$ on the unfriendly good becomes small and for simplicity is ignored in our calculations. Furthermore, by assuming a highly inelastic supply curve for friendly goods (as appears to be the case of certified timber, at least in the short to medium term), the change in the revenues between the pre-labelling and post-labelling situations can be approximated by $(p_f - p) \cdot q_f$.

Notes

1. This paper is an abridged version of the original report presented at the UNCTAD Workshop on Ecolabelling and International Trade, Geneva, June 1994.
2. Other potential benefits of TC often mentioned incude: (i) improved control over illegal logging; (ii) internalization of the externalities or social costs caused by timber production; (iii) rationalization of investment in the timber industry; and (iv) improved efficiency in timber-based industry.
3. International Tropical Timber Organization (ITTO), *Report of the Working Party on Certification of all Timber and Timber Products* (Cartagena: ITTO, May 1994).
4. J. R. Vincent, "The Tropical Timber Trade and Sustainable Development", *Science*, 256 (1992) p. 1651.
5. Data for logs, sawnwood and wood-based panels are from FAO *Yearbook of Forest Products*. For wood furniture and wood manufacture the data are from United Nations trade statistics. Because for the latter we only have data for the major exporters, we extrapolated the world total for wood manufacture and wood furniture based on the share of logs plus sawnwood plus wood panel exports revenues of these exporters in the world export revenues (for logs plus sawnwood plus wood based panels). All data are for 1991.
6. Defined here as logs, sawnwood and wood-based panels.
7. General Agreement on Tariffs and Trade, "Increases in Market Access Resulting from the Uruguay Round", *News of the Uruguay Round*, April 1994.
8. D. Winterhalter and D. L. Cassens, *United States Hardwood Forests: Consumer Perception and Willingness to Pay* (Purdue University, Department of Forestry, 1993).
9. Baharuddin Haji Gazali and Markku Simula, *Certification Scheme for All Timber and Timber Products* (Cartagena: ITTO, May 1994).
10. A comparison with the results of a survey on organic food may help put the "green premium" for tropical timber issue in perspective. Based on a national survey, Van Ravensway and John Hoehn reported that the increased price that consumers in the United States are willing to pay for health and environmental attributes is between 5 and 7 per cent on average. See Van Ravensway and John Hoehn, "Consumer Willingness to Pay for Reducing Pesticides Residues in Food: Results of a Nationwide Survey",

Department of Agricultural Economics, Michigan State University, mimeo, March 1991.

11. There may also be additional financial gains through the recapture of market that currently ban the use of tropical timber.
12. Johnson and Cabarle report that demand for wood from sustainable sources presently barely influences the Japanese local market. See N. Johnson, and B. Cabarle, *Surviving the Cut: Natural Forest Management in Humid Tropics* (Washington, DC: World Resources Institute, 1993).
13. On high-value markets for tropical sawnwood, plywood and veneer in the European Community, see FAO, *High-value Markets for Tropical Sawnwood, Plywood and Veneer in the European Community* (Rome: FAO, October 1991).
14. This has already happened in one retail store in the United States which has actually cut the price of timber products made from certified timber because it is buying direct from the producer.
15. The reduced trade intermediation will result in lower production costs that will shift the supply curve (S_f) for certified timber to the right.
16. This can be seen as a shift to the right of the supply for non-certified timber.
17. P. N. Varangis, C. A. Primo Braga and K. Takeuchi, "Tropical Timber Trade Policies: What Impact Will Ecolabelling Have?", *Wirtschaftspolitische Blatter*, vol. 3/4 (1993), pp. 338–51.
18. This is not just a valid description of only the intermediate dynamics, as noted by A. Mattoo and H. V. Singh, "Eco-Labelling: Policy Considerations", *Kyklos*, vol. 47 (1994), pp. 53–65. These authors assume that the demand for certified tropical timber is greater than the supply at the pre-labelling price. However, available estimates suggest that this is not an accurate description of the current situation. With supply of certified timber estimated at around one million cubic metres, demand is tentatively estimated to be at least two to three times as much. Thus, the situation of the existence of excess demand for certified timber described in the Annex is a more accurate representation of the tropical timber market.
19. The assumption here is that tropical, temperate and softwood timber products have a high elasticity of substitution, at least in the long run, and that there is a low elasticity of substitution between timber products and non-timber products. In such a scenario, the rejection of tropical timber in Europe will increase prices of temperate and softwood timber products, in which case Asian importers will substitute tropical timber products for the latter.
20. The formula applied for the calculation is:

$$\alpha R = \left(1 - \frac{1}{e}\right) \frac{\alpha Q}{Q} \cdot \mathrm{R}$$

    where, R is the revenue (PQ), Q is the quantity (exports) and e is the price demand elasticity.

21. See Johnson and Cabarle, op. cit., and "The Greening of Protectionism", *The Economist*, 27 February–5 March 1993, p. 28.
22. European countries included are the EU12 and EFTA countries.

23. These incremental revenues are the product of $(p_f - p)q_f$ as shown in Figure 15.4.
24. This section draws mainly on M. Ahmad, "The Importance of Eco-labeling and Timber Certification for Indonesia's Export Markets", Department of Agricultural Economics, Michigan State University, mimeo, 1994.
25. Haji Gazali and Simula, "Certification Scheme for All Timber and Timber Products", op. cit.
26. See Paris and Ruzicka, "Barking Up the Wrong Tree: The Role of Rent Appropriation in Sustainable Forest Management", Environmental Office Occasional Paper, no. 1, Asian Development Bank, Manila, 1991.
27. According to Ahmad, op. cit., another rough estimate of the cost of sustainable forest management in Indonesia is to take the official forest plantation planting cost of $1000 per hectare divided by about 30 cubic metres of log harvested per hectare concession. It generates the estimated additional costs of about $35 per cubic metre of log harvested.
28. Jaakko Pöyry, "Tropical Deforestation in Asia and Market for Wood", Consultant's Report to the World Bank, 1993.
29. Ani Septiani and Joana Elliot, "Viability of Eco-Labeling Indonesian Wood Products as a Means of Enabling Sustainable Forest Management", NRMP, Jakarta, 1994.
30. See Ahmad, op. cit.
31. See World Bank, "Strategy for Forest Sector Developing in Asia", Asia Technical Department Series, Technical paper no. 182, 1992.
32. Mattoo and Singh, op. cit.

16 Certification and Eco-Labelling of Timber and Timber Products

David P. Elliott

In recent years, there has been intense interest and concern about deforestation and degradation of the world's forests with consequent environmental damages – at the global level, loss of biological diversity and climate change, and at the national and local levels, harm to the provision of products and services derived from forests. Initiatives for certification and eco-labelling of timber and timber products have been motivated by these concerns and by the possibilities of acting in the near term to foster better forest management and complementing long-term efforts to improve forestry policies and practices. It is also widely recognized that timber is an important commodity in trade and that forest industries provide income and employment in producing countries.

As with other trade-related incentives that influence forest use, there are limits to the scope of effectiveness of certification and eco-labelling of timber and timber products. Forests used for the production of timber comprise only a part of all forests and account for only a part of the whole problem of forest loss and degradation. Further, only a part of the logs harvested in production forests are destined for international trade as logs or in the form of sawnwood, plywood and veneer, or more highly manufactured products made of these commodities.[1]

For consumers, eco-labelling constitutes one of the very few means by which the public can, through buying decisions, have some influence on the management of forests. Certification and eco-labelling could be used in domestic markets of producing countries as well as in international trade.

I CONCEPTS OF CERTIFICATION AND LABELLING

In the context of this paper, certification refers to documentary evidence that certain standards have been met with regard to origin and environmental aspects, as validated by an independent certifier.[2] A key aim in establishing standards is the sustainability of forest management as, for example, in the protection of biological diversity.[3] Another important aspect of certification is its use in later stages of processing and trade, in connection with verification and monitoring procedures.

Labelling of timber and timber products may be thought of as a means to provide information to the final consumer on certified products or products manufactured from certified timber. The name of the certifier and other more specific information might be included in a label. A common international label might also be used. Certification and labelling are conceptually similar in that they identify a product as meeting standards, but they have physically separate documents. Eco-labelling is particularly important for identification in sales of consumer goods such as furniture to the general public. Some other form of documentary evidence might be used in the case of large volumes of sawnwood or plywood for use in construction, since individual labels would be impractical.

II STANDARDS FOR SUSTAINABLE MANAGEMENT

The multiple uses of forests and the wide variety of conditions under which timber is grown make it impossible to set down a clear and simple set of globally applicable standards for the sustainable management of forests. Efforts at the multilateral level have, instead, focused on formulating and agreeing on broader principles, guidelines and criteria. A precise and detailed definition of the term "sustainable management" is also difficult for similar reasons. The International Tropical Timber Organization (ITTO), an intergovernmental organization having both producing and consuming countries as members, has put forward the following definition:

> Sustainable forest management is the process of managing permanent forest land to achieve one or more clearly specified objectives of management with regard to the production of a continuous flow

> of desired forest products and services without undue reduction of its inherent values and future productivity and without undue undesirable effects on the physical and social environment.[4]

For the purposes of certification and labelling, the term "sustainably produced timber" refers to timber originating from forests that are managed with the aim of sustainability from that point in time onwards. However, a stricter use of the term could refer only to timber grown under conditions of sustainable management through its entire life cycle. The latter use of the term would seriously restrict the scope of its application, as supplies would be considerably smaller here.

Standards may be set by sponsoring organizations, be they non-governmental or governmental. Guidance for standard-setting is drawn from a wide range of principles, guidelines and criteria, as well as the growing body of research and practical knowledge in this area. Multilaterally agreed principles are of particular interest here, as they may form a common basis for setting standards. Furthermore, they may facilitate the harmonization of standards and the mutual recognition of national certification and labelling schemes, leading to wider and increased application of schemes.

Chief among the multilaterally agreed principles are those in the "Non-legally binding authoritative statement of principles for a global consensus on the management, conservation and sustainable development of all types of forests", agreed at the United Nations Conference on Environment and Development (UNCED) in 1992.[5] The "Forest Principles", as they are informally known, represent a first global consensus on forests, and their guiding objectives are to contribute to the management, conservation and sustainable development of forests, and to provide for their multiple and complementary functions and uses. A number of these principles are relevant to the process of standard-setting for certification and labelling. For example, the Forest Principles provide that sustainable forest management and use should be carried out in accordance with national development policies and priorities, and on the basis of environmentally sound national guidelines. Another example is that the Principles specify that account should be taken, as appropriate and if applicable, of relevant internationally agreed methodologies and criteria in the formulation of such guidelines.

With regard to internationally agreed methodologies and criteria, the "Guidelines" and "Criteria" recommended by the ITTO give a broad orientation for setting standards. They cover issues related to the sustainable management of natural and planted tropical production forests and the conservation of biological diversity in tropical production forests (see Box 16.1).

Box 16.1 ITTO guidelines and criteria for setting standards

"ITTO Guidelines for the sustainable management of natural tropical forests" (December 1992);

"Criteria for the measurement of sustainable tropical forest management" (March 1992);

"ITTO Guidelines for the establishment and the sustainable management of planted tropical forests" (January 1993); and

"ITTO Guidelines on the conservation of biological diversity in tropical production forests" (September 1993).

As regards temperate and boreal timbers and forest management, two resolutions in the form of general guidelines on sustainable management of forests in Europe and conservation of biological diversity in European forests were agreed at the Ministerial Conference on the Protection of Forests in Europe held in Helsinki in June 1993. In September 1993, a seminar was held in Montreal on sustainable development of temperate and boreal forests for the purpose of exchanging views on criteria and indicators of sustainable forestry. A follow-up meeting was held in December 1993. The United Nations Conference for the Negotiation of a Successor Agreement to the International Tropical Timber Agreement, 1983 was held in four parts from April 1993 to January 1994. It resulted in the adoption of the International Tropical Timber Agreement, 1994, under which the ITTO will continue to operate. In this conference, a group of consumer countries of temperate, boreal and tropical timbers issued a formal statement committing themselves to implement appropriate guidelines and criteria for sustainable management of their forests comparable to those developed by the ITTO for tropical forests.[6] In May 1994, the ITTO convened a Working Party on Certification of All Timber and Timber Products. A wide-ranging discussion took place on key issues in the area.

There is a continuing initiative from UNCED for negotiating an international instrument or convention on forests in the future. The matter is still under consideration, and if it materializes, the terms of the proposed convention could provide much guidance for the certification and eco-labelling of timber.

The process of agreeing on broad guidelines which could be used for setting standards is of crucial importance. From a multilateral perspective, arrangements for the participation of all concerned are essential, and consensus-building often takes time. Matters of equitability in the distribution of responsibilities between developed and developing countries, as well as efficiency, equal sharing and global partnership are especially relevant here. In other words, the stress needs to be on avoiding unilateralism and double standards (one set for tropical countries and another, less stringent set for non-tropical countries) with respect to time-frame, definitions, guidelines, criteria and indicators. A collective effort in an international process could lay the necessary legal and equitable basis for concerted international action.

Practical action has not, however, awaited developments at the multilateral level. For instance, the Forest Stewardship Council, a body whose members are non-governmental organizations with diverse interests, has been established with the aim of providing an international framework for various certification schemes through global principles and criteria agreed on by its members.

However they are agreed on, guidelines or principles can only be general, and more specific criteria and standards are needed for local conditions. In Canada, for instance, it is foreseen that several sets of criteria and standards are needed for sustainable forestry at local levels, on account of the heterogeneity in physical conditions, ownership, etc.

III PRINCIPLES FOR TRADE IN TIMBER PRODUCTS

While considering certification and eco-labelling of timber and timber products, account should be taken of trade principles and their linkages with issues related to environment and development. In this regard, the UNCED Forest Principles include the following elements:

> 13. (a) Trade in forest products should be based on non-discriminatory and multilaterally agreed rules and procedures consistent with international law and practices. In this context, open and free international trade in forest products should be facilitated.
> (b) Reduction and removal of tariff barriers and impediments to the provision of better market access and better prices for higher value-added forest products and their local processing should be encouraged to enable producer countries to better conserve and manage their renewable forest resources.
> (c) Incorporation of environmental costs and benefits into market

forces and mechanisms, in order to achieve forest conservation and sustainable development should be encouraged both domestically and internationally.

(d) Forest conservation and sustainable development policies should be integrated with economic, trade and other relevant policies.

(e) Fiscal, trade, industrial, transportation and other policies and practices that may lead to forest degradation should be avoided. Adequate policies, aimed at management, conservation and sustainable development of forests, including, where appropriate, incentives, should be encouraged.

14. Unilateral measures, incompatible with international obligations or agreements, to restrict and/or ban international trade in timber or other forest products should be removed or avoided, in order to attain long-term sustainable forest management.[7]

IV CERTIFICATION AND ECO-LABELLING SCHEMES

At present, the certification schemes in operation are few and their total coverage of trade small, but they are expected to grow in number and share of trade. A recent study by Ghazali and Simula reported that only four of the certification systems surveyed could be considered operational and that the timber and timber products certified in 1993 amounted only to an estimated 1.5 million cubic metres. Although all of the certified timber did not enter international trade, this quantity is the equivalent of less than 0.5 per cent of world trade in industrial logs, sawnwood, plywood and veneer. A total of about 35 suppliers were certified. Most of the certified timber was of tropical origin and sold in the United States market.[8]

As an example of the organization and operation of a scheme, Box 16.2 provides information on the Rainforest Alliance's "Smart Wood" certification programme. It is estimated that the output from sources certified under the Smart Wood programme is over one million cubic metres per year.[9] A novel form of certification was suggested in a study by the London Environmental Economics Centre for the ITTO.[10] Given the difficulties with product labelling and certification of logging concessions, it was felt that the most appropriate scheme, at least initially, would be country certification. The main point of such a country certification scheme would be to ensure that a producer country is implementing policies, regulations and management plans that ensure substantial progress towards the ITTO's Year 2000 Target.[11] The Target refers to the organization's priority objective of bringing tropical production forests under sustainable management so that the total exports of tropical timber products come from sustainably managed resources by the year 2000.

Box 16.2 Smart Wood Certification Programme*

Background

Smart Wood was established as the first independent forest management certification program in the world in 1990. The Program is managed by a core staff of forestry specialists, with assistance from Smart Wood advisors and local consultants and cooperating organizations in producing countries throughout the Americas, Europe, Asia, Africa and the Pacific. Smart Wood is part of the Rainforest Alliance's ECO-OK product certification effort.

Purpose

The purpose of Smart Wood is to provide objective third-party evaluation of forest products sources and companies, enabling consumers to identify products whose harvesting does not contribute to the destruction of forests. Smart Wood certifies forest products that come from "sustainable " or "well-managed" forestry operations, or "sources". Sources could include a natural forest, a plantation, a large commercial forestry concession or a small-scale community project. Through certification, Smart Wood hopes to increase forest managers' incentives to adopt sustainable forestry practices that meet long-term environmental, economic and social needs.

Eligibility

Smart Wood is a voluntary program working with the forestry industry and with wholesalers or retailers of forest products. All sources of timber, or companies involved in selling forest products, in all types of forests, are eligible to apply for certification. At the request of applicants, Smart Wood staff or advisors conduct a field evaluation (and subsequent field audits) of forestry activities, pertinent records and facilities as necessary to verify the quantity of forest management at the source, or clarify the sources of a trading company's forest products. All information is held in strict confidentiality.

Cost

All certified sources and companies are requested to pay an annual, non-reimbursable program management fee. No organization shall be refused participation in the Program due to an inability to pay the annual management fee or cover certification costs. However, because Smart Wood must raise funds to cover assessments for such organizations, they will usually take longer to perform. All payments made to Smart Wood are solely for the purpose of covering program costs.

Criteria for Certification

Smart Wood certification is based on field review using either the "Smart Wood Generic Guidelines for Assessing Natural Forests", "Smart Wood Generic Guidelines for Assessing Forest Plantations", or, when available, country- or region-specific guidelines. In general, candidate operations must meet the following broad principles: maintenance of environmental functions, including watershed stability and biological conservation; sustained yield of forestry production; and positive impact on local communities. Smart Wood companies are certified according to whether all or some of their wood products come from certified Smart Wood sources.

Evaluation/Audit Process

When a potential Smart Wood source is first identified, an information search on that operation is conducted. In most cases, Smart Wood will conduct an initial field evaluation, using its own staff or personnel from a cooperating regional or local organization, or independent consultants. In all field evaluations, a local specialist from that country will be involved. Field evaluations are reviewed by Smart Wood staff and members of an independent review panel. After input from review panel members, the Smart Wood Program makes a final decision as to certification. Whether certified as a Smart Wood source or company, periodic field audits are conducted. Separate Smart Wood company and source "Certification Assessment and Audit Protocols" provide more detail on field procedures.

International Networking

To facilitate evaluation and monitoring of sources, Smart Wood is developing an international network of certification professionals, called regional Forestry Field Agents, and local collaborating organizations.

---

* *Source*: Rainforest Alliance, "Description of the 'Smart Wood' Certification Programme", 30 September 1993.

A particularly important consideration is the role of governments in certification and labelling schemes. Most schemes are conceived of as voluntary. If they are mandatory, the issue of compatibility with the rules of the General Agreement on Tariffs and Trade (GATT) arises, as distinguishing products on the basis of production methods is not permitted under GATT rules at present. Governments can, however, play a sponsoring role for voluntary schemes, as these are not incompatible with the GATT rules. Austria and the Netherlands already have schemes in place. Indonesia has taken steps to develop a certification system for timber products, and the European Union is considering an eco-labelling scheme for timber. Another function for governments could be the regulation of schemes in order to prevent illegitimate certification programmes, false advertising or counterfeit certificates.

V SOME PRELIMINARY POLICY CONCLUSIONS

A thorough analysis of the implications of certification and eco-labelling is not yet possible since few schemes are in operation and others are still being developed. Many problem areas remain to be solved. Ghazali and Simula considered a number of aspects of timber certification and the available, very limited information on their implications for costs of forest management and certification, their implications for demand, prices and trade, and their impact on forest production and forest industries.[12]

As with other market-oriented measures, the purpose of certification and eco-labelling should be to reinforce the positive incentives for sustainable management, and not to penalize or restrict production and trade in timber not meeting standards. These and other improvements of mechanisms between markets and forest management should also complement policies and practices in producing countries for the sustainable management of their forests. In this regard, internalization of the costs of sustainable management of forests in production costs is an important issue.

Certification and eco-labelling could create a price premium and an additional quantity of timber sold. There is some empirical evidence that consumers are willing to pay a premium for "green" timber, although it is uncertain whether they would do so in actual buying situations.[13] Additional revenue from a price premium and an expanded sales volume, if passed back through the long chain of processing, marketing and trade, should provide a financial incentive for the sustainable management of forests.

Another possible outcome is that, given the competition from non-wood products in consumer markets and in the construction industry, there may be neither a price premium nor expanded sales. Nevertheless, certification and eco-labelling could be useful in gaining access to markets or market segments where environmentally sensitive buyers are important, while products that are not certified or labelled could fare worse. In an extreme situation, certification and eco-labelling, by allowing some timber and products to gain access, would be preferable to total bans and boycotts that would cut off revenues and financial incentives for sustainable forest management.

Countries which do not meet certification standards could lose markets and revenue from sales, unless they could divert trade to other equally remunerative markets where certification and labelling would not be essential. This problem highlights the need for national and international policies and programmes for sustainable forest management that would help those countries to meet standards. This action would be particularly important for developing countries which are highly dependent on timber for export earnings and domestic income and employment as, for example, is the case for some African countries.

Suppliers that meet standards of sustainable management will have their share of difficulties as well. Production costs are likely to rise with sustainable management. Firstly, harvesting with low-intensity and selective felling systems yields considerably lower volumes of timber on a per-hectare basis. Secondly, there is a higher cost per hectare of logging, resulting from more stringent protection of the environment, including the residual stands of trees and their regeneration. These two factors imply that the cost per cubic metre of producing timber will rise with sustainable management. Improvements in technology could, however, be a factor which would reduce production costs. An additional cost of producing timber sustainably could reduce or eliminate the gains from a "green" price premium and from the extra sales resulting from the supply of certified timber.

It should be noted that the factors that affect the cost of sustainable production are inherent to sustainable management, and are not merely limited to logging in connection with certification and eco-labelling schemes. These factors will, of necessity, accompany the implementation of schemes. In addition, there would be additional costs that are specifically related to participation in certification schemes, such as the costs of periodic inspections.

The international community could be supportive in discussing and, where possible, agreeing on appropriate elements for certification and eco-labelling, such as guidelines and standards for sustainable forest management, practical aspects of implementation of schemes at the producer level, and monitoring and verification of flows of "green" timber in trade, processing and marketing. Other supportive areas could be the harmonization of schemes or the mutual recognition of schemes and labels, to increase the scope of application and credibility of schemes.

In considering certification and eco-labelling as policy instruments to promote sustainable forest management, account should be taken not only of their effectiveness in reaching improved forests management while ensuring access to markets, but also other international obligations and commitments. Equitability or fairness in the distribution of responsibilities between countries, respect for national sovereignty and compatibility with other international obligations, such as the agreements at UNCED and ITTO's Year 2000 target for sustainable management, are important in the consideration of policy. Reduced tariffs and greater access to markets for sustainably produced timber may foster improved forest management, but possible use of certification in connection with trade policy, such as bans, quotas or tariffs on unsustainably produced timber, needs consideration.

Notes

1. However, in some cases, there are close links between logging and offtake as exports. For example, in the Sarawak state of Malaysia, about four-fifths of logs are destined for exports in some form.
2. For a more detailed discussion of the concepts of certification and labelling, see Markku Simula, "Timber Certification Initiatives and their Implications for Developing Countries", in this volume.
3. See section II, below.
4. International Tropical Timber Organization, "Sustainable Forest Management", Decision 6(XI) of the International Tropical Timber Council, 4 December 1991.
5. United Nations Conference on Environment and Development, *Report of the United Nations Conference on Environment and Development*, A/CONF.151/26 (vol. III), 14 August 1992, pp. 111–16.
6. UNCTAD, "Formal statement by consumer members", TD/TIMBER.2/L.6, 21 January 1994. The formal statement is also included in the Introduction to document TD/TIMBER.2/16, which contains the text of the International Tropical Timber Agreement, 1994 (United Nations publication, Sales no. 94.II.D.23).
7. United Nations Conference on Environment and Development, op. cit., p. 116.

8. B. H. Ghazali and M. Simula, *Certification Schemes for all Timber and Timber Products*, study prepared for the International Tropical Timber Organization, 15 April 1994, p. 32.
9. Details of other certification schemes and views of governments and organizations are given in Ghazali and Simula, op. cit.
10. London Environmental Economics Centre, *The Economic Linkages between the International Trade in Tropical Timber and the Sustainable Managment of Tropical Forests*, main report to the International Tropical Timber Organization, 19 March 1993, p. 123.
11. International Tropical Timber Organization, "ITTO Action Plan: Criteria and Priority Areas for Programme Development and Project Work", November 1990, p. 3.
12. Ghazali and Simula, op. cit., pp. 71–82.
13. See also, Simula, "Timber Certification Initiatives", in this volume.

17 Eco-Labelling and GATT

Janet Chakarian[1]

This chapter discusses some of the general orientations that have emerged from the work carried out by the General Agreement on Tariffs and Trade (GATT) on eco-labelling. This work has been conducted in the context of the Group on Environmental Measures and International Trade, a working group which was convened in November 1991 on the basis of an agenda of three items, one of which concerned the trade effects of new forms of labelling and packaging requirements aimed at protecting the environment.

Discussions in the Group have concentrated on trying to identify the trade effects of these measures and on analysing to what extent they might differ from the trade-related technical regulations and standards that are more familiar to GATT contracting parties through the Agreement on Technical Barriers to Trade. Discussions were assisted to a great extent by information supplied by contracting parties on their own national labelling and packaging schemes, the majority of which were voluntary in nature. Although not mandatory, it was considered that such eco-labelling schemes could still have a major influence on conditions of competition in a market. The group considered that effective access to foreign suppliers to participate and raise their trade concerns in the process through which product criteria and threshold levels for awarding eco-labels were decided was critical, as was having access to certification systems and the awarding of labels on the same terms as domestically produced goods.

It was also observed in the Group that both the choice of products to be labelled and the criteria that a product must meet in order to obtain the label tend to reflect local environmental conditions, such as resource constraints and local preferences for specific environmental product attributes, which may be difficult for foreign producers to meet or result in overlooking positive environmental qualities of imported products. The influence of local industry in the choice of products or criteria should not result in inadvertent protective consequences, and the importance of basing the criteria on sound scientific evidence was stressed. The choice of which environmental qualities to highlight in awarding labels, particularly in the context of life-cycle analysis where usually only a few of the product's attributes are highlighted, inevitably involves value judgements, and can have an important influence on the trade effects of the measures. Therefore, it was viewed as critical that foreign suppliers have access to the design stage of the scheme.

Eco-labelling criteria based on processes and production methods (PPMs), which are often used in schemes that involve life-cycle analysis of products, may prove particularly difficult and even environmentally inappropriate for overseas suppliers to meet. There are legitimate reasons for diversity in environmental regulations across countries, not least of which is that environmental concerns and priorities vary among countries. As these are often reflected in PPMs, foreign suppliers' access to an eco-label may be restricted if their own preferred PPMs are not the same as those required in the overseas market, or if establishing that they meet the process standards involves substantial additional cost. Although many contracting parties recognize that eco-labelling schemes based on life-cycle analysis will inevitably have to take into account the environmental impact of the PPMs used, some have raised the concern that specifying trade restrictions in terms of PPMs can imply exporting domestic environmental standards and raise issues of extraterritorial application.

There has been some discussion on the potential inconsistencies between article III of the General Agreement and mandatory eco-labelling schemes that involve life-cycle analysis. While it is true that article III only applies to products and that discrimination between products based on PPMs is inconsistent with the General Agreement, it is not clear whether such eco-labelling schemes would constitute discrimination according to the meaning of this term in the General Agreement. The language of article III:1 explicitly recognizes that such "internal taxes and other internal charges, and laws, regulations and requirements affecting the internal sale, offering for sale, purchase, transportation, distribution or use of products" exist, and should not be applied to imported and domestic products so as to afford protection to domestic production. In any consideration of consistency between a measure and article III of the General Agreement, there are a number of analytical steps that must be carried out, such as the aim and effect of the measure, and whether the measure would change the conditions of competition in the domestic market for this product. In addition, article XX – the exceptions article – might be invoked, which would bring in the concepts of necessity and unjustifiable discrimination into the analysis. As each case would need to be examined on its own merits, general statements of consistency or inconsistency may often do justice neither to the measure nor to the GATT system.

Further, the newly created World Trade Organization (WTO) Committee on Trade and Environment will continue to examine the issues in a generic fashion as the item of packaging and labelling schemes will be carried over from the Group into the new Committee. Some of the issues identified for further analysis include:

- the practical distinction between voluntary and mandatory measures and their implications for trade;
- approaches to the setting of criteria and threshold levels in the design of the measure;
- the scope for standardization or harmonization and mutual recognition;
- complications that can arise for trade through the setting of requirements in terms of product PPMs rather than product characteristics; and
- special difficulties and costs that small-size foreign suppliers, especially from developing countries, may face.

Note

1. The views expressed are those of the author and do not necessarily reflect the views of the WTO member States or Secretariat.

18 Eco-Labelling and the WTO Agreement on Technical Barriers to Trade

Vivien Liu[1]

I THE AGREEMENT ON TECHNICAL BARRIERS TO TRADE

Among non-tariff measures, technical regulations, standards and conformity assessment procedures are areas which can create technical barriers to trade. Under the Technical Barriers to Trade (TBT) Agreement, measures that are mandatory are called technical regulations and those that are voluntary are called standards. They fall under different provisions of the Agreement. Technical regulations, standards and conformity assessment procedures can be prepared by central governmental, local governmental, non-governmental or regional bodies. Given this fact, the Agreement builds upon different levels of obligations. There is a first level of obligation for central government bodies, and second level obligations for local, non-governmental and regional bodies.

The TBT Agreement, while recognizing the freedom of members to take measures for the protection of human, animal and plant life or health or the environment, takes the following four principles to minimize unnecessary obstacles to trade that might result from the preparation, adoption and application of technical regulations, standards and procedures for conformity assessment:

- non-discrimination;
- avoid the creation of unnecessary barriers to trade;
- encourage the use of international standards where appropriate for local needs, accepting equivalent standards and mutual recognition; and
- create a very high degree of transparency by prior notifications, affording opportunity for comments and consultations, as well as establishing enquiry points.

II ECO-LABELLING SCHEMES AND THE TBT AGREEMENT

Eco-labelling schemes are becoming increasingly important tools of environmental policy implemented at the local, national, regional or international level. They can be mandatory technical regulations or voluntary standards with conformity assessment procedures established for determining whether the criteria are met.

Eco-labelling schemes that are mandatory, either at a national level or sub-national level, come under articles 2 and 3 of the TBT Agreement. Voluntary eco-labelling standards established by central government, local government, non-governmental bodies and regional bodies are covered by article 4 and annex 3 (Code of Good Practice for the Preparation, Adoption and Application of Standards) of the Agreement. The provisions relating to the conformity assessment procedures of eco-labelling programmes are articles 5, 6, 7, 8 and 9 of the Agreement. Article 5 provides detailed disciplines for central government bodies in cases where a positive assurance of conformity with technical regulations or standards is required. Article 6 encourages central government bodies, wherever possible, to accept the results of the conformity assessment procedures of other members.

Articles 7 and 8 related to the procedures for the assessment of conformity by local government and non-governmental bodies provide obligations for members not to take measures which require or encourage their local government and non-governmental bodies to act in a manner inconsistent with the provisions of articles 5 and 6. Members shall take such reasonable measures as may be available to them to ensure that their local government bodies comply with the provisions of articles 5 and 6, and to ensure that their central government bodies rely on non-governmental bodies only to the extent that these bodies comply with the provisions of articles 5 and 6.

Article 9 of the Agreement encourages members to formulate and participate in international systems for conformity assessment. When formulating and adopting international systems for conformity assessment, members should try their best to ensure that the system in which relevant bodies within their territories are members comply with the provisions of articles 5 and 6 of the Agreement, as applicable.

Although eco-labelling programmes are usually voluntary, it is recognized that trade effects can arise, particularly for small suppliers from developing countries. Their main concerns relate to:

- availability of information on criteria or procedures in order to

adjust products or production methods according to the programme;
- possibility of involvement in the preparation of eco-labelling standards and criteria, especially those in the developed countries;
- possibility of harmonization and the availability of international standards and guidelines;
- possibility of access to the programme or scheme;
- possibility of reaching mutual recognition agreements with importing countries; and
- possibility of receiving technical assistance.

III POSSIBLE RESPONSES

A Transparency

Foreign suppliers might not be aware of an eco-labelling programme or might not possess details of its criteria due to inadequate availability of information. An appropriate response would be to increase the transparency of eco-labelling programmes in importing countries.

Articles 10.1 and 10.3 of the TBT Agreement oblige members to set up enquiry points to provide information to and answer queries from interested parties of other members on technical regulations, standards and conformity assessment procedures. Articles 2.9, 2.10, 3.2, 5.6, 5.7 and 7.2 of the Agreement provide obligations to notify technical regulations and conformity assessment procedures prepared by central and local governmental bodies to other members through the secretariat of the WTO. Articles 2.11 and 5.8 require members to publish or make available all adopted technical regulations and conformity assessment procedures to enable interested parties in other members to become acquainted with them. Articles 2.12 and 5.9 state that members shall allow a reasonable interval between the publication of technical regulations and their entry into force so that producers in exporting members, and particularly in developing-county members, can adapt their products or methods of production to the requirements of the importing members.

Regarding voluntary standards, annex 3 – the Code of Good Practice for the Preparation, Adoption and Application of Standards – also provides provisions on transparency, such as the obligations to notify, provide copies of work programmes on draft standards and to publish adopted standards.

B Participation of Other Countries

Articles 2.9 and 5.6 of the TBT Agreement provide for obligations to notify and provide opportunities for comments from parties of other WTO members before the adoption of technical regulations or conformity assessment procedures and to take those comments into consideration. This can help guard against the misuse of eco-labelling programmes and prevent the requirements from being unjustifiably costly or difficult for foreign producers to meet, thus making access to the programme equally available to all suppliers.

Standardization bodies adhering to the Code of Good Practice are also obliged to allow a period of at least 60 days for the submission of comments on draft standards by interested parties within the territory of a member of the WTO and to afford opportunity for consultation and make objective efforts to solve any problem.

C Harmonization of Eco-Labelling Programmes

The Agreement does not prevent members from setting regulations or standards at the levels it considers appropriate. However, articles 2.4, 2.5 and 2.6 of the TBT Agreement encourage members to use international standards as a basis for their technical regulations if it is possible and to participate in the preparation of international standards in relation to specific products. The use of standards, criteria, terms, labelling symbols and guidelines prepared by international standardizing bodies may minimize consumer confusion and promote economic efficiency. The same wording can be found in Clause F of annex 3 of the Agreement, encouraging the use of international standards.

D Acceptance of Equivalent Standards or Regulations

Another approach to harmonization could be the acceptance of equivalent standards among countries, based on reciprocity. This would presuppose a study of the foreign criteria and an assessment of their suitability for use in the country. Article 2.7 of the Agreement encourages members to give positive consideration to accepting technical regulations of other members as equivalent, provided that they are satisfied that these regulations adequately fulfil the objectives of their own regulations.

E Non-discrimination

The TBT Agreement, in articles 2–4, requires that members shall accord national treatment and most-favoured-nation (MFN) treatment to imported products so that the same technical regulations and standards are to be met by imported products as well as domestic products. Non-discriminatory treatment is also applied in granting access to testing facilities and receiving marks or certifications under article 5 of the Agreement, so that foreign manufacturers may apply for labels for their products under conditions no less favourable than those accorded to domestic products.

F Mutual Recognition

It would increase the costs for producers if they have to meet a variety of labelling requirements in the different markets they supply. Article 6 of the Agreement encourages mutual recognition of conformity assessment by central government bodies. It is recognized that prior consultations may be necessary in order to arrive at a mutually satisfactory understanding regarding the competence of the relevant conformity assessment bodies in the exporting member. This can be done, for instance, through accreditation using relevant international guidelines or recommendations.

G Technical Assistance to Developing Countries

Article 11 of the TBT Agreement encourages members to provide technical assistance to other members, if requested, regarding the methods by which their technical regulations can best be met and the steps that should be taken by foreign producers who wish to have access to systems for conformity assessment operated by their governmental and non-governmental bodies. Some of the eco-labelling programmes are regional programmes and the question is whether they are open to participation by non-regional manufacturers. Article 11.7 of the Agreement states that members shall encourage bodies within their territories which are participants in international or regional systems for conformity assessment to advise other members, especially the developing-country members, regarding the establishment of the institutions which would enable the relevant bodies to fulfil the obligations of membership or participation.

Note

1. The views expressed are those of the author and do not necessarily reflect the views of the WTO member States or Secretariat.

19 ISO and Eco-Labelling

John Henry

INTRODUCTION

The International Organization for Standardization (ISO) first became involved in trying to standardize the tools used in environmental management when the ISO Committee of Council on Consumer Policy (COPOLCO) became concerned about the proliferation of eco-labelling schemes in the late 1980s and their lack of compatibility with one another. ISO's subcommittee on environmental labelling, ISO/TC 207/SC3, is attempting to establish agreed procedures and principles to underpin all current and future eco-labelling schemes, and this is aimed at providing some of the infrastructure necessary for the schemes to move closer together. This is a long-term project and, for the present, there is still considerable diversity among operating schemes.

I WHAT IS ENVIRONMENTAL LABELLING?

ISO recognizes that there are many different ways in which a product can be labelled to show that it is environmentally preferable. There are claims made by the manufacturer, called Type II labelling in ISO. There is a separate stream of work in ISO/TC 207/SC3 dealing with Type II labelling.

There are also the third-party schemes, which come in many forms. By far the most important form is what is called Type I labelling in ISO. It is also known as 'eco-labelling', but this is difficult to translate into some languages, hence the numerical classification system.

A Type I labelling scheme has the following characteristics.

- It is a voluntary, third-party scheme.
- It involves the awarding of a label when the product in question meets certain criteria.
- The scheme aims to identify and promote products which exhibit

environmental leadership, i.e. criteria are set at a level above the average environmental performance.

- The parameters and the pass/fail criteria are pre-set for each category of products, and are publicly available.
- The criteria are set after consideration of the environmental impacts over the life cycle of the product. This is normally done by a Board, using a consultative process.

In essence, Type I labelling involves a body of some standing in the community making a decision, based on scientific principles, on what constitutes an environmentally preferable product. Consumers are then relieved of the task of evaluating competing environmental claims and having to decide what kinds of impact are more important. They merely need to decide whether or not they have confidence in the body operating the scheme.

Type I schemes are distinct from single-attribute schemes, like energy labelling, by virtue of the fact that they are based on the use of multiple criteria and on an analysis of the entire life cycle of the product.

The schemes tend to be run by independent organizations, with the support and close cooperation of the national government, although this may not always be the case. The Canadian scheme is run by a government agency and the European Union (EU) scheme was established by EU regulation. At the other end of the spectrum, the United States Green Seal programme is operated totally independently of any government recognition.

II ANALYSING THE SCHEMES

There are probably about 20 schemes in operation today around the world that fit the Type I classification. The first scheme of this kind was the Blue Angel, which began labelling products in Germany in 1979. Most of the other schemes emerged in the late 1980s or early 1990s. Eco-labelling schemes in the Asia-Pacific region include the Japanese Eco-Mark, Singapore Green label, Korean Ecomark, Environmental Choice of Canada, United States Green Seal, and Environmental Choice of New Zealand.

The schemes vary markedly in terms of both their processes and their detailed technical requirements. The former area is one where ISO is mainly focusing its attention. Quite often the schemes are criticized for failures in their methodologies of both criteria-setting and conformity assessment, and it is acknowledged that the very nature of the schemes calls for a degree of subjective decision-making at some level.

By far the most rigorous scheme, when it comes to applying life-cycle inventory techniques to criteria setting, is the French Marque NF– Environnement. It involves a very thorough use of numerical data provided by industry members of a panel, in order to establish criteria. In this, as well as in certification, the French system is difficult to fault. However, the criteria-development process is long and resource-intensive. To date, the scheme has only produced criteria for two groups of products – (a) paints and varnishes, and (b) garbage bags.

By contrast, the most successful schemes in terms of cost recovery and numbers of products certified are the Blue Angel and Japan's Eco-Mark. Both rely solely on declarations made by manufacturers for conformity assessment, and the Blue Angel, in particular, has been criticized in recent years for not being rigorous enough in its life-cycle review.

III TECHNICAL CRITERIA

The area which causes the greatest concern for international trade is the disparity among schemes with respect to technical criteria. The schemes tend to be built around addressing national environmental issues, reflecting the adage "think globally act locally". This may be the appropriate procedure when examining the usage phase of the product's life cycle, but when the criteria also cover the raw materials and manufacturing phases, the potential arises for imported products to be treated differently from locally made products.

For example, a highly industrialized European country may have a very sensitive aquatic ecosystem, where the local river system is both the principal source of drinking water and the recipient for liquid factory effluent. Under these circumstances, the product criteria of a European scheme might reflect the tight national standards for liquid effluent that are mandatory in the country. By contrast, a less industrialized country at the opposite side of the world may have a long sea coast and a marine environment which can readily absorb quite concentrated effluents, particularly if there are relatively few factories producing liquid effluent in significant quantities.

Here, the question arises: "should the products from the second country be eligible for the environmental mark in the European scheme, provided the manufacturer works to the possibly less stringent environmental standards of the second country?" The question becomes even more difficult to answer when one considers, on the one hand, the ability of transnational corporations to transfer their manufacturing operations between countries and, on the other hand, the premise that the environmental gains to be made in developing countries are of a scale of magnitude larger than those to be made in industrialized countries. This is a fairly simple example of how environmental labelling can affect trade. A more controversial and complicated area would be that of products made from rainforest timbers.

IV THE ISSUE OF INTERNATIONAL TRADE

The Agreement on Technical Barriers to Trade (TBT), in article 2.2, allows for the protection of the environment to be considered as a legitimate objective of trade-restrictive technical regulations. It has generally been agreed within the Working Group of ISO/TC 207/SC3, which deals with General Principles of Environmental Labelling, that Type I labelling schemes need to address this issue rather than simply rely on this apparent "let-out" under GATT.

Similarly, an argument is often raised that, in a typical labelling scheme, no more than 15–20 per cent of the products on the market could meet the environmental criteria for awarding the label. Thus, it might be said that the scheme discriminates against 80 per cent of the products on the market, the majority of which will be locally made. This is a sound argument when one looks at the criteria developed in order to cover aspects of the usage and disposal phase, but it becomes less valid when one looks at the manufacturing and raw materials aspects of the life cycle. Local manufacturers are often already legally compelled to meet requirements on factory emissions etc. in the criteria. However, for overseas manufacturers, the technology to meet such criteria may not even be available.

The trade question is one of the most difficult issues facing the General Principles Working Group, and it goes to the very heart of the principles which underlie eco-labelling. Environmental labelling, by definition, is a tool for influencing the market and, in the modern world economy, markets do not operate in isolation from each other. If a Type I scheme is to address the raw-materials phase, then it is my view that the Board setting the criteria needs to undertake that part of the life-cycle review using worldwide data. Similarly, for the manufacturing phase, compliance with the local environmental regulations where the product is made seems more relevant than regulations where the product is sold. Some schemes agree with this position, while others do not.

V CONCLUSION

Environmental labelling schemes do have the potential to affect trade. However, to date, the most powerful schemes, such as Blue Angel, have concentrated on the usage phase of the product life-cycle and this has moderated the effects on international trade. Type I schemes may, in future, need to pay more attention to the global environmental situation when setting criteria, particularly as the schemes move from strictly a national coverage to more regional schemes. ISO has a major role to play in laying down principles against which schemes can measure their criteria-development systems. However, the schemes themselves need critically to review their procedures if they are to continue to be relevant in the 1990s and beyond.

20 Eco-Labelling Initiatives as Potential Barriers to Trade: A Viewpoint from Developing Countries

Veena Jha and Simonetta Zarrilli[1]

INTRODUCTION

Eco-labelling means the use of labels in order to inform consumers that a labelled product is environmentally more friendly relative to other products in the same category. Eco-labelling programmes aim to protect the environment through raising consumer awareness about the environmental effects of the products and thus changing consumer behaviour as well as the manufacturing design of products in favour of relatively environmentally friendly products and technologies.

In markets with consumer preferences for "green" products, a label serves as a promotion instrument. Governments and ecological interest groups tend to support eco-labelling schemes since the promotional effect of a label sets incentives for producers to improve the environmental qualities of their products, and may help meet environmental objectives. Moreover, labelling is conceived as a market-oriented instrument which does not establish any binding requirements or bans.

The criteria for the award of such labels, at least in theory, call for an overall assessment of the ecological impact of a good during its life cycle, including production, distribution, use, consumption, and disposal. This process is termed the "cradle-to-grave" approach. Therefore, eco-labels differ from "single-issue labels" which address only one environmental quality of a product, for instance biodegradability. They also differ from "warning labels" indicating that the use of the product may be dangerous, such as warnings regarding toxicity on pesticide or fungicide packaging.

Comparing the different types of environmental impacts associated with the product's life cycle is very difficult to do in a satisfactory manner. For instance, it is difficult to compare a product which uses an energy-intensive production process but emits few pollutants with one which uses less energy in its production process but emits more pollutants. Equally, it may be difficult to compare a product which is durable but difficult to dispose of, with one which has a shorter life span but is more easily biodegradable. Thus, in practice, there is general agreement neither on how to weight different types of environmental impacts, nor on a procedure for evaluating the net or total environmental impact of a product.

In principle, eco-labelling programmes are voluntary and open to both domestic and foreign suppliers, including those from developing countries. However, domestic producers can more easily influence the development and implementation of national eco-labelling programmes. For example, domestic producers may influence the selection of new product categories which may be eligible for labelling, thus not including (by default) product categories which are of interest to foreign suppliers, particularly those from developing countries. The selection of criteria and thresholds may also focus on narrow domestic concerns and policies, thus not giving due consideration to other environmentally friendly processes applicable in developing countries. Lastly, methods of plant inspection or testing may be difficult or expensive for foreign firms, particularly from developing countries. Thus eco-labelling may act as a *de facto* barrier to trade.

I OPERATION OF ECO-LABELLING SYSTEMS

The selection of product categories for eco-labelling may be more easily guided by the interests of consumer and of the industry in the importing country, since they participate in the process of product selection while foreign firms do not. Foreign companies, particularly from developing countries, may find it difficult to represent their interests in national eco-labelling schemes of OECD countries because, first of all, they do not participate in the process of selection of product categories and, secondly, they may be unable to provide finances to the labelling authorities in the OECD countries for conducting research on product categories of export interest to them.

Another concern of foreign producers is that the selection of product categories may be so narrow as to exclude other like products in the same category. For example, the labelling schemes on tropical timber exclude temperate woods and other comparable woods. Thus, while eco-labelled tropical timber may get a market advantage over all other unlabelled woods, failure to qualify for a label may put tropical timber at a market disadvantage by comparison to other woods. Given that the setting of the criteria for the labelling of tropical timber may not involve them, producing countries may face some difficulties in complying with the criteria for labelling (see section II.C).

Proposals for the granting of environmental labels to new product categories are generally suggested by the manufacturers. For example, in Canada and Germany, more than 70 per cent of the proposals come from industry, even though in theory anyone can propose a product category for labelling.[2] Thus it is likely that the criteria and thresholds will be developed in response to domestic environmental concerns, in many instances in response to the domestic manufacturer's environmental and commercial concerns. These may or may not correspond to the most environmentally friendly options available. This is shown by the eco-labelling criteria developed by EU on paper products (see section II.A).

Eco-labelling may also impact on the competitiveness of products exported from developing countries in two other ways. First of all, a number of schemes set their criteria in such a way that initially only the most environmentally friendly products (the top 15–20 per cent) within a particular product category would qualify for the label. In some cases, the selection of criteria and thresholds may be so narrow that it may actually mandate a particular technology or a particular production process. For example, in the case of a private labelling proposal on textiles in Germany, environmentally friendly chemicals used in dyeing are defined so narrowly as to exclude natural dyes which in most cases are environmentally friendly (see section II.B).

Secondly, the idea behind some eco-labelling schemes[3] is not to induce consumers to buy eco-labelled products at a premium price, but to keep the labelled and the non-labelled products at the same price. In such schemes it is hoped that the increase in the market share of the labelled products will compensate for cost rises that may have been incurred in the process of qualifying for an eco-label. As the relative costs of compliance are likely to be higher for developing countries, eco-labelling may adversely affect the competitiveness of their products.

Plant inspection may pose particular problems in developing countries, because a number of products which are exported to the OECD countries and continue to remain competitive are manufactured in the informal sector with very small, often household-level units. While plant inspection would be a problem for all foreign producers, big or small, it is unlikely that small firms would either be able to sponsor a product for eco-labelling or to pay for on-site plant checks, required by several OECD eco-labelling schemes.

The necessity of applying eco-labelling criteria to foreign products is almost a foregone conclusion, because even if eco-labelling programmes wish to be internally directed, the foreign content of domestic products will necessitate international involvement. So far, this issue has not been examined in most eco-labelling programmes as they have not used a true cradle-to-grave approach.

As the objective of eco-labelling schemes is to promote environmental goals, different environmental goals should be given due consideration. For instance, since waste reduction is one of the environmental priorities in the European Union (EU), the EU eco-labelling scheme for paper products rewards the use of recycled paper. However, another country may target reforestation as a primary environmental objective and may thus feel that virgin pulp from planted forests which follow a pattern of reforestation should also be rewarded by eco-labelling systems. Thus eco-labelling schemes should be flexible enough to take account of different ways and different environmental goals, as long as the ultimate effect on the environment is positive.

This section has pointed out ways in which eco-labelling schemes may in practice constitute a barrier to trade. The next section will analyse in more detail a few cases where eco-labelling could be an actual or a potential barrier to trade, particularly for products exported from developing countries. Section III examines the provisions in the General Agreement on Tariffs and Trade (GATT) and its associated instruments which are applicable to eco-labelling. Section IV suggests ways in which eco-labelling schemes could be improved in order to meet their environmental objectives, as well as facilitate trade flows.

II CASE STUDIES

The impact of eco-labelling on exports from developing countries does not appear as yet to be very significant as only few products of export interest to developing countries are covered. However, proposals for including in some eco-labelling schemes products of primary export interest to developing countries, such as textiles, clothing, tropical timber and tropical timber products, paper, and footwear have already been passed or are under investigation in the EU and in other OECD countries. This section presents a preliminary consideration of the possible impacts of eco-labelling schemes on trade from developing countries for three product categories: pulp and paper, textiles and tropical timber.

A Pulp and Paper

In March 1992, the Council of the European Communities adopted a regulation for a Community eco-labelling award scheme.[4] Six member countries have been acting as "lead countries", and have developed or are in the process of developing criteria for the granting of the European eco-label to certain selected product categories. Denmark has been chairing the working group responsible for developing criteria for paper products (toilet paper, kitchen rolls, copying paper, writing paper).[5]

The "environmental goals" that the criteria developed by Denmark for paper products aim at are increased use of recycled materials and clean technology, as well as minimal waste generation in the production process. To qualify for a label a product should have not more than a stipulated number of load points (penalties), which are awarded on the basis of several parameters.

Brazilian manufacturers/exporters of pulp have expressed their concern regarding some of the criteria put forward by Denmark.[6] According to them, the way in which load points related to the following criteria – consumption of renewable and non-renewable resources, waste generation, and sulphur emission – are calculated, would largely benefit European paper producers and would put foreign firms manufacturing final (paper) or intermediate products (pulp) in a less favourable position.[7]

However, Brazilian manufacturers/exporters have been unsuccessful in voicing their concern, since their proposal to participate, either directly or indirectly (through the International Chamber of Commerce) in the discussions for the setting of criteria has been rejected.

According to the Brazilian exporters, criteria based on consumption of renewable resources[8] would allot them more load points than comparable European producers for the following reasons:

- Waste paper is not counted in the calculations of the consumption of renewable resources. This gives an advantage to companies using recycled paper, which are mostly European.
- No distinction is made between wood coming from planted forests, which generally are sustainably managed, and other kinds of wood.

- The beneficial environmental and social effects of planted forests have not been considered.
- The definition of "sustainable forest management" has been given by Denmark, instead of being elaborated in an international forum. A characteristic of a sustainably managed forest is, according to the Danish criteria, that it should contain a variety of species. This concept, if strictly applied, would imply that planted forests (usually based on a single species of tree) would not be regarded as "sustainably managed".

Brazilian companies felt that they may be charged with load points which do not correspond to their actual consumption of non-renewable resources (mainly fossil fuels),[9] since in calculating this consumption, the implicit assumption is that all countries have an energy grid similar to that in Europe.

The way in which waste generation is calculated and load points are attributed would also mainly benefit European companies, since their use of recycled pulp is greater than that of Brazil, and they are allowed to subtract it from the amount of waste generated.[10] Brazilian manufacturers/exporters expressed their discontent with the fact that producers outside Europe would be charged with load points corresponding to the amount of sulphur emitted during pulp and paper production. A reduction of sulphur emissions in Europe would alleviate the phenomenon of "acid rains", that affects some countries in Europe. A parallel reduction of these emissions in other geographical areas will be of no use to Europe (which will be too far away to benefit from it). Countries outside Europe which have to reduce their sulphur emissions in order to comply with the eco-labelling criteria (such as Brazil), will probably never experience a similar phenomenon. Brazilian producers/manufacturers of paper and pulp felt that the working group chaired by Denmark had developed the criteria keeping in mind solely the patterns of European production, and rewarding only environmental efforts made in Europe. No attention was paid to the fact that in non-EU countries positive environmental results might be reached in ways different from those that represent a priority in Europe and that solutions that are appropriate in Europe may not be used in other regions.

In establishing criteria, eco-labelling authorities should consider and reward all equivalent environmental efforts and achievements of manufacturers. The Danish proposal could have better environmental and trade impacts if it rewarded not only companies involved in recycling (as it contributes to less deforestation and waste reduction, regarded as major environmental goals in Europe), but also companies involved in other environmental efforts, like reforestation (which represents an environmental priority in Brazil).

B Textiles

A number of schemes for labelling textiles have been proposed in different countries. Only a few of them will be analysed here. Those are private labelling schemes and not government sponsored national schemes. However, private schemes may have similar effects on consumer choice as national labelling schemes and may thus affect textile imports from developing countries.[11]

The textile labelling schemes which will be examined here include a scheme proposed by the German textile industry, and a scheme developed by German and Austrian Research Institutes.

The German textile industry associated in the union "Gesamttextil" is investigating the possibility of introducing two green labels for textiles.[12] For this purpose Gesamttextil has established an association for consumers and environmentally friendly textiles producers of the EU and EFTA. Trade associations and suppliers for the textile and clothing industry can also become sponsoring members.

Of the two labels proposed, one is a product label, MST (*Marke scadstoffgeprufter Textilien*) and the other is a process-related label, MUT (*Marke umweltschonender Textilien*). MST is geared to the final consumer and involves tests for chemicals, dyes, etc. MUT relates to the production process and is meant to be used only by garment and textile manufacturers. In the draft list of criteria for the MST seal, norms are set for chemicals and other factors which relate to the final use of the product. Seven different tests are needed to check the quantity of formaldehyde, chemicals (pentachlorophenol or PCP), heavy metals, azo-dyes, pesticides, etc., in garments.[13]

The MUT label sets norms for production processes and it is granted exclusively to intermediate products. All processing operations need to be analysed in order to determine the degree of permitted levels of pollution of air, water, and soil. Attention will particularly be focused on reduction of chlorine and chrome-based dyestuffs, as well as other chrome and allergenic compounds.

In order to comply with the national legislation,[14] the German textile industry has already introduced processes which save energy, chemicals and costs by reducing the discharge of waste and polluted water which has later to be cleaned. It is expected that in the long run existing eco-standards will be tightened, some substances not as yet considered will be included and eco-standards relating to processing will become increasingly important.

There are several ways in which this initiative could constitute a trade barrier for developing countries. First of all, it may be easier for the German textile industry to comply with the criteria as the draft criteria were developed by them, and they already have the technical competence to meet higher environmental standards as defined by these criteria.

Secondly, there are some specific problems which developing countries can be expected to encounter with respect to the permitted dyestuffs in the MST label. After examining all the criteria for the eco-labelling of textiles, at the moment the most binding criteria narrow down to a few concerns, the most important of which relate to the use of PCP and formaldehyde. These requirements imply that in order to meet the criteria for MST or other such labels, in practice, dyestuffs may have to be imported from Germany or other EU countries; this will increase the cost of textiles from developing countries. Moreover, natural dyes produced and used in developing countries are not regarded as an ecological alternative by the scheme.[15]

The verification procedures associated with award of the MUT label may be difficult to implement in practice, particularly in developing countries, as they may involve on-site plant inspection. Moreover, as the process adjustments have already begun in Germany, their trading partners who have not started such environmental innovations may be put at a comparative disadvantage, as their adjustment costs are likely to be higher.

Another system, the Eco-Tex Standard 100, has been developed by an international association for research on eco-textiles established by German and Austrian research institutes. The standard is largely based on the possible impact of the use of textiles on human health. Ecological impacts of the production process are not included as it is recognized that international monitoring will need to be organized before standards are formulated. Eco-Tex will not itself issue a label but will provide a basis for the issue of labels: a list of criteria and check and control methods will be made available to the textile industry. Even though the criteria are fewer than those of Gesamttextil, the product norms of Eco-Tex and Gesamttextil are similar. Thus, labels based on Eco-Tex Standard 100 can be expected to have effects on exports from developing countries similar to those of the MST label.

The influence of these criteria on trade is further reinforced by the so called "selective evasion strategy"[16] of innovative retailers who try to "by-pass" suppliers with low eco-standards, many of which may be from developing countries. However, retailers in their long-term strategy may also provide their low-cost suppliers with technical assistance that will enable them to meet the eco-standards required by Germany. But this may be a time-consuming process and thus in the short run it is likely that developing countries may face a trade barrier.

Eco-labelling can lead to a situation where both final consumers and retailers prefer to buy and stock only labelled products as was evidenced by the "selective evasion strategy" of innovative retailers in Germany. Thus exporters may find it difficult to find buyers for their non-labelled products. In such a situation eco-labelling schemes, even if they are voluntary, will have the same effect as mandatory schemes.

C Tropical Timber

There are several proposals for the introduction of eco-labels for tropical timber and tropical timber products. These proposals respond to consumer concern in Europe and North America about deforestation of tropical woods. Moreover, as eco-labelling schemes are voluntarily adopted, they avoid the implementation of measures such as boycotts and bans. At the moment, Austria is the only country that has already included these products in its eco-labelling programme.

The eco-labelling of tropical timber and its products is likely to create difficulties for producing countries, if some basic problems are not solved before the implementation of the programmes. These are:

- lack of a common definition of sustainably managed forests (even though most countries seem to use the International Tropical Timber Organization (ITTO) guidelines on sustainable forest management as a basis for the definition); and
- lack of involvement of producing countries in the formulation of the definition.

Several definitions of sustainably managed forests have already been proposed. Some of them refer to the concept of "sustained yield", meaning that harvesting should not exceed the forest's growth rate. Other definitions are wider, covering also water quality, biodiversity and non-wood forest products. Some definitions include social issues in relation to forest management, such as local participation in project planning, employment generation and profit sharing.[17]

The European Commission has defined sustainable forest management as the planned utilization of forests in a manner compatible with the conservation of forest ecosystems for future generations.[18] The lack of a common definition of sustainable forest management will probably lead to a situation in which several countries will develop their own definition and thus different criteria will develop for different eco-labelling programmes for tropical timber.

The divergence of criteria is particularly inappropriate as the common goal, sustainable exploitation of forests, can best be achieved through international cooperation and consensus between producing and consuming countries. If eco-criteria are developed without any participation of foreign producers, the cost of compliance for them may be high and may be even economically unviable. In the case of tropical timber, producing countries tend to react negatively to environmental standards imposed from outside. This is because they feel that countries which do not produce tropical timber may not have a practical knowledge of some aspects of tropical timber forestry and may thus formulate inappropriate definitions and set standards which may not be acceptable to producers. However, some efforts which deserve mention have been made to formulate labelling systems and criteria on the basis of cooperation between producing and consuming countries.

The German forestry and timber industries, jointly with a trade union, an importers' organization and the Germany Forestry Association, formulated the "Projekt Tropenwald",[19] with the aim of contributing to forest protection by labelling tropical timber and other tropical forest products stemming from sustainable management.[20] Labels will be granted on the basis of ITTO guidelines. In order to make labelling acceptable to producer countries, inspection procedures should be agreeable to them and testing authorities in the exporting countries should be made responsible for the procedures. The German government has been urged to provide technical and financial assistance to producing countries in order to help them to implement sound forest management.

Another initiative for the labelling of wood, the Forest Stewardship Council (FSC),[21] has been promoted by a diverse group of environmental organizations, concerned people from the forestry industry, community forestry representatives, and forest certification organizations from several countries in the world. The two aims of the project are to develop a set of principles[22] and criteria of good forest management and create a single and widely recognized system of certification. The FSC will not itself be a "certifier"; local certifying organizations will instead be the "certifiers". They will grant the label to companies that comply with the principles and criteria developed by the FSC. Local certifying organizations are also called upon to play an active role in setting criteria, by adding to the general framework, specific requirements related to local conditions. The FSC aims at establishing criteria for all kind of forests, temperate, tropical and boreal.

III ECO-LABELLING SYSTEMS AND THEIR GATT COMPATIBILITY

There are certain provisions in the articles of the General Agreement on Tariffs and Trade (GATT) and in the Technical Barriers to Trade (TBT) Agreement which may imply that eco-labelling schemes may be subject to GATT/WTO obligations.[23] One important case which sets a precedent for the GATT consideration of eco-labelling systems is the Austrian legislation on tropical timber,[24] and the same considerations may apply to other eco-labelling schemes.

It could be argued that eco-labelling requirements could be considered as a form of a certification system to which provisions of Article 7 of the TBT Agreement apply. Article 7 requires that such systems should be formulated or applied in a way that they do not "have the effect of creating unnecessary obstacles to trade".

In order to avoid certification systems causing barriers to trade, the TBT Agreement requires that national standardization authorities use the guidelines and recommendations developed by international standardization bodies. In addition, the TBT requires that certification systems should be published in draft form with a view to giving countries having an export interest an opportunity to comment on the draft. It further imposes the obligation to take such comments into account before finalizing the systems. In order to provide transparency, countries are also required to notify the WTO secretariat the product to which such systems would apply.

The "Code of Good Practice for the Preparation, Adoption and Application of Standards", which is part of the revised TBT text, requires autonomous bodies to apply the same principles and rules as are required to be followed by central government bodies. However, where a system is being elaborated by voluntary bodies, the notification obligations should be made to the ISO/IEC information centre.

An eco-labelling system may thus be considered as causing unnecessary barriers to trade under the provision of the TBT Agreement if:

- the determination of the criteria to which the product must conform in order to qualify for the label, in particular with regard to use of raw materials and production and processing method, is not based on objective or scientific consideration or fails to take into account adequately the production processes prevailing in other countries;
- procedures for verification in granting the label are unnecessarily strict or rigorous, thereby making it almost impossible for a foreign producer to obtain the label;
- the system is prepared and adopted for a product which is almost entirely imported, and the right to grant an eco-label rests entirely with the authorities of the importing countries.

IV CONCLUSIONS

The preceding section has indicated possible ways in which the formulation and implementation of eco-labelling systems could cause a barrier to trade from developing countries. The criteria developed by the eco-labelling systems often take account only of domestic concerns and may or may not be the only way of achieving environmental goals, as was shown by the case of pulp and paper. In other cases the testing procedures may be difficult and expensive. In order to mitigate some of the problems associated with eco-labelling specially for developing countries, the following suggestions are being made.

A Transparency, Consultation and Market Access

Eco-labelling schemes, specially when developed on the basis of a wider participation of all interested parties, may contribute to environmental preservation, without disrupting international trade. They may also create new market opportunities for all environmentally conscious producers some of whom may be from developing countries. In order to make environmental objectives and trade mutually compatible, some principles should be kept in mind while developing eco-labelling systems.

- Countries may have different environmental priorities, objectives and methods of achieving them. Eco-labelling schemes should give due consideration to different environmental objectives and also to the diverse methods of achieving these objectives.[25]
- Eco-labelling schemes could be of greater benefit to developing

countries and better achieve environmental objectives if developing countries were consulted in the process of setting criteria for eco-labelling programmes in OECD countries. This could be facilitated if developing countries obtain early information about the product categories that are being considered for labelling.

B Internationally Based Labels

Internationally based labels developed with the participation of foreign countries, particularly developing countries, in the process of establishing eco-labelling programmes may partly alleviate the trade problems associated with eco-labelling programmes. International labels may also reduce consumer confusion which can arise because of the coexistence of several different national labels.

Labels granted on the basis of an international consensus are likely to be more successful with producers and consumers than those based on national initiatives. National labelling initiatives are likely to be less successful in making trade and environment mutually compatible, because they may not be acceptable to some producing countries and may rely on multiple and occasionally conflicting environmental solutions. National labels are also more likely, for the reasons discussed in the previous chapter, to be (or to be perceived as being) "unfair" or discriminatory towards foreign producers.

Examples of attempts at the international formulation of labels and criteria are the "Projekt Tropenwald" and the "Forest Stewardship Council" (FSC). It is noteworthy that the members of the FSC founding group are conducting country assessments in different parts of the world to evaluate the feasibility of accreditation and certification and to solicit inputs on the principles and criteria for eco-labelling forest products.

Some general principles should apply when internationally based labels and criteria are formulated:

- countries which play a key role as producers or consumers of a product for which an eco-label is envisaged should be consulted;
- countries from different geographical areas and at different levels of development should be consulted; and
- countries which will base their eco-labelling programmes on principles and criteria different from those internationally agreed should prove to have acceptable reasons for doing so (the burden of proof should lie with them).

C Mutual Recognition

Mutual recognition will also represent a viable alternative in making trade and environmental objectives compatible. This is because mutual recognition of eco-labels will mitigate the trade restrictive impacts of eco-labelling programmes while maintaining their environmental goals.

Some developing countries have already started their own eco-labelling programmes.[26] In order to gain recognition for their eco-labelling schemes, an initiative at the international level is needed to develop a framework and rules on the basis of which importing countries recognise as equivalent the eco-labels issued by the exporting country.

Some lessons can be drawn from precedents of systems which can be used for mutual recognition, e.g. the procedures laid down in the International Convention on Mutual recognition of Pharmaceutical products, developed by EFTA. The EFTA and EU member countries are also investigating schemes which closely resemble either harmonized or mutual recognition systems of eco-labelling.

The EFTA Ministers for Consumers Affairs have expressed their hope for the establishment of a common eco-labelling system among the EFTA and the EU member countries.[27] Representatives from the Nordic eco-labelling bodies have been participating in the work of the EU aimed at the establishment of the eco-criteria. The basic purpose of this initiative is to exchange information and to ensure that the principles that have led to the establishment of the criteria in the Nordic countries are taken into account in the determination of the criteria for the EU label. In 1997, when the EU eco-labelling programme will be reviewed, a decision will probably be taken on whether the "White Swan" (the Nordic countries eco-label) should be replaced by the eco-label of the Union.

Another phenomenon that may suggest closer collaboration between different countries on eco-labelling programmes is the following: producers from a few EU countries have asked for a license to use the "White Swan" in the European Union. This is because for certain products, such as paper, consumers have shown a clear preference for eco-labelled products. If a national eco-label is not available (as is the case with non-recycled paper in Germany), producers use foreign labels to promote the environmental qualities of their products. Again this is not a case of mutual recognition, but indicates that consumers, if well informed, may recognize and accept foreign labels. This also shows how complex the labelling issue can be, since the very reason for not awarding eco-labels may be subverted if foreign eco-labels are accepted. This reinforces the need for international consensus on labelling. Another example is Switzerland which has decided to use the EU label, even though it is not a member of the European Union, for products produced and sold in Switzerland.

A similar argument can be made in support of the recognition of labels from developing countries. Eco-labelling schemes in developing countries are normally based on the eco-labelling programmes existing in developed countries, even though the exact scope and nature of the programmes respond to their specific domestic needs. For instance, the Eco-mark programme in India was developed in consultation with the Environmental Choice Program in Canada. The fact that the eco-labelling systems in developing countries adapt (in keeping with their goals) the criteria developed by the better-known schemes in the OECD countries implies that it may be easier to make these systems mutually acceptable. However, recognition of national eco-labelling schemes will require efforts by national governments to popularize their schemes on a wider basis and beyond their national boundaries.

D Technical Assistance

A major problem in developing countries is the testing and verification of products and plants. This problem could partly be alleviated by training the standardization institutes in developing countries to conduct on-site plant tests. Training can also be conducted through agencies appointed by international standardization bodies such as ISO. For example, the ISO 9000 mark is used by several exporters in developing countries. ISO designates testing agencies for verifying whether the product meets the requirements of the ISO 9000 mark in the exporting countries themselves. Similar arrangements could be made for meeting eco-labelling criteria.

In general, national certification bodies in the exporting countries should be allowed to undertake testing and verification. However, in cases where this is not possible or uneconomic, international certification firms could also undertake the job of on-site plant testing, and could thus certify whether a particular product meets the criteria required for the eco-label; e.g. in the US Green Seal programme, the testing of products is conducted by a New York based Underwriters Laboratories. This group has more than 90 branches throughout the world, and thus the nearest Underwriters laboratory can be contacted for testing and certification that the product meets the criteria required for obtaining a label. However, if monopoly rights are awarded to a few international certification firms, these may also obtain monopoly profits. The cost of certification may thus in some cases be unduly high for developing countries if they need the help of international certification firms for obtaining foreign labels. In order to avoid this situation, eco-labelling authorities in OECD countries should try to unify the costs of certification whether carried out by national or international certification firms. The ISO has set a precedent for this with its ISO 9000 mark.

Moreover, consultancy firms are emerging in the EU countries which will provide technical assistance to developing countries, particularly those in Africa, to enable them to meet the criteria set for eco-labelling. These consultancy firms will be authorised by the various eco-labelling schemes to conduct verification procedures in the exporting countries. Thus, though the parent companies will be based in the OECD countries, subsidiaries will be located, for example, in African countries. Cost estimates for the provision of such services are not yet available. If the costs are not so high as to cancel the competitive edge, developing countries may wish to avail themselves of such services.

Notes

1. The authors would like to thank René Vossenaar, Serafino Marchese and Vinod Rege for their comments.
2. See OECD, *Environmental Labelling in OECD Countries* (Paris: OECD, 1991).
3. This was stated in an interview with officials in the French Ministry of Environment, and in another interview with a private company which has been granted the "White Swan" in Sweden.
4. Council Regulation no. 880/92, *Official Journal of the European Communities*, no. L 99/1 of 11 April 1992.
5. The criteria proposed by Denmark for kitchen rolls and toilet paper were adopted in December 1994.
6. Most of the information regarding the case of the Brazilian pulp industry was collected in an interview with the manager for environmental affairs of one big pulp producing and exporting company in Rio de Janeiro. See also Associaçao Brasileira de exportadores de celulose, "Danger of Trade Barriers against Pulp Exporters to the EEC", April 1993; and International Environment Reporter, "EC Eco-label Program Raises Concerns for Brazilian Business", 27 January 1993. See also ABECEL, "EU Eco-labelling of Tissue and Towel Paper Products: A Brazilian Perspective", in this volume.
7. Intermediate products are not eligible for eco-labelling, but their environ-

mental impact is assessed when the eco-label is requested for the final product, by applying the life-cycle analysis.

8. Renewable resources are defined as the vegetable fibres, mainly wood, used in the production of tissue/paper. Load points are attributed on the basis of the amount of wood used per tonne of tissue/paper products, regardless of whether wood comes from natural or planted forests. However, waste paper, forest waste and wood waste are excluded from the calculations of load points. Virgin pulp will only be eligible for labelling if it originates from "sustainably managed forests". Sustainable forest management is defined by the scheme and includes management of forest areas after wood felling.
9. The consumption of non-renewable resources includes direct consumption of fossil fuels as well as its indirect consumption through the use of electricity. The indirect consumption of fossil fuels is based, among other factors, on the number of kWh of electricity used. The consumption of fossil fuels per KWh of electricity is higher in the Europe by comparison to Brazil, which is more dependent on hydroelectricity.
10. The use of recycled fibres is considered as "removal of waste". Therefore, the amount of recycled fibres used for production of tissue/paper must be subtracted from the amount of waste generated during production.
11. There are many eco-labelling proposals for the textile sector besides those presented here (such as "Clean fashion" and "Steilmann"). The proposals examined in the paper are listed mainly for illustrative purposes in order to analyse their possible implications for developing countries.
12. See Sportswear International, *Ecology and Fashion – Greener Still*, 1992. Note that these labelling schemes are being sponsored by the German textile industry and are not included in the "Blue Angel" eco-labelling programme of Germany.
13. At present the known effects of the production and processing of natural fibres include the following: production requires large areas of land, uses fertilisers and toxic pesticides and causes soil erosion; fibre processing requires chemicals and large quantities of water; textile processing requires bleaching, dyeing and special finishing which releases chemicals into the water and the air, and the use of textiles for clothing may require the use of buttons, containing azo-dyes or chrome which are known allergenic substances. The proposals for the eco-labelling of textiles try to address these environmental problems. In a proposal put forward by the "Good Environmental Choice" of Sweden (this is an eco-labelling programme sponsored by an environmentalist NGO), the criteria will probably relate to the use of fertilizers and pesticides during production, and to the release of chemicals during processing. In the two German labels, the proposed criteria are mainly related to air, soil and water pollution during production processes, while the criteria of the Eco-Tex Standard 100 (this system is being developed by German and Austrian research institutes) are based on the possible impact of the use of textiles on human health. See Bunning, Danne, Hagenmaier, Kölling, Siller, Wender and Wiernann, 1993, "International Eco-Standards as a New Challenge for Industries in Developing Countries: the Case of Indian Textile Industry", paper written for the GDI.
14. The use of PCP was banned in November 1990.

15. See Sewekow, 1988, as quoted in Bunning *et al.*, 1993, op.cit.
16. Ibid.
17. See Panayotis N. Varangis, C.A. Primo Braga and Kenji Takeuchi, 1993, "Tropical Timber Trade Policies: What Impact will Ecolabelling Have?", *Wirtschaftspolitische Blatter*, vol. 3/4 (1993).
18. Proposal for a Council Regulation on Operations to Promote Tropical Forests (COM(93) 53 final), *Official Journal of the European Communities,* no. C 78/8, 19 March 1993.
19. See Projekt Tropenwald, "Protection and Conservation of Tropical Forests by Sustainable Management", 1992.
20. Two types of labels are being considered: a country label that will be issued to countries that adopt sustainable land-use plans, expand their forest authorities and ratify the ITTO guidelines; and a company label for firms whose logging operations coincide with ITTO guidelines and to products produced according to these guidelines.
21. See "The Forest Stewardship Council: A Fact Sheet", 1992. See also Markku Simula, "Timber Certification Initiatives and their Implications for Developing Countries", Box 14.2, in this volume.
22. Contrary to other eco-labelling initiatives in which the eco-criteria are supposed to be revised every two/three years, the FSC aims at establishing a long-lasting set of criteria for good forest management.
23. See Vinod Rege, "GATT Law and Environment Related Issues Affecting Trade of Developing Countries", *Journal of World Trade*, June 1994, vol. 28, no. 3, pp. 95–169.
24. The Austrian law came into force in September 1992 and provided for a double system of mandatory and voluntary labelling of tropical timber and tropical timber products being placed in the Austrian market. The mandatory labelling consisted of the obligation to indicate on the product "made of tropical timber" or "contains tropical timber", while the voluntary label (quality mark) indicated that tropical timber or tropical timber products originated from forests that had fulfilled effective exploitation. The definition of "effective exploitation" was given by the law, and applicants had to prove compliance with the definition. The legislation was introduced as a response to the growing concern in the country on deforestation in tropical areas. The Austrian legislation was challenged in GATT by the ASEAN countries on the grounds that (a) labelling provisions did not apply to other like products such as temperate wood products and (b) the definition of sustainable forestry was provided by Austria exclusively, and was not based on international norms or consultations. Before an official decision was taken within the GATT, Austria decided to withdraw from the law the mandatory labelling requirement, while keeping the voluntary labelling provisions.
25. In the case of criteria for paper and pulp, if sustainable forest management through plantation forestry were given as much importance as recycling, then Brazilian exporters would face fewer difficulties in meeting the criteria for eco-labelling. Similarly, in the case of textiles, if natural dyes which may be as ecologically sound as environmentally friendly chemical dyes are accepted by eco-labelling programmes, some Asian countries may meet the criteria more easily.

26. India, the Republic of Korea and Singapore have established their own eco-labelling programmes. Other developing countries such as Brazil, Colombia and the ASEAN countries are working on such programmes.
27. EFTA Ministerial Meeting on Consumer Policy, Vienna, 19 November 1992.

21 Dealing with the Trade Barrier Issue

Environmental Choice Programme,
Environment Canada

Environmental improvement can be achieved through the use of a number of policy tools, alone or in concert with one another. These include environmental regulation, information and education programmes, and an array of economic instruments such as fiscal incentives and market-based approaches. While eco-labelling programmes are often thought of as economic instruments, they are not usually confined to any one of these policy tools. They could be implemented by regulation as part of a broader environmental regulatory programme, as any of the variety of economic or market instruments, or as a public information or education programme. Each approach or model usually has its specific implementation methodology. For example, information programmes often operate on an awards basis, while market-based programmes operate on some degree of cost recovery. However, it must be noted that regardless of the type of programme developed, different countries have different environmental priorities and policy requirements.

The underlying premise of most of the eco-labelling programmes now in place is that the strong environmental values of consumers can be used as a market force to leverage environmental improvement. These programmes, therefore, were developed as market-based programmes in order to reduce the stress on the environment by encouraging the demand for and supply of environmentally responsible products and were designed to operate on the basis of cost recovery and eventual self-sufficiency.

Environmental labelling, at present, includes three different kinds of programmes:

- *Type I – Criteria-based, third-party certification programmes*: these are owned and operated by a third party, i.e. not the industries being licensed, and often they are run by governments;

- *Type II – Information self-declaration programmes*: these are run by the companies themselves, and specific environmental attributes are identified and included on the product labels;
- *Type III – Qualified product information label programmes, using preset indices*: these are in effect report cards against a predetermined set of life-cycle-related indices. Any product in any sector could be labelled this way.

The first third-party certification eco-labelling programme was introduced in Germany in 1977. The second programme of this kind, the Canadian Environmental Choice Programme, was launched in 1988. Others have followed in rapid succession. So far, over 20 eco-labelling programmes have been launched in countries such as the United States, Australia, New Zealand, India, Japan, China, South Africa, Sri Lanka, and most West European countries. Interest in such programmes has been expressed by countries such as Malaysia, Colombia, Argentina and Brazil. The European Union (EU) has also developed an eco-labelling programme which, it hopes, will eventually replace existing national labelling programmes within the EU.

With the growth of eco-labelling programmes, a number of questions and concerns related to barriers to trade has arisen. This paper attempts to define the trade problem that relates to eco-labelling,[1] and proposes an approach for dealing with this in a viable and pragmatic way.

I DEFINING THE PROBLEM

There are a number of possible trade barriers that could be created in the development of any eco-labelling programme. These include:

- *Extrajurisdictional requirements*: the requirement that all licensees must meet the environmental (or other) laws of the country in which the programme operates could be considered an extrajurisdictional trade barrier.
- *Accessibility to the label*: the limitation of authorized use of the label to domestic companies alone could be considered a trade barrier.
- *Transparency of process*: any guideline or criteria development process that is in any way not open and transparent could be considered a trade barrier.

- *Open to consultation*: the exclusion of foreign input into the guideline-development process could be considered a trade barrier.
- *Production and process methods*: programmes which have criteria or guideline requirements related to the production and process methods (PPMs), as opposed to just the use and disposal aspects of the product being certified, could be accused of creating a trade barrier.

These issues are being discussed in a number of fora, including the World Trade Organization (WTO), the Organization for Economic Co-operation and Development (OECD), and the International Organization for Standardization (ISO) and the newly formed Global Eco-labelling Network (GEN).

II OECD

The OECD joint experts group on trade and environment has been examining a broad range of issues with a view to increasing the mutual compatibility of trade and environment policies. The group's analytical work has three main objectives: to raise the level of understanding of the issues; to provide inputs into the work of other fora such as GATT, the World Trade Organization (WTO) and the United Nations Environment Programme (UNEP); and to lead to policy conclusions and possible guidelines where appropriate.

The issue of eco-labelling and trade arises in the context of a number of the items on the group's work programme, and in particular in discussions on PPMs and on life-cycle management. In the case of PPMs, eco-labelling is seen both as a potential alternative to the use of trade measures, and as an instrument which itself raises PPM-related questions. In the case of life-cycle management, eco-labelling is seen as an approach which recognizes that environmental impacts can arise at different stages of a product's life cycle, and which, in some cases, makes use of life-cycle review and assessment techniques.

While the importance of the eco-labelling and trade issue has been recognized by the OECD joint experts group, the group has not yet undertaken an in-depth analysis of the issue. However, there is interest on the part of some members of the OECD in having the group focus on eco-labelling as one of its priorities over the coming year.

III WTO

The issue of eco-labelling and trade was, together with packaging, one of the three agenda items of the former GATT Working Group on Environmental Measures and International Trade.[2] Discussions in the GATT Working Group have been analytical in nature, seeking to elucidate the various trade-related aspects of the issue. Many interventions focused on the different types of trade barriers, mentioned above, that could be created by an eco-labelling programme. Developing countries, in particular, were concerned that these programmes could have the effect of reducing their access to developed-country markets, with no benefit to the environment. Other interventions pointed out the environmental rationale of these programmes and the difficulty of finding solutions that addressed the trade problems while preserving the integrity of the programmes. While no conclusions were reached, common themes were the need for transparency and access to the label for imports, and the role that increased international cooperation between programmes could play in reducing trade barriers.

Eco-labelling is also one of the items on the initial agenda of the new Trade and Environment Committee of WTO. The Committee's mandate directs it to identify the relationship between trade measures and environmental measures, and to make appropriate recommendations on whether any modification to the provisions of the multilateral trading system is required. Initial work in the Committee also could be analytical in nature.

IV ISO

Following the success of the ISO 9000 standards on total quality management, which in itself was a departure for ISO, work began around 1992 on a new series of standards related to environmental management systems. One element of this work has been related to eco-labelling. Three different types of eco-labelling programmes have been identified, and these were described earlier in this chapter. Most of the world's formal eco-labelling programmes are considered Type I programmes, and ISO has begun the development of a set of guiding principles for Type I eco-labelling. These principles have two major purposes:

- to eliminate or avoid barriers to trade; and

- to provide guidance to countries which wish to develop such programmes.

At the ISO meeting in Australia in May 1994, a draft set of principles was reviewed, and eleven principles were elaborated. These related to:

- the voluntary nature of the programme;
- regulatory requirements – product compliance with market requirements;
- life-cycle approach – labelling should incorporate the life-cycle concept;
- selectivity – degree of selectivity should take into account the potential for environmental improvement;
- effectiveness – market penetration must be sufficient to be visible in the marketplace;
- review of criteria – criteria must be reviewed periodically, once every three years or so;
- consultation – processes should allow for wide input of views;
- transparency – processes must be visible and comprehensible;
- funding – independence from commercial interest so no conflict of interest;
- international aspects – programme must be internationally accessible; and
- compliance assessment – internationally recognized tests should be used where possible.

Principles are not, by themselves, sufficient to eliminate or avoid trade barriers, nor are they sufficient to guide or instruct countries in the development of eco-labelling programmes. The latter issue is being addressed by a proposal to situate the principles in a broader document which would serve as a step-by-step guide to developing an eco-labelling programme. This was notionally accepted by the ISO in its meeting in May 1994. The former issue, related to trade barrier concerns, forms the focus of the present paper.

V GEN

Since the creation of Germany's Blue Angel programme in 1977 and Canada's Environmental Choice Programme in 1988, more than 20 similar programmes have been developed worldwide. With this growth came opportunities to discuss methodologies and other policy and technical issues. At a meeting of twelve country programmes in Washington, a Global Eco-labelling Network (GEN) was created as a vehicle for exchanging information and enhancing cooperation. The twelve countries also identified ten elements that would be typical of a *bona fide* eco-labelling organization, and these were related to:

- voluntary for potential licensees;
- run by a not-for-profit organization without commercial interests;
- funding shall not create a conflict of interests;
- independent from commercial interests;
- seeks advice from and consults with stakeholder interests;
- legally protected logo;
- criteria based on assessment of overall life of a product;
- open access to potential licensees from all countries;
- criteria levels reduce damage to the environment; and
- periodic review and update of criteria and categories.

Most of these elements were taken into account in the ISO exercise, but the ISO principles include several important additions: regulatory compliance, selectivity and transparency.

VI ELEMENTS OF A PROPOSED SOLUTION

While the work under way at WTO, OECD and UNCTAD is contributing to finding a better definition of the issues at stake, the work at ISO and at GEN offers opportunities to serve as part of a broader solution to the trade barrier problems. ISO intends to publish the guiding principles for eco-labelling which are being developed in the context of a handbook on developing eco-labelling programmes, as a standard. These principles, at least in the current draft form, address four of the five trade barriers defined in section I: extrajurisdictional requirements, accessibility, transparency and openness. They do not address the issue of PPMs.

The PPM issue could also be addressed by a principle that requires foreign-made products to meet only the use and disposal requirements of the programme in the country where the product is to be marketed. However, the major environmental impact of many products is at the manufacturing stage. Therefore, providing a label to these products would be reasonable only if these were certified by the exporting country's programme and if this programme met the eco-labelling principles standard.

Reciprocity or mutual recognition forms the focus of another approach that is beginning to be discussed, and which may be capable of dealing with the PPM issue more effectively. It would require some form of multilateral agreement. Requirements of the agreement could include, by way of example, one or more of the following:

- acceptance of the exporting country's programme certification of products, provided that the eco-labelling principles standard is met;
- acceptance of the exporting country's programme certification of products against the requirements of the programme in the country where the product is to be marketed, provided the exporting country's programme meets the eco-labelling principles standard; or
- acceptance of the exporting country's programme PPM requirements, but the use and disposal requirements would be that of the programme in the country where the product would be marketed, provided that its programme meets the eco-labelling principles standard.

Dealing substantively with trade barriers requires that the principles (and related standards) be adhered to in practice. Because ISO is a non-governmental body and most eco-labelling programmes are governmental programmes, the application of standards set by the ISO may create some difficulties. However, if the standard could be developed in concert with labelling programmes, most logically through GEN, and applied by GEN, then the identified trade barrier issues could be dealt with.

However,. GEN is still in its infancy. It has not yet developed any institutional capacity. Institutional capacity will be required in order to deal effectively with a range of issues, including those related to information exchange and trade. The tasks could include the following:

- convening annual meetings;
- undertaking research on topics of common interest;
- developing and managing relevant international agreements;
- developing and managing an international eco-labelling database consisting of the principles, operations, activities, guidelines and background technical work of the programmes of different countries;

- serving as a clearing house for information exchange; and
- representing eco-labelling interests at environmental and trade meetings.

With the number of international institutions currently in existence, most countries have strongly resisted the creation of more new institutions. Given this view and the existence of a number of organizations already doing work on environment and trade issues, it is difficult to foresee GEN developing into or creating the kind of institution that could deal with the tasks outlined above.

None the less, the following criteria are considered to be necessary features of any institution that undertakes work on behalf of eco-labelling interests:

- global membership;
- a primarily environmental mandate;
- capability to deal with trade and development issues;
- ability to provide a forum for international discussion and negotiation;
- experience in developing and managing international agreements;
- an established network of and contact with national environment programmes around the world;
- experience and capability in database management; and
- forward-looking and action-oriented nature.

These criteria could be used in designing or choosing an appropriate organization to take on the international eco-labelling job.

VII CONCLUSION

In addressing the issue of trade barriers posed by eco-labelling programmes, while each country should have the flexibility to design and implement programmes that meet local needs, broad principles and multilateral agreements can be effectively used for dealing with this issue.

A potential solution to the trade barrier problem thus could have three components:

- an eco-labelling programme standard based on a broad set of principles;

- a multilateral mutual recognition agreement; and
- an international institution capable of and willing to serve eco-labelling interests.

If this is seen as a reasonable approach, the two key steps that should follow will be:

- ISO engaging GEN in the development of the eco-labelling programme standard; and
- GEN discussing the institutional issue.

Notes

1. For the purposes of this paper, eco-labelling refers only to Type I third-party certification programmes.
2. See also Janet Chakarian, "Eco-labelling and GATT", and Vivien Liu, "Eco-labelling and the Agreement on Technical Barriers to Trade", in this volume.

22 Environmental Product Requirements: A New Trade Barrier?

Poul Wendel Jessen

In recent years, consumers have seen a growing number of products with labels providing information on environmental aspects. However, often the information provided does not appear well-grounded. To tackle this problem, several countries have taken initiatives to set up official eco-labelling schemes for providing consumers with objective and reliable information on the environmental impact of products. Many schemes analyse the entire life cycle of products, which means that, in the establishment of environmental product requirements, the evaluation covers all stages from raw material via production and use, to the discarded product in the form of waste. Not all labelling systems are equally thorough, though, but the parties involved cooperate worldwide to exchange ideas and experience.

Eco-labelling schemes are voluntary, leaving the producers free to request the use of the label for marketing purposes. Formally speaking, the label does not constitute a trade barrier; all products can still be marketed, whether labelled or not. However, if labelled products are supported, for instance, by public "green" procurement policies, it could become important for a producer to be able to meet the labelling criteria. In countries where eco-labelling schemes have been operational for some time now, it is evident that labelling is a valuable and reliable marketing tool, contributing to increased market shares. Some producers may find it difficult to maintain their market shares without an eco-label.

Official eco-labelling schemes were first set up in advanced industrialized countries, and labelling schemes are now operational in developed market economies such as the United States, Canada, Japan and many European countries. Recently, labelling schemes have also been introduced in a number of developing countries, e.g. Brazil, Chile and Colombia. In international fora, these countries have argued for the mutual recognition of eco-labels, so that they may overcome the "barriers to trade" experienced in developed-country markets on account of environmental requirements.

This paper attempts to take a closer look at the functioning of eco-labelling systems, and to examine the risk that the systems may make it more difficult for some developing countries to sell their products in markets where the issue of sustainability gains growing importance. Basically, most of the voluntary labelling schemes are designed along the same lines, with a view to promoting the development of products with reduced environmental impact over their entire life cycle, and to giving the consumers unbiased information on the labelled products. The European Union (EU) being by far the most important market for products exported from a number of developing countries, the debate on possible obstacles to trade caused by environmental labelling has focused mainly on the EU eco-label.

I THE ECO-LABELLING SCHEME OF THE EU

The EU eco-labelling scheme, which was adopted by the Council of Ministers in March 1992, is based on Council Regulation 880/92 on a Community eco-label award scheme. The preamble draws attention to the importance of developing a common European policy for cleaner products. The motivation underlying the adoption of a common European eco-labelling scheme was, first, the need for reliable consumer guidance and, second, the wish to avoid the proliferation of national systems which might obstruct the implementation of the Single Market, which later came into effect on 1 January 1993. The decision-makers were aware of the risk that varying environmental product requirements within the Community might result in barriers to trade among the member States. Technical barriers to trade need not reflect deliberate policy measures, but may be motivated by differing environmental conditions (geographical or biological) or by politically motivated infrastructural decisions. For example, the ranking of environmental priorities in national product policies may differ, depending on whether the waste policy priorities focus upon incineration or landfilling. In Denmark, more than 70 per cent of household waste is incinerated, and it is therefore essential to substitute PVC-containing products and packaging in order to avoid the serious environmental problems related to incineration. Another example is that of differences in the development of sewage treatment plants. In countries where the treatment plants are fitted with phosphate precipitation equipment, it is not essential to avoid phosphate in detergents. On the other hand, in countries where problems of phosphate separation in connection with sewage treatment facilities have not been solved, phosphate separation is essential.

II RELATIONS WITH THIRD COUNTRIES

Producers in and outside the EU are free to apply for a permit to use the eco-label. As regards producers outside the Union, article 4 (3) of the Regulation reads:

> Products imported into the Community, for which the award of an eco-label in accordance with this Regulation has been requested, must at least meet the same strict criteria as products manufactured in the Community.

In other words, no matter where the product was manufactured, it must meet the requirements laid down in the criteria relevant to the product type in question. It is therefore very important that work to establish environmental criteria takes place openly, to give relevant interest groups outside the Union access to information and to allow them to comment on the proposed criteria. The open procedure was introduced in 1994, in response to criticism, particularly from industrial interests outside the Union. This kind of openness is remarkable as far as labelling schemes are concerned.

III TECHNICAL BARRIERS TO TRADE

Although eco-labelling schemes are voluntary and do not constitute trade barriers in the strict sense, technical requirements used in the formulation of environmental criteria may have unintended trade effects outside the Union. For instance, general references to EC directives on emissions to water, air or soil, or the so-called Seveso Directive on dangerous chemicals, may imply that unless the product fulfils most of the Community environmental legislation, it may not be eligible for an EU eco-label. The purpose of the eco-labelling scheme, however, is not to export the entire Community legislation in the field of the environment to the rest of the world. Therefore, specific product requirements would need to be formulated in the criteria documents. Where possible and appropriate, reference should be made to internationally recognized standards and definitions (e.g. requirements for sustainable forestry with respect to certain paper products).

IV ECO-LABELLING OF PAPER PRODUCTS

Work on defining environmental criteria for paper products was initiated in 1990, when the Commission and the member States asked Denmark to be the lead country for criteria work in this field. Representatives from the member States, relevant European interest groups, a number of independent experts, and the Commission, were invited to take part in the work on criteria. In 1991, the *ad hoc* working group presented its provisional results in the report "Eco-labelling of Paper Products". More than a thousand copies of the report were printed and circulated internationally, and comments were published in a large number of English-language journals. The report discussed the possibility of establishing a methodology for setting up environmental criteria based on the cradle-to-grave approach. A concrete proposal was presented, dealing with criteria for xerographic copying paper and kitchen rolls.

On the basis of the results presented in the report and the comments received, it was decided that the working group would continue its work and prepare the final proposals for the criteria for two tissue products and for copying and writing paper for office use. As regards tissue paper, work was completed by the end of 1992, and the criteria were approved by the member States in March 1993. Final proposals for criteria for copying and writing paper are expected to be submitted to the EU Commission at the end of 1994. Acting as the lead country, Denmark has received comments from relevant interest groups from all over the world.

V CONSUMER CONFIDENCE

The general issue of political and ethical criteria with respect to issues such as occupational requirements, child labour, animal testing, etc.

may – in spite of their significance – be difficult to handle in connection with work on an eco-labelling scheme. The question of animal tests, however, was resolved in the EU: the Community Directive on cosmetics, to which reference is made for relevant product groups, provides for gradually phasing out the use of animal tests by not later than 1 January 1998. Moreover, the Union has recently prepared a proposal for future trade agreements providing for 30 per cent customs reductions, on condition that a number of international requirements, including on health and safety at work and child labour, are met.

It remains to be seen how consumers will react to labelled products, manufactured under acceptable conditions with respect to the environment, but under occupational conditions that the consumers deem unacceptable and consider as social dumping. Similar issues arise with respect to T-shirts bought from factories in countries where environmental conditions are under control, but where the workers, including children, work 12–14 hours a day in unacceptable conditions. There are several issues of this kind that may be difficult to handle within eco-labelling schemes, and other tools may need to be found for ensuring consumer confidence in the label.

VI THE NEED FOR DIALOGUE

Although many consumers understand the need to support the economy of developing countries by purchasing their products, it may be difficult to convert this goodwill through labelled products, if the issues mentioned above are not tackled adequately. This dilemma may be solved if there is constructive dialogue with these countries before identifying the product fields to be included in the labelling scheme. Developing countries can perhaps point out a number of products made from renewable resources or "natural" products which may be marketed as products with reduced environmental impact. There have been suggestions that the field of application of eco-labels be extended to a number of service activities such as tourism. The idea was brought forward by countries in Southern Europe, who requested that the economically vital tourist sector be subject to an environmental evaluation.

Obviously, the debate on more environmentally friendly products has only just started. Developing countries need to play an important role in this debate, in order to underline the global dimensions of a product strategy based on the active participation of consumers, contributing to a better environment.

23 Harmonization and Mutual Recognition: Are They Feasible?

Veena Jha

INTRODUCTION

The rationale behind the development of guidelines on harmonization and mutual recognition of eco-labelling schemes is to ensure that they are effective in promoting environmental improvements and that they do not constitute an unnecessary obstacle to trade. On the environmental side, improvements will generally result if a large number of producers use the eco-labels and the maximum number of consumers recognize and value the eco-label. Both goals will be better encouraged through harmonization and mutual recognition.

The existing eco-labelling schemes in both developing and developed countries indicate that consumer response has been more satisfactory where the criteria are simple, few and understandable. In several cases, the criteria are also aligned to the national environmental regulations. Moreover, product categories which are clearly associated to global environmental goals, such as energy efficiency or deforestation, are more likely to be sensitive to eco-labelling. In developing countries the lack of a market for eco-labelled products may be a serious handicap to its development. Thus schemes of mutual recognition and harmonization which lead to expansion of markets, or address global environmental concerns are likely to gain more consumer acceptance.

From a trade point of view, harmonization and mutual recognition may substantially lower transactions costs associated with eco-labelling. It will also make the process more transparent, open and participatory. One way of harmonizing eco-criteria would be to base them on internationally agreed standards. However, international standards may not fully take account of the technologies and production methods used in the manufacture of such products in the developing countries. From an environmental perspective, it may often be preferable to have diverse criteria. In this case the diverse criteria could possibly be reconciled through a scheme of mutual recognition.

In deriving conditions under which mutual recognition may be beneficial and those under which harmonization would be more useful, it may be necessary to distinguish between local and global environmental problems. With respect to global environmental problems, the broad criteria for environmental labelling should, as far as possible, be internationally agreed. These criteria could be negotiated under an international environmental agreement, or alternatively by international standardization bodies with the active participation of national standardization bodies, particularly from developing countries. As a starting point, these criteria could be established on the basis of product characteristics. One good example of such a standard is the establishment of standstill levels of chlorofluorocarbon (CFC) emissions negotiated under the Montreal Protocol.

Local environmental problems in the producing country may require a different approach. In the case of global environmental problems, goals and thresholds are unique; by contrast, in the case of local environmental problems, disparate environmental goals and thresholds are the norm. For example, pollution thresholds differ, based on such variables as climate, soil characteristics, pollution assimilative capacities, as well as ability and willingness to pay. Even to achieve identical environmental quality between two nations, their individual standards need not be the same. In this case, mutual recognition may be a useful initiative.

Harmonization and mutual recognition also pave the way for constructing eco-labelling schemes in a way so as to incorporate different levels of technological and socio-economic development and take into account the uniqueness of the environmental conditions in each country, as well as recognition of global environmental responsibilities.

While harmonization and mutual recognition may be laudable goals for eco-labelling schemes, they may be extremely difficult to operationalize, particularly under conditions of diverse environmental and developmental priorities. This chapter sets out some criteria which may be useful to bear in mind while developing schemes for harmonization and mutual recognition. The approach adopted is to distinguish between the two concepts and the contexts in which they may be relevant. Specific cases, namely tropical timber for harmonization and textiles for mutual recognition, have been considered. The purpose of examining these specific cases is to derive some of the generalizable aspects which may then be used as a basis to develop guidelines for harmonization and mutual recognition.

I MUTUAL RECOGNITION – THE CASE OF TEXTILES

The case of textiles is an interesting one from the point of view of the fact that the processes of production, the scale of production and the raw materials used differ between nations and even within nations. The market for textiles is segmented in terms of price, quality and fashion. Trade contributes an important share of the total production of textiles and undoubtedly the different stages of textile production, consumption and disposal have significant impacts on the environment. However, whether environmental features of textiles will be an important factor influencing consumer choice remains a debatable issue. Thus desired environmental improvements would only result from eco-labelling of textiles if the producers see the real benefits of labelling and are able to influence consumer choice in favour of the environmentally friendly alternative.

The European Union is in the process of developing an eco-label for textiles, which relies to a large extent on process-related criteria. In addition, there are several private schemes for the labelling of textiles. For example, the German textile industry associated in the union "*Gesamttextil*" is investigating the possibility of introducing two green labels for textiles. Trade associations and suppliers for the textile and clothing industry can also become sponsoring members.

Of the two labels proposed, one is a product label, the "MST", and the other is a process-related label the "MUT". The MST (*Marke scadstoffgeprufter Textilien*) is geared to the final consumer and involves tests for chemicals, dyes, etc. Seven different tests are needed to check the quantities of formaldehyde, chemicals (pentachlorophenol (PCP)), heavy metals, azo-dyes, pesticides, etc., in garments. The MUT (*Marke umweltschonender Textilien*) relates to the production process and is meant to be used only by garment and textile manufacturers.

The MUT label sets norms for production processes and it is granted exclusively to intermediate products. All processing operations need to be analysed in order to determine the degree of permitted levels of pollution of air, water and soil. Attention will particularly be focused on reduction of chlorine and chrome-based dyestuffs, as well as other chrome and allergenic compounds. The verification procedures associated with award of the MUT label may be difficult to implement in practice, particularly in developing countries, as they may involve on-site plant inspection.

Another system, the Eco-Tex Standard 100, is being developed by an international association for research on eco-textiles established by

German and Austrian research institutes. The standard is largely based on the possible impact of the use of textiles on human health. Ecological impacts of the production process are not included, as it is recognized that international monitoring will need to be organized before standards are formulated. Even though the criteria are fewer than those of Gesamttextil, the product norms of Eco-Tex and Gesamttextil are similar. Thus, labels based on Eco-Tex standard 100 can be expected to have effects on exports from developing countries similar to those of the MST label.

In these cases, mutual recognition based on the fact that local environmental conditions should determine process requirements, may be a viable alternative. As far as product-related requirements go, it may be useful to look for environmentally friendly alternatives which are locally available. For example, natural dyes or different threshold levels for certain chemicals may be regarded as viable alternatives. Formaldehyde is one such contentious chemical. However, since the criteria developed by the above-mentioned systems are unlikely to reflect local alternatives in terms of raw materials or processes, it may be better to institute a system of mutual recognition as this is more likely to reflect environmental improvements and be more cost-effective.

Establishing equivalence of eco-labelling criteria may be a useful way of dealing with developing country concerns, as well as facilitating mutual recognition. Where environmental aspects are addressed through regulatory approaches, compliance with the domestic exporting country's regulation could be considered as equivalent to compliance with the regulation in the importing country. Where non-regulatory PPM-related criteria are used to define environmentally superior products, for specific process-related criteria addressing intrinsically local environmental problems in the producing country, the eco-labelling programme of the importing country might accept as *equivalent*, PPMs which are friendly to the domestic environment of the producing country.

In a life-cycle analysis, equivalencies may also exist between product- and process-related criteria. For example, if the issue at stake is waste generation, the volume and type of waste generated during production could be weighed against biodegradability of the product after disposal. In the context of textiles, this may imply the equivalence between fabrics made of mixed fibres in a cleaner way with those made with 100% cotton which is biodegradable. It is to be noted that such a scheme already exists in a limited way in the load-points system of granting eco-labels. (See Jha and Zarrilli in this volume).

Mutual recognition in the context of eco-labelling generally would imply that, provided certain conditions are met, qualification for the eco-label of the exporting country is accepted as a basis for awarding the eco-label used in the importing country. Mutual recognition would normally apply to identical or similar product categories.

Mutual recognition tends to be easier between countries which have comparable levels of development and which are already involved in other kinds of trade arrangements. In fact, the few proposals for mutual recognition of eco-labelling schemes which have been formally discussed so far involve, on the one hand, the European Union and the EFTA countries and, on the other, the United States and Canada. In addition, the present experience is limited to certain aspects of eco-labelling such as conformity assessment procedures.

Mutual recognition of eco-labelling programmes implemented by countries at different levels of economic development may involve programmes which vary more substantially from each other in terms of environmental criteria. Mutual confidence, based on the previous harmonization of technical requirements, such as testing and inspection methods, would be a prerequisite for mutual recognition. Work on internationally agreed guidelines for eco-labelling could also contribute to creating conditions for moving towards mutual recognition of eco-labels.

II HARMONIZATION OF CRITERIA ON LABELLING OF TROPICAL TIMBER

Tropical timber presents an interesting case because the markets for this product are eroding rapidly because of consumer concern about deforestation. Eco-labelling schemes are voluntarily adopted, and thus they may avoid the implementation of measures such as boycotts and bans. Eco-labelling may also be an instrument for restoring markets, but the proliferation of labels on tropical timber and the difficulties in defining sustainable forestry makes a case for an internationally based label.

There are several proposals for the introduction of eco-labels for tropical timber and tropical timber products, all of which attempt to define sustainably managed forests. Some definitions, admittedly few, refer to the concept of "sustained yield", meaning that harvesting should not exceed the forest's growth rate. Other definitions are wider, covering also water quality, biodiversity and non-wood forest products. Some definitions include social issues in relation to forest management, such as local participation in project planning, employment generation and profit sharing. The lack of a common definition of sustainable forest management, has led to the development of different criteria for different eco-labelling programmes for tropical timber.

In the case of tropical timber, producing countries tend to react negatively to environmental standards imposed from outside. This is because they feel that countries which do not produce tropical timber may not have a practical knowledge of some aspects of tropical timber forestry and may thus formulate inappropriate definitions and set standards which may not be acceptable to producers.

However, some efforts which deserve mention have been made to formulate labelling systems and criteria on the basis of cooperation between producing and consuming countries. The German forestry and timber industries, jointly with a trade union, an importers' organization and the Germany Forestry Association, formulated the "*Projekt Tropenwald*", with the aim of contributing to forest protection by labelling tropical timber and other tropical forest products stemming from sustainable management. Another initiative for the labelling of wood, the Forest Stewardship Council (FSC), has been promoted by a diverse group of environmental organizations, concerned people from the forest industry, community forestry representatives and forest certification organizations from several countries in the world. The two aims of the project are to develop a set of principles and criteria of good forest management and create a single and widely recognized system of certification. The FSC will not itself be a "certifier"; local certifying organizations will instead be the "certifiers". They will grant the label to companies that comply with the principles and criteria developed by the FSC. Local certifying organizations are also called upon to play an active role in setting criteria, by adding to the general framework, specific requirements related to local conditions. The FSC aims at establishing criteria for all kind of forests, temperate, tropical and boreal.

Internationally based harmonized labelling schemes would be beneficial in cases such as tropical timber. However, even in this context it should be realized that criteria relate to environmental, social and economic features of forestry. While it may be possible, through the international convention on forestry, to obtain broad guidelines on environmental criteria, it would be difficult to understand the social and economic criteria relating to sustainable forestry, as these would be specific to the context to which they apply. Therefore, even in such cases, harmonization would have to incorporate divergences of social and economic goals of sustainable forestry which will have to be generated locally.

In this context, it is worth mentioning an Indonesian initiative which at its inception has tried to associate all the eco-labelling schemes and to learn from the existing schemes on eco-labelling. Indonesia is conducting several pilot tests of projects which will enable it to devise criteria which are workable and verifiable. They also recognize the fact that labels which are ideal in terms of their environmental attributes may not be accepted by the industry. Thus the problem is to strike the right balance between the two interests. Regional certification schemes or certification of an entire area is also being investigated as a facilitating mechanism. It may be possible to apply the same concept to small-scale tanners or to small-scale producers of textiles.

III CONCLUSIONS

This chapter has outlined instances where mutual recognition may prove to be a useful mechanism for reconciling trade, environment and development interests. These include cases where environmental problems are dispersed, local and where production conditions differ substantially between nations, where the stage of development imposes different scales of production, and where eco-labelling is an important aspect of competitiveness. In cases where the problem is global, where criteria are relatively simple to devise and relate to a few aspects of production process, where eco-labelling is an important aspect of market access, and where single issue labels can be devised with international cooperation, harmonization may be a more viable initiative. However, harmonization should also be accompanied by a procedure of mutual recognition of some criteria where such criteria are best resolved locally. These processes may also promote commercial interests by enlarging markets for eco-labelled products.

It is also to be noted that eco-labelling has so far not been significant in influencing consumer behaviour, except in the case of some products, such as pulp and paper. However, the issues raised by eco-labelling are also relevant for many other forms of environmental standard-setting, as they involve several contentious issues relating to the use of PPMs, involve value judgements, and incorporate several other dimensions besides the environmental virtues of a product, in determining the eco-criteria. Moreover, in some new schemes eco-criteria are actually set at levels which are consistent with regulations in particular countries. In others, eco-criteria later become regulations, as in the case of phosphate-free detergents. Thus a study of the trade and other effects of eco-labelling would be of relevance in other situations where compliance is not necessarily voluntary, but may become mandatory.

24 International Environmental Standards: Their Role in the Mutual Recognition of Eco-Labelling Schemes

Laura B. Campbell

Eco-labelling schemes, as economic instruments aimed at environmental improvement, are increasingly being used in order to generate consumer preference for environmentally friendly products. The proliferation of eco-labelling schemes has fostered concerns in both developed and developing counties over the potential effects of such schemes on international trade and market access, due in part to the tendency of eco-labelling schemes to focus on domestic products and domestic environmental standards.

One way to achieve the environmental goals of eco-labelling without discriminating against imported goods is to rely, when possible, on international environmental standards[1] in establishing environmental criteria on which an eco-label is based. This chapter outlines some existing international environmental standards, and discusses how they might be utilized in defining environmental criteria used in the award of eco-labels. As discussed below, establishing environmental criteria using international standards could also promote the mutual recognition of national eco-labelling schemes.

Most eco-labelling schemes use a limited life-cycle analysis, in which the key environmental effects of producing, using and disposing of the product are considered in awarding the eco-label. Based on the limited life-cycle model, many environmental criteria which serve as the basis for granting an eco-label are process-related, i.e. they relate to the environmental impacts of the product manufacturing process rather than those of the final product. For imported goods, the environment affected by the production process is that of the producing country. At the same time, eco-labels are usually awarded based on environmental criteria that reflect only the environmental concerns and national environmental standards of the importing country.

Two related issues must be addressed to ensure that eco-labelling schemes achieve their environmental purpose without imposing an unfair burden on international trade. First, all affected parties, including foreign producers, should have an opportunity to participate in the process of selecting and defining the environmental criteria on which eco-labels are awarded. Currently, foreign producers, especially those in developing countries, may not have access to the process of selection and definition of the environmental criteria for eco-labels. Secondly, the environmental standards underlying eco-labelling criteria should be based on sound scientific data and reflect varying environmental, economic and social concerns in different countries. One way of ensuring that eco-labelling criteria are transparent and scientifically sound is to base them on international standards that have been developed with wide participation by developed and developing countries, and are based on scientific risk management.

Following the Uruguay Round, the General Agreement on Tariffs and Trade (GATT) shows a strong preference for the use of international standards, particularly in areas concerning health and environment, to avoid the possibility of national standards creating non-tariff trade barriers. The relationship between international environmental standards and trade under the General Agreement is discussed below.

I INTERNATIONAL ENVIRONMENTAL STANDARDS AND TRADE: THE GENERAL AGREEMENT

As the GATT negotiations have been increasingly successful in reducing tariffs, concerns have arisen over the use of non-tariff trade barriers. In order to avoid the potential for national technical standards to operate as non-tariff barriers to trade, the revised Agreement on Technical Barriers to Trade (TBT Agreement) and the new Agreement on the Application of Sanitary and Phytosanitary Measures (SPS Agreement) require the use of international standards as the basis for national standards where relevant international standards exist.

Both the TBT and the SPS Agreements require adherence to the following principles:

- non-discrimination against imported products;
- transparency in the development and implementation of standards;
- acceptance of "equivalent" technical standards of other countries; and
- special and differential treatment for developing countries.

Both agreements require that a scientific justification serve as the basis for standards. The SPS Agreement further requires that scientific justification be based on risk assessment procedures and that, where available, the risk assessment procedures developed by international organizations should be taken into account.

The SPS Agreement designates Codex Alimentarius as the international standard to be applied in matters concerning food safety. In anticipation of this designation during the Uruguay Round, the operation of Codex Alimentarius was examined carefully since 1991, and a great deal of work has been done to ensure that it meets the requirements of the SPS Agreement. This paper describes the development and the operation of the Codex in some detail because it serves as a good model of how existing international environmental standards might be further developed to play a role similar to the Codex in other areas of environmental protection.

Under the TBT Agreement, technical standards that have an impact on trade are permitted only to the extent that they constitute the least trade-restrictive measure necessary in order to fulfil a "legitimate objective". A "legitimate objective" is defined so as to include the prevention of deceptive practices, protection of human health or safety, animal or plant life or health, or the environment. If a technical standard is created to fulfil one of these legitimate objectives, and is based on an international standard, it is presumed not to be an unnecessary obstacle to international trade, and therefore consistent with GATT.

Article 2.7 of the TBT Agreement states:

> Members shall give positive consideration to accepting *as equivalent* technical regulations of other Members, even if these regulations differ from their own, provided they are satisfied that these regulations adequately fulfil the objectives of their own regulations. (Emphasis added)

Eco-labelling schemes are not technical standards. However, mutual recognition of national eco-labelling schemes requires that the environmental criteria on which eco-labels are awarded are viewed as equivalent. As discussed below, selecting and defining eco-labelling criteria will be the central issue in determining whether national schemes are equivalent and therefore worthy of mutual recognition.

II INTERNATIONAL STANDARDS AND MUTUAL RECOGNITION

In the context of eco-labelling, the term "mutual recognition" means that products that have been awarded an eco-label under one country's scheme will be presumed to meet criteria for granting an eco-label in a corresponding country. Where countries mutually recognize national eco-labelling schemes, the labels awarded under the schemes of different countries may be used interchangeably.

Mutual recognition can take place on a bilateral or on a multilateral level. Mutual recognition on a multilateral basis would normally be accomplished through accreditation by an independent international authority.

For example, on a bilateral level, if Germany and Brazil mutually recognize each other's eco-labelling schemes, a product granted an eco-label in Brazil could apply the German eco-label on products exported to Germany. On a multilateral level, if Brazil's eco-labelling schemes were accredited by an international authority, Brazil's eco-label would be interchangeable with those of any country which participated in the international accreditation process.

In essence, mutual recognition of an eco-labelling scheme will be based on a determination that the environmental criteria on which eco-labels are awarded are equivalent. To the extent that their underlying eco-labelling criteria are based on international standards, with acceptable variation reflecting differences in economic, social, health and environmental concerns of countries, national eco-labelling schemes could be deemed equivalent.

III CODEX ALIMENTARIUS

Codex Alimentarius is a set of internationally adopted standards, codes of practice and guidelines aimed at the protection of consumer health and at facilitating international trade in food and food products. Codex

Alimentarius includes standards covering food additives and contaminants, methods of food analysis and sampling, labelling, hygiene in food production, pesticide residues in foods, food import and export certification and inspection systems and standards for specific classes for foods and food products. Codex Alimentarius standards cover both product quality and production process. The standards are not legally binding, but they serve as the basis for the enactment of national requirements and procedures.

Codex standards, codes and guidelines are elaborated by the Codex Alimentarius Commission, and proposed to the Food and Agriculture Organization (FAO) and the World Health Organization (WHO), which together administer the joint FAO/WHO Food Standards Programme. Membership in the Commission is open to all members and associate members of FAO and WHO. Members of the United Nations who are not members of either FAO or WHO may attend meetings of the Commission as observers. As of 1993, there were 144 developed and developing country members in the Codex Alimentarius Commission.

IV WHO'S ENVIRONMENTAL HEALTH GUIDELINES AND CRITERIA

WHO has issued non-binding guidelines for drinking water and air quality. These guidelines, exclusively based on scientific data, are intended to serve as the basis for the development of national standards and regulations. Local or national environmental, social, economic and cultural conditions are expected to be considered during the development of national standards.

WHO environmental quality guidelines are developed with the participation of hundreds of experts from developed and developing countries, and are extensively reviewed for scientific accuracy. WHO officials stress that the guidelines are based solely on scientific data on the health and environmental effects of pollutants, and that they do not take into account technological, political or economic factors.

WHO also has an Environmental Health Criteria Programme, which it initiated in 1976. The programme is now the joint responsibility of WHO, United Nations Environment Programme (UNEP) and the International Labour Organization (ILO), under the framework of the International Programme on Chemical Safety (IPCS). The aim of this programme is to provide national authorities with information concerning chemical hazards so as to enable them to develop appropriate national standards on chemicals.

A Guidelines on Drinking Water Quality

In 1993, WHO issued global guidelines for drinking water quality intended to serve as the basis for developing binding national standards. Over 200 experts from nearly 40 developed and developing countries participated in the formulation of the guidelines over a period of several years. While the guidelines include recommended concentration levels for microbial and chemical contaminants, the experts who drafted the guidelines did not advocate the adoption of binding international standards, and stressed the importance of national priorities and economic factors for setting up national standards. In illustrating the need for national risk–benefit analysis as the basis for standard setting, the drafters of the guidelines emphasized that the fact that chemical contaminants are not normally associated with acute health effects places them in a position of lower priority for most developing countries than microbial contaminants, the effects of which are usually acute and widespread.

One difficulty in basing environmental criteria for eco-labelling on international water quality guidelines is the indirect relationship between pollution emissions during the manufacturing process and water quality. Emissions by a single industrial source are usually one of the many potential influences on overall water quality.

B Air Quality Guidelines

WHO first published global air quality criteria and guidelines for urban pollutants in 1972. These guidelines, which covered the major conventional pollutants – sulphur dioxide, particulates, carbon monoxide, photochemical oxidants and nitrogen dioxide – have been very influential over the past 20 years in developing national ambient air quality standards. Global air quality guidelines have not been reissued since 1972, but WHO published regional air quality guidelines for Europe in 1987, and this is currently being updated for global use.

One of the difficulties with using compliance with global or even national ambient air quality standards as an indication of a specific product's environmental friendliness is the indirect relationship between a factory's air pollution emissions and an area's overall ambient air quality. The ambient air quality will depend on a number of factors such as the number of other factories in the area and meterological conditions.

V CODE OF ETHICS ON INTERNATIONAL TRADE IN CHEMICALS

In April 1994, following a series of informal consultations among developed and developing countries, agreement was reached on adopting a Code of Ethics on International Trade in Chemicals, a non-binding set of principles governing environmentally sound management of chemicals in international trade. The Code is primarily addressed to industry and other private sector parties, and covers production and management of chemicals in international trade, taking into account their entire life cycle. The Code includes provisions on minimizing health and environmental risks from chemicals, packaging and labelling, testing and risk assessment, and quality assurance. The Code is aimed at ensuring the safe management of chemicals during the manufacturing process and by the final consumer. Adoption of the Code of Ethics represents an important step forward in promoting safe management of chemicals in international trade.

VI OTHER VOLUNTARY CODES OF CONDUCT

A Responsible Care Programme

"Responsible Care" is the title of the programme and codes of management practice originally initiated in Canada and adopted by the European Chemical Industry Council (CEFIC) and the United States Chemical Manufacturers's Association (CMA). This voluntary set of guiding principles and codes of practice is aimed at recognizing and responding to community concerns about chemicals which can be manufactured, transported, used and disposed of safely, as well as at working with government officials, customers and the public to ensure chemical safety. Codes of management practice dealing with specific concerns related to the health and environmental effects of chemicals such as process safety, waste and release reduction, community awareness and emergency response and chemical distribution have been adopted. The Responsible Care Programme also includes procedures for self-evaluation and assessment, which could serve as a useful example of ways in which certification of compliance with international standards could be measured.

B OECD Guidelines for Manufacturers and Traders Exporting Chemicals

The Business and Industry Advisory Committee (BIAC) is an independent organization serving as a consultative body to the Organization for Economic Cooperation and Development (OECD), representing business and industry. In 1985, BIAC issued guidelines addressed to manufacturers and traders exporting chemicals which are intended to promote the safe use, handling and disposal of chemicals in importing countries.

BIAC developed the guidelines as a supplementary contribution to the work of OECD governments on information exchange related to the export of banned or severely restricted chemicals. The guidelines set forth a voluntary scheme for chemical manufacturers and exporters supplying their direct customers with information about hazards associated with chemicals and safety practices for minimizing risk.

C UNEP: Voluntary Environmental Standards for Banks

As of April 1994, 55 major international banks have adopted a nonbinding set of principles under which they have agreed to promote sustainable development and environmental protection as an integral part of all banking activities. UNEP's negotiation of this joint statement by banks reflects its recognition of the importance of incorporating environmental considerations in financial decision-making, and represents important progress towards the internationalization of environmental costs in commercial business transactions. The voluntary set of principles on incorporating environmental principles in lending transactions creates a framework for environmentally sound business practices within the banking industry.

VII CONTROLS ON OZONE-DEPLETING CHEMICALS: THE MONTREAL PROTOCOL

The use and production of ozone-depleting chemicals are controlled in two basic ways under the Montreal Protocol: by placing limits on consumption (which is defined as production plus imports) in countries which are parties to the Protocol and by restricting trade with non-parties. Under the Protocol, limits on production of ozone-depleting chemicals are phased in over time, with different time frames for developed and developing countries.

The Montreal Protocol is an example of binding international environmental standards negotiated with extensive participation from both developed and developing countries. The standards reflect the different economic circumstances among countries which are parties to the Protocol.

In order to ensure that industry in countries which comply with the production and consumption limits of the Protocol are not placed at a competitive disadvantage, the Protocol imposes restrictions on trade with non-parties. In keeping with the principle of non-discrimination under the General Agreement, non-parties can avoid being subject to these trade restrictions by showing compliance with the control measures in the Protocol.

VIII ISO: ENVIRONMENTAL MANAGEMENT STANDARDS

In 1991, the International Organization for Standardization (ISO) and the International Electrotechnical Committee (IEC) jointly established the Strategic Advisory Group for the Environment (SAGE) to make recommendations relating to international standards. Following the establishment of SAGE, a working group was created to make recommendations on international standards for environmental management systems.

The ISO/IEC working group plans to develop a model environmental management system based on the general principles of environmental responsibility and voluntary codes of conduct issued recently by various trade organizations such as those discussed in section IV of this paper. The environmental management model envisioned will not specify performance criteria but rather will rely on voluntary standards. The basic purpose of the model environmental management system would be to enable an organization to ensure that its environmental performance met policy requirements.

IX CONCLUSION

Existing international health and environmental standards could be used in establishing environmental criteria for the mutual recognition of eco-labelling schemes. Codex Alimentarius serves as one of the best examples of how international cooperation in setting standards which are both process- and product-related can be done in a manner which effectively promotes human health and the environment and international trade. In several areas of environmental concern, however, no international guidance exists which could serve as the basis for mutual recognition and certification of environmentally friendly products, especially on energy consumption and forest and water resource management.

Note

1. The term "international environmental standard" includes non-binding standards, guidelines, codes of conduct and guiding principles which apply either to governments or industry.

25 Trade in Eco-Labelled Products: Developing-Country Participation and the Need for Increased Transparency

Simonetta Zarrilli

INTRODUCTION

The effects of eco-labelling on developing-country exports so far have been modest, especially because of the limited number of products included in the schemes and because most of the items considered for labelling are not of particular export interest to them. However, developing countries are becoming more exposed to the effects of eco-labelling since some of the new product categories which are being selected for inclusion in the eco-labelling programmes are of great export interest to them.

If this trend continues, it will become crucial for foreign manufacturers/exporters to be aware of the new products included in the eco-labelling programmes and to become familiar with the eco-criteria which apply to them. In certain cases, it would be suitable to involve foreign manufacturers/exporters in the development of criteria, since this would ensure that the views and concerns of those who have a clear export interest in that product group are taken into account when the environmental characteristics of a specific product group are discussed. Foreign-producer participation would be of particular value when the criteria are PPM-related, since the environmental and developmental conditions of the producing country may be significantly different from those of the importing country, and the producing country may rely on production processes which are dissimilar to those of the importing country, even if they are equally sound from an environmental point of view.

Statistical data about eco-labelling programmes are very rare. Little or no information is available at present on the market shares of eco-labelled products, probably because most eco-labelling schemes have been implemented only in recent years.

This paper analyses, in its first part, eco-labelling-related trade flows between developing countries and three OECD importing markets: Canada, the Nordic countries[1] and the European Union (EU). The product categories taken into account are those which have already been included in the eco-labelling programmes of these countries, as well as some of those which will be included in the near future (see Box 25.1).

Box 25.1 Number of product categories under different eco-labelling programmes

Countries	*Canada*	*EU*	*Germany*	*Japan*	*Netherlands*	*Nordic countries*	*Total*
Product groups							
Packaging	–	–	–	2	6	–	19
Cosmetics	–	–	3	1	–	–	4
Vehicles and parts thereof	–	–	8	–	–	–	8
Paints, coatings and varnishes	3	–	5	1	1	1	11
Recyclable/recycled/reusable made of paper	5	2	7	10	7	5	36
Recyclable/recycled/reusable other than paper	2	–	9	7	–	–	18
Batteries	2	–	2	–	–	1	5
Boilers and gas burners	1	–	7	–	1	–	9
Insulating materials/products	2	–	4	2	–	–	8
Water economizing machinery/products	1	–	4	3	1	–	9
Household equipment and office appliances	3	2	8	7	3	3	26

Lubricants/fuels and oils	2	–	3	7	–	1	13
Footwear	–	–	–	–	–	1	1
Textiles/clothes	–	–	–	1	1	–	2
Carpets	–	–	–	–	1	–	1
Other	9	1	14	10	11	7	52
Total	30	5	76	55	27	19	212

Source: UNCTAD.

While the analysis leads to the conclusion that, on average, developing-country participation in the trade of potential eco-labelled products is rather limited, for certain product categories imports from developing countries represent a high share of total imports. Moreover, evidence shows that in certain cases exports in specific products are very significant for the exporting country. The second part of the paper addresses the issue of foreign manufacturers/exporters' participation in the development of the eco-criteria, in order to assess whether existing transparency rules which apply to voluntary measures, including eco-labelling, are adequate and contribute to minimize the potential negative trade impact that these measures may have. Some possible criteria for encouraging foreign participation in the setting up of eco-criteria are suggested, and some examples of foreign participation based on the proposed criteria are given.

I METHODOLOGY

It should be mentioned that it is difficult to estimate the incidence of eco-labelling in international trade. The principal reason is that in order to link eco-labelling with information on international trade flows, there is a need to identify products covered by eco-labelling programmes in terms of the Harmonized System nomenclature (HS). In most cases, however, the definition of the product categories included in eco-labelling schemes is either too broad,[2] or too specific[3] to allow correspondence with the HS. The data are therefore based on a *tentative* tariff classification of the products included, or under consideration, in the three eco-labelling programmes mentioned above. In some cases the list of products included in the analysis is larger than the products actually included in the eco-labelling schemes. This is because:

- according to the HS, it is not possible to distinguish products on the basis of some "environmental" characteristics, such as recyclability, recycled content, rechargeability and reusability, and therefore all products in a specific product category have to be considered, regardless of their environmental attributes;[4]
- the definition of the product category is very broad or does not correspond to any specific HS code;[5]
- the definition is too detailed, therefore there is no precise correspondence to any specific code.[6]

In some exceptional cases the definition is too vague to lead to any classification of the corresponding product.[7] It is also important to keep in mind that since traders have the option to either applying for eco-labels or selling unlabelled products, the trade data presented in this paper provide an indication of trade in products for which eco-labelling programmes exist or are planned, whether or not exporters have applied for the label. However, considering that, for example, products having a recycled content compete with similar products not having a recycled content, the data collected provide a meaningful indication of the importance that imports of a product category have in a specific market.

II MAIN FINDINGS

In the three markets analysed, the imports of products included in the eco-labelling schemes represent a small percentage of total imports: 1.2 per cent for Canada; 2.5 per cent for the Nordic countries; and 3.3 per cent for the EU. Developing-country share of total imports of "potential" eco-labelled products is quite low in Canada (5.8 per cent), is as negligible as 0.9 per cent in the Nordic countries, but it is considerably higher in the EU, where it reaches 44.9 per cent (see Table 25.1).

A Canada

For just one product category included in the Canadian eco-labelling programme, imports originating in developing countries represent a high

Table 25.1 Participation of developing countries in trade in products planned to be included or already included in eco-labelling programmes

	Imports of eco-labelled products (million US$)	*Total imports (million US$)*	*Share of eco-labelled products in total imports (%)*	*Imports of eco-labelled products from developing countries (million US$)*	*Share of eco-labelled products from developing countries in total imports of eco-labelled products (%)*
Canada (1992)	1512	129 200	1.2	88.7	5.8
Nordic countries (Finland, Norway, Sweden) (1990)	2422	97 000	2.5	21.5	0.9
EU (1992)	20 794	636 300	3.3	9343	44.9

share of total imports: textile bags (78.4 per cent), plastic bags (20.9 per cent) and paper bags (15.0 per cent). For lamps, batteries and wood pulp, imports from developing countries account for 13.3 per cent, 7.5 per cent and 6.5 per cent, respectively, of total imports, while for the other product categories developing-country exports are negligible (see Table 25.2).

B Nordic Countries

Imports from developing countries of "potential" eco-labelled products are very limited, the only exception being lamps (37.4 per cent), for which Hong Kong is the main supplier (see Table 25.3).

C European Union

For three product categories which will soon be included in the eco-labelling programme of the EU, developing countries represent the main foreign suppliers of the EU market with a substantial market share: 80.1 per cent for shirts and 84.6 per cent for T-shirts; 79.0 per cent for bed linen; and 74.6 per cent for footwear.

In another three product groups developing countries also account for a significant share of total imports: lamps (34.4 per cent), wood pulp (9.2 per cent), and hair lacquers (6.6 per cent). However, for the remaining product groups developing countries have a small share in the EU market (see Table 25.4).

Table 25.2 Developing countries' participation in trade in specific product categories included in eco-labelling programmes: Canada, 1992

HS heading	*Description*	*Total imports (US$000)*	*Imports from developing countries (US$000)*	*Share of developing countries in total (%)*	*Major supplies*
3208 3209 3210	Paints and varnishes	224 262	14	–	USA Germany UK
3401 3402	Soap and detergents	206 223	2 585	1.2	USA UK Germany
3923.21 3923.29	Plastic bags	57 437	12 011	20.9	USA Hong Kong China
4701 4702 4703 4704 4705	Wood pulp	140 222	9 133	6.5	USA South Africa Brazil
4801	News print	16 473	–	–	USA France
4810.11 4810.12 4810.21 4810.29	Paper and paperboard	254 143	2 253	0.9	USA France Italy
4818.40	Diapers	58 717	66	0.1	USA Austria Hungary
4819.30 4819.40	Paper bags	21 719	3 255	15.0	USA Korea (Rep. of) China
6305	Textile bags	19 114	15 022	78.6	Brazil Haiti China
8506	Primary cells and primary batteries	62 556	4 738	7.5	USA Japan Germany
8513	Electric lamps, filament, fluorescent and ultra violet lamps.	222 651	29 725	13.3	USA Republic of Korea Japan
8516.10	Water heaters	12 350	117	0.9	USA Germany Italy
9009.90	Toner cartridges	216 571	9 799	4.5	USA Japan Germany

Table 25.3 Developing countries' participation in trade in specific product categories included in eco-labelling programmes: Nordic countries,[a] 1990

HS	*Description*	*Total imports (US$ 000)*	*Imports from developing countries (US$000)*	*Share of developing countries in total imports (%)*	*Major suppliers*
3208 3209 3210	Paints and varnishes	197 546	–	–	Germany Sweden UK
3401	Soap and detergents	301 505	–	–	Denmark Germany UK
4701 4702 4703 4704 4705	Wood pulp	184 602	9784	5.3	Sweden Norway Finland
4801	Newsprint	4210	–	–	Denmark Finland Sweden
4810.11 4810.12 4810.21 4810.29	Paper and paperboard	200 127	–	–	Finland Sweden Germany
4817.10	Envelopes	19070	–	–	Sweden Denmark Finland
4818.10 4818.20	Toilet paper, tissue and towels	95 885	403	0.4	Sweden Finland ex-Yugoslavia
49	Books, newspapers, pictures and other products	758 221	–	–	Germany UK Denmark
8407.21 8407.29 8408.10	Marine engine	171 426	–	–	Japan USA Finland
8416	Furnace burners	24 595	74	0.3	Germany UK Denmark
8422.11 8422.19	Dishwashers	88 812	–	–	Germany Sweden Italy
8506	Primary cells and primary batteries	65 818	1494	2.3	Belgium Germany Japan

8513 8539	Electric, filament, ulta violet and fluorescent lamps	13 881	5190	37.4	Hong Kong Germany USA
9009.11 9009.12 9009.21 9009.22	Photocopying machines	194 906	3762	1.9	Japan Netherlands UK
9009.90	Toner cartridges	101 309	770	0.7	USA, Japan and UK

[a] Finland, Norway and Sweden, including trade among these countries.

Table 25.4 Developing countries' participation in trade in specific product categories planned to be included or already included in eco-labelling programmes: European Union, 1992 (excluding intra-EU trade)

HS	*Description*	*Total imports US$000*	*Imports from developing countries (US$000)*	*Share of developing countries in total imports (%)*	*Major suppliers*
3208 3209 3210	Paints and varnishes	290 068	3282	1.1	Switzerland Sweden USA
3305.10	Shampoo	41 777	853	2.0	USA Switzerland Austria
3305.30	Hair lacquers	6453	432	6.6	USA Switzerland Austria
3402	Detergents	352 358	5926	1.7	Switzerland USA Sweden
4701, 4702, 4703, 4704 4705	Wood pulp	5 522 603	512 890	9.2	USA Sweden Canada
4810.11 4810.12 4810.21 4810.29	Copying and writing paper (paper and paperboard)	2 598 403	2361	0.1	Finland Sweden Austria
4818.10 4818.20	Toilet paper, tissue and towels	201 757	3847	1.9	Sweden Austria Finland
6109.10 6109.90	T-shirts of cotton or other textile materials knitted or crocheted	1 850 406	1 566 422	84.6	Turkey Hong Kong India
6205.20 6205.30	Men's and women's shirts of cotton and				Hong Kong India

6206.30 6206.40	man-made fibres	3 541 666	2 836 333	80.1	Bangladesh
6302.10 6302.21 6302.31 6302.32	Bed linen, of cotton or other textile materials	582 849	460 291	78.9	Pakistan Turkey India
6401, 6402 6403, 6404, 6405	Footwear	5 112 734	3 815 586	74.6	China Republic of Korea Indonesia
8422.11 8422.19	Dishwashers	57 838	413	0.7	Sweden Switzerland USA
8450.11 8450.12 8450.19 8450.20	Washing machines	126 659	541	0.4	Sweden USA ex-Yugoslavia
8513 8539	Lamps	623 745	214 656	34.4	USA China Japan

III TRANSPARENCY RULES IN THE INTERNATIONAL TRADING SYSTEM

In the international trading system, transparency is regarded as a means to:

- build confidence in and provide security and stability to the multilateral trading system;
- help minimize trade restriction and distortion;
- assist private sector operators to adjust to changing trade policies; and
- prevent misunderstanding and trade disputes from arising.[8]

The main transparency provisions applying in the international trading system are GATT Article X; the 1979 Understanding Regarding Notification, Consultation, Dispute Settlement and Surveillance; the Uruguay Round Decision on Notification Procedures; and the notification provisions of the Agreement on Technical Barriers to Trade (TBT). Article X requires that measures applied by WTO members that can have a significant effect on trade shall be published promptly to enable governments and traders to become acquainted with them. The 1979 Understanding requires notification, to the maximum extent possible, of the adoption of trade measures affecting the operation of the General Agreement, where possible in advance of implementation. The Decision on Notification Procedures provides a general obligation for members to notify policy actions. An illustrative list of policy actions which are agreed to be notifiable is annexed to the Decision. It also recommends the establishment of a central registry of notifications under the responsibility of the WTO secretariat. The notification provisions of the TBT Agreement require publication and notification of standards and regulations prior to their entry into force, or, where that is not possible, immediately after their adoption. They also require comments from other members on proposed or adopted standards and regulations to be taken into account and enquiry points to be established to provide information and answer enquiries from other members. The *ex-ante* notification obligations of the TBT Agreement are regarded as particularly valuable; however, *ex-post* publication and notification is the GATT norm.

As far as voluntary measures, including eco-labelling are concerned, it is generally felt that none of the provisions mentioned before, but those of the TBT Agreement, cover them, in particular voluntary measures administered by the private sector. Therefore the question is whether the obligations of the TBT Agreement provide for an adequate level of transparency.

The general feeling emerging from the international debate on this issue seems to be that transparency should be commensurate with a measure's trade effects: the greater the potential for a measure to have significant trade effects, the more transparent it should be to a country's trading partners.[9] The issue at stake is therefore whether the present transparency rules which apply to eco-labelling are adequate and help minimize trade restriction and distortion.

The experience seems to indicate two possible risks: inadequate compliance with existing transparency obligations and inadequacy of present transparency provisions. On the first point, a further distinction should be made between negligence in fulfilling transparency obligations and differences in the interpretation of the transparency obligations. In the case of eco-labelling, countries have been very reluctant to notify their eco-labelling programmes because of several reasons: they felt that the programmes were not going to have a significant impact on trade; the fact that most eco-labelling schemes were administered by non-governmental bodies was regarded as a reason for leaving them outside the scope of the GATT notification system (pending the implementation of the Uruguay Round TBT Agreement); and concerns were raised about the suitability to extend the application of WTO rules to eco-labelling programmes which include PPMs criteria not related to the final characteristics of the product.

On the other hand, full compliance with existing transparency provisions may prove to be insufficient, especially when the programmes heavily rely on PPM-based criteria, and other mechanisms, such as consultation with potentially affected trading partners and availability of information related to the programmes at the earliest possible stage of their development may prove to be useful to secure the environmental goals of eco-labelling without adversely impacting international trade.

IV THE NEED FOR INCREASED TRANSPARENCY

According to the ISO working draft on "Guiding Principles for Environmental Labelling, Practitioner Programmes and Systems",[10] transparency in environmental labelling programmes of Type I[11] entails the clear and open-for-examination availability of the rationale and details on which the programmes are based; the availability for inspection and commenting to stakeholders of information on criteria, certification and award procedures; periodic revision of criteria and the funding sources for the programme development. Transparency also involves the participation of stakeholders in developing criteria and certification as well as early notification of concerned domestic and foreign producers about the product categories and criteria. Practitioners should make available to the public a summary of the responses and considerations to stakeholders comments. Transparency would thus include a new aspect, namely the ability, for certain countries, to participate in the discussions leading to the adoption of the eco-criteria. The issue at stake is therefore to find out to whom the debate should be extended.

A possible option for extending the debate to foreign producers, especially from developing countries, would be to identify those products which are of export interest to developing countries and making sure that when criteria related to these products are discussed, the main suppliers among developing countries become involved.

Considering that agricultural products as well as raw materials, intermediate and capital goods normally are not earmarked for eco-labelling, only the so-called "consumer products" can be included in the eco-labelling schemes. In order to assess when consumer products may be considered of export interest to developing countries, some possible parameters to use could be to look at the import share (more than 50 per cent) and the export value (more than one million US$) that developing countries as a group have for a specific product in a specific importing country.

An analysis has been carried out on the basis of these parameters, taking as an example imports into the EU (extra-EU imports) in 1992. The EU has been chosen since eco-labelling in this market has by far the largest potential effect on developing countries. According to trade statistics, there are 444 products at 6-digit level of the HS where exports from developing countries as a group exceed 1 million US$ and 50 per cent import share. These products include, among others, leather articles, wooden frames, tableware and kitchenware, textiles and clothing, footwear, jewellery, cooking appliances, sewing machines, electro-mechanical and electro-thermic domestic appliances, cassette players, radios, TV receivers, bicycles, motorcycles, clocks and watches, toys, and combs. One option for increasing transparency would be to make sure that when the eco-criteria for one of these products/product groups are discussed, the first suppliers among developing countries are invited to participate in the debate (see Table 25.5).

When schemes are based on the life-cycle approach, the question of whether a product qualifies for a label may depend to a large extent on the materials used; for example, leather for shoes, cotton for T-shirts and bed linen, and pulp for tissue products. The question is then whether, in addition to the manufacturers of the product categories subject to eco-labelling, the principal suppliers of the raw materials should also be involved in the process of establishing criteria, since the final product would be eligible for labelling only if the raw materials comply with the eco-criteria related to them. For example, the Russian Federation is the main supplier of cotton to the EU among developing countries and countries in transition, while Brazil is the main supplier, among developing countries, of both leather and pulp. Therefore, it would probably be worth exploring the possibility of including the representatives of the Russian Federation and Brazil in the discussions leading to the setting up of the eco-criteria for leather, textiles and paper products.

There could be, however, other options to identify those countries which should be consulted when the eco-criteria are set up. In a different field – modification of tariff schedules – international trade rules have been established to rule the participation of countries in the negotiations.

According to the GATT Agreement, when a contracting party wants to modify or withdraw a concession for a specific product, it has to

Table 25.5 Major developing country suppliers to the EU for some industrial consumer products,[a] 1992 (thousand US$)[b]

HS	*Description*	*Total imports*	*Developing*	*Import share (%)*	*Main suppliers*
4202.11 4202.12 4202.19	Trunks, suitcases of leather, plastic or other materials	505 284	430 048	85.1	China Taiwan, Prov. of China Republic of Korea
4202.21 4202.22 4202.29 4202.31 4202.32 4202.39	Handbags and articles carried in pocket or handbags of leather or plastic	746 110	691 663	92.7	China India Thailand
5701.10 5701.90 5702.10 5702.20 5702.31 5702.32 5702.39 5702.41 5702.42 5702.49 5702.51 5702.59 5702.91 5702.99 5703.10	Carpets and other textile floor coverings	1 516 347	1 235 133	81.4	Islamic Republic of Iran India China
6103.32 6103.33 6103.39 6104.32 6104.33 6104.39 6203.31 6203.32 6203.39 6204.32 6204.33 6204.39	Men's or boys', women's or girls' jackets and blazers	1 337 902	922 644	68.9	China Turkey Poland
6302.40 6302.51 6302.52 6302.53 6302.59 6302.60 6302.91	Toilet linen and kitchen linen	650 518	507 868	78.0	China Brazil Turkey
6401.99 6402.19 6402.20 6402.91 6402.99 6403.11	Footwear	4 758 444	3 783 294	79.5	China Republic of Korea Indonesia

6403.19 6403.51 6403.91 6403.99 6404.11 6404.19 6404.20 6405.10 6405.20 6405.90					
7323.91 7323.92 7323.93 7323.94 7323.99	Table, kitchen or other household articles of iron or steel	465 606	330 008	70.8	China Republic of Korea Taiwan, Prov. of China
8452.10	Sewing machines	238 304	136 254	57.1	Taiwan, Prov. of China, Brazil China
8516.40	Electric irons	128 290	110 370	86.0	Singapore China Taiwan, Prov. of China
8516.50	Microwave ovens	503 111	324 007	64.4	Republic of Korea Thailand China
8527.11 8527.19 8527.21 8527.31 8528.32 8528.10 8528.20	Radio and television receivers	5 514 533	3 809 899	69.0	China Malaysia Republic of Korea
9102.12 9102.29 9103.10 9105.11 9105.19 9105.21 9105.29 9105.91 9105.99	Watch, clocks, alarm clocks	515 089	359 917	69.8	China Taiwan, Prov. of China Hong Kong
9503.41 9503.49 9503.50 9503.60 9503.60 9503.70 9503.80 9503.90	Toys	2 303 655	2 120 775	92.0	China Thailand Taiwan, Prov. of China

[a] Industrial consumer products were defined according to the broad, economic categories listed in the SITC Document, Series M, NO 53, Rev.2, p. 10.
[b] Exports: more than 1 million US$; market share: more than 50 per cent.

negotiate it with two categories of countries: the contracting party with which the concession was initially negotiated (initial negotiating rights); and the contracting party which has a principal supplying interest. The applicant party has also to consult any other contracting party which has a substantial interest in the negotiations (Article XXVIII).

The country having a principal supplying interest is the country which has had, for the specific product and for a reasonable period of time prior to negotiations, a larger share in the market of the applicant contracting party than a contracting party with which the concession was initially negotiated.[12]

The country or countries having a substantial interest are those which have a significant share in the market of the country seeking to modify or withdraw the concession.[13] During the meeting of the Committee on Tariff Concessions in July 1985, it was agreed that a country having 10 per cent share can be regarded as a "substantial supplier".[14]

Exceptionally, if for a specific country the concession in question affects trade which constitutes a major part of its total exports, this country may be regarded as having a principal supplying interest.[15] This provision has been further spelt out during the negotiations of the Uruguay Round. Therefore the country which has the highest ratio of exports of the product to the market of the country modifying or withdrawing the concession to its total exports to that market shall be deemed to have a principal supplying interest.[16] This is to secure a redistribution of negotiating rights in favour of small and medium-sized exporting countries.

Even though these principles apply in a field rather different from eco-labelling, it may be worth exploring the suitability to extend their application to eco-labelling, considering that the two cases – modification of tariff schedules and inclusion of a new product group in an eco-labelling programme – have at least an element in common: the need to distinguish those countries which have a concrete trade interest in a specific product (and therefore should get involved in the negotiations/consultations), from those whose trading interest is rather remote or insufficiently significant to justify their involvement.

In the case of eco-labelling, there will probably be a limited number of cases in which a developing country is the first supplier of a new product group. In more cases a developing country will be asked to participate in the discussions because the product under consideration is a crucial one for its exports, independently from the importance that these exports have for the importing country (highest ratio of exports out of total exports). By applying the principle of "substantial interest" (that in the case of modification of schedules gives those countries which have at least 10 per cent market share the right to be consulted), more countries would get the chance to be involved in the discussions for the setting up of the eco-criteria.

Tables 25.6–25.10 give some examples, related to the EU eco-labelling programme, of what would happen in terms of country participation in the eco-labelling discussions if the above-mentioned principles were to apply. In the case of T-shirts (which, because of classification problems, have been split in two groups), Turkey and the Maldives would be invited to participate in the discussions, Turkey being the first suppliers (principal supplying interest) and the Maldives because of the share that exports of T-shirts have in their total exports (highest ratio of exports out of total exports). In the case of shirts, Hong Kong would be invited because of its position as first supplier, India because it has more than 10 per cent market share (substantial interest), and Cambodia due to the ratio that the exports of shirts have out of its total exports. When discussing bed linen, Pakistan would be invited because is the first supplier, and Turkey and India because they have more than 10 per cent market share. For footwear, the People's Republic of China would be invited being the first supplier, the Republic of Korea because it has more than 10 per cent market share, and Indonesia because of the principle of the highest ratio of exports out of total exports. In the case of tissue paper, Sweden would be invited being the first supplier, Austria and Finland[17] because they have more than 10 per cent market share, and Slovenia because of highest ratio of exports out of total exports.

V CONCLUSIONS

It is doubtful that transparency alone would be able to avoid all the trade-related problems which may arise from the implementation of eco-labelling programmes, however it can provide a substantial contribution to the solution of these problems.

Eco-labelling agencies in developed countries may wish to analyse the actual and potential market and trade shares of developing countries in new product categories being considered for eco-labelling, and may wish to invite those foreign producers whose trading interest might be substantially affected by eco-labelling to participate in the development of eco-criteria, in particular PPM-related criteria. Such consultations

Table 25.6 EU eco-labelling programme: T-shirts (HS 6109.10–6109.90) (1992; thousand US$)

Exporting country	*Exports*[a]	*Share in total EU imports*[b]	*Share (%)*[c]	*Rank*[d]
Turkey	395 055	21.3	4.6	7
Hong Kong	139 072	7.5	1.8	16
India	117 279	6.3	1.8	15
Bangladesh	115 949	6.2	11.9	3
Mauritius	100 772	5.4	9.3	4
....	....	....	....	....
Maldives[e]	4569	0.2	18.7	1

[a] EU imports originating in the exporting country for the specific product.
[b] Share in EU imports originating in the exporting country for the specific product.
[c] Share of exports for the specific product over total exports to the EU originating in the exporting country.
[d] Ranks of share as defined above.
[e] Country selected because of rank.

Table 25.7 EU eco-labelling programme: shirts (HS 6205.20–6205.30–6206.30–6206.40) (1992; thousand US$)

Exporting country	*Exports*[a]	*Share in total EU imports*[b]	*Share (%)*[c]	*Rank*[d]
Hong Kong	613 048	17.3	8.0	6
India	452 808	12.7	7.2	7
Bangladesh	294 110	8.3	30.3	2
Turkey	264 979	7.4	3.1	17
Poland	223 319	6.3	2.4	19
....	....	....	....	....
Cambodia[e]	10 936	0.3	31.2	1

[a] EU imports originating in the exporting country for the specific product.
[b] Share in EU imports originating in the exporting country for the specific product.
[c] Share of exports for the specific product over total exports to the EU originating in the exporting country.
[d] Ranks of share as defined above.
[e] Country selected because of rank.

Table 25.8 EU eco-labelling programme: footwear (HS 6401–6402–6403–6404–6405) (1992; thousand US$)

Exporting country	*Exports*[a]	*Share in total EU imports*[b]	*Share (%)*[c]	*Rank*[d]
China	936 984	18.3	4.3	6
Republic of Korea	814 470	15.9	8.5	2
Indonesia	490 135	9.5	8.7	1
Thailand	419 541	8.2	5.7	4
Taiwan, Prov. of China	348 319	6.8	2.5	15
Austria	287 419	5.6	0.9	30
Brazil	281 138	5.5	2.4	17
USA	168 005	3.2	0.1	55
Czechoslovakia	141 578	2.7	1.9	20
Hungary	135 263	2.6	2.6	14

[a] EU imports originating in the exporting country for the specific product.
[b] Share in EU imports originating in the exporting country for the specific product.
[c] Share of exports for the specific product over total exports to the EU originating in the exporting country.
[d] Ranks of share as defined above.

Table 25.9 EU eco-labelling programme: bed linen (HS 6302.10–6302.21–6302.31–6302.32) (1992; thousand US$)

Exporting country	*Exports*[a]	*Share in total EU imports*[b]	*Share (%)*[c]	*Rank*[d]
Pakistan	124 478	22.5	6.0	1
Turkey	105 962	19.1	1.2	3
India	73 508	13.3	1.1	5
Thailand	27 893	5.0	0.3	11
China (P.R.)	24 994	4.5	0.1	31

[a] EU imports originating in the exporting country for the specific product.
[b] Share in EU imports originating in the exporting country for the specific product.
[c] Share of exports for the specific product over total exports to the EU originating in the exporting country.
[d] Ranks of share as defined above.

Table 25.10 EU eco-labelling programme: tissue paper (HS 4818.10–4818.20) (1992; thousand US$)

Exporting country	*Exports*[a]	*Share in total EU imports*[b]	*Share (%)*[c]	*Rank*[d]
Sweden	68 446	33.9	0.2	3
Austria	39 683	19.6	0.1	7
Finland	26 173	12.9	0.1	5
Slovenia	17 054	8.4	0.8	1
Switzerland	17 030	8.4	0.0	12

[a] EU imports originating in the exporting country for the specific product.
[b] Share in EU imports originating in the exporting country for the specific product.
[c] Share of exports for the specific product over total exports to the EU originating in the exporting country.
[d] Ranks of share as defined above.

would help to assess the potential trade, environmental and developmental effects of eco-labelling in the producing countries, and would give foreign producers the opportunity to clarify the environmental and developmental problems they have to face and the priorities they have to respect according to their national environmental and developmental policies.

Notes

1. Finland, Norway and Sweden have a common eco-labelling scheme. Therefore, for the purpose of this study, they are regarded as a single market. Since data were collected before 1 January 1995, Finland and Sweden are not regarded as EU member countries.
2. Canada has, for example, in its programme "major household appliances", while the EU has "packaging".
3. For instance, "Fine paper from recycled paper" (Canadian scheme); "Rechargeable batteries" (Nordic country scheme).
4. In the case of the product category "newsprint from recycled paper", for example, all the codes corresponding to "newsprint" have been taken into account, since there are no specific codes which distinguish newsprint from recycled paper from other kinds of newsprint.
5. There are no codes corresponding to the definition "copying and writing paper", for instance. Therefore several codes, which include copying and writing paper as well as other paper products, have been considered.

6. For example, there is not a specific code covering "toner cartridges", while there is a code for all parts and accessories of photocopying machines.
7. This is, for example, the case of compost.
8. World Trade Organization, "The Provisions of the Multilateral Trading System with Respect to the Transparency of Trade Measures used for Environmental Purposes and Environmental Measures and Requirements which have Significant Trade Effects", WT/CTE/W/5, 23 March 1995.
9. WTO, op. cit.
10. ISO/TC 207/SC 3/WG 1, "Working Draft", ISO/WD 14024, January 1995.
11. Type I labelling programmes rely on multiple criteria, are voluntary and third-party-based.
12. "Notes and Supplementary Provisions", Ad Article XXVIII, Paragraph 1, 4.
13. Ibid., Ad Article XXVIII, Paragraph 1, 7.
14. TAR/M/16, p. 10.
15. "Notes and Supplementary Provisions", Ad Article XXVIII, Paragraph 1, 5.
16. "Understanding of the interpretation of Article XXVIII of the General Agreement on Tariffs and Trade, 1994".
17. Since the analysis is based on 1992 trade flows, Austria, Finland and Sweden are not regarded as EU member countries.

26 Environmentally Preferable Commodities

Mehmet Arda

INTRODUCTION

Eco-labelling in the importing markets can both provide opportunities for and be a constraint to the exports of developing countries. In this respect, there are two important questions which are discussed in the other chapters in this volume. Firstly, how to benefit from the existing eco-labelling schemes and, secondly, how to devise eco-labelling schemes that take into account the legitimate environmental and/or economic interests of the developing countries.

The issue of eco-labelling, as it is generally applied now, is relevant only to a part of developing-country exports. This stems from the principal rationale behind eco-labelling schemes, namely, the protection of the environment of the importing country where the scheme is implemented, and the protection of global commons. Moreover, eco-labelling schemes are designed with specific products or product groups in mind. Products exported by developing countries that are subject to eco-labelling schemes constitute two main groups which are not mutually exclusive: the first includes products which are also produced in the importing countries, and the second comprises products the production of which directly affects global commons. Examples of the first group include items such as flowers, textiles and leather goods. The second group comprises goods such as tropical timber and products containing chloroflurocarbons.

There are several products produced and exported – or that could potentially be exported – by developing countries that fall outside customary eco-labelling schemes, but have environmentally preferable characteristics that could be emphasized by producers and used in export promotion. Thus, opportunities exist for increasing export earnings while protecting the environment. The first step here would be to identify products that have an export potential based on their environmentally preferable characteristics. Some of these characteristics will be more relevant to consumers than to producers. Eco-labels and certification procedures could be developed by producing countries, preferably in concert, for these latter products that escape the interests of importing-country authorities. This can be viewed as a "bottom-up" approach to eco-labelling.

I ENVIRONMENTALLY PREFERABLE CHARACTERISTICS

In principle, products with environmental advantages cause less environmental stress during their life cycles compared to other products that serve the same purpose. They may have been produced in an ecologically preferable production process and/or they may have an ecologically preferable end to their useful life. Products which have less harmful or more beneficial effects on human health (not because of their intrinsic characteristics but because they contain less harmful residues or less harmful foreign items) are also included in this definition.

Undisputed scientific proof for environmental advantages is very difficult, if not impossible, to obtain. In spite of the advances achieved in life-cycle analysis, ranking of products according to their environmental impact remains controversial on account of the variety of environmental effects generated and the necessity to put them all into comparable units or to assign priorities. As this paper intends to provide only some initial information on product types that developing countries can export on environmentally preferable grounds, undisputed scientific proof has not been sought. Natural products with claims to environmental advantages in at least one stage of their life cycle are given as examples. There may be situations where environmental advantages with respect to one aspect (e.g. biodegradability) may coexist with environmental disadvantages on another count (e.g. water pollution at the production stage). Whether, overall, the product may be considered environmentally beneficial depends on the relative importance attached to the different criteria.

Claims to environmental advantages are made for many products produced by developing countries. These products merit particular attention because their increased use and trade would contribute not only to environmental protection but also to development and poverty alleviation. Inadequate development and poverty are seen by many as the principal causes of environmental degradation in developing countries. Therefore, products supplied by developing countries should be considered to have indirect environmental advantages even when they have the same direct environmental impact as those originating in more developed countries.

II ENVIRONMENTALLY PREFERABLE PRODUCTS FALLING OUTSIDE ECO-LABELLING SCHEMES

Some of the environmentally preferable products falling outside eco-labelling schemes in industrialized countries can be substituted for goods with environmentally less desirable characteristics currently used in developed countries. These include natural fibres which can have expanded utilization in several industrial areas. Some of the products (such as organically grown tropical beverages) will compete with other products exported by developing countries, while others have the potential to be used instead of products produced in importing countries. Apart from products that developing countries may have to promote actively, there are products for which the demand may increase, on account of environmentally based regulations in the main markets.

A Agricultural Inputs

Agriculture is one of the main sources of water pollution in places where external inputs into agriculture are used intensively. This is particularly the case in some developed countries. Several organic agricultural inputs perceived to have no or very little negative impact on the environment are produced in developing countries. Pyrethrum, mostly produced in East Africa, and neem, a tree native to India and Burma but also grown in Africa, are among such products.

Some entomologists now conclude that neem has such remarkable powers that it will usher a new era in safe, natural pesticides. Perhaps the most important quality of neem is that neem products appear to have little or no toxicity to warm-blooded animals.[1] It is on account of these characteristics that such inputs are seen as acceptable for use in organic agriculture. There are also other advantages associated with using plants as a source of pest control. The carbon absorption capacity of plants while they grow, as well as their contribution to controlling soil erosion and deforestation, should also be recognized.

There are several problems, however, in expanding the use and trade of these products. Firstly, chemical companies are in the process of developing synthetic substances which have characteristics similar to these natural products. Secondly, the supply of these products may not be as reliable as would be required for their expanded use. Thirdly, and perhaps most importantly, the greatest impediment to commercial development may simply be a general lack of credibility, or even awareness of what these products are and what they can do.[2] Information on these products is not adequately available to facilitate the building up of public opinion. This makes enhancement of scientific research a prerequisite for the large-scale commercial exploitation of these products and for fully utilizing their environmental characteristics in promotion.

B Natural Fibres as Industrial Inputs

Natural fibres have a large potential for use in many branches of industry. Work in this area is being undertaken in the United States and in the European Union, mainly as a means of alternative employment opportunities for using surplus agricultural land, as well as for emphasizing the environmentally preferable characteristics of natural fibres. There is scope for developing countries producing and exporting natural fibres to benefit from this trend. The main environmental advantage of using natural fibres as industrial inputs rests in their being biodegradable and safe to burn. Thus, important environmental benefits exist in the area of waste management. These products are also less harmful to the workers who use them. Industrial areas where natural fibres can claim environmental advantages over currently used items include composites and geotextiles.

1 Composites

Flax, cotton and jute are most frequently used as substitutes for glass fibres in reinforced polymer matrix composites. The principal environmental advantage of natural fibres over glass fibres in this area is their biodegradability and combustibility. Burning of glass fibres leaves much ash, and recycling is possible for only a very limited range of composites containing glass fibres.

A related area where natural products can claim environmental advantage is in building materials. Despite environmental problems, asbestos fibres are still the most applied reinforcement fibre in inorganic matrix composites (IMC) such as cement and concrete. In developed countries wood pulps and flax are the main products with environmental advantages used as substitutes for asbestos. Among such products of developing countries, bamboo, sisal and reed have the desirable qualities.[3]

2 *Geotextiles*

In civil engineering, large quantities of geotextiles, mainly based on synthetic materials, are used in road construction and hydraulic engineering in erosion control systems, drains, foundations and soil separations. In cases where geotextiles are not permanently required, or as temporary support for rooting plants on civil constructions, plant geotextiles can be applied. In the latter case, jute, coir and straw have a large potential. Being biodegradable, when they disintegrate they turn into humus, thus eliminating the need for post-installation work at the end of their useful life. The potential to employ geotextiles based on plant fibres will be increased as biodegradability is designed or programmed into the product.

C Pulp and Paper Products

The pulp and paper industry is currently based, to a large extent, on wood and waste paper as raw material. Many other crops, such as bagasse from sugar cane stalks, flax, various kinds of grass, reeds, straw, hemp, jute and kenaf are also potential raw materials for the paper industry. The environmental implications of using annual crops as against pulp from sustainably managed forests can be the subject of much discussion. However, it has been noted that kenaf paper requires minimal chemical inputs in either field or mill operations, reducing costs and environmental concerns. Furthermore, it uses 15–25 per cent less energy than pine, and the treated wastewater can be used for irrigating nearby fibre fields.

Materials which are normally wasted and disposed of in an environmentally undesirable manner, for example thrown into waterways or burned, can be used as environmentally preferable alternatives to wood. Such materials in developing countries include rice husks and straw. Similarly, various plants considered as environmental nuisance, including water hyacinths and several kinds of grass, can be identified as environmentally preferable raw materials for paper because their use prevents potential environmental problems.

D Non-traditional Timber

Non-traditional timber and other wood products have a wide variety of potential uses ranging from construction to furniture manufacturing. Traditionally, certain types of trees such as rubber and coconut trees have been destroyed when they become too old. Latex for the former and coconuts for the latter were considered the only useful parts of these trees. The wood of these trees is non-durable in its natural form. However, recent research in the producing countries has resulted in processes through which this wood can be treated and preserved. Increased utilization of these trees leads to environmental benefits on two accounts: firstly, they can be substituted for other types of trees that come from forests, thus helping in the conservation of forest resources; and, secondly, the atmospheric pollution caused by their burning on site can be eliminated.

E Non-wood Products from Forests

Sustainably managed forests provide a large number of non-wood products, apart from their main output, timber. These include tradeable food products such as nuts and fruit, raw materials such as bamboo and rattan, and health-care ingredients. Increased earnings from these products can add considerable value to the returns of the local residents and increase their interest in sustainable management of the resource. However, these products have not received much attention so far, as their value in terms of export earnings has been rather small in comparison to timber. For example, "90 per cent of world production of rattan amounts to only 10 per cent of the value of timber production in the leading rattan producing country", namely Indonesia. The value of nut exports from Brazil amounts to about 10 per cent of the country's export earnings from tropical roundwood. Recognition of the importance of potential earnings from such products for encouraging forest conservation by local populations could considerably increase the attractiveness of these products to consumers who are concerned about the effects of deforestation on global commons.

F Biomass Fuels

There are several types of biomass fuels which can be produced from a wide range of inputs. Ethanol is produced mainly from sugar-rich agricultural products. Methanol can be made from natural gas or any carbon-rich material. Biodiesel fuels are mostly based on vegetable oils. All these fuels can be made from abundant agricultural crops in developing countries. Their environmental advantages derive from the neutral carbon dioxide cycle (with a one-off reduction in carbon dioxide up front) and savings on exhaustible resources.

Demand for biomass fuels is crucially affected by government regulations in industrialized countries. In the United States, the Clean Air Act requires the use of reformulated gasoline in smoggy cities, and has proposed that 30 per cent of the additives should come from renewable resources, that is ethanol made from corn in the United States. In Europe, there are tax advantages in using biodiesel. Although the use of biomass fuels is still in its early stages, and the trend is influenced as much by finding useful employment for surplus agricultural production as environmental concerns, an increased use of this fuel resource appears very likely in the future.

G Organically Grown Agricultural Products

Organically produced goods exported by developing countries are subjected to certification programmes that generally apply to products of the industrialized countries. There are also certification schemes concerning "fair trade" practices. These include a variety of social factors as well.

Markets for organic products have, so far, been niche markets. Organic food producers expect this to change, however, as health-related awareness increases. For example, the market for baby food has been turning to organically produced inputs fairly rapidly. While many foodstuffs have been sold upon organic grounds mainly related to health for a considerably long period of time, new markets are emerging for other organically grown crops. These include fibres such as cotton and foodstuffs such as sugar, whose production processes were not of much interest to consumers until recently. A factor that may increase consumer demand for organically grown produce is the ongoing efforts by certain industrialized-country governments to switch their own agriculture to organic methods. As consumer awareness increases, the demand for imported organic products is likely to increase as well.

Organically grown products of developing countries that benefit from certification schemes include coffee, cocoa, bananas and, increasingly, cotton. Possibly the best known example of an organic product coming from developing countries is Max Havelaar coffee which is often sold at prices between 50 and 100 per cent higher than the price of regular coffee.

It can be argued that as more and more producers attempt to benefit from this price differential, the premium may become narrower and make organic production less attractive. However, organic production has been found to lead to a reduction of production costs in many instances, once the initial switching costs have been amortized.

III CONCLUSIONS

Although the market for environmentally preferable natural products appears to have considerable potential, there are important problems that remain to be tackled:

- *Price competitiveness*: This arises at two levels – at the production of the raw product, and at the utilization of the raw material when the product is an input into some finished item. In both cases, the initial switching costs are likely to be more important than the long-run variable costs. This initial handicap, however, acts as a significant barrier to the acceptance of the specific product by the consumer or the industrial user.
- *Scientific information about quality*: This is particularly important for products with potential use as inputs in agriculture or industry. It is unlikely for potential users to initiate a scientific inquiry if the necessary basic information is not supplied by the producer. In many instances, cooperation among producing countries could facilitate such research.
- *Information on environment-friendly characteristics*: Many of the claims are based on anecdotal evidence, and environmentally negative aspects of products are sometimes ignored. Although undisputed scientific proof should not be a prerequisite for the acceptance of the product as environmentally preferable, credible claims are necessary. For several products, such as organic produce, this function is performed by certification agencies.
- *Marketing*: In introducing an environmentally preferable product to a new market, public-opinion groups such as consumer groups and other non-governmental organizations could play a crucial role. Industrial organizations could also play a major role with respect to the marketing of environmentally preferable inputs.

Notes

1. National Research Council, *Neem: A Tree for Solving Global Problems* (Washington, D.C.: National Academy Press, 1992) pp. 1, 4.
2. Ibid., p. 15.
3. See also International Trade Centre, "Certification of 'Environmentally Friendly' Products from Developing Countries: The Case of Sisal", in this volume.

27 Certification of Environmentally Friendly Products from Developing Countries: The Case of Sisal

International Trade Centre, Geneva

Environmental considerations in export promotion constitute one of the global priorities for the medium-term plan of the International Trade Centre (ITC) for the period 1992–7. Global priorities are defined as issues of universal concern, which should be taken into account in all ITC subprogrammes and activities as recurrent themes.

ITC has a unique potential within the United Nations system to provide concentrated export-development support to developing countries in environment-related areas. ITC has undertaken, for the benefit of developing countries, initial activities related to the development of trade in environmentally clean equipment over the past six years.

ITC has accumulated experience in a number of areas:

- Firstly, ITC has been assisting developing countries to take advantage of new opportunities created by a greater awareness of the need for environmental protection by providing them with advice and help on the export development and promotion of environmentally sound products, services and technology.
- A second area of ITC activities is information and advice to the developing countries on the legal framework and operational procedures for the import of potentially hazardous products for the environment.
- Thirdly, ITC informs developing countries on environment-related legislation, procedures, legal assistance, standards, etc., applicable to the exporting industries in developing countries.

Periodical newsletters and bulletins disseminated in both developed and developing countries by ITC's export packaging and export quality management services are examples of this activity. These publications have addressed issues such as standards, quality and the environment, and the impact of environmental legislation on export packaging from developing countries. In addition, a manual is under preparation on quality requirements for textiles and clothing in selected markets in Europe and North America, and this will specifically refer to the environmental regulations regarding eco-labelling requirements. The central database PACKDATA continues to expand its subjects related to environment, recycling, reuse, eco-packaging, eco-labelling, etc. As these subjects evidently warrant wider capacities in terms of consultancy, research and documentation, a new interregional project on safe and environmentally acceptable export packaging has been submitted to a donor country for financing.

• Quality embodies the totality of characteristics that bears on a product's ability to satisfy explicit (contractual) or implicit needs, including such sensitive aspects as health, safety and environmental protection. Therefore, environmental considerations have, quite naturally, been one of the major concerns of the ITC Export Quality Management Service.

Respect for the environment is becoming increasingly a new market imperative, a *sine qua non* for entering international markets. Consequently, the programme has started research on the major environmental requirements that may affect products from developing countries, including environmental management systems, eco-auditing and eco-labelling requirements. A database is being established on these requirements and on the major eco-labelling schemes, with a view to informing and assisting developing-country exporters on ways and means to comply with the stringent regulations and trade practices that are emerging in this area.

ITC continues to participate, as an observer, in the Technical Barriers to Trade meetings and work in the General Agreement on Tariffs and Trade (GATT), which increasingly deal with environmental issues. It also has liaison status in the International Organization for Standardization (ISO) Technical Commitee 207 (ISO TC 207) on Environmental Management.

Furthermore, ITC is considering broadening its work in the area of trade and environment to cover eco-labelling aspects in the following ways:

- ITC's work in the dissemination of information on environmental regulations and measures that have an impact on trade would also include information on eco-labelling systems that have been adopted or are being developed, in developed and developing countries as well as in countries with economies in transition. This work would include awareness creation and training activities.

- In relation to selected products in which developing countries have an export interest, the ITC would disseminate information on the criteria and the procedures (including those for inspection of the production unit) that would have to be followed by producers in exporting countries to meet the standards for eco-labelling, and assist them in upgrading products for this purpose.
- ITC would also simultaneously start examining whether it could provide assistance to interested developing countries (and to economies in transition) in establishing and developing their own eco-labelling systems. As a first step for work in this area, ITC could provide information and advice to interested developing countries on organizations in other countries (both developed and developing) with which they can collaborate in developing eco-labels for the product or products in which they have an export interest.
- At a later stage, the ITC could possibly act as the United Nations focal point for assisting developing countries in developing eco-labelling systems, by obtaining, where appropriate, assistance from organizations that have developed such systems for the products concerned.
- Eventually, one may also envisage the possibility of ITC playing a role with respect to inspection and certification, in close coordination with other organizations.

Any activity that ITC will embark on in this area will be carried out in close consultation and coordination with the United Nations Conference on Trade and Development (UNCTAD), the World Trade Organization (WTO) and the ISO. Obviously, the implementation of any expanded ITC role in the field of eco-labelling will greatly depend upon the support this plan receives in both developed and developing countries. Informal consultations with several countries have evoked a very positive response.

I SISAL: THE ISSUE

Sisal is extracted from the leaf of a cactus in the Agave family that grows in desert-like areas where no other form of agriculture is possible.

The largest producing countries are Brazil, Mexico, Kenya and Tanzania. Sisal twine was traditionally used in harvesting machines almost exclusively. However, synthetic substitutes were developed in the late 1960s, which have now taken over half of the market. In addition, new silage methods using plastic sheeting directly in the field have further reduced the use of sisal twine. Recent years have also seen the introduction of machines that prepare giant high-density bales which require the elasticity of synthetic twine. Both sorts of twine, however, can be used in the large variety of small and medium-sized machines, including for big round bales, and it is here that the competition between them mainly takes place.

The German environmental institute, Environmental Protection Encouragement Agency (EPEA) has made a study of both types of twine from raw material to waste products for the United Nations' Food and Agricultural Organization (FAO). The greatest difference of course is that sisal is a natural product which is biodegradable, whereas polypropylene is *not.* Sisal twine coming from renewable resources only requires land and human effort. Synthetic twine requires money and petroleum, as both a raw material and a source of energy.

Based on this preliminary comparison alone, EPEA can cite a list of ways in which manufacturing synthetic twine seriously damages the environment. Approximately ten times as much energy is needed to produce one tonne of polypropylene as one tonne of sisal. The raw material, petroleum, is a non-renewable fossil fuel and, during the manufacturing process, sulphur dioxide and nitrogen oxides are released, contributing to the acidification of soil. Health hazards, such as the emission of carcinogens, also result from the manufacture of polypropylene.

But the problems do not end with the production phase. After polypropylene twine is used, there is waste. And it creates problems wherever it ends up. Synthetic twine does not decompose and therefore cannot be composted, and it is both difficult and economically not viable to recycle. Waste is also left from the production phase. EPEA calculates that producing one tonne of synthetic twine generates more than five tonnes of non-degradable waste if all phases, including the extraction of petroleum, are taken into account.

Synthetic twine residue can end up in the stomachs of cows. Because synthetic twine is not biodegradable, it remains there until the cow is slaughtered. Heavy clumps weighing up to 20 kg have been found in the first stomach of cows. Sisal twine residue, on the other hand, is excreted naturally.

Problems also arise with ensilaging directly in the field, when hay and straw are baled with polypropylene twine and plastic sheeting. There is also the risk that the chemicals used in ensilage will leak out and threaten the ground water.

Such a life-cycle analysis makes it clear that sisal twine is the obvious winner when it comes to being safer for the environment. That does not mean, however, that producing sisal twine is without problems. Artificial fertilizers and pesticides are used, especially in Africa, although to no greater extent than in other types of farming. Producing sisal twine requires large quantities of water, and the current production methods often lead to water pollution. Large quantities of organic waste also result. A certain amount of mineral oil is also added during the production phase. EPEA's view, however, is that this problem can be solved rather easily. Since the pollutants in the washing water consist in the main of organic material, the water can be purified biologically. One can also have closed purification systems. The waste can be used as a fertilizer, and vegetable oil can be substituted for petroleum, something certain manufacturers are already doing. Although sisal twine is the winner in terms of safeguarding the environment, polypropylene twine has until now been more successful when it comes to gaining market shares. Today, the price of the two competing products is about the same, but EPEA thinks that the future belongs to the natural fibre in an economic sense as well. Increasingly, strict laws regarding waste disposal and environmental taxes based on the principle that "the polluter should pay", will favour sisal twine, in their view. Polypropylene twine and plastic sheeting for ensilage in the field will become considerably more expensive.

A comparison of the properties of agricultural twine is provided in table 27.1.

II ITC'S SISAL EXPORT PROMOTION PROJECT

This project was undertaken in the light of the serious problems faced by the sisal industry in developing countries and following repeated requests and recommendations by the FAO Intergovernmental Group on Hard Fibres and by the trade and industry in producing and consuming countries to undertake a generic promotion campaign for sisal harvest twine. ITC, in close collaboration with the representatives of sisal trading communities, the Secretary of the FAO Intergovernmental Group and relevant government agencies in Brazil and Tanzania,

Table 27.1 Sisal and synthetic twine: a comparison

Properties and other considerations	*Sisal*	*Synthetics*
Natural	Yes	No
Biodegradable	Yes	No
Harmful to cattle	No	Yes
Produced from renewable resources	Yes	No
Prevents erosion	Yes	No
Farmers economically dependent on production	Yes	No
Consumption of energy for production	Negligible	Very high
Polluting waste	Negligible	Very high

took the initiative to design a three-year pilot promotion campaign for implementation by ITC. Core financing for the project of US$450 000 was obtained from the Government of Sweden and this was complemented by US$20 000 from the Brazilian Exporters' Association of Sisal manufacturers (ABEMS) as well as additional support from the London Sisal Association, the trade and industry, and the cooperative movement in the countries where the campaign was implemented.

The objectives of the project were:

- to increase the awareness of farmers' cooperatives and agricultural machinery manufacturers in selected Western European countries regarding the ecological and technical advantages of using sisal harvest twine in lieu of polypropylene and, in this respect, to obtain the support of opinion leaders for each target group;
- to reassure importers, distributors and end-users in those importing countries as to the availability, consistent quality and continuing competitiveness of sisal harvest twine; and
- to increase the natural solidarity between farmers in developed and producing developing countries, thus awakening them to the need for joint promotion efforts.

While carrying out market promotion activities for sisal harvest twine, farmers were to be persuaded of the technical and environment advantages of using sisal harvest twine in view of the following features.

- sisal twine is biodegradable, and does not remain in the soil;
- it is less likely to jam the agricultural machines;

- it has a less abrasive effect on the moving parts of agricultural machinery.
- it is user-friendly to farmers (it does not cut their hands while handling);
- sisal has a greater knot strength, given the same breaking strain of the twine, and thus avoids stoppage of machinery and loss of harvest time;
- it is particularly well-suited for conventional baling;
- since it is recognized that the use of hay instead of silage for cattle feed has a positive effect on the quality of milk, the increased use of hay will lead to an increase in the use of baling of hay, as well as in the use of twine.

The main activities of the project, which started in 1990, were:

- the development of an overall implementation strategy in collaboration with the trade and industry;
- the development of a "SISAL-Natural" logo;
- the dissemination and use of the logo by sisal twine producers in Brazil, Tanzania, Madagascar, Kenya and Cuba;
- the preparation and dissemination of instructions for use of the logo in promotion campaigns for sisal products in selected markets, namely France, Germany, Sweden, Denmark and Finland;[1]
- implementation of publicity campaign in target markets;
- work with manufacturers of harvesting machinery to adapt their machines to sisal twine; and
- publication of technical articles in selected newspapers and magazines.

III CONCLUSIONS AND RECOMMENDATIONS

Due to the limitations in resources, the critical mass for promotional activities in some of the target markets was not reached and, therefore, the visible results of the campaign were difficult to discern. Measuring the effect of the campaign was, in general, found to be difficult on account of several factors affecting consumption, such as shrinkage of the agricultural sector, shrinkage of baling, hay and straw in general due to inroads of new techniques (increasing silage), climate conditions, carry over of stocks from one season to another, and the instability of prices for sisal and variations in currency rates – US dollars to European currencies.

Among the achievements, the following can be highlighted:

- In spite of the difficulties in measuring the effects of the campaign, there is evidence that the campaign has had a positive effect on consumption in France and Finland.
- Farmers were increasingly made aware of the environmental benefits of using sisal through technical messages and folders. The information received from the farmers' cooperatives provides evidence of their concern as well as willingness to participate in this promotional campaign.
- The campaign also created improved solidarity between farmers in producing and consuming countries. A broader understanding has been created for the impact that reduced consumption of sisal will have on the producing developing countries. The cooperative movement and the trade and industry in the target markets have fully joined in the campaign.
- The information-providing role of the project on environmental issues concerning synthetic fibres *vis-à-vis* the use of natural fibres has had a broader effect in the farming circle than just relating to the use of sisal.
- Much of the basic promotional material required for a bigger campaign was developed by the pilot phase. This includes the creation of a basic promotional message, the development of basic promotional material, including information folders, posters, advertisements for newspapers and professional magazines, promotional material for product packs, articles on environmental issues, etc. The availability of such basic promotional material will help in making a larger campaign more cost-effective.

In the light of the positive results of this campaign, implemented with very limited resources, it is felt that the promotion of sisal harvest twine is a worthwhile activity, particularly in the traditional markets and for traditional baling. Although technological changes will continue to affect the overall consumption of sisal twine adversely, it should be possible to maintain the traditional baling segment of the market for sisal twine with effective marketing and promotional actions.

Note

1. Examples of these instructions include: (a) the objective of the symbol is to project an image around sisal as a high quality and environmentally friendly product; (b) users must avoid the use of adulterated batching oils; (c) users should comply with applicable technical regulations in target markets, particularly concerning the use of certain chemicals or dangerous elements; and (d) ITC, in close collaboration with the concerned associations in producing countries, will monitor the correct application of the scheme, and reserves the right to withdraw the use of the logo if obvious misuse is found.

Index